World Chr

Se   ...rreto

MIGRATION AND PUBLIC DISCOURSE
IN WORLD CHRISTIANITY

World Christianity and Public Religion Series

Series Editor: Raimundo C. Barreto

MIGRATION AND PUBLIC DISCOURSE IN WORLD CHRISTIANITY

AFE ADOGAME

RAIMUNDO C. BARRETO

WANDERLEY PEREIRA DA ROSA

FORTRESS PRESS

MINNEAPOLIS

To Óscar Alberto Martínez Ramírez and his
23-old-month daughter, Valerie, who lost their lives
seeking a better life in the U.S.,
and to all migrant families who see themselves
pictured in them

CONTENTS

THE WORLD CHRISTIANITY AND PUBLIC RELIGION SERIES

During the latter half of the twentieth century, scholars began to pay attention to the truly worldwide, polycentric, and culturally diverse world of Christianity. The rapid growth in the number of Christians living in the Global South caught the attention of Western scholars as a trend that would not be reversed in the near future.

A number of books have been written in an attempt to offer clues on how these drastic demographic changes affect the shape Christianity will take in the coming decades. Beyond the fascination with the exciting numbers, one might notice that as Christianity rapidly spreads in the Global South and its diaspora, the rise of a new-world Christian consciousness brings along deep cultural, social, and economic consequences, which demand further scholarly attention. In regard to the cultural sphere, it is worth stressing that as more people all around the world have access to the gospel in the vernacular, they are embracing Christianity as their own. As a consequence, Christianity can no longer be conceived only from a Western perspective. We have stepped into the threshold of a new era. New and creative theological insights have emerged, debunking homogenic understanding of World Christianity. Conversion to Christianity, especially in former Western colonies, did not result in the westernization of converts as some missionaries expected. Instead, indigenous cultures and their spiritualities remain alive and well. This series engages a number of the emerging voices from within the many indigenous Christianities around the world, paying attention not only to their histories and practices, but also to their theological articulations, and their impact upon the societies where they exist.

While during the modern era, the study of Christianity has tended to be predominantly informed by Western perspectives and priorities, World Christianity in the beginning of the twenty-first century is more often understood in the context of contextual relationships with other religions of the world. No religion is hermetically sealed. Mass migration, which has become increasingly characteristic of the current era, has increased the exchanges among different peoples and cultures, giving rise to a growing demand for studies that take intercultural communication, intercultural theologies, and interfaith dialogue more seriously. Likewise, there has been a growing interest in issues of hybridity, liminality, border thinking, cultural interweaving—particularly in the context of formerly colonized cultures.

Old problems still linger. Scientific and technological advances have not reduced the existing injustices and power asymmetry. Rather, socioeconomic injustice is as fiercely prevalent as when the first theologies of liberation emerged in the 1960s. According to Indian theologian Felix Wilfred, the demographic shift of World Christianity is not simply a shift "from the West to the South, but a shift of Christianity from the rich and middle classes to the poor." In other words, "those with below $500 dollars as annual income are the ones who will be, if not already, the most numerous Christian disciples in our world."[1]

In a context of such economic disparity, standing in solidarity with the poor is extremely important. Yet, it is not enough. Christians emerging in contexts of poverty and injustice in different parts of the world have been asking challenging and complex questions about the reasons for such inequality. The persistence of mass migration, and the grave problems related to the inhuman treatment many migrants, refugees, asylum seekers, and stateless persons receive when crossing borders, help increase awareness of the indivisibility of concerns with justice, requiring renewed moral commitments and creative responses to what is amounting to a global human calamity. Likewise, unjust relations based on race, gender, and sexuality, along with important land-related disputes and environmental concerns are part of the public agenda Christians are called to engage in, both in the Global North and South. The postcolonial rise of identity claims of previously silenced voices, combined with the fear of difference, and economic insecurity has contributed to the recent revitalization of nationalist and xenophobic ideologies, which are poisoning societies across the world.

All these facts, combined with enlarged worldviews—which do not conceive of sharp separations between the sacred and the secular—informing particularly non-Western Christians in their relationships with the world, make the public face, voice, and reason of World Christianity unavoidable. Christians from the Global South and its diaspora are key actors in what we commonly refer to as the public sphere in the West. As such, they are producing new perspectives on the impact of religion on public life and an array of approaches on issues related to citizenship, public witness, peace, justice, environmental relations, and contemporary migration.

---

[1] Felix Wilfred, "Christianity between Decline and Resurgence," in *Christianity in Crisis?* Edited by Jon Sobrino and Felix Wilfred. Concilium 2005/3. London : SCM Press, 2005, 27–37 (31).

This series, which stems from a partnership between Princeton Theological Seminary and Faculdade Unida, aims to provide a unique space for sustained dialogue on all those issues. It blends a number of methods and approaches from the emerging field of World Christianity, in conversation with other fields of study, including studies on religious reasoning in the public sphere, public theologies, postcolonial/decolonial theories, intercultural studies, migration studies, critical gender studies, critical race studies, queer theory, and globalization theories. The series intentionally brings religious scholars and theologians from varied Christian traditions and countries into conversation with one another. At its root are two schools from the Reformed tradition, one in South America and the other in North America, and one which is young and the other with a tradition spanning over 200 years.

In the first half of the twentieth century, Princeton Theological Seminary appointed John Mackay as president after he lived for years as a missionary in Latin America, a period which deeply influenced him. Mackay himself, by turning ecumenics into a mandatory field of study for the church in the twentieth century, anticipated the emergence of the field we know today as World Christianity:

> A new reality has come to birth. For the first time in the life of mankind the Community of Christ, the Christian Church, can be found, albeit in nuclear form, in the remotest frontiers of human habitation. This community has thereby become "ecumenical" in the primitive, geographical meaning of that term. History is thus confronted with a new fact.[2]

In turn, Faculdade Unida has a history marked by a commitment to the retrieval of a particular memory. Such memory is linked to theologians such as Richard Shaull and Rubem Alves. Shaull was a pioneer in encouraging young Latin-American Christians such as Rubem Alves, Jovelino Ramos, João Dias de Araújo, Joaquim Beato, Beatriz Melano, and others to think theologically from their own social and cultural location, that is, as Latin-Americans. Encouraging ecumenical solidarity, he contributed to the rise of liberation theology in Brazil. Shaull's student, Rubem Alves, wrote the first book-length treatise on liberation theology,[3] while living in exile in the United States. He was one of the most creative thinkers of his days, having also contributed to the rising interest in emerging fields such as theopoetics.

---

[2]   John Mackay, *Ecumenics: The Science of the Church Universal* (Englewood Cliffs, N.J.: Prentice-Hall, 1964), vii.

[3]   Rubem Alves, "Towards a Theology of Liberation: An Exploration of the Encounter between the Languages of Humanistic Messianism and Messianic Humanism" (Ph.D diss., Princeton Theological Seminary, 1968).

This series is, therefore, deeply rooted in a long tradition, which is renewed by the circumstances of a new era. It enables a dialogue that places priority on voices from the Global South, but which invites participants from the centers of modern Christianity in Europe and North America to engage with their peers from the South.

The series is published in English and Portuguese. Its bilingual nature garners an inclusionary approach. A number of texts originally produced in Portuguese, which otherwise wouldn't be available to English readers are, through this series, made more visible and accessible for Anglophonic readers. Similarly, the work of authors known in the English-speaking world who had previously been unexplored in studies on religion and theology among scholars working in Portuguese or Spanish in Latin America are engaged in this dialogue, becoming more easily available for Latin American readers. Above all, it shows that it is possible to promote this type of transnational and transcultural dialogue without placing priority on any one language as *lingua franca*.

The series has six volumes planned. The first volume, published in Brazil in 2016 and in the United States in 2017, approaches World Christianity as a form of public religion, identifying areas for possible intercultural engagement. Each of the other five volumes focuses on more specific topics of concern for a public agenda for World Christianity in the twenty-first century. Volume Two addresses questions of migration and public discourse in World Christianity. Volume Three discusses current approaches to urbanization and identity in World Christianity. Volume Four focuses on World Christianity and interfaith relations. Volume Five turns our attention to pressing environmental concerns in World Christianity scholarship. Finally, volume Six places varied perspectives on race, ethnicity, gender, and sexuality in World Christianity.

It is our hope that this series can become a platform for intercultural and intergenerational dialogue, creating opportunities for greater interaction between senior and emerging scholars and writers from the Global South and its diaspora, and between them and scholars from other parts of the world.

Raimundo C. Barreto, Jr.
General Editor

ACKNOWLEDGMENTS

A book project of this magnitude involves the cooperation of many hands and minds. Our deepest gratitude to Princeton Theological Seminary and Faculdade Unida for the support they have provided to this series, which has made it possible to assemble authors from diverse linguistic backgrounds and regional contexts for such a robust conversation. It is only because of the financial support from these institutions that we are able to make this book available to English and Portuguese readers alike (its Portuguese edition will be available soon).

Our very special gratitude to Dean James F. Kay, who recently retired after decades of service at Princeton Theological Seminary. His enthusiastic support from the moment we first discussed the idea of this series with him was key for us to be able to bring it into existence.

We are equally grateful to all the authors who gave a significant amount of their busy time to this project. Their work is the reason of our enthusiasm about the volume we are putting in the hands of our readers. We owe a great debt to Melissa Martin, who assisted the editors in the early stages of putting this volume together, and to Sun Yong Lee and Stephen DiTrolio for their thorough proofreading of the final draft. Lee also did a wonderful job creating the book's index. Four chapters of this book were originally written in Portuguese. Thanks to the translating skills of Saulo Adriano, the reader has access to them in English.

Last but not least, the editors appreciate all the support Fortress Press and its editors have offered to us throughout the process of putting this volume together. More than anything else, we appreciate, the keen understanding Fortress Press has demonstrated as for the relevance of a multilingual and transcontinental project like this to address the impact on public reasoning of the ongoing changes in the contemporary demographic and cultural makeup of Christianity worldwide. We thank, in special, Fortress Press' Acquiring Editor Jesudas Athyal, himself a scholar of World Christianity, for his warm support and the competent editorial assistance he and his team have offered to us. Likewise, the editors appreciate all the support they have received from Editora Unida toward the publication of the Portuguese version of this volume in Brazil.

CONTRIBUTORS

Afe Adogame is the Maxwell M. Upson Professor of Christianity and Society at Princeton Theological Seminary. A leading scholar of the African diaspora, he holds a PhD in history of religions from the University of Bayreuth in Germany and has served as associate professor of World Christianity and religious studies, and international director at School of Divinity, New College, at The University of Edinburgh in Scotland. His teaching and research interests are broad but tend to focus on interrogating new dynamics of religious experiences and expressions in Africa and the African Diaspora, with a particular focus on African Christianities and new indigenous religious movements; the interconnectedness between religion and migration, globalization, politics, economy, media, and the civil society. He has widely published; he is the author of *The African Christian Diaspora: New Currents and Emerging Trends in World Christianity* (Bloomsbury Academic, 2013), and the editor/co-editor of books such as *The Public Face of African New Religious Movements in Diaspora: Imagining the Religious 'Other'* (Ashgate, 2014), *Africa in Scotland, Scotland in Africa: Historical Legacies and Contemporary Hybridities* (Brill, 2014), and *Engaging the World: Christian Communities in Contemporary Global Societies* (Regnum Edinburgh Centenary Series. Regnum, 2014).

Edmond Akwasi Agyeman is a lecturer in African Studies at the University of Education, Winneba (UEW), Ghana. He holds a PhD degree in Migration Studies from the Comillas Pontifical University in Madrid, Spain. Prior to joining the UEW, he was a COE Fellow at the Center for the Study of Social Stratification and Inequality, Tohoku University, Japan. His research interest focuses on ethnicity, social stratification, migration, religion, and ethics.

Eduardo Albuquerque Nunes holds a Master's degree in Political Science, and PhDs in Political Science (USP-Yale Law School) and Economics (USP-Norwegian School of Economics, NHH). He is the Regional

Strategy Director in World Vision International and an Associate Professor at Advanced Studies Institute, University of Sao Paulo, Brazil.

Fabio Baggio is a missionary priest of the Scalabrinian Congregation. He obtained a Baccalaureate in Theology and a Licentiate and PhD in Church History at the Pontifical Gregorian University. In his first years of mission, Fr. Baggio served as advisor for migrations to the Chilean Bishops' Conference and as director of the Department for Migration in the Archdiocese of Buenos Aires. He taught in different universities in Europe, Latin America, and Asia. From 2002 to 2010, he was director of the Scalabrini Migration Center (SMC) in Quezon City (Philippines) and editor of "Asian and Pacific Migration Journal." In 2010, he was appointed director of the Scalabrini International Migration Institute (SIMI), incorporated to the Pontifical Urban University in Rome. From January 1, 2017 he is under-secretary of the Refugees and Migrants Section of the Dicastery for the Promotion of Integral Human Development in the Vatican.

Raimundo C. Barreto is assistant professor of World Christianity at Princeton Theological Seminary. He earned degrees from the Seminário Teológico do Norte do Brasil, Escola Superior de Teologia, and McAfee School of Theology. He has a PhD degree in Religion and Society from Princeton Theological Seminary. His publications include *Evangélicos e Pobreza no Brazil: Pistas para uma Ética Social Evangélica Brasileira* (Rio de Janeiro, Brazil: Novos Diálogos, 2013) and the co-edited volumes, *Engaging the Jubilee: Freedom and Justice Papers of the Baptist World Alliance* [2010–2015] (Falls Church, VA, USA: Baptist World Alliance, 2015) and *World Christianity as Public Religion*; it also includes the series: World Christianity and Public Religion (Minneapolis, MN: Augsburg Fortress Press, 2017).

Moses O. Biney is associate professor of Religion and Society and director for the Master of Divinity (M.Div.) program at New York Theological Seminary. He holds a PhD from Princeton Theological Seminary. He is also an ordained Presbyterian Minister currently serving as pastor for Bethel Presbyterian Reformed Church, Brooklyn, N.Y. Dr. Biney's research and teaching interests include the religions of Africa and the African Diaspora, religion and migration, religion and culture, urban ministry and congregational studies. He is the author of *From Africa to America: Religion and Adaptation among Ghanaian Immigrants in New York* (New York University Press, 2011).

Gioacchino Campese is a member of the Missionaries of St. Charles (Scalabrinians) currently serving as professor of pastoral theology of human mobility at the Scalabrini International Migration Institute (SIMI), Pontifical Urbaniana University, Rome. He has been ministering with migrants and refugees in Mexico, United States, and Italy. Among his recent publications are: D. Groody and G. Campese (eds.), *A Promised Land, A Perilous Journey: Theological Perspectives on Migration*, 2008; G. Campese, "The Irruption of Migrants. Theology of Migration in the 21st Century" in *Theological Studies*, 2012; "Mission and Migration" in Stephen B. Bevans (ed.), *A Century of Catholic Mission. Roman Catholic Missiology 1910 to the Present*, 2013; and "One Does not Live of Bread Alone...(Matt 4:4): The Relational Turn of Theologies of Migration in the Twenty-First Century," in Michael L. Budde (ed.), *Scattered and Gathered. Catholics in Diaspora*, 2017.

João Chaves is a native of Brazil and has a PhD in Religion from Baylor University. He is the author of *Evangelicals and Liberation Revisited* (Wipf & Stock, 2013) and is currently working on his second book, *The Global Mission of the Jim Crow South* (Mercer University Press). His research deals with the intersection of migration and denominational identity and he has done extensive ethnographic work on Latinx immigrant communities in the United States.

Sonia Maria de Freitas has a PhD in Social History from the Universidade de São Paulo/USP, with specialization in Oral History at the University of Essex, UK. A researcher for twenty-five years, she was the curator of several exhibitions, taught courses in museums of the State Department of Culture, and implemented and coordinated two oral history projects at the São Paulo Museum of Image and Sound (MIS) and the Museum of Immigration. In addition to participating in collective works, she has published articles in scientific journals both in Brazil and abroad. Among her published books are *Reminiscências*; *O Café e a Imigração*; *História Oral: Possibilidades e Procedimentos*; *Vida e Obra do Comendador Montenegro: um lousanense visionário no Brasil*; *A Saúde no Brasil: do Descobrimento aos dias atuais*; *Médicos do Brasil: histórias de vidas extraordinárias dedicadas à Saúde*; and *Presença Portuguesa em São Paulo*, for which she received the Clio History Award in 2007.

Christine J. Hong is assistant professor of Educational Ministries at Columbia Theological Seminary in Decatur, GA. She holds a BA from University of Washington, ThM and MDiv degrees from Princeton Theological Seminary, and a PhD from Claremont School of Theology. Her interests include de-colonial approaches to religious and interreligious education. Hong's interests also include Asian American spiritualities, and the spiritual and theological formation of children and adolescents among communities of color. Hong is a Teaching Elder in the

Presbyterian Church (U.S.A.) and has spent time both as a religious educator and youth and young adult minister in New York and Southern California.

Henrietta Nyamnjoh is a research fellow at Environmental and Geographical Science, University of Cape Town. She was a 2017 Carnegie Fellow through the African Humanities Program, and during her tenure researched on religion and healing among Cameroonian migrants in Cape Town. Her research interests include migration and mobility, transnational studies, and migration and health. Additionally, she is also interested in understanding religion in the context of migration and migrants' experiences of seeking biomedical health care in Cape Town and Johannesburg. Henrietta has researched and published on migrants' appropriation of Information and Communication Technologies, Hometown Associations and migrants' everyday lives.

Janice McLean-Farrell is the Dirk Romeyn Assistant Professor of Metro-Urban Ministry at New Brunswick Theological Seminary. She holds a Doctor of Philosophy degree from the University of Edinburgh. Dr. McLean-Farrell is the author of *West Indian Pentecostals: Living their Faith in New York and London* (Bloomsbury, 2016) as well as several articles on urban youth, religion, immigrant churches, global cities, and the Caribbean. She is also the coeditor of *Understanding World Christianity: The Vision and Work of Andrew F. Walls* (Orbis, 2011) and *Engaging the World: Christian Communities in Contemporary Global Societies* (Regnum, 2014).

David Mesquiati de Oliveira has a PhD degree in Theology and teaches Religious Studies at UNIDA (Faculdade Unida de Vitoria). He has carried out post-doctoral studies in Theology at PUC-Rio and Faculdades EST. His research focuses on Pentecostalism in Latin America, Mission Theology and Indigenous Issues. He has published five books, including *Experiência e Hermenêutica Pentecostal* (CPAD, 2018) and *Diálogo e Missão nos Andes* (Garimpo/PUC-Rio, 2016), being the editor of *Pentecostalismo e Transformação Social* (Fonte, 2013), *Pentecostalismo e Diálogo* (Fonte, 2014), *Pentecostalismo e Unidade* (Fonte, 2015), and *Reformas e Pentecostalismos* (Unida, 2017). In 2018, he was Visiting Scholar at Princeton Theological Seminary. He is the coordinator of the *Rede Latino-americana de Estudos Pentecostais* (RELEP – Latin American Network of Pentecostal Studies) and a member of the steering committee of the Latin American and Caribbean Pentecostal Forum (FPLyC). He is also part of the steering committee of the Latin American Theological Fellowship.

Justice Richard Kwabena Owusu Kyei holds a PhD degree in Sociology and he is a lecturer in the Department of Sociology and Social Work in Kwame Nkrumah University of Science and Technology, Kumasi, Ghana. His research interests are: transnationalism, social theory, migration, sociology of religion, urban sociology, political sociology, African traditional religion and gender.

Shalon Park, a PhD student in the Department of History and Ecumenics (World Christianity and History of Religions) at Princeton Theological Seminary, works on the relationships between language development and religious history of Korea, with particular concentrations in the history of vernacular translations and Protestant missions of the nineteenth and twentieth century Korea. Her article can be found in the *Journal of Church and State*: "The Politics of Impeaching Shamanism: Regulating Religions in the Korean Public Sphere" (2018). Her research spans Korean literature, theories of translation, religion-state relations, nationalism, migration, and Asian-American Studies.

Francisco Pelaez-Diaz is a PhD candidate in Religion and Society at Princeton Theological Seminary. His research focuses on the appropriation of the notion of the crucified peoples—as coined by Latin American theologian Ignacio Ellacuría—by Central American migrants in their journey to the United States through Mexico. More broadly, he is interested in the religious and ethical aspects of the causes and effects of human migration in the context of globalization. Francisco has worked as an ordained pastor among immigrants in a multiethnic/multiracial PC(USA) congregation in Dayton, Ohio. He taught and served as the Academic Dean of the Presbyterian Theological Seminary of Mexico, where he earned his bachelor's degree in theology. He earned his Master of Theology in Christian Ethics at Princeton Theological Seminary.

Wanderley Pereira da Rosa holds a bachelor's degree in theology from the Presbyterian Seminary Rev. José Manoel da Conceição of São Paulo / SP (1991), a graduate degree in Philosophy from the Federal University of Espírito Santo (2002), a Master's degree in Theology from EST Colleges of São Leopoldo / RS (2010) and PhD in Theology from the Pontifical Catholic University of Rio de Janeiro / RJ (2015). He is a professor of History of Christianity and of Religion, Democracy and Public Sphere at Faculdade Unida de Vitoria where he has also been the President since 1997. His main research interests are the social and political theology of the Reformation and the history of Protestantism in Brazil. Currently he coordinates the Group of Research "Intellectual Origins of Brazilian Protestantism." He is a member of SOTER—Society of Theology and Science of Religion and the AAR—American

Academy of Religion. He is also the Executive Editor for publications at Editora Unida.

Fábio Py teaches Social Policy in the Graduate Program at Universidade Estadual do Norte Fluminense (UENF). He holds a doctoral degree in Theology from Pontifica Universidade Catolica (PUCC-RIO), and his publications include a number of articles and edited volumes. He is currently developing the Collective Common House of progressive evangelicals open for religious dialogue in Campos, Rio de Janeiro. He also collaborates with the Comissão Pastoral da Terra (CPT) of Norte Fluminense, Rio de Janeiro.

Luis N. Rivera-Pagán is the Henry Winters Luce Professor of Ecumenics and Mission Emeritus at Princeton Theological Seminary. He received his Doctorate in Philosophy (PhD) at Yale University, in 1970, and is the author of several books, among them: *A la sombra del armagedón: reflexiones críticas sobre el desafío nuclear* (1988), *Senderos teológicos: el pensamiento evangélico puertorriqueño* (1989), *Evangelización y violencia: La conquista de América* (1990), *A Violent Evangelism: The Political and Religious Conquest of the Americas* (1992), *Los sueños del ciervo: Perspectivas teológicas desde el Caribe* (1995), *Entre el oro y la fe: El dilema de América* (1995), *Mito exilio y demonios: literatura y teología en América Latina* (1996), *La evangelización de los pueblos americanos: algunas reflexiones históricas* (1997), *Diálogos y polifonías: perspectivas y reseñas* (1999), *Fe y cultura en Puerto Rico* (2002), *Essays From the Diaspora* (2002), *God, in your Grace... Official Report of the Ninth Assembly of the World Council of Churches* (2007) [Editor], *Teología y cultura en América Latina* (2009), *Ensayos teológicos desde el Caribe* (2013), *Peregrinajes teológicos y literarios* (2013), *Essays from the Margins* (2014), *Voces teológicas en diálogo con la cultura* (2017) [Editor], and *Evocaciones literarias and sociales* (2018).

INTRODUCTION:
MIGRATION AND PUBLIC DISCOURSE IN
WORLD CHRISTIANITY

Afe Adogame, Raimundo Barreto, Wanderley P. da Rosa

This book advances a conversation placed at the juncture of three important concerns: first, the concern with the role of religion in shaping public discourses; second, the concern with the increased flow of populations around the contemporary world and the role of religion in reshaping identities, creating transnational networks, and assisting migrants to cope with the numerous challenges involved in the process of displacement and relocation; and third, the phenomenon of World Christianity, which is connected with the major demographic shift in worldwide Christianity in the past several decades. This entails, among other things, the reversal of the flow of Christianity. From the sixteenth century until the first half of the twentieth century, the Christian faith tended to move from the North to the South and from the West to the East. Since the second half of the last century, however, World Christianity has become gradually polycentric.[1] Consequently, an increasing number of Christian migrants and missionaries originating in Africa, Latin America, and Asia have been moving not only from South to the North (a movement often referred to as reverse mission), but also among different regions in the South (through South–South relations). Furthermore, in many parts of the West, religion has often been boxed into a private sphere, whereas World Christianity and other religious traditions have remained visible in the public sphere historically and in the contemporary era.

This volume, the second in the series "World Christianity and Public Religion,"[2] has gathered fifteen authors from five continents whose works

---

[1]   See Klaus Koschorke and Adrian Hermann, eds., *Polycentric Structures in the History of World Christianity* (Wiesbaden: Harrassowitz, 2014).

[2]   The first of this six-volume series appeared in 2017. See Raimundo Barreto, Ronaldo Cavalcante, and Wanderley P. da Rosa, eds., *World Christianity as Public Religion* (Minneapolis, MN: Fortress Press, 2017).

reinforce the understanding that most Christians—as well as religious peoples around the world[3]—do not subscribe to an understanding of their faith that keeps their convictions and practices confined to the sphere of their individual lives. Instead, their religious faith and practices more often than not play a significant role in shaping public discourse.[4] It is not only that religious convictions and values are important components of an individual's worldview, which, therefore becomes an inevitable variable in the shaping of values that affect public life, but it is also that they often become, as Jung Mo Sung reminds us, a moral-theological imperative, which prompts people of faith, when faced with suffering and injustice, to engage in movements and initiatives struggling to overcome those situations.[5]

In this book, such conversation focuses particularly on people of faith on the move; that is, displaced peoples and other sorts of migrants who unavoidably carry their faith as they move from one place to another. Their faith, in return, contributes to strengthening their resilience and capacity to cope with adversity, becoming a source for renewed meanings and identities as they navigate the hybridity of living in-between, or on the borders—existential and physical ones. As migrants tend to exist on the move, they do not radically break with original homelands and their past experiences, memories, and relationships. On the contrary, they mostly expand their world by forming transnational networks, which are important for their survival and development. Such processes of relocation and reinvention of life, culture, and community hardly occur in a social vacuum nor take place without a relationship with contexts and systems that are foreign to them, and many times difficult to navigate. More often, migrants are met with fear, insecurity, and hostility by at least significant sectors of the host populations, who perceive new arrivals as a threat to their existence, or at least as competitors for limited resources. Thus, the process of migration itself raises several questions which are of public concern, such as matters related to the protection of human rights, child rights, women rights, freedom of religion and belief, war, climate change and environmental degradation, cultural clashes and ethnic violence, xenophobia, gender violence, and the conditions of work and education, among others.

---

[3] For a view on the public presence of other religious movements—in this case, the African New Religious Movements in diaspora—see Afe Adogame, ed., *The Public Face of New African Religious Movements in Diaspora* (Oxon and New York: Routledge, 2014).

[4] Miroslav Volf, *A Public Faith: How Followers of Christ Should Serve the Common Good* (Grand Rapids, MI: Brazos Press, 2011). See Volf's introductory chapter in particular.

[5] Jung Mo Sung, "Christianity as Public Religion: Pluralism and Dialogue," in *World Christianity as Public Religion*, edited by Raimundo Barreto, Wanderley P. da Rosa, and Ronaldo Cavalcante (Minneapolis, MN: Fortress Press, 2017), 64–80. Kindle version.

Although migration is not a new phenomenon in the human experience—human beings have always migrated in search of water, food, security, better conditions of life, or to escape natural disasters and wars—the world has never seen the large scale of mass migration that exists today. The globalization of capital, significant development in the areas of transportation and communication, and unsolved sharp economic imbalances—and the conflicts that emanate from them—have all contributed to intensify migration flows in the past century. Of relevance to the studies of World Christianity are the flows of people from formerly colonized parts of the world to the lands that formerly colonized them. Whereas migration flows are undeniably multidirectional, being found in any particular continent of the world and among all of them, it is indisputable that, particularly since the last quarter of the twentieth century, the movement of people from countries formerly colonized—whose wealth and natural resources were expropriated by colonial powers—to the very metropoles that colonized them drastically intensified.[6] Puerto Rican scholar and journalist Juan Gonzalez[7] interprets this current movement of people following the capital and wealth extorted from their lands by the colonial powers as a consequence of the imbalance between work and capital. According to him, it is a paradox that the current world order has made it so easy for capital to move instantaneously from one part of the world to other, whereas immigration laws make it increasingly harder for workers to follow suit without proper consideration of the fact that the search for work tends to follow the flow of capital. Such perspective is helpful as one examines current tensions and conflicts, in the midst of intensified xenophobic sentiments in all regions of the world, especially in Europe, the United States, and Australia, in relation to the threat posed by immigrants coming from formerly colonized countries in the Global South. It is this unsustainable situation that partly explains the recent rise of ugly nationalism. This is a paradox because North American and European countries cannot boast of economic survival and mobility without immigrants, especially when they prefer documented and skilled to undocumented immigration. The reality is that you cannot have skilled labor at the expense of the other; one is a magnet for the other. The dire quest and need by any country for the skilled and economically mobile labor, with the total exclusion of unskilled labor is a mirage. Nonetheless, in such a complex and multifaceted context that migrants

---

6   See, for instance, Ana Paula Beja Horta and Paul White, "Postcolonial Migration and Citizenship Regimes: A Comparison of Portugal and the United Kingdom", *Revista Migrações* 4 (2009): 33–57.

7   Juan Gonzalez, "Reaping What We Sow: Roots of Central American Migration," *Nuestra Herencia Lecture Series*, Princeton Theological Seminary, Princeton, NJ, October 5, 2018. Video available at https://www.ptsem.edu/news/the-2018-herencia-lectures.

move and live, their faith empowers them to move forward, even in spite of adversities.

As part of the bilingual nature of this series, all chapters originally written in English have also been translated into Portuguese and will be made available to Portuguese-speaking audiences. The cross-fertilizing impact of the interaction among scholars from Africa, Asia, the Pacific, Latin America, and the Caribbean with "Western" scholarship, often mediated by the former's diasporic voices, is in itself significant to producing a shift in public discourse through the construction of transnational networks, the recovery of forgotten and suppressed aspects of collective memory, and the relocation in the locus of discourse—through the development of border thinking—or thinking in between.

This volume seeks to promote a worldwide, multifaceted, and interdisciplinary conversation on the theme of migration and public discourses in World Christianity. However, despite the variety of contexts it examines, the editors have privileged the Latin American experience with migration. More than half of the contributions to this volume are written by authors from Latin America and the Caribbean or who have lived and worked in the region. Such apparent asymmetry is uttered instead as a corrective of an imbalance noticed in the field of World Christianity,[8] considering the limited numbers of scholars in that region who have contributed to the foundations of this field. There are three contributions on Africa and the African immigrants, two on Korea and the Korean immigrants, two on migratory flows from and to Europe, and three involving migratory flows to and from the United States.

Keeping with the spirit of this series, this volume provides opportunity for the crossing of cultural and language borders. Of the five Brazilians contributing to this volume, four of them live and work in a Portuguese-speaking environment. One contributor writes from the Caribbean, while three others speak from diasporic Latin American and Caribbean communities in the United States. Although some of those whose contributions were made primarily in another language than English are prolific writers in their native language, very little of their scholarship has been previously available in English.

Finally, in line with the interdisciplinarity that has become increasingly characteristic in World Christianity scholarship, our authors represent different disciplines, fields, and subfields in the study of religion. A few of them write from a more theological perspective. Diverse historiographical and

---

8   This gap is articulated in Raimundo C. Barreto, "The Epistemological Turn in World Christianity: Engaging Decoloniality in Latin American and Caribbean Christian Discourses," *Journal of World Christianity* 9/1 (2019): 48–60.

ethnographic methods can be identified in these studies of migration and World Christianity, shedding new light on little known experiences of migration—like that of the Russian Orthodox in Brazil—and on multifaceted transnational networks such as that formed among migrants of the Central American Northern Triangle and Evangelical churches in Texas.

This volume identifies key topics in need of scholarly attention within the study of World Christianity and migration. An intergenerational mix of scholars of migration from all regions of the world contribute chapters on topics such as the feminization of international migration, theologies of migration, migrant narratives, south-south migration, and migration and civic responsibility. A particular concern common to many authors in this volume is the engagement of migrants' narratives as important sources for public reason and theology in the twenty-first century.

The book is divided into five sections. The first part, comprising three chapters, focuses on the impact of transnational networks and cross-cultural interactions in shaping religious identities and theologies. In chapter one, Edmond Agyeman and Justice Richard Kwabena Owusu Kyei employ the concept of religious field to explain the cross-border religious engagement by second-generation migrants in Amsterdam, focusing on the activities of Ghanaian-led Christian churches. Drawing from ethnographic fieldwork among Ghanaian second generation in Amsterdam between 2014 and 2015, the authors argue that second-generation Ghanaians in Amsterdam strongly support and interiorize the shared essence and religious beliefs of their parents with a transnational optic that connects them to Ghana and other Ghanaian communities across Europe.

Eduardo Albuquerque Nunes, in chapter two, explores elements of the mutual influence on the social and political behavior of non-Catholic Christians mediated through pendular migration flows between Central America's Northern Triangle and the United States, starting in 1990. The author points to new migration patterns—pendular and urban middle-class—which are related to the phenomenon of Northern Triangle megachurches, and to US megachurches as well. He argues that deeper understanding of pendular religious exchanges can also shed light on the possible relations between the increasing reactionary political responses and the phenomenon of religious Neo-Conservatism in both regions.

In chapter three, Moses Biney examines the relationship between transnationalism, religious participation, and civic responsibility in the context of African immigrants in North America. Post-1965 African immigrants in North America participate in civil duties of all kinds in multiple places—that is, in their "host countries" (United States and Canada), and other countries where they have their roots. This chapter both interrogates the common understanding of civic responsibility as solely a local endeavor linked to territory and place of residence and shows how these African immigrants in North America understand and execute their global civic responsibilities through their transnational social and religious networks and activities.

The second part of the book highlights the reshaping of religious identities and theologies in migrants' experiences within different environments. In chapter four, João Chaves examines how the challenges posed by undocumented parishioners push Latin American pastors and denominational leaders in the United States to revise their theological and political conservatism. This chapter looks primarily at Brazilian Baptists, disclosing the way in which Brazilian Baptist pastors and denominational workers who migrate to the United States in order to pastor faith communities comprised of primarily migrant parishioners often change their stance on theology, American immigration policy, and political affiliation because of their exposure to the conundrums created by the presence of undocumented parishioners. The chapter draws on dozens of interviews, church minutes, church newsletters, sermons, and periodicals to demonstrate progression in the theopolitics of ministers. Paradoxically, the author shows that when Latin American Evangelicals become the neighbors of their American "founding fathers," they move further away from their politically conservative disposition. The challenge of undocumented presence, therefore, deeply affects the dynamics of immigrant churches in terms of leadership ideology, and given the influence of these leaders in their communities, it informs the public witness of Evangelical immigrants.

Continuity and transformation can also impact subjectivity in connection with reminiscences of the culture of origin, as reinterpreted and reconceived in a different context. In chapter five, Shalon Park challenges common assumptions that represent the high conversion rate of North Korean migrants in South Korea through the narrative of South Korean Protestants' political aspiration. In this narrative, the different aspects of North Korean migrants' stories—from the transnational boundary crossing to social resettlement—"arrive" at the confluence of Christianity and liberation. North Korean converts are portrayed as subjects who transitioned from being victims of Juche ideology to be the liberated new subjects, becoming potential agents of Christianization of the imagined reunified nation. This chapter deals with the issues of representation, while exploring the possibilities of continuity in the migrants' conversion narrative. By situating the North Korean migrants' conversion to Christianity in the discourse of Juche, the chapter highlights the ways in which conversion signifies social, political, and religious transformation intertwined with the migrants' reflexivity.

In chapter six, Sonia Maria de Freitas highlights the relationship between matters of identity, religion, and the resistance of Russian immigrants in Brazil. This chapter addresses some dimensions of the Russian immigration to Brazil— more specifically to São Paulo City—between the 1880s and the 1950s. It probes the characteristics of the integration of this ethnic group into Brazilian society, its strategies for organizing itself as a community and for reshaping its identity, mainly through religion.

Finally, in chapter seven, Janice A. McLean-Farrell turns the reader's attention to the intricacies and complexity that characterize the feminization of migration. Considering the lives of Afro-Caribbean women living in New York City as an integrated whole where seemingly "compartmentalized" components influence and are influenced by each other, the author focuses on the intersection of family, faith, and personal development to investigate how Afro-Caribbean females' lives are being shaped in the diaspora. On top of inquiring into change and continuity of the women's understanding of themselves, this chapter contributes to the understanding of how the expressions of Afro-Caribbean faith in New York City and the Caribbean are shaped by those women's lives. This chapter results from ethnographic research the author conducted among Afro-Caribbean women in New York City. Her approach broadens the scope of studies on the feminization of migration, providing the reader with more integrational portrayal of what life is like for Afro-Caribbean women in New York City.

Part three focuses on migrants' narratives as theology, with priority given to migrants' own voices and meaning-making as theological resources for the development of theologies of migration. Focusing on the experience of Korean migrants, Christine J. Hong discusses in chapter eight the power and influence of narratives and stories in the lives of immigrants, asserting that the story and its transmission for immigrant communities not only helps to preserve culture, language, and heritage but creates alternate spaces for different generations to relate to homeland, experiences of trauma, and to one another in ways that cultivate wholeness and community. This chapter further focuses on the importance of intergenerational story co-formation as a form of resilience, resistance, and survival amid human movement and other migratory legacies.

In chapter nine, Henrietta M. Nyamnjoh shows, based on her study of the experience of Cameroonian migrants in Cape Town, South Africa, that the migrant's experience is often fraught with challenges in the host country, especially in cases where they are relegated to the margins or face healthcare problems or failures with business. She examines how migrants in Cape Town face these challenges by turning "to God for intercession via Pentecostal churches." Drawing from ethnographic research among Cameroonian migrants in Cape Town, this chapter explores various challenges that migrants face and how they use religion and spirituality to understand and cope with the various forms of duress. She concludes that, in the face of diverse challenges, migrants have taken to religious mobility in search of prophetic men/women of God to seek healing and deliverance.

In chapter ten, Fabio Baggio, a Scalabrinian missionary priest who currently serves as under-secretary of the Refugees and Migrants Section of the Dicastery for the Promotion of Integral Human Development in the Vatican, recounts four stories of migrants and refugees in different regions of the world to highlight how the encounter between "locals" and "newcomers" has deeply transformed their lives. Applied to migrants' narratives, the parable of the Good Samaritan suggests a theological reflection on the transition from "neighbourhood" to "proximity." His reflections are placed in dialogue with Pope Francis's magisterial statements and the four verbs (welcome, protect, promote and to integrate) that summarize the Catholic Church's response to the challenges of contemporary migration.

Part four presents theological responses to current challenges and crises involving migration, public policy and civil discourse. In chapter eleven, Luis Rivera-Pagán offers a renewed reflection on migration and xenophobia as serious social quandaries, in response to the increasingly charged and polarized climate migrants face in different parts of the world, underlining some urgent challenges to the ethical sensitivity of religious people and persons of good will. The author challenges the reader to perceive this issue from the perspective of the immigrants, to pay cordial (that is, deep from our hearts) attention to their stories of suffering, hope, courage, resistance, ingenuity, and death, as so frequently happens in the wildernesses of the American Southwest.

In chapter twelve, Gioacchino Campese provides a provisional map of the so-called "refugee crisis" in Europe, which he describes as a "value crisis," with crucial theological and missionary/pastoral implications, rather than a "capacity and resource crisis." In this context, the author discusses the role of God's memory as a central theological category with a special connection with the suffering of a migrant and oppressed people. This represents an imperative call to today's people of God in Europe to nurture a "responsible culture of remembrance" that is one of the most urgent tasks Christians have taken on against the hostility and xenophobia that are afflicting the continent.

In chapter thirteen, Francisco Pelaez-Diaz addresses one of the most serious migrant-related crisis in the Americas, namely the journey of millions of Central Americans who, since the civil wars of the 1980s and early 1990s, and the perils of a grueling journey north to the Mexican/US border. His essay focuses on the role of faith in such a journey. He brings attention to the reenactment of the Way of the Cross performed by Central American migrants in their journey through Mexico, a social phenomenon that shows the centrality of the religious element in the process of breaking boundaries to protest the effects of structural violence. The situation of violence in certain Central American countries (the so called Northern Triangle) constitutes one of the main reasons behind the decision by hundreds of thousands of people to migrate every year. Such violence continues in the journey through Mexico, where these migrants endure hardened immigration policies, corruption, crime, rejection, discrimination, social marginalization and in many cases, death. Since 2011, migrants have been reenacting the Way of the Cross in different parts of Mexico evoking the image of the "crucified peoples." This particular reenactment has its origin not only in the popular representation that occurs in Latin America, but also in the notion of the crucified peoples as coined and proposed by the theologian and philosopher Ignacio Ellacuría, who was murdered in 1989 in El Salvador. The notion of the crucified peoples was conceived as a hermeneutical tool to denounce the violence directed against the Salvadoran and Central American population. The notion of the crucified peoples that is implied in the reenactment of the Way of the Cross enables migrants to cross not only the political/geographical boundaries that separate modern states, but also religious and social boundaries.

The book concludes with two essays focusing on migration in the context of Brazilian Pentecostalism, underlining, however, two distinct migratory flows. The first one is a case study of two Pentecostal expressions in a landless workers' settlement in Rio de Janeiro. In chapter fourteen, Fabio Py highlights the interface between Christianity and the organization of rural social movements in Campos dos Goytacazes, the northern part of the state of Rio de Janeiro, with attention to the migratory flows in the region. More specifically, he examines the Pentecostal expansion in the largest settlement of the Landless Workers Movement (MST) in the region, the Zumbi dos Palmares settlement, using two cases of migrants who formed the settlements to highlight two Pentecostal responses to that context: one that he describes as "closed" for the possibility of religious dialogue, linked to expressions of prosperity theology; and another that he sees as a more "open" form of Pentecostalism, which, being more ecumenical, collaborates more closely with the Pastoral Commission of the Earth (CPT). This chapter seeks to debunk any reductionism of the Pentecostal

experience, pointing to the complexity of the migrations that formed this specific settlement—the product of agrarian reform—and the diversity of modula-
tions in the field of rural Pentecostalism in Brazil.

The final chapter by David Mesquiati de Oliveira focuses on the diaspora
of Brazilian Pentecostalism. There are around three million Brazilians living
abroad, half of whom are in the United States. Mostly based on literature
review, de Oliveira analyzes the missionary motivations of these immigrants as
well as their practice of caring for others in their new locations. As a result of
their strong sense of community, their intense religious experiences, and their
deep connection with Brazilian culture, Brazilian Pentecostal churches create
a special foothold for Brazilian migrants. De Oliveira argues that an analysis
of the diaspora of Brazilian Pentecostalism corroborates the inseparable links
between migration and mission, affirming that, for most Brazilian Pentecostals,
migration is a theological project.

The combination of voices, themes, interests, and networks present in the
chapters of this book, along with its interdisciplinary and inter-contextual
makeup, makes this volume an important and unique contribution for students,
scholars, and religious leaders seeking to understand the links and relations involving the triple emphasis present throughout the book.

We hope that the readers will enjoy reading this book, a product of
two years of hard work, commitment and dedication by the editors and
contributors.

BIBLIOGRAPHY:

Adogame, Afe, ed., *The Public Face of New African Religious Movements in Diaspora*.
 Oxon and New York: Routledge, 2014.
Barreto, "The Epistemological Turn in World Christianity: Engaging Decoloniality
 in Latin American and Caribbean Christian Discourses," *Journal of World
 Christianity* 9/1 (2019): 48–60.
Barreto, R., Ronaldo Cavalcante, and Wanderley P. da Rosa, eds., *World Christianity
 as Public Religion*. Minneapolis, MN: Fortress Press, 2017.
Gonzalez, Juan. "Reaping What We Sow: Roots of Central American Migration,"
 Nuestra Herencia Lecture Series, Princeton Theological Seminary, Princeton,
 NJ, October 5, 2018. Video available at https://www.ptsem.edu/news/
 the-2018-herencia-lectures.

Horta, Ana Paula Beja and Paul White, "Postcolonial Migration and Citizenship Regimes: A Comparison of Portugal and the United Kingdom", *Revista Migrações* 4 (2009): 33–57.

Koschorke, Klaus and Adrian Hermann, eds., *Polycentric Structures in the History of World Christianity*. Wiesbaden: Harrassowitz, 2014.

Sung, Jung Mo. "Christianity as Public Religion: Pluralism and Dialogue," in *World Christianity as Public Religion*, edited by Raimundo Barreto, Wanderley P. da Rosa, and Ronaldo Cavalcante (Minneapolis, MN: Fortress Press, 2017), 64–80.

Volf, Miroslav. A Public Faith: How Followers of Christ Should Serve the Common Good. Grand Rapids, MI: Brazos Press, 2011.

PART I

SHAPING IDENTITIES: TRANSNATIONAL NETWORKS AND RELIGIOUS DISCOURSE

CHAPTER 1

RELIGIOUS IDENTITIES AND TRANSNATIONAL RELIGIOUS PRACTICES OF SECOND-GENERATION GHANAIAN MIGRANTS IN AMSTERDAM

Edmond Akwasi Agyeman & Justice Richard Kwabena Owusu Kyei

INTRODUCTION

This chapter investigates the engagements in the transnational religious field by second generations of Sub-Saharan African descent in Europe. The study seeks to contribute to the literature on the intergenerational transnational religious activities of Sub-Saharan Africans in Europe, using the case of second generation Ghanaians in Amsterdam. Even though there is no consensus in the literature as to who qualifies to be called second generation,[1] the term is used in migration studies as an umbrella term to classify different categories of immigrant children. The chapter conceptualizes second generation as any child born in the Netherlands or who entered the Netherlands at/before the age of six with at least one parent being of Ghanaian origin and is eighteen years and above as at the time of the data collection. The age of arrival in the host country has always been considered an important factor in the study of the adaptation of immigrant children.[2] Immigrants who enter the host country at a tender age

---

[1]   Rosa Aparicio, "The Integration of the Second and 1.5 Generations of Moroccan, Dominican and Peruvian Origin in Madrid and Barcelona," *Journal of Ethnic and Migration Studies* 33, no.7 (September 1, 2007): 1169–93, https://doi.org/10.1080/13691830701541713; G. Favaro and M. Napoli, *Ragazze e ragazzi nella migrazione. Adolescenti stranieri: identità, racconti, progetti* (Milano: Guerini e Associati, 2004); Christian Timmerman, E. Vanderwaeren, and Maurice Crul, "The Second Generation in Belgium," *International Migration Review* 37, no.4 (2003): 1065–1090.

[2]   Elena Caneva and Maurizio Ambrosini, "Le seconde generazioni: nodi critici e nuove forme di integrazione," *Sociologia   E Politiche Sociali*, no.1 (2009): 25–46, https://doi.org/10.3280/SP2009-001003.

are less likely to be handicapped compared with those who arrive in the host country in their teens.[3]

Some scholars of immigrant integration doubt the persistence of transnationalism among immigrants across generations. [4] Others also hold that the phenomenon is not widespread among immigrants as only a small proportion of first-generation immigrants are involved.[5] These scholars argue that there is less likelihood that immigrants' transnational practices extend beyond first-generation immigrants as transnational parents may not generate transnational children.[6] However, some studies have found that second generations actively engage in different forms of transnational practices.[7] Mugge noted in her study of transnational politics of Turkish, Surinamese, and Moroccan immigrants in the Netherlands that second generations are involved in varied forms of transnational political practices.[8] Arthur argued in his work on female second-generation Africans in the United States of America that some of them construct identities that are transnational in nature to contest the marginalized connotations attached to blackness. [9] The cross-border political engagement by second-generation Ghanaians in Amsterdam has also been evidenced in some

[3]   Sandy Baum and Stella M. Flores, "Higher Education and Children in Immigrant Families," *The Future of Children* 21, no.1 (2011): 175, https://doi.org/10.1353/foc.2011.0000.
[4]   Michael Jones-Correa, *Between Two Nations: The Political Predicament of Latinos in New York City* (Ithaca, NY: Cornell University Press, 1998); Marcelo M. Suárez-Orozco, ed., *Crossings: Mexican Immigration in Interdisciplinary Perspectives* (Cambridge, Mass.: David Rockefeller Center for Latin American Studies, 1998).
[5]   Alejandro Portes, Luis E. Guarnizo, and Patricia Landolt, "The Study of Transnationalism: Pitfalls and Promise of an Emergent Research Field," *Ethnic and Racial Studies* 22, no.2 (January 1, 1999): 217–37, https://doi.org/10.1080/014198799329468.
[6]   Richard Alba and Victor Nee, *Remaking the American Mainstream: Assimilation and Contemporary Immigration* (Cambridge, Mass.: Harvard University Press, 2003); Philip Kasinitz, John H. Mollenkopf, and Mary C. Waters, "Worlds of the Second Generation," in *Becoming New Yorkers: Ethnographies of the New Second Generation* (New York: Russell Sage Foundation, 2004), 1–19.
[7]   Cecilia Menjívar, "Living in Two Worlds? Guatemalan-Origin Children in the United States and Emerging Transnationalism," *Journal of Ethnic and Migration Studies – J ETHN MIGR STUD* 28 (July 1, 2002): 531–52, https://doi.org/10.1080/13691830220146590; Rhacel Salazar Parreñas, "Long Distance Intimacy: Class, Gender and Intergenerational Relations Between Mothers and Children in Filipino Transnational Families," *Global Networks* 5 (2005): 317–36, https://doi.org/10.1111/j.1471-0374.2005.00122.x; Robert Smith, *Mexican New York: Transnational Lives of New Immigrants* (Berkeley: University of California Press, 2006).
[8]   L. Mügge, *Beyond Dutch Borders: Transnational Politics Among Colonial Migrants, Guest Workers and the Second Generation*, IMISCOE Research (Amsterdam University Press, 2010).
[9]   John A. Arthur, *African Diaspora Identities: Negotiating Culture in Transnational Migration* (Lanham, MD: Lexington Books, 2010).

recent studies.[10] This study seeks to contribute to the literature by examining how second-generation Ghanaians in Amsterdam form religious identities in the transnational religious field.

Data for this study are drawn from ethnographic research involving in-depth interviews, participant observation and informal interviews which took place in Amsterdam between January 2014 and January 2015. Snowball sampling technique was adopted in recruiting the second-generation respondents. Fifty second-generation Ghanaians participated in the research out of which thirty-five were females and fifteen were males. In addition, nine African Initiated Christian Churches (AICCs) in Amsterdam were purposively sampled for interview. This was based on the religious affiliation of majority of the second-generation participants. They include Wesley Methodist Church of Ghana, Resurrection Power and Living Bread Ministries, Christ the King Baptist Church, Redemption Faith International Ministries, Amsterdam Seventh Day Adventist Church, Emmanuel Presbyterian Church of Ghana, Pentecost Revival Church International, Love Christian Centre and Church of Pentecost. These churches are located in the South-east Municipality of Amsterdam where the Ghanaian population in Amsterdam is largely concentrated.

TRANSNATIONAL RELIGIOUS FIELD AND PRACTICES

In migration studies, the concept of social field has widely been used to explain the activities of migrants across borders.[11] By the term social field, we mean a "set of multiple interlocking networks of social relationships in which ideas, practices, and resources are [...] exchanged, organised and transformed".[12] Within the domain of religion, transnational religious field is conceptualized as

---

10 Mary Boatemaa Setrana and Justice Richard Kwabena Owusu Kyei, "Transnational Paradigm within Immigrant Political Integration Discourse. The Case of Ghanaians in the Netherlands," *Afrique Contemporaine* 256, no.4 (2015): 91–101; Richard Kwabena Owusu Kyei and Mary Boatemaa Setrana, "Political Participation Beyond National Borders: The Case of Ghanaian Political Party Branches in the Netherlands," in *Migration and Development in Africa: Trends, Challenges, and Policy Implications*, ed. Steve Tonah, Mary Boatemaa Setrana, and John A. Arthur (Lanham: Lexington Books, 2017), 41–56.

11 See Nina Glick Schiller, "Transmigrants and Nation-States: Something Old and Something New in the U.S. Immigrant Experience," in *The Handbook of International Migration: The American Experience*, ed. C. Hirschman, P. Kasinitz, and J. Dewind (Russell Sage Foundation, 1999), 94–119; Nina Glick Schiller and Georges E. Fouron, "Terrains of Blood and Nation: Haitian Transnational Social Fields," *Ethnic and Racial Studies* 22, no.2 (January 1, 1999): 340–66; Nina Glick Schiller, "The Centrality of Ethnography in the Study of Transnational Migration: Seeing the Wetland Instead of the Swamp America Arrivals," in *American Arrivals: Anthropology Engages the New Immigration*, ed. Nancy Foner, Illustrated Edition (Santa Fe: School for Advanced Research Press, 2003), 99–128.

12 Peggy Levitt and Nina Glick Schiller, "Conceptualizing Simultaneity: A Transnational Social Field Perspective on Society," *International Migration Review* 38, no.3 (2004): 1009.

the fluid social space within which immigrants are simultaneously embedded in cross border multi layered socioreligious relations.[13]

In this chapter, we employ the concept of religious field in order to discover and explain the intensity of the cross border engagement of the second-generation Ghanaian migrants in Amsterdam. Transnational religious field is operationalized as linkage between host-home countries as well as host-host countries.[14] The study investigates the multifarious relations in the transnational religious field of the AICCs in Amsterdam that result in the construction of identity among second-generation Ghanaians.

GHANAIAN IMMIGRATION IN THE NETHERLANDS

During the 1980s, the Netherlands suffered shortage of manual labor in their factories and service sectors but the Dutch government did not want to enter into a guest worker agreement with any country. However, asylum seekers and labor migrants entered the Netherlands with little restrictions and got absorbed into the Dutch manufacturing and service sectors where unskilled labor was needed.[15] Mass movement of Ghanaians to the Netherlands began during this period and most of them settled in the Bijlmer district of Amsterdam and to a lesser extent in The Hague.[16]

Moreover, some Ghanaian migrants who had already established in other European countries also moved to the Netherlands due to its flexible immigration policies. In several of the interviews, some of the second-generation (SG) Ghanaians recounted that they were born in other European countries before their parents moved to the Netherlands. A female respondent whose parents first settled in Belgium said: "I was born in Belgium in 1989 but my mother decided to move to Amsterdam when I was almost one year old and it was because the living conditions and opportunities for immigrants were more favorable here in the Netherlands (SG. 23)." Another female interviewee (SG. 21) also said her parents moved from Belgium (where she was born) to the Netherlands while she was only a year old "to seek for residence permit and also

13   Levitt and Schiller, "Conceptualizing Simultaneity: A Transnational Social Field Perspective on Society."
14   Edmond Akwasi Agyeman, "Religion, Race and Migrants' Integration in Italy: The Case of Ghanaian Migrant Churches in the Province of Vicenza, Veneto," *Deusto Journal of Human Rights*, no.8 (2011): 105, https://doi.org/10.18543/aahdh-8-2011.
15   Rijk A. Van Dijk, "Religion, Reciprocity and Restructuring Family Responsibility in the Ghanaian Pentecostal Diaspora.," in *The Transnational Family: New European Frontiers and Global Networks*, ed. Deborah Fahy Bryceson and Ulla Vuorela (Oxford/New York: Berg Publishers Limited, 2002), 173–96.
16   Ton Dietz et al., "Ghanaians in Amsterdam, Their 'Good Work Back Home' and the Importance of Reciprocity," *Journal of Global Initiatives: Policy, Pedagogy, Perspective* 6, no.1 (June 1, 2011), https://digitalcommons.kennesaw.edu/jgi/vol6/iss1/7.

to look for work." Similar stories were recounted by interviewees SG 6 and SG 27, whose parents migrated to Amsterdam from Paris and Berlin respectively while they were children. These multiple origins also explain the complexity of fields within which the second generation constructs their religious identities. Within this context, second-generation Ghanaians define their social fields and identities not only in respect of their current country of residence and that of their parents' origin country, but also in connection with several other countries in Europe and beyond where Ghanaian communities have been established.

According to the Amsterdam Bureau for Research and Statistics, Ghanaians were about 12,480 in 1996 but by 2014, the total Ghanaian population in the Netherlands had increased to 22,556.[17] These official figures do not capture Ghanaian migrants living in the Netherlands without a legal status of residence. In 2014, the number of second-generation Ghanaians in the Netherlands was estimated to be around 8,871.[18] More than half of the Ghanaian populations in the Netherlands live in Amsterdam and they are the fifth largest immigrant group in Amsterdam after the Moroccans, Turkish, Antilleans and Surinamese. They are largely employed in semi-skilled and unskilled jobs mainly due to low proficiency in the Dutch language, discrimination in the labor market and the cumbersome process of foreign diploma recognition by the Dutch government.

The Ghanaian-led Christian Churches

In the Netherlands, a growing number of AICCs were started mostly by Ghanaian immigrants in the 1990s. According to Ter Haar, by 1995 there were about seventeen Ghanaian Christian churches in Amsterdam and forty African-led churches in Amsterdam alone.[19] As of 2013, AICCs in the Netherlands were estimated to be around 150.[20] Whereas most of these churches were established by members of the migrant community, some Ghanaians who founded churches in Ghana also reached out to Ghanaian migrant communities in Europe to establish their churches in order to attain an international status.[21]

For first-generation Ghanaian migrants, the presence of co-ethnic churches in the host country provided a space to be at home in a foreign country and to maintain ties with the country of origin. The churches, at the same time, offered avenues for new arrivals to meet people with similar language

---

[17]   "Statistics Netherlands. 'Population; Sex, Origin and Generation.,'" accessed August 1, 2017, https://opendata.cbs.nl/statline/#/CBS/en/dataset/37325ENG/table?fromstatweb

[18]   "Statistics Netherlands. 'Population; Sex, Origin and Generation.'"

[19]   Gerrie ter Haar, *Halfway to Paradise: African Christians in Europe* (Cardiff: Cardiff Academic Press, 1998), 6.

[20]   Dirk Van den Bos, "Kerken in de Bijlmer zijn parels in Amsterdam-Zuidoost.," accessed June 27, 2013, https://www.rd.nl/kerken-in-de-bijlmer-zijn-parels-in-amsterdam-zuidoost-1.320217

[21]   Akwasi Agyeman, "Religion, Race and Migrants' Integration in Italy."

and worldview, fit into the new society, and construct new identities.[22] Some AICCs in Amsterdam provided the opportunity for some Ghanaian first-generation migrants to meet and share their experiences with the aim of helping them shed off the stress and trauma that their migration trajectories generated. They provided psychosocial support and an organizational structure to first generation immigrants which consequently led to shaping the identity of Ghanaian migrants in the Netherlands.

Most of the Ghanaian AICCs operate within a transnational field. This was evident during the interviews with church leaders. A founding member of the Wesley Methodist Church of Ghana said:

> As a mission circuit of the church we have a financial quota that we contribute to the headquarters of the church in Ghana. Apart from the obliged contribution, we also support financially the running of the church's university in Ghana. The church in Amsterdam has adopted some of the local churches in Ghana and we remit financially to them regularly. Apart from the pastor who is an employee of the church, all of us work on voluntary basis and we do not expect any financial returns (interview on November 16, 2014).

The head pastor of Pentecost Revival Church International also recounted:

> In the year 2000, Pentecost Revival Church International started here in Amsterdam and it has remained a vibrant church. We have sister churches in different parts of Belgium and also in Ghana. In each of the countries, we have a national coordinator and I am the general overseer with my office here in Amsterdam (interview on August 15, 2014).

The transnational field within which these churches operate allows pastors and other church leaders in Ghana to influence the activities of their members in the Netherlands. Additionally, the co-ethnic nature of the churches enables migrants to perpetuate their language and culture in the Netherlands.

CREATING CHRISTIAN IDENTITY IN THE TRANSNATIONAL RELIGIOUS FIELD

The engagement of second-generation Ghanaians in the socio-religious space which the IACCs provide affects their identity construction. This is because, the transnational religious field of most of the AICCs provides the avenue for the creation of a transnational Christian identity by the second-generation. Most of the second-generation participants define themselves in reference to their membership in AICCs. Some of the second-generation respondents maintain strong cross-border ties with their parent's country of origin through

---

[22]   Akwasi Agyeman, "Religion, Race and Migrants' Integration in Italy."

their participation in the transnational religious field. This came up in several of the narratives during the interview sessions:

> I am a member of Moment of Glory Prayer Army (MOGPA) headquartered in Ghana. Every morning the head pastor organizes morning devotion with members around the globe through internet radio. We engage in intercessory prayers, sharing of the word of God and then we conclude with final blessing. On Saturdays, the members here in Amsterdam gather at a rented place and we have direct encounter with the pastor via Skype video conferencing. Items like necklaces, scarves, and banners are blessed by the pastor and members buy them. Some people also bring their own personal items (SG. 18).

The practice of participating in morning devotions organized by pastors in Ghana through internet radio or Skype is very popular among Ghanaian migrants in Amsterdam. Another respondent who is a member of another church narrated her experiences in relation to the MOGPA morning devotion:

> I do join MOGPA morning devotion around 4:30 am through the MOGPA mobile application which I have downloaded on my phone. I do not attend the Skype meetings on Saturday because I do not want to go public with my participation. My church has vehemently prohibited the attendance and participation of such spiritual exercises but the practice is spreading widely among Ghanaians in Amsterdam. Some people adorn themselves, their cars and homes with stickers, banners, bracelets and scarves of MOGPA (SG. 7).

From the interviews, it becomes clear that advancement in communication technologies like internet radio, internet television, and Skype calls reveals the uniqueness of transnational practices in recent times. Therefore, in many situations, second-generation migrants do not need to physically translocate, yet they are still able to engage in the transnational religious field due to time–distance compression facilitated by the use of modern communication technologies. Intriguingly, none of the interviewees mentioned MOGPA as their prime religious institution, meanwhile in their narrative, they recounted their participation in the religious activities of MOGPA. The practice questions belongingness and adherence to a particular religious institution and points to the possibility of maintaining multiple religious identities in the transnational religious field.

Some of the second-generation interviewees, however, operated within the same religious field even as they travel back and forth between host country and parents' country of origin. This was evidenced in some of the interviews as explained in the following narrative:

> Whenever we go to Ghana we attend the same church as we do here in
> Amsterdam. I used to complain to my mum on the frequency with which we
> went to church. But now because I am personally convinced of my spiritual
> growth; I love to pray and fast. The last time we went I was the one reminding
> my mum of the prayer meetings and I do not care if we stay in church praying
> for five days. I am going back home this summer (SG. 13).

CREATING UNLIMITED SPACE IN TRANSNATIONAL RELIGIOUS PRACTICE

The intensity of religious transnationalism among the second-generation migrants was examined in terms of transnational living and transnational practices.
Even though transnational migrants may not produce transnational children,
this chapter found that the transnational religious engagement of some of the
respondents were categorized as transnational living due to the intensity of
cross-border religious activities. From the data, the social space within which
second-generation Ghanaians live their religious life encompasses not only
their country of residence or that of origin, but also other host communities
where Ghanaians have settled. In other words, while some second-generation
Ghanaians are involved in witnessing their Christian faith within the Dutch
public space, some extend it to other European countries like Belgium and the
United Kingdom. This was evidenced in this interview:

> For me Christianity is a way of life. I try to live my life in the likeness of Christ
> and in so doing I preach Christ with my life. Together with the youth group, I
> go out to public places, hospitals and rehabilitation homes to preach the word
> of God. We sometimes travel to the cities of Brussels, Antwerp and Liege in
> Belgium to evangelize and try to plant new branches of the church (SG. 33).

Another respondent who is a member of a music group also recounted how
through music she has contributed to spreading the gospel across countries in
Europe through the network of her church:

> I am a member of the youth choir and we evangelize through singing. We have
> performed in several Dutch churches and in other branches of my church in
> Belgium and the United Kingdom. The Lord has manifested in these occa-
> sions. We have had native converts through our song ministration (SG. 39).

Another respondent narrated his experience in the transnational religious
social field in the following words:

> Almost every year, the youth groups in the branches of our church in the
> Netherlands and in some other countries in Europe go for a week-long camp-
> ing. Last year we went to Cologne, Germany and this year we are likely to go to

Belgium. We do different recreational and religious activities to strengthen our spirituality. We also build friendship networks and they are all aimed at our physical and spiritual wellbeing (SG. 11).

The fact that these youth groups claim to draw people, including natives, into their religious folk and also build friendship networks across countries, also helps in understanding the salient role of religious fields not only in terms of physical space that they create but also in terms of level of networks and interactions that they are able to construct.

Moreover, a lot of the participants also recounted that their participation in transnational religious fields have helped to attain new status and recognitions that transcend national boundaries. A participant recounted that she is given similar social status and recognition when she travels home or elsewhere in Europe as a deaconess in the church of Pentecost. She said:

> I am a deaconess in my church and I am sometimes sent on mission to minister in other branches of the church. I am acknowledged as a deaconess and treated as such. When I go home, I only need to exhibit my card which identifies me as a deaconess and I am allowed to sit among the deaconesses. The recognition of the hierarchical position of members of the presbytery outside their jurisdiction is the normal practice in my church. Sometimes some of the presbytery from Ghana visit us and they also enjoy the same treatment and privileges according to their position in the church (SG. 7).

Another area where the second-generation respondents manifested an aspect of transnational practice was their role in financial remittances. In fact, while some studies on remittances of immigrants concluded that second generations do not have strong connections with their home countries as such they have no obligations to remit financially,[23] this was not confirmed by our study. On the contrary, data from this research show that at the organizational level, some of the respondents are obliged to contribute toward the financial needs of their churches back home. The obligation is born out of their sense of belongingness and identification with the religious field which is not confined to the nation-state but transcends the territorial boundaries of the Netherlands. The following narratives from two of our respondents elucidate this point:

> The paying of the tithe at the end of the month is very painful. As a student I receive very little money from my part-time job but I am encouraged to pay one tenth as tithe in church. Sometimes my contribution is not up to one tenth of the salary but I am doing my best. I do believe in the Christian doctrine of

23   Ntokozo Nzama and Brij Maharaj, "Honouring the Dual Commitment: Remittance Strategies of Ghanaian Migrants in Amsterdam," *Migracijske i Etničke Teme* 30, no.2 (2014): 193–213.

offering which is why I continue to give notwithstanding the difficulties. It is my belief that the Lord will reward me spiritually for my financial contributions to the church. The money is also needed to support the church here in Amsterdam and at home for its pastoral and developmental projects (S.G. 41).

I do pay tithe in church because I work. Growing up, I translate certain Christian values that I acquired from childhood into my day to day lifestyle. I am aware that there is more blessing in giving than in receiving. As such I make financial offerings to the Lord to atone for my sins and to pray for the Lord's blessings. My financial contributions to the church foster the pastoral work of the church back home (S.G. 14).

In fact, majority of interviewees were in support of their church's transnational obligation. There were only few instances where some had opposing views. But this was largely due to financial and time constraints associated with such obligations. For example, one participant lamented about the persistent demand for money in his church. He said:

When I get to church always there is a preaching about money, Oh God, give them money to pay their tithe, always it is like give money, money and all that the church does is to preach and pray to God for money, to support the work of God. The church has a lot of developmental projects both home and abroad and it needs to enrich its finances in order to carry out the activities. I am interested in the wellbeing of the church members in Amsterdam not those outside, as such I am against the church's approach (SG. 3).

Another participant recounted the cumbersome nature of the second-generation engaging in the church's transnational missionary work:

My church did not have any branch outside the Netherlands and even though it tried to go on mission in other countries as a way of recruiting new members, the exercise was cumbersome so I could not take part in it. Moreover, I could not abandon my schooling for the missionary activities (SG. 8).

However, our observation from the data collected indicated that the fluid and unrestricted boundaries of the Christian community connect the second-generation Ghanaians in Amsterdam to geographical locations outside their place of residence as they remit financially toward the pastoral projects in the transnational religious field. From this perspective, financial remittances in the transnational religious field are not perceived as mere acts of charity but they are embedded with religious and spiritual connotations. The data challenge the literature that describes remittances as merely the financial or material transfer of migrants' resources to their country of origin without taking into consideration the motivations and benefits of the sending agents.[24] Such mono-causal simplification of remittances relegates to the background the social and religious interaction between migrants and their home countries.

Moreover, this study shows that the second-generation Ghanaians in Amsterdam interiorize the shared essence and religious beliefs of their parents with a transnational optic that transcends the nation state.[25] As social actors in the religious field, they reconstruct and give fresh meaning to the identities befitting of the lifestyle in the host country. Although the studied second-generation Ghanaians have been brought up in the Dutch society, they are conscious of their ethnic identity. Identities formed by some of them are not monolithic but multifaceted and they are a melange of several identities encompassing a wide space. Furthermore, the involvement of some second-generation Ghanaians has ensured the sustainability of transnational religious practices initiated by their parents. Individuals think and act in ways that are expected of them and with time they internalize these norms as their own.[26] The research shows that religious socialization from infancy has formed some of the studied second generations to perceive Christianity as a way of life.

Conclusion

In this chapter, we examined the transnational religious identities and practices among second-generation Ghanaian immigrants based in Amsterdam. We conceptualized second-generation Ghanaians as any child born in the Netherlands or was brought to the Netherlands at or before the age of six with at least one parent being of Ghanaian origin and was at least eighteen years and above at the time of this research.

The study found that, the Ghanaian immigrant churches that were established in the Netherlands from the late 1980s operated within a transnational field. This has created a space for the creation of a transnational religious identity among the second generation. The transnational space created by these religious groups encompassed the country of origin of the respondents' parents as

[24] Hein De Haas, "International Migration, Remittances and Development: Myths and Facts," *Third World Quarterly* 26, no.8 (November 1, 2005): 1269–84, https://doi.org/10.1080/01436590500336757; Ronald Skeldon, "International Migration as a Tool in Development Policy: A Passing Phase?," *Population and Development Review* 34, no.1 (2008): 1–18, https://doi.org/10.1111/j.1728-4457.2008.00203.x.

[25] Arthur, *African Diaspora Identities*, 162.

[26] Darren E. Sherkat, "Counterculture or Continuity? Competing Influences on Baby Boomers' Religious Orientations and Participation," *Social Forces; Oxford* 76, no.3 (March 1998): 1087–1114, http://yeshebi.ptsem.edu:2103/10.1093/sf/76.3.1087; Darren E. Sherkat and John Wilson, "Preferences, Constraints, and Choices in Religious Markets: An Examination of Religious Switching and Apostasy," *Social Forces* 73, no.3 (March 1, 1995): 993–1026, https://doi.org/10.1093/sf/73.3.993.

well as other countries in Europe where Ghanaian communities are found. The second generation maintained a strong cross-border ties within these spaces through their participation in the transnational religious environment provided by the churches.

Some of the transnational religious practices of the participants included participation in the morning devotions organized by pastors in Ghana through internet radio and Skype, participation in the evangelizing activity of the church to spread the gospel across Europe, creating religious networks and friendship ties across Europe and making financial contribution toward the churches' missionary and social activity in the parents' country of origin. From the study, it was clear that advancement in communication technologies like internet radio, internet television, and Skype calls, which have been appropriated by the youth has actually shaped and revealed the uniqueness of modern transnational religious practices among the second-generation migrants.

The chapter showed that, although most of the second-generation were brought up in the Netherlands, their participation in the transnational religious field has helped them to construct a complex ethnic identity encompassing the different spheres within which they operate.

Finally, we found the majority of participants (48 out of 50 second-generation interviewees) to be strongly in support of the transnational activities of their churches. In a few instances where there were opposing views, we found that they could largely be attributed to the financial burden and the time constraints that the second generation is confronted with as a result of their participation in the transnational activity of their church.

BIBLIOGRAPHY:

Akwasi Agyeman, Edmond. "Religion, Race and Migrants' Integration in Italy: The Case of Ghanaian Migrant Churches in the Province of Vicenza, Veneto." *Deusto Journal of Human Rights,* no.8 (2011): 105-116. https://doi.org/10.18543/aahdh-8-2011.

Alba, Richard, and Victor Nee. *Remaking the American Mainstream: Assimilation and Contemporary Immigration.* Cambridge, Mass.: Harvard University Press, 2003.

Aparicio, Rosa. "The Integration of the Second and 1.5 Generations of Moroccan, Dominican and Peruvian Origin in Madrid and Barcelona." *Journal of Ethnic and Migration Studies* 33, no.7 (September 1, 2007): 1169–93. https://doi.org/10.1080/13691830701541713.

Arthur, John A. *African Diaspora Identities: Negotiating Culture in Transnational Migration*. Lanham, MD: Lexington Books, 2010.

Baum, Sandy, and Stella M. Flores. "Higher Education and Children in Immigrant Families." *The Future of Children* 21, no.1 (2011): 171–93. https://doi.org/10.1353/foc.2011.0000.

Boatemaa Setrana, Mary, and Justice Richard Kwabena Owusu Kyei. "Transnational Paradigm within Immigrant Political Integration Discourse. The Case of Ghanaians in the Netherlands." *Afrique Contemporaine* 256, no.4 (2015): 91–101.

Caneva, Elena, and Maurizio Ambrosini. "Le seconde generazioni: nodi critici e nuove forme di integrazione." *SOCIOLOGIA E POLITICHE SOCIALI*, no.1 (2009): 25–46. https://doi.org/10.3280/SP2009-001003.

Dietz, Ton, Valentina Mazzucato, Mirjam Kabki, and Lothar Smith. "Ghanaians in Amsterdam, Their 'Good Work Back Home' and the Importance of Reciprocity." *Journal of Global Initiatives: Policy, Pedagogy, Perspective* 6, no.1 (June 1, 2011). https://digitalcommons.kennesaw.edu/jgi/vol6/iss1/7.

Favaro, G., and M. Napoli. *Ragazze e ragazzi nella migrazione. Adolescenti stranieri: identità, racconti, progetti*. Milano: Guerini e Associati, 2004.

Haar, Gerrie ter. *Halfway to Paradise: African Christians in Europe*. Cardiff: Cardiff Academic Press, 1998.

Haas, Hein De. "International Migration, Remittances and Development: Myths and Facts." *Third World Quarterly* 26, no.8 (November 1, 2005): 1269–84. https://doi.org/10.1080/01436590500336757.

Jones-Correa, Michael. *Between Two Nations: The Political Predicament of Latinos in New York City*. Ithaca, NY: Cornell University Press, 1998.

Kasinitz, Philip, John H. Mollenkopf, and Mary C. Waters. "Worlds of the Second Generation." In *Becoming New Yorkers: Ethnographies of the New Second Generation*, 1–19. New York: Russell Sage Foundation, 2004.

Kyei, Richard Kwabena Owusu, and Mary Boatemaa Setrana. "Political Participation Beyond National Borders: The Case of Ghanaian Political Party Branches in the Netherlands." In *Migration and Development in Africa: Trends, Challenges, and Policy Implications*, edited by Steve Tonah, Mary Boatemaa Setrana, and John A. Arthur, 41–56. Lanham: Lexington Books, 2017.

Levitt, Peggy, and Nina Glick Schiller. "Conceptualizing Simultaneity: A Transnational Social Field Perspective on Society." *International Migration Review* 38, no.3, (2004): 1002–39.

Menjívar, Cecilia. "Living in Two Worlds? Guatemalan-Origin Children in the United States and Emerging Transnationalism." *Journal of Ethnic and Migration Studies – J ETHN MIGR STUD* 28 (July 1, 2002): 531–52. https://doi.org/10.1080/13691830220146590.

Mügge, L. *Beyond Dutch Borders: Transnational Politics Among Colonial Migrants, Guest Workers and the Second Generation*. IMISCOE Research. Amsterdam University Press, 2010.

Nzama, Ntokozo, and Brij Maharaj. "Honouring the Dual Commitment: Remittance Strategies of Ghanaian Migrants in Amsterdam." *Migracijske i Etničke Teme* 30, no.2 (2014): 193–213.

Portes, Alejandro, Luis E. Guarnizo, and Patricia Landolt. "The Study of Transnationalism: Pitfalls and Promise of an Emergent Research Field." *Ethnic and Racial Studies* 22, no.2 (January 1, 1999): 217–37. https://doi.org/10.1080/014198799329468.

Salazar Parreñas, Rhacel. "Long Distance Intimacy: Class, Gender and Intergenerational Relations Between Mothers and Children in Filipino Transnational Families." *Global Networks* 5 (2005): 317–36. https://doi.org/10.1111/j.1471-0374.2005.00122.x.

Schiller, Nina Glick. "The Centrality of Ethnography in the Study of Transnational Migration: Seeing the Wetland Instead of the Swamp America Arrivals." In *American Arrivals: Anthropology Engages the New Immigration*, edited by Nancy Foner, Illustrated Edition, 99–128. Santa Fe: School for Advanced Research Press, 2003.

———. "Transmigrants and Nation-States: Something Old and Something New in the U.S. Immigrant Experience." In *The Handbook of International Migration: The American Experience*, edited by C. Hirschman, P. Kasinitz, and J. Dewind, 94–119. Russell Sage Foundation, 1999.

Schiller, Nina Glick, and Georges E. Fouron. "Terrains of Blood and Nation: Haitian Transnational Social Fields." *Ethnic and Racial Studies* 22, no.2 (January 1, 1999): 340–66.

Sherkat, Darren E. "Counterculture or Continuity? Competing Influences on Baby Boomers' Religious Orientations and Participation." *Social Forces; Oxford* 76, no.3 (March 1998): 1087–1114.

Sherkat, Darren E., and John Wilson. "Preferences, Constraints, and Choices in Religious Markets: An Examination of Religious Switching and Apostasy." *Social Forces* 73, no.3 (March 1, 1995): 993–1026. https://doi.org/10.1093/sf/73.3.993.

Skeldon, Ronald. "International Migration as a Tool in Development Policy: A Passing Phase?" *Population and Development Review* 34, no.1 (2008): 1–18. https://doi.org/10.1111/j.1728-4457.2008.00203.x.

Smith, Robert. *Mexican New York: Transnational Lives of New Immigrants*. 1st ed. Berkeley: University of California Press, 2006.

"Statistics Netherlands. 'Population; Sex, Origin and Generation.'" Accessed August 1, 2017. https://statline.cbs.nl/StatWeb/publication/?DM=SLEN-&PA=37325ENG&D1=0&D2=a&D3=0&D4=0&D5=0,85&D6=11-17&LA=EN&HDR=G2,G3,G4,T&STB=G1,G5&VW=T.

Suárez-Orozco, Marcelo M., ed. *Crossings: Mexican Immigration in Interdisciplinary Perspectives*. 1st ed. Cambridge, Mass.: David Rockefeller Center for Latin American Studies, 1998.

Timmerman, Christian, E. Vanderwaeren, and Maurice Crul. "The Second Generation in Belgium." *International Migration Review* 37, no.4 (2003): 1065–1090.

Van den Bos, Dirk. "Kerken in de Bijlmer zijn parels in Amsterdam-Zuidoost." Accessed June 27, 2013. http://www.refdag.nl/kerkplein/kerknieuws/ kerken_in_de_bijlmer_zijn_parels_in_amsterdamzuidoost_1_749924.

Van Dijk, Rijk A. "Religion, Reciprocity and Restructuring Family Responsibility in the Ghanaian Pentecostal Diaspora." In *The Transnational Family: New European Frontiers and Global Networks*, edited by Deborah Fahy Bryceson and Ulla Vuorela, 173–96. Oxford/New York: Berg Publishers Limited, 2002.

CHAPTER 2

MIGRATIONS AND RELIGIOUS CONFIGURATION AMONG "EVANGELICALS" IN LATIN AMERICA'S NORTHERN TRIANGLE IN THE FIRST DECADE OF THE TWENTY-FIRST CENTURY

Eduardo Albuquerque

"We are a travelling species."

Jorge Drexler
Movimiento, Salvavidas de Hielo, 2017

INTRODUCTION

Human migrations are an age-old phenomena; and their reverberations on our cultural, social and religious makeup have been extensively studied. What each population eats, how they organize themselves, the way they speak, what they believe in and how they express their beliefs have some degree of correlation with migration flows which have shaped us and which influence new cycles.

However, although migrations are as old as history itself, their flows vary, and so do their parameters. Thus, the impact they exert on society varies. Not only does people's movement help shape population, but the configuration of such movement is also an important factor to be taken into account. Evolution in the means of transportation and communication has given birth to a floating and oblique version of migratory movements, creating new mechanisms of influence which make the migration flows more fluid. While in the past, migrants used to carry with them influences from their points of origin which would later interplay with others from their destination (or even from other migrants), modern migration allows the opening of more dynamic channels,

31

which put the influences from the point of origin and those from the host destination in constant interchange. The same holds true for religion.

It is not in the scope of this chapter to provide a conceptual analysis of migration and religious dynamic. That has already been evidenced and analyzed by others in the academia.[1] My goal here is to identify possible elements of migration influence on the social and political behavior among non-Catholic Christians in migration flows between Central America's Northern Triangle and the United States.

MIGRATIONS AND RELIGION

The history of humankind, including its preliterate phase once called prehistory, can be told through an account of the multiple waves of migration. There is not a single period in history without record of human movement flows. Migrant populations have carried, along with their baggage, seeds, farming techniques, knowledge, and numerous cultural manifestations—including religious beliefs and manifestations. At every migration flow, the human foundation brought along in the migrant's baggage is also transformed. Encounters with a new land and new cultures generate hybrid elements, which in turn are soon moved around by subsequent migration flows.

It would be no exaggeration to say that migration and change are synonyms as far as history is concerned. Human history can be studied through the map of migration flows. Such flows, in most cases, are driven by the search for resources. Triggered by conflicts (for resources, hegemony, or natural crises), migrations in their turn bring forth other disputes. Thus, whereas migrations can be described as synonyms of change, one cannot neglect that they also produce clashes—with a higher or lesser degree of violence.

The religions of the world have both contributed to and been influenced by such clashes. Migration flows are part of the founding identity and functioning dynamics of the various religious traditions. All major world religions have expanded on the path of migration. Some were born in the wake of migration waves. At the very onset of Judaism, Islam, Buddhism and Christianity, migration (with spatially concentrated origin and destination points) and diaspora (dispersed across different destinations) were decisive.

---

[1]   Some of the most recent works on the issue include: Stephen Castles, Hein de Haas, and Mark J. Miller, *The Age of Migration: International Population Movements in the Modern World*, 5th ed. (London: Palgrave Macmillan, 2014). Peter Beyer and Lori Beamen, *Religion, Globalization, and Culture* (Boston: Brill, 2007). Maria Elo, "Understanding Transnational Diaspora Entrepreneurship and the Role of Values", in *Diasporas and Transnational Entrepreneurship in Global Contexts*, ed. Sonja Ojo (Hershey: IGI Global, 2016), 45–65.

The Americas, since the sixteenth century, were the scene of a violent migration event linked to colonization, a process through which the religion of the colonialist metropolis was transplanted into the colonies. This process undoubtedly took place also in Asia and Africa, but it was in the Americas that there was the largest population transplant, not only from the metropolitan countries, but also from Africa (through the Transatlantic slave trade). Transplant, miscegenation, and extermination of native populations: that was how the colonial project succeeded in suppressing and replacing (at least formally) native religions. The American colonies were formed under the religious aegis of their metropolises. Religion was used as a formative element of a new, subaltern identity, which aimed to suppress other unyielding identities (indigenous, African, etc.). In the Americas, displaced and enslaved Africans, along with uprooted indigenous populations forced to serve in the European settlements, were Christianized by force. The Christianity that resulted of that imposition, though, was never a docile reproduction.

The process of forced Christianization, totally merged in the colonial project, received a new component at the end of the eighteenth century. In the wake of economic growth and political autonomy—which would result in the independence of the colonies—new migrations of populations from countries other than the original metropolises (other European countries, Middle East, Far East, etc.) began to take place.

The poor living conditions of large sectors of the populations in the countries of origin met the need of the American elites for labor to expand the agricultural frontiers (and find a demographic "balance" to counter the danger of the then-preponderant ethnic majority of indigenous and Afro-descendant peoples). This new flux increased in the post-colonial period in the nineteenth century, and reached new peaks in the postwar periods of the twentieth century. These migration flows brought new religious elements to Latin America—especially Protestantism, absent in the vast majority of colonial enterprises—initially restricted to specific ethnic groups, but which eventually influenced and were influenced by the religious stock they found.

In this nonstop course of migration waves, two types of migration flows—which started in the seventeenth century, being, however, sporadic then—have intensified since the 1960s: interregional and urban migration. In the last five decades, the population flow from rural areas to cities, and to neighboring countries, has increased, in particular, the march from Central America to the United States. Triggered by economic (boom of prosperity in the USA and rapid industrialization in the major regional economies) and political (warfare and totalitarian governments) factors, this peculiar migration flow has also had an unprecedented impact on the exchange of religious goods.

This chapter focuses on the ramification of this last flow, considering in particular its transmutation starting in the early 1990s, with new demographic, economic, and communication parameters which converged into an unprecedented migratory pattern, which I call *the urban middle-class pendulum*. Before analyzing it, it is important to briefly recap the religious profile and environment in both the countries of origin and the countries of destination.

THE NORTHERN TRIANGLE CONTEXT

The focus of this chapter is the region in Mesoamerica known as the Northern Triangle (due to its map shape), formed by Guatemala, Honduras, El Salvador, and Nicaragua. Although a structural analysis of this region is beyond the scope of this chapter, it is necessary to summarize the context in which those migrants left their homelands between the 1970s and 1990s. This panorama can be summed up in two terms: civil war and economic stagnation.

The Northern Triangle was deeply affected by the "arrival" of the Cold War in Latin America and the Caribbean, especially its main landmark, the Cuban Revolution in 1959.[2] The United States felt that its long-term economic dominance in the region was threatened as Cuba and the USSR developed close ties and Mexico pursued a policy of active non-alignment. Thus, the less powerful Northern Triangle countries saw their internal conflicts escalate exponentially because of the global geopolitical dispute that triggered and fueled armed conflicts, leaving a toll of over three hundred thousand dead and displacing about three million people.

Guatemala had the longest armed conflict in the region, outlasted only by the one in Colombia, which formally ceased in 2017. There had been armed outbreaks since 1964. But the 1970s and the 1980s were the most intense years. In that period, around 140,000 people died in clashes involving the guerrilla (some among guerrilla groups themselves), government forces, and the civilian population. Besides the death toll, 44,000 people went missing and 50,000 peasants were forced out of their lands. In the late 1980s, the intensity of the conflicts decreased. But a permanent ceasefire agreement was only signed in December 1996.[3]

---

[2]   As it is beyond the scope studied here, I will not address the conflicts and the situation in Belize, but they could be discussed in the context of the same scenario of instability. Also out of the scope of this chapter is the Mexican context, as the Mexico–USA migration dynamics has its own characteristics, and its history started before the borders of these countries were drawn the way they are now.

[3]   See Berthold Molden, "La Guerra Civil Guatemalteca: Historias y Memorias Cruzadas en el Entorno Global de la Guerra Fría," *Anuario de estudios centroamericanos* 41 (2015): 67–91.

While Guatemala experienced the longest lasting conflict in the region, El Salvador witnessed the most dramatic one. Between 1980 and 1992, upto 75,000 civilians were killed and other 9,000 went missing.

Honduras did not have guerrilla groups, but it was deeply influenced by the region's volatility. It was marked by deep political unsteadiness, continual interference by the United States and growing military prominence. Ruled by elected presidents or not, the country went through decades in which civil rights were harshly restricted. Amnesty International estimates that over 8,000 politicians disappeared in Honduras in the 1970s and 1980s. Honduras has become the main ally of the United States and an intermediary for anti-socialist governments and paramilitary groups. Its support of the war on guerrillas has not produced a stable alliance with the neighboring governments. Dozens of military skirmishes were recorded. The most anecdotal one was the "Soccer War," a clash with El Salvador lasting 100 days, sparked during a match between Salvadorans and Hondurans.

Nicaragua has a peculiar history in this region. It is the smallest of the four countries, and it also experienced armed conflict. But a far-reaching alliance (with strong support from sectors of the Catholic Church and minority urban Protestant groups) ended up quickly overthrowing the dictatorial regime and installing a socialist-oriented government. Then the roles were reversed and the United States, which had supported pro-government groups in El Salvador and Guatemala, set up a guerrilla force there. Cuba, an ally of neighboring guerrilla groups, partnered with the government. Despite the peculiarity of its ideological traits, the effects of those elements on forced immigration were similar to the events in its neighbors.[4]

Such conflicts worsened the rural exodus, creating a huge wave of *desplazados*, internally displaced people who lost their lands and were forced away. In 1985, almost 20 percent of the population of those countries experienced forced displacement. Starting in the mid-1960s on, but mainly in the 1970s and 1980s, armed conflicts in many Latin American countries and in the Caribbean set off migrations to Europe and the Americas (Mexico, Spain, Costa Rica, Canada, but mainly to the United States). Those populations carried their religion with them.

The immigrant waves up to 1980 had as an important characteristic an apparent religious transplantation, facilitated by the double isolation experienced

---

4   Celestino Andrés Arauz and Patricia Pizzurno. "José Antonio Remón Cantera: Militarismo, Oligarquía y Guerra Fría," *Crítica*, March 11, 2010, http://www.critica.com.pa/archivo/historia/f11-03.html.

by those communities, aliens in their host countries and exiled from their countries, taking the form of "ghetto" churches.

When the conflicts ended, between the late 1980s and early 1990s, the economy of the region was devastated by the aftermath of years of warfare, the oil economic crisis and the ensuing American recession in the late 1970s. As the region had always depended economically on the US demand, the prices of its export products fell, leading an already precarious economy, exhausted by the cost of war, to near collapse.

Re-democratization came along with economic crisis, political instability, and weakened institutions. The region—which in the 1960s had average indicators close to those of other countries in the continent—by 1990 represented the poorest group of countries along with Haiti and Bolivia.

While poverty and war struck historically poor rural populations who had constituted the bulk of the migratory flow until the end of the 1980s, the economic collapse of the 1990s hit the growing urban and educated middle class (in the large and mid-sized cities) that grew in the 1970–1990 period. There was no space in the traditional primary-export economy or in an industrial/services economy (as in other countries of the continent) to absorb them and respond to their desire for progress and social mobility.

It has already been noted that when it comes to migration, it is not only the number of those migrating that matters, but also their reasons.[5] This group from the Northern Triangle migrating in the 1990s had primarily economic motivations.

While between 1990 and 2010, the migration flow of Mexicans to the United States decreased until it turned negative; the number of immigrants from the Triangle rose almost by 150 percent during the same period. The end of armed conflicts in the Northern Triangle did not reverse the migration flow (except for Nicaragua, where there was some stabilization). Rather, the flow intensified in the 2000s, impelled by endemic violence (drugs, organized gangs and militias) and chronic poverty. Conflicting official data and estimated statistics show that around 20 to 35 percent of the population in the Northern Triangle migrated between 1980 and 2000.[6]

---

[5]   "Yet our era is qualitatively different. It is not just the number of people on the go, nor their reasons, though these matter." James V. Spickard and Afe Adogame, "Introduction: Africa, the New African Diaspora, and Religious Transnationalism in a Global World," in *Religion Crossing Boundaries: Transnational Religious and Social Dynamics in Africa and the New African Diaspora*, ed. Afe Adogame and James V. Spickard (Leiden/Boston: Brill, 2010), 1–28 (8).

[6]   United Nations. Social & Economic Affairs Division. *International Migrant Stock: Reports 1980–2015*. Available at http://www.un.org/en/development/desa/population/migration/publications/migrationreport/index.shtml.

Thus, communities fleeing wars would be followed by migration flows caused mainly by economic crises. If we confine our analysis to intra-regional migrations in the Americas, the migrant flow from Central American countries to the United States in only 15 years (1985–2000) was equivalent to the numbers recorded in the previous 50 years (1935–1985).[7]

Socioeconomic Profile

The phenomenon of a group of migrants changing their religious tradition and/or adhering to another, and in turn bringing the elements of the old religion into this new one, is not something new. This is basically the script of the history of religions. What this article highlights, though, is the specificity of religious exchanges in a Northern Triangle contingent at the end of the twentieth century whose characteristics differ from their forerunners in terms of its socioeconomic aspects and migratory dynamics.

In the socioeconomic aspect, as seen above, this group of Latinx migrants is different from their forerunners in terms of income, schooling, context of origin, and age (the same phenomenon may also be associated with Southern Asians or even with Africans, but that is out of the scope here). Among Latinas/os who migrated to the United States between 1990 and 2000, 38 percent had a college degree, and 57 percent were in the middle class in their countries of origin; 11 percent of those migrants were among the 20 percent wealthiest people of their home countries, and continued to maintain active economic ties with them; 82 percent came from cities and 54 percent from the three largest cities of their countries. Most of them (64 percent) were under 35. For the sake of comparison, while in 1984 less than 60 percent of Latinos/as were proficient in English, in 2012, almost 70 percent communicated well in the language of the country of destination.[8]

Their ties with their home countries can be noticed in the fact that they send most of their income back to their countries of origin. The so-called remittances reveal the first change in migration after the 1980s civil wars in the region. The postwar migrants maintain active ties with their home countries. Insignificant before 1990, remittances increased considerably between 1992

---

7   US Border Patrol. *South Border Consolidated Report, 2014.* Census Bureau, Immigration & United Nations, Department of Economic and Social Affairs, Population Division (2013). *International Migration Report 2013.* ST/ESA/SER.A/346, available at https://www.cbp.gov/newsroom/stats.

8   Jens Manuel Krogstad et al eds., "English Proficiency on the Rise Among Latinos: U.S. Born Driving Language Trends," Pew Research Center, Washington, D.C., May 2015, available at http://assets.pewresearch.org/wp-content/uploads/sites/7/2015/05/2015-05-12_hispanics-english-proficiency_FINAL.pdf.

and 2008,[9] becoming vital for the Northern Triangle economies, mainly El Salvador and Guatemala where 28 percent and 24 percent of the adults, respectively, depended primarily on remittances for their survival.

This flow also differs from the previous ones by bringing in immigrants with weaker traditional religious ties, coming from more urban, educated contexts, and with a disillusioned view of politics (for them, politics means war). If remittances reveal strong ties with those who stayed, this group is part of a typical phenomenon of the turn of the century: pendular migration. Immigrating and returning in regular cycles was rare before. For this group, however, it is the standard behavior, as 61 percent of the Latino/a migrants coming to the United States after the 1990s (or their family members) have engaged in commuting journeys.[10] Remittances, thanks to communication technologies and income level, among other factors, enabled this migratory group to maintain active and dynamic ties with their home countries. It was no longer a matter of staying here or there; it was about being in both places and nowhere at the same time.

The contingents already established in previous waves tended to religious conservatism, as they tried to maintain the culture of origin (aided by a retrospective frozen image of their home countries), as if building their identity in the country of destination based on their old memories. Consequently, most Hispanic immigrants tended to attend exclusively Latino/a churches.[11] More recent migrants have turned the exchanges between their home and host countries (in this case the United States) into dynamic channels. But, before turning our attention to that, we need to briefly examine the religious context of the United States at the time when the pendular migratory wave from the Northern Triangle started.

North-American Religious Context

Immigrants coming from different religious traditions, dispersed and weak European religious institutions, and wide freedom of religion and anti-monopolistic legislation converted the United States into the first large open religious market. An unprecedented religious dynamics was established. Individuals were not just able to choose their religious affiliations. Those choices could be different from their parents' or their ethnic group's religion. And, after transitioning to another religion, they could change religion again.

---

[9]   Multilateral Investment Fund of the IDB Group, Map Database. IDB, Washington, 2012. Also, "Remittances to Latin America and the Caribbean in 2012: Differing Behavior Across Regions," available at https://publications.iadb.org/bitstream/handle/11319/5919/Remittances%20to%20Latin%20America%20and%20the%20Caribbean%202012.pdf?sequence=2.

[10]   US Border Patrol. *South Border Report, 2014*, https://www.cbp.gov/newsroom/stats

[11]   UAM Prensa, *Comportamiento regliososo Hispanico*, Mexico DF: UAM Prensa, 2011).

The Evangelical movement and its Pentecostal ramifications into multiple churches are expressions of this dispute that changed the North American religious map. It created the ability one sees in many American churches today to understand and react quickly to market changes—an ability to adapt vocabulary, architectures, clothing, media, liturgies, and homilies to survive and grow. That greater capacity of some groups to adapt to particular contexts became an important factor in a competitive religious market. In the nineteenth and twentieth centuries alone, more churches emerged in the United States than probably in all previous centuries in the history of Christianity. The aggressive dispute for religious consumers continues to be a key trait of that movement to this day.

Conservative theologian David Wells coined a concept to describe this adaptation model. He distinguishes churches that are traditionally "producers" (with a slow changing pace, and with clearly defined products waiting to be discovered by their audience) from those he classifies as "consumers" (active search groups, which shape their religious products to suit the markets emerging around them).[12]

Although in Wells' work such division is both value-based (for producing groups) and pejorative (for consumers), we can apply Wells' idea using a Weberian economic sociological logic. Thus, as in other economic markets, successful consumer churches tend to move toward operating as producers, becoming then stagnant, and losing market to new consumer groups, in a dynamic economic market cycle. From the perspective of non-stagnant roles, Wells' division can be seen not as a dichotomy, but as a gradient. Groups vary not only in their capacity to shape themselves, but in the way they adapt. For example, consumer liturgies and architectures may coexist with producer homilies and discourses. Many other combinations arise as in a construction toy, like a religious Lego, becoming overwhelmingly expansionist, and adapting in response to the aggressive dispute for market share typical of capitalist economies.

Thus, it is important to recognize this open characteristic of a religious market and its contrast to Central American scenario in the 1980s. Even though the Catholic Church no longer held the status of official church in most of Latin America, and the freedom of religion and belief was legally established, the Centro American countries studied here were still religious arenas where Catholicism was hegemonically dominant. The precariousness of official statistics in this regard hinders accuracy, but it is safe to say that by 1985 less than 8 percent of the population of the region could be classified as Protestant,

---

12   David F. Wells, *Above All Earthly Powers: Christ in a Postmodern World* (Grand Rapids: William B. Eerdmans Publishing Company, 2005).

Evangelical, or Pentecostal. Moreover, outside the capital cities (where 72 percent of immigrants came from) this figure was close to 3 percent.[13]

Thus, migrants in the Northern Triangle pendular flows came from a hegemonic religious space with very low change. But perhaps partly because of the violence underlying such hegemony, they also came from a highly adaptable tradition of religious practice. There were not many religious groups openly vying for the faithful, but a religious fluidity can be seen in the popular practices (absorbed into or only tolerated by the Roman Catholic Church), which expressed a diversity differing from hegemonic practices either through updating or syncretizing elements not only from Native American and/or African-derived religions but also from other forms of Catholicism and religious traditions. Religious adaptation (which some identify as resistance) made those immigrants not only less adherent to Catholic orthodoxy but also open to changing their religious affiliations. In other words, Central-American immigrants, accustomed to a sort of marginalized religious dynamics, quickly converted into a religious market niche in the United States.

Unidirectional and Pendular Exchanges

A specific element of this market dynamics is central for my analysis: free megachurches (groups of thousands of consumers not linked to traditional denominations). This branch, in its somewhat neo-Pentecostal versions, was the group displaying the most aggressive consumer behavior toward the market of Northern Triangle migrants in the late twentieth century and early twenty-first century.

Megachurches began to show interest in the Northern Triangle migratory flow in a singular moment in the dispute for the religious market in the United States. Televangelism had been growing since the 1970s, and was already exhausting its first phase, focused on the insertion into a market complementary to the ecclesiastical parish and large evangelistic events often associated with "3D churches" or traditional parishes. In the 1980s, "televangelist" churches slowly changed their strategy and started using mass media as a platform to build and expand their own local "retail" network nationwide. Mass media, however, remained their main stage, and mass market—either unexplored or under-explored—their main focus. The strategy was to create and expand a network of local small "outlets." Nothing, though, would overshadow the centrality of the electronic pulpit as the main sales channel.

---

[13]   Percentages extrapolated retroactively by the author, using the Albuquerque-Rochmann, model based on the data of 1980 and 2005.

Megachurches learned from televangelists the importance of television and the professional and television-oriented religious spectacle. But mass media was for them an advertising strategy, not a primary delivery channel. Local experience remained its main product; so the worship event was expected to be as spectacular as possible in size and special effects to create a unique experience.

Megachurches linked the centrality of the "live" product to two new factors. The first was the market-oriented focus on growing suburban areas (other than the focus on small cities and marginalized urban populations used by televangelists) and the middle class. Thus, megachurches developed an experience with specific products aimed at reaching the whole family (differently from the mass products of televangelist churches). They no longer limited themselves to going after the remnants of the traditional churches; those who were not consuming religious products. Instead, their target now included those dissatisfied with the religious products from the other churches, i.e., those using a traditional liturgical religious format—the "producers" format, in Wells' classification.

The second new element in megachurches was the import of techniques hitherto applied exclusively to non-religious products. The late twentieth century witnessed the consolidation of the perception of management and marketing as "sciences." It became common for governments, civil society organizations and churches to apply principles of administrative rationality from the private sector in their management practices. Modern capitalism broke once and for all the boundaries of economic relations and took over the management posts of human undertakings hitherto regarded as "not-for-profit."

Because of its market focus, megachurches have grown mainly in the most economically dynamic states in the US south (California, Colorado, Texas, and New Mexico) and in the suburban regions with the highest population growth (conurbations in the Eastern-Central states), which is precisely the main destination of the Northern Triangle migration. Texas is the state with the largest concentration of megachurches: seventeen of the largest and fourteen of the fastest growing megachurches are located there.[14] The destinations are distinct from those of previous flows, with a heavier urban presence in the East Coast and Florida, and some rural presence in the South.[15]

In 1970, there were ten megachurches in the United States. In 1990, 250 fitted that definition, and in 2003, 740. The number rose to 1,416 in 2011. The top 100 together have over one million members or consumers. Half of them consider themselves non-denominational, that is, they are not associated with

---

[14]   Data from the Hartford Institute for Religion Research, available at http://hirr.hartsem. edu/megachurch/megachurches.html.
[15]   Pew Research Center, 2015. US Census Bureau, https://www.census.gov/data.html.

any older or larger movement.[16] This phenomenon of growing megachurches in the United States ended up crossing paths with the large migratory flows from the Northern Triangle.

At the end of the twentieth century, as Northern Triangle immigrants began to achieve economic stability, they entered the radar of the US religious market. There is no specific data by home countries, but here are some facts: a) Northern Triangle immigrants were the fastest growing group at the turn of the century (when the Mexican migration flow stagnated and then receded); b) megachurches have grown more among Hispanics than among other groups. In California and Texas, for example, the Hispanic contingent is 21.3 percent higher in megachurches than among the general population. Nationwide, Hispanics account for nearly $1/4^{th}$ of megachurch members against a share of just over $1/10^{th}$ of the general population.[17] Between 2000 and 2015, the percentage of Evangelical Latinos in the United States more than doubled—the highest growth rate recorded within the Evangelical segment.

Another factor that points to the strong participation of Northern Triangle migrants in American megachurches is a phenomenon from across the border: the emergence of megachurches in the Northern Triangle countries. Since the turn of the century, a number of new churches have formed in Nicaragua, Honduras, El Salvador, and mainly in Guatemala.[18] Northern Triangle Evangelical groups of pendular configuration have become an active channel of influence in the religious expressions in their home countries. The authority exercised by missionaries (associated with large denominations and agencies) since the nineteenth century has undergone a dramatic decline.

Evangelical churches have been experiencing a vertiginous growth in the twenty-first century in those countries, having come to occupy a place of significant political and social influence among the urban middle class in their countries of origin. Religious statistics are precarious, but some figures are striking. From less than 10 thousand people in 1995, the largest Northern Triangle churches accounted together for over 1.5 million people in 2015.[19] Some of those churches are: Hosanna in Nicaragua; El Shaddai, Casa de Dios and Fraternidad Cristiana, in Guatemala; Tabernáculo do Avivamiento Internacional and Ministerio COMPAZ, in El Salvador; and Ministerio Internacional La Cosecha, Ministerio Apostólico y Profético Mi Viña, Centro

---

[16]   Jose Luis Rocha, *Meglaiglesias en Centro America* (Manágua: Editora de la UCA, 2014).

[17]   University of Texas in El Paso. "Latin American and Border Studies," El Paso, 2015. See also Pew Research Center, "The Shifting Religious Identity of Latinos in the United States: Nearly One-in-Four Latinos Are Former Catholics," available at http://www.pewforum.org/2014/05/07/the-shifting-religious-identity-of-latinos-in-the-united-states/.

[18]   Some of them are older churches undergoing some form of re-engineering.

[19]   Rocha, *Meglaiglesias*.

Cristiano Internacional, Casa del Alfarero, Reunión del Señor, Iglesia Cántico Nuevo, Ministerio Internacional Shalom, and Vida Abundante, in Honduras.[20]

On top of these developments, by the end of the 1990s another wave of religious import came to the region from the South: the so-called *invasión Brasileña* (Brazilian invasion), a Brazilian version of North-American faith healing neo-Pentecostalism. While the exchange of influences is undeniable, this group differs from pendular migrant churches as they, at least initially, turned to the lower classes, to intra-regional immigrants, and to small towns. In common, both groups share an entrepreneurial vision of the religious enterprise. Whereas the Brazilian churches were not a result of migratory flows, they benefited from the religious diversity they had brought about, the growing flow of South-South trade, and the Brazilian desire to bolster their geopolitical standing in the region. Despite its success, this segment did not grow as much as the pendular megachurches. The largest multinational Brazilian religious enterprise, the Universal Church of the Kingdom of God, saw its membership jump from 269 thousand to 3 million between 1991 and 2010, an annual growth rate of 28 percent. In the same period, pendular megachurches grew upto 37 percent a year.[21]

In effect, as those megachurches flourish on both ends, pendular migration facilitates the establishment of a religious trade balance. Continual and complex exchanges reflect on both ends. In what follows, I highlight some of the possible religious effects of this encounter, of this new populational migratory dynamics.

THE NON-PLACE IN THE BALANCE

My aim here is to highlight that pendular migration, a situation in which populations can live in two different places at the same time, leads paradoxically to a dynamics of non-place in the exchanges, including the religious ones. It is no wonder that these groups, whether in the United States or in the Northern Triangle region, reinterpret cultural (a discourse of individual material success as a proof of divine favor, the belief in the possibility of manipulating immaterial conflicts, and so on) and political elements (reducing the political sphere to an individual moral agenda) of their context to create a political discourse camouflaged by a culturally detached religiosity.

The concept of place is transversal, informed by multiple human, social, political, and economic factors. Thus, the capacity for instantaneous dissemination of information, the rapidity of economic flows, and advanced

---

20   Most of them have branches also in neighboring countries, and some in the United States.
21   Rocha, *Meglaiglesias*. Growth projection estimated by the author, based on linear logs.

transportation systems have contributed to shorten distances, having profound implications on the way space is perceived. Place is norm and power; it belongs in the domain of strategy and indicates a position of stability, a configuration of positions. In its turn, non-place occurs in a construction of meanings linked to practices or tactics that are capable of changing established meanings. Space is the practice of the place, or the ways subjects change it by appropriating, occupying, or experiencing it. Space presupposes a place animated by displacement; it is "a crossing of bodies in movement;" being, therefore, a "practiced place." Migrations create space by replacing previously fixed places, that is, places artificially built with deliberately arranged elements.

Some authors have pointed to the construction of non-places or the creation of artificial places in the context of flows of people, products and information. These non-places are in high demand among groups in search of community, rootedness, historical sense, and identity. Spaces deliberately homogenized, built on the ideals of production and consumerism, and subjected to transient use.[22] A shopping mall is an example of a non-place. All shopping malls offer the same ambience, no matter where they are; an artificial bubble created for the purpose of keeping people isolated from external factors for the longest time possible so that they consume the maximum they can.

When megachurches occupy non-sacred places, they take ownership of secular elements that create a non-place, a place for consumption, artificially detached from its political, social, and national context. Everything in a megachurch is built to fit any context and as many consumers as possible. The option for desacralized religious spaces, symbolic ambivalence, and individualistic discourse are elements of this non-place. Their leaders use business names for their activities, not accepting religious labels. Such strategy maintains open the possibilities for pleasing a broad range of people, and to accept a plethora of religious practices. For instance, 40 percent of the members of El Shaddai, a Northern Triangle megachurch, identify themselves as "Catholic."[23]

This pendular, bidirectional movement of megachurches thus entails the paradox of acknowledging the non-place, through the solely individual message, the practice of intense cultural absorption, and through political action

---

[22]   For an analysis of the concepts of place and non-place, see: Luiz Carlos Schneider, "Lugar e Não-Lugar: Espaços da Complexidade," *Ágora* 17/1: (2015): 65–74; Milton Santos, *A Natureza do Espaço: Técnica e Tempo, Razão e Emoção* (São Paulo: Editora da Universidade de São Paulo, 2002); and Michel de Certeau, *A Invenção do Cotidiano: Artes de Fazer* (Petrópolis, RJ: Vozes, 1994).

[23]   Universidade Centroamericana (UCA). *Iglesias en Centro America* (Viento, UCA, Managua, 2014).

both passive (as it regards any proposal for social reform) and active (when electing candidates with agendas focused on individual morality).[24]

Religious Balance of Trade in Discourse and Structure

Some scholars stress that what defines a megachurch is not only its size, but also its strategy.[25] In the case of pendular megachurches, their strategic configuration and exchanges can be summarized in two aspects: discourse and structure. Both in discourse and structures, pendular megachurches do their best not to cause political disruption, being conservative by nature, markedly cloning business elements. The discourses and structures of those megachurches on the US end (oriented toward their consumers) are influenced by the demands and views of Northern Triangle immigrants. On the other hand, Northern Triangle megachurch leaders also absorb American discourses and the management structures and emphases of North-American megachurches.

Discourse

The dominant discourse in pendular megachurches stresses economic success (prosperity), being individualistic, commercial (possibility of manipulative exchange with the sacred), politically conservative (strict sexual morality, but loose social and economic morality), and with a consumerist emphasis (on consuming religious products as a sign of belonging, to the detriment of following rules and customs or even the need to regularly attend services). The prosperity discourse that marked some Evangelical groups in the United States during the robust postwar economic growth had a setback during the 1976–1980 economic crisis. However, American megachurches updated that discourse to the new wave of economic growth in the 1990s. This growth was sustained by increased capital gains, the entrepreneurial boom, growing competition, new forms of employment (shorter, multiple contracts), and more skilled employees (higher schooling level). Such growth led paradoxically to an increase in both wealth and inequality. The Northern Triangle migration flows in the 1990s reacted positively to a discourse that associated faith to economic growth, and economic progress to boldness and a forward-looking and bellicose attitude (strengthened by competition).

Economic success has been traditionally seen in the Anglo-Saxon Protestant culture as a sign of divine blessing. But one thing that is characteristic

---

[24] Ibid.

[25] See, for instance, Roberto Bazanini and Ernesto Michelangelo Giglio "The Role of Stakeholders in Solomon's Temple: An Exploratory Study," *Organização & Sociedade* 24/83 (2017): 674–690; and Scott Thumma, "The Kingdom, the Power, and the Glory: Megachurches in Modern American Society" (PhD diss., Emory University, 1996).

in the prosperity gospel that one finds in the Northern Triangle tradition, as in most Latin America, is the association of opulent signs of economic superiority with divine favor. Economic success, seen as a sign of divine favor, thus met the immigrants' aspirations of getting rich and exhibiting it. In such context, the discourse of success disengaged itself from traditionally austere Protestant ethics to meet the necessity of immigrants to exhibit their success. In pendular megachurches, money takes the center stage in ways that a Calvinism based on shame and guilt would not allow.

Less common elements in Anglo-Saxon religious traditions also grow exponentially in American megachurches where Hispanic people are strongly represented. Catholic and Native American elements are given more emphasis than in the "Anglo-Saxon" versions of these churches. Spiritual warfare and the consequent need to guarantee protection (through objects, chains, campaigns, and so on) are exacerbated. It is known that Anglo-Saxon and Eastern religions also make symbolic use of objects, whereas Latin American religiosity also has its own rational instrumentation of the religious enterprise and the emphasis on the sacred for success. However, it is reasonable to state that in a symbolic "trade balance," those immigrations have imported and exported elements of discourses from one place to another.

Pendular megachurches tend to embrace and encourage moral, economic, and social ideas, of which some associate with postmodern secularism (open competition, instrumental relationships, economic success as a goal, consumption as a social activity, vague institutional affiliation, and so on). A message focusing on positive thinking, concern with persecution against Christians, and economic success commonly heard in US megachurch pulpits was thus tailored to the demands of incoming Northern Triangle populations, and adapted to include Northern Triangle components.

The refusal to provide their own political responses does not mean that megachurches on both ends are apolitical. On the contrary, they are extremely active and eager for power. Political power is seen as an asset to be acquired through competition and exhibited. However, it is not accompanied by a broader social and political philosophy. Rather, it tends to replicate liberal economic ideology while oddly combining it with anti-liberal elements such as the support of repressive practices by the state against the poor and other "deviants," the imposition of religious symbols in the public space (along with the struggle against lay education and the imposition of religions limits to science), the primacy of individual power (as long as people profess the same faith) in private spaces (opposition to children's and women's rights, among others), and the diffusion of conservative individual moral values (against same-sex unions or "non-traditional" families).

It is curiously noticed that the process of formatting a religiosity contained within aspects of sexual morality (which reinforce economic, gender-based and ethnic inequalities) subordinated to the interests of the powerful is something old in Latin America. It is an advanced "technology" in the history of the continent. However, it is possible to say that Northern Triangle migrants have contributed to strengthen a moral framework that associates pragmatism to an emphasis on individual morality.

Structure

If in the case of discourse, transnational exchanges have established a mutual trade of influences, it is not much different when we think about structure. The pendular structure is based on a tripod: aesthetics of modernity (non-religious mimicry); management and marketing strategies; and religious business models.

All these elements, alien to or at least uncommon in the Northern Triangle tradition, have emerged and acquired dominant status in the megachurches that have popped up throughout the Triangle. However, paradoxically, American elements are "contextualized," and once returned to the United States with the migratory flows, they influence their own creators.

In the aesthetics aspects of modernity, the structure of Northern Triangle megachurches is conceived to break with traditional religious aesthetics. Temples, titles, liturgies, and practices are all shaped so they do not look religious. As a consequence, they concomitantly avoid traditional competition and expand their potential market. Here an American matrix is clear. However, it also undergoes adaptations in the Northern Triangle. While in the United States megachurches tend to contrast with traditional Evangelical groups, generating an unpretentious lay aesthetics, in the Northern Triangle they tend to emphasize an overtly lay aesthetics that is both anti-Catholic and ostensibly luxurious. Such aesthetics also embodies the unabashed use of technology as a sign of modernity, contrasting the "analogical" style of traditional religious culture. Northern Triangle aesthetics is designed to show both luxury and modernity.

The management matrix is also clearly North American, characterized by streamlined administrative management, competition, emphasis on revenue as a critical success indicator, and on the production and sale of a myriad of religious products. Managers take the stage; their wisdom and ability are evidenced by successful numbers. These business components gain Northern Triangle tones and shadings as they are used to emphasize the personalist figure of the leader (the religious CEO), and to promote a spectacularization of power in the pursuit of monopolistic control and pragmatic opacity.

As for the religious models, dynamic migratory flows facilitated the replication in Northern Triangle countries of religious formats (theologies, ecclesiologies, liturgies, training materials, and communication styles) transplanted from megachurch groups (pervasive among migrants) in the United States. Thus, the presence of official religious franchises and some "pirate" versions, established and developed in the shadows of their North American matrices, drastically expanded. The control and influence previously exerted by denominations or missionary agencies were pulverized and recast according to business models. Paradoxically, megachurches of Latin American origin, structured within a corporate logics, have spread their operations to the United States, where that model originated, thus establishing a kind of faith multinational enterprise.

CONCLUSION

This chapter does not aim to draw broad conclusions. However, based on a number of religious phenomena associated with recent migration, it seeks to identify possible symbolic and material exchanges which created a religious trade balance at the beginning of the twenty-first century between the Northern Triangle countries and the United States, especially through megachurches in both regions.

I do not aim to state in a simplistic or reductionist way that these exchanges are exclusive. There are other global cultural elements, influences from changes in the social and economic contexts, along with other simultaneous migratory flows which also need to be accounted for. Nevertheless, it seems clear that new migration patterns, pendular and urban middle class, are related to the phenomenon of Northern Triangle megachurches, having likely impacted the American megachurches as well. Thus, moving beyond the commonly assumed paradigm of smaller countries that are subservient to and emulating major powers, consequently standing always on the receiving end, the observation of Northern Triangle pendular migration helps us inquire the extent to which religious phenomena in the United States are influenced by exchanges with economically subaltern neighbors. The fact that these countries are small in size, population, or economic power does not mean that they are not able to export religious products and re-signify what they import in their exchanges with the United States.

A deeper understanding of pendular religious exchanges can also shed light on possible relations between the increase of reactionary political responses in both regions and the increasing phenomenon of religious neo-conservatism seen in both ends.

BIBLIOGRAPHY:

Arauz, Celestino Andrés and Patricia Pizzurno. "José Antonio Remón Cantera: Militarismo, Oligarquía y Guerra Fría," *Crítica*. March 11, 2010. http://www.critica.com.pa/archivo/historia/f11-03.html.

Castles, Stephen, Hein de Haas, and Mark J. Miller. *The Age of Migration: International Population Movements in the Modern World*. 5th ed. London: Palgrave Macmillan, 2014

Bazanini, Roberto, and Ernesto Michelangelo Giglio "the Role of Stakeholders in Solomon's Temple: An Exploratory Study," *Organização & Sociedade*. 24/83 (2017): 674–690.

Beyer, Peter, and Lori Beamen, *Religion, Globalization, and Culture*. Boston: Brill, 2007.

Certeau, Michel de. *A Invenção do Cotidiano: Artes de Fazer*. Petrópolis, RJ: Vozes, 1994.

Data from the Hartford Institute for Religion Research, http://hirr.hartsem.edu/megachurch/megachurches.html.

Elo, Maria. "Understanding Transnational Diaspora Entrepreneurship and the Role of Values." *In Diasporas and Transnational Entrepreneurship in Global Contexts*. Edited by Sonja Ojo, 45–65. Hershey: IGI Global, 2016.

Krogstad, Jens Manuel et al (eds.). "English Proficiency on the Rise Among Latinos: U.S. Born Driving Language Changes," *Pew Research Center*. May 2015. https://www.pewresearch.org/wp-content/uploads/sites/5/2015/05/2015-05-12_hispanics-english-proficiency_FINAL.pdf

Molden, Berthold. "La Guerra Civil Guatemalteca: Historias y Memorias Cruzadas en el Entorno Global de la Guerra Fría," *Anuario de Estudios Centroamericanos* 41 (2015): 67–91.

Multilateral Investment Fund of the IDB Group. Map Database. IDB, Washington, 2012.

———. "Remittances to Latin America and the Caribbean in 2012: Delivering Behavior Across Regions." https://publications.iadb.org/bitstream/handle/11319/5919/Remittances%20to%20Latin%20America%20and%20the%20Caribbean%202012.pdf?sequence=2.

"The Shifting Religious Identity of Latinos in the United States: Nearly One-in-Four Latinos Are Former Catholics." *Pew Research Center*. https://www.pewforum.org/2014/05/07/the-shifting-religious-identity-of-latinos-in-the-united-states/.

Rocha, Jose Luis. *Meglaiglesias en Centro America*. Manágua: Editora de la UCA, 2014.

Santos, Milton. *A Naturezado Espaço: Técnica e Tempo, Razão e Emoção. São Paulo*: Editora da Universidade de São Paulo, 2002.

Schneider, Luiz Carlos. "Lugare Não-Lugar: Espaços da Complexidade," *Ágora* 17, no.1 (2015): 65–74.

Spickard, James V. and Afe Adogame. "Introduction: Africa, the New African Diaspora, and Religious Transnationalism in a Global World." In *Religion Crossing Boundaries: Transnational Religious and Social Dynamics in Africa and the New African Diaspora*. Edited by Afe Adogame and James V. Spickard. 1–28 (8). Leiden/Boston: Brill, 2010.

Thumma, Scott. "The Kingdom, the Power, and the Glory: Megachurches in Modern American Society." PhD diss., Emory University, 1996.

UAM Prensa, *Comportamiento Regliososo Hispanico,* Mexico DF: UAM Prensa, 2011.

United Nations. *Social & Economic Affairs Division*. International Migrant Stock Reports 1980–2015. http://www.un.org/en/development/desa/population/migration/publications/migrationreport/index.shtml.

Universidade Centroamericana (UCA). *Iglesias en Centro America*. Viento, UCA, Managua, 2014.

University of Texas in El Paso. *Latin American and Border Studies*. El Paso, 2015.

US Border Patrol. *South Border Consolidated Report*, 2014.

Census Bureau, Immigration & United Nations, Department of Economic and Social Affairs, Population Division, 2013. International Migration Report 2013. ST/ESA/SER.A/346. https://www.cbp.gov/newsroom/stats

Wells, David F. *Above All Earthly Powers: Christ in a Postmodern World*. Grand Rapids: William B Eerdmans Publishing Company, 2005.

CHAPTER 3

TRANSNATIONALISM, RELIGIOUS PARTICIPATION, AND CIVIC RESPONSIBILITY AMONG AFRICAN IMMIGRANTS IN NORTH AMERICA

Moses Biney

INTRODUCTION

On September 18, 2016, CTV News headlined the story "King of West African tribe returns to landscaping job in Canada."[1] According to the story, Eric Manu, a thirty-two-year-old Ghanaian Chief (King), had returned to Canada and resumed his previous job as a landscaper. Manu had married a Canadian woman he met in Ghana and migrated to Langley, BC in 2012. Three years later, upon the demise of his uncle, he was recalled by the elders of his tribe in Ghana to be installed as the chief (king) of Adansi Aboabo Number 2.[2] His return to Canada was therefore only temporary. According to the report, he had come to work, raise money, and procure school and medical supplies for the people of Aboabo No. 2. It states:

> Manu and his Canadian boss Susan Watson started a foundation that packed a shipping container with medical supplies, school supplies, and clothing that arrived in Ghana this spring. The *To the Moon and Back Foundation (*italics mine*)* hopes to continue raising money and donations to send a second shipment and improve the local medical clinic.

Though sensational, this story is not an isolated case. In October 2009 for instance, the story of Charles Wesley Mumbere, a former nurses' aide who was crowned King in Uganda was reported by the Daily Telegraph. He had worked

---

[1]   See http://www.ctvnews.ca/canada/king-of-west-african-tribe-returns-to-landscaping-job-in-canada/ Last accessed October 15, 2017

[2]   This is the name of a village in southern Ghana. The No. 2 distinguishes it from another nearby village with the same name.

for years as a nurse's aide in Maryland and Pennsylvania. Mumbere, aged 56, who was a US permanent resident and had a son and daughter in Harrisburg had to relocate to Uganda and travelled back and forth between Uganda and the United States.[3] I have heard several other anecdotal accounts of African royals who do "less than royally" jobs in cities and towns in the United States and Canada but play very important political and social roles in their countries of birth. Aside from royals such as Eric, there are many African immigrants living in North America who play vital social and political roles in their countries of origin. I recount these stories for two reasons. First, to point to the transnational life of many Africans in the North American diaspora and, second, to show that immigrants perform their civic responsibilities both in their country of origin and country of residence.

Very little is known about the nature and extent of civic engagement among the post-1965 African immigrants in North America.[4] Many times, in discourses with colleagues about the religious institutions and practices of African immigrants, I have often had to answer questions such as, "Do African immigrant congregations in the United States engage in issues of social justice and advocacy?" "Are members progressive or conservative?" These questions hint at a larger and crucial question, which is, "What is the nature and function of African Diaspora Christianity in the public sphere?" We need to have a fuller understanding of these matters especially as we look at African diaspora Christianity within the context of public religion.

I seek to do two main things in this chapter. First, it interrogates the common understanding of civic responsibility as solely a local endeavor linked to territory, place of residence, rather than to global and human needs—everywhere and anywhere. Second, it shows how post-1965 African immigrants in North America understand and execute their global civic responsibilities through their transnational social and religious networks and activities.

What is Civic Responsibility?

Civic responsibility or citizens' responsibility to the state or country, is an old and perennial concept. Though its meaning is still contested,[5] and often

---

3   See http://www.telegraph.co.uk/news/worldnews/africaandindianocean/. Last accessed November 16, 2017.

4   Not much is known about the civic engagement of Post-1965 immigrants in America in general. A few publications that briefly touch on the subject include: Michael W. Foley and Dean Hoge, *Religion and the New Immigrants: How Faith Communities Form Our New Citizens* (New York: Oxford University Press, 2007); R. Stephen Warner, *A Church of Our Own: Disestablishment and Diversity in the American Church* (New Brunswick: Rutgers University Press, 2005).

5   Corwin E. Smidt et al. *Pews, Prayers, & Participation: Religion and Civic Responsibility in America* (Washington, DC: Georgetown University Press, 2008), 25.

renegotiated,[6] it generally refers to the engagement of citizens in activities which promotes the civic life and governance of their respective country or state. Examples of such activities include voting, volunteering for community projects, picking up litter, and maintaining a sanitary environment. The origin of civic participation is often traced to ancient Rome and specifically to Lucius Quintus Cincinnatus (519–430 BC), a Roman statesman and military leader whose selfless and devoted service to the Roman empire is considered the very epitome of selflessness and love of country.[7] For many democratic nations, civic responsibilities are considered essential that are often enshrined in constitutions and engrained in the lifestyles of a large percentage of the populace. In the United States, for instance, civic responsibility has its strongest endorsement in the nation's constitution ratified in 1787. The preamble to the constitution states:

> We the people of the United States, in order to form a perfect union, establish justice, insure domestic tranquility, provide for the common defense, promote general welfare, and secure the blessings of liberty to ourselves and the prosperity do ordain and establish this constitution for the United States of America.[8]

The wording and intent of this preamble, among other things, establishes a link between citizenship and civic responsibility, a symbiotic relationship between civic liberties and political structures, and a dependence of individual freedoms, liberty, and welfare on constitutional democracy. In other words, civic virtues, citizenship, and political participation are critical to promotion of social responsibility. Citizenship, or belongingness to the Union (United States of America) therefore constitutes the basis for enjoying the full liberties and welfare available. On the other hand, citizens are expected to undertake certain responsibilities to enhance the "perfect union." Prominent among these responsibilities are political participation, and civic engagement activities such as associational involvement, volunteering, philanthropy, and civic education. American citizens therefore are generally believed (and even expected) to be more socially responsible than non-citizens. Whether this is truly the case is debatable. But for now, we need to look at the more pressing question of citizenship.

Who then belongs to the Union? Constitutionally, the answer to this question is easy. Socially and politically, however, it is not so. It is complicated

---

6   Alexander W. Astin, "The Civic Challenge of Educating the Underprepared Student" in *Civic Responsibility and Higher Education*, ed. Thomas Ehrlich (Westport, CT: The American Council on Education and The Oryx Press, 2000), 124–48.

7   https://www.britannica.com/biography/Lucius-Quinctius-Cincinnatus, last accessed September 13, 2018.

8   The Constitution of the United States (Carlisle, MA: Applewood Books), 1.

by the lack of knowledge of immigration laws and conventions by a large percentage of the American populace and the chicanery of politicians and opinion leaders who exploit this ignorance and associated fears.[9]

The Citizenship Clause of the US Constitution's 1868 Fourteenth Amendment specifies that a person can gain US citizenship either by birth or through naturalization. The process of naturalization allows any person born outside of the United States irrespective of race, gender, or country of birth to apply for citizenship if he or she: (a) has lived continuously in the United States as a green card holder[10] for at least 5 years immediately preceding the date of filing the application (b) is physically present in the United States for at least 30 months out of the 5 years immediately preceding the date of filing the application (c) is able to read, write, and speak English and has knowledge and an understanding of US history and government (civics), and (d) has good moral character, accepts the principles of the constitution of the United States, and is well-disposed to the good order and happiness of the United States during all relevant periods under the law.[11] Whoever qualifies after going through the rigorous naturalization process is granted citizenship. Citizenship through naturalization confers on a person almost the same rights, and exacts the same responsibilities from him or her as born citizen.[12] The responsibilities include (i) supporting and defending the constitution (ii) staying informed of the issues affecting one's community (iii) participating in the democratic process of the United States (iv) respecting and obeying federal, state, and local laws (v) respecting the rights, beliefs, and opinions of others (vi) participating in one's local community (vii) paying income and other taxes honestly, and on time, to federal, state, and local authorities, (viii) serving on a jury when called upon, and (ix) defending the country should the need arise.[13] The rights also include the permission to vote and be voted for in state and federal elections, receiving fair and just treatment under the law, the opportunity to practice one's religion without any fear of intimidation, etc. Though these are legally protected and

---

[9] Much fear mongering and lies about immigrants and the dangers they pose were peddled during the 2016 political campaigns particularly on the side of the Republican Party (GOP) whose presidential candidate Donald J. Trump has intensified the suspicions of and hatred of immigrants and foreigners in general. Racists and bigots have also become more blatant in their physical and verbal attacks.

[10] Green card holders are those who have been issued with permanent residency cards. They are authorized to stay and work in the United States and are also able to travel back and forth between the US and other countries.

[11] United States Citizenship and Naturalization Service, https://www.uscis.gov/us-citizenship/citizenship-through-naturalization/path-us-citizenship, accessed November 12, 2017.

[12] A major difference is that a naturalized citizen cannot stand for or be voted for as the president of the United States.

[13] https://www.uscis.gov/us-citizenship/citizenship-through-naturalization/path-us-citizenship, accessed November 12, 2017.

even mandated, not all Americans, know or accept this fact. It is not uncommon for some Americans to perceive all people born outside the United States (irrespective of status) and their American-born children as "immigrants" who must be deported. Social media platforms such as Facebook, Twitter, and others are replete with comments and arguments by scholars, politicians, and social commentators, that continually reinforce the debunked notion that immigrants are merely "takers," that is, they feed off the taxes of citizens by accessing government-assisted programs such as welfare and charity without contributing politically, socially, and financially to the life of America.[14]

For many non-white naturalized citizens, their legal statuses do not automatically translate into full social acceptance.[15] Ironically, descriptors such as "foreign-born," "alien," and "second-generation immigrants" used in US census and immigration classification connote a less than equal relationship between born and naturalized citizens and deepen the perception mentioned earlier.

Debates regarding citizenship in America have often revolved around issues of assimilation, multiculturalism, globalization, and nationalism. Assimilationists call for an America which is a "melting pot" of all cultures. One of its chief proponents the late Samuel P. Huntington, who for many years taught at Harvard University and directed its Center for International Affairs, for instance, argued that immigration without assimilation was a problem for America and all wealthy industrialized cities.[16] To him, the "salience and substance of American identity" has and continues to diminish due largely to the presence of immigrants who have failed to assimilate fully into the American culture.[17] He blames this situation and what he calls the "erosion of the importance of citizenship" on the allowance of dual citizenship in the United States. Here are his words:

> The concept of dual citizenship is foreign to the American constitution. . . . Yet many Americans have homes in two States. Under existing law and practice however, Americans can be citizens of two countries. Dual citizens with

---

[14] If Facebook, Twitter and other social media platforms were considered true barometers of American racial, cultural, political and religious relationships, then it is obvious that racism, ethnocentricity and bigotry masquerading under the guise of patriotism and "anti-Political Correctness" remain high.

[15] Some Ghanaians I interviewed in an earlier research for instance, indicated that although they are naturalized American citizens, they feel often treated as second- class citizens due to their race and because they were not born in the United States. See *From Africa to America: Religion and Adaptation among Ghanaian Immigrants in New York* (New York: New York University Press, 2011), 25–2.

[16] Samuel P. Huntington, *Who Are We? The Challenges to America's National Identity* (New York: Simon Schuster Paperbacks, 2004), 178.

[17] By "American culture" he essentially meant Anglo-protestant culture which he considered the best for democratic governance.

residences in Santo Domingo and Boston can vote in both American and Dominican elections, but Americans with residences in New York and Boston cannot vote in both places.[18]

This quote is striking for two important reasons. First, it oversimplifies the US law on dual nationality as described in the Immigration and Nationality Act. Second, it exaggerates and critiques the transnational lifestyles of many naturalized American citizens and especially their ability to exercise civic responsibilities in both the United States and other countries. It cannot be overemphasized that globalization and its attendant crossing of borders has become part of the common reality of our times. Improvements in technology and transportation have considerably enhanced inter- and intracontinental travel making it comparatively easy for legal residents and naturalized citizens to move between the United States and their countries of birth. For Huntington and others, this weakens national identity and must not be encouraged. Granted that that may occur, what they often fail to acknowledge however, is the benefits the United States derives from these "unofficial ambassadors" who by virtue of their "dual citizenship" are able to influence policies in other countries and foster American interests.

Unfortunately, such views as expressed by Huntington have not remained merely part of an academic discourse. Practically, they appear to have influenced considerably the thoughts and actions of nationalists and many white supremacists who view citizenship through the prism of "blood and soil." A clear evidence of this is a "Unite the Right" rally held in Charlottesville, Virginia, on August 12, 2017. Far right groups—white supremacists, white nationalists, neo-Nazis, Klansmen and militias—converged on Charlottesville, Virginia, supposedly to protest the removal of the statute of the late confederate general Robert E. Lee from the Emancipation Park. Marchers, some carrying rifles, swastikas and confederate flags, and different kinds of Fascist memorabilia chanted anti-Muslim, anti-Semitic, anti-immigrant, and racial slogans and threatened violence. At a vigil organized the night before, Klansmen dressed in white and carrying torches chanted repeatedly, "Jews will not replace us," "blacks will not replace us," "blood and soil." "Antifa," a conglomeration of anti-fascist groups, also organized to protest the rally. The verbal exchanges and physical confrontation that ensued quickly degenerated into violence leading to several injuries and one fatality. As one reporter calls it, "it was a war zone."[19]

---

18   Samuel P. Huntington, *Who Are We?*, 213.
19   See "Blood and Soil," https://www.bing.com/videos/search?q=chants+of+%22jews+will+not+replace+us&vie;   https://www.theguardian.com/us-news/2017/aug/16/charlottesville-neo-nazis-vice-news-hbo

The chant "blood and soil" at this "protest" is instructive not only because of its historical connections with Nazism but more importantly; it is indicative of the resurgence in twenty-first century America, of the notion that ethnicity is bound to blood descent and territory and that true citizenship requires an ethnic and religious test. Not all Americans subscribe to this notion as revealed in the late Senator John McCain's rebuttal in his remarks at the 2017 Liberty Medal Ceremony.[20]

The Charlottesville incident provides a context for our current discussion of civil responsibility in North America as it serves as a pointer to the general ascendancy in the scapegoating and vilification of minorities and "foreigners" in North America and the chilling effects they have on African immigrants. Though shocking, the incident was not unexpected. Events and the nature of much of public discourse before, during and after the 2016 presidential elections in the United States have been boiling up to this point. More so, statements and policy proposals directed against immigrants and minorities by politicians and powerful voices in the society have emboldened white supremacists and other hate groups to verbally and physically attack persons they consider foreigners.[21]

For many African immigrants I interviewed, this and other such instances were proof of the lack of true acceptance of non-white persons in America. Marda, a fifty-five-year-old woman from Liberia responded this way when I asked her how she felt: "I have lived in this country (US) for 35 years. I have never felt so fearful for my life and anxious for my children." When I asked if she would want to go back to Liberia, she emphatically said "No!" After a short pause, she continued, "I'm a citizen of the United States. This is where I belong. I want to remain here, so I can support the family back in Liberia." Mama

---

[20]   He reminds Americans, particularly its leadership that: "We live in a land made of ideals, not blood and soil. We are the custodians of those ideals at home, and their champion abroad. We have done great good in the world. That leadership has had its costs, but we have become incomparably powerful and wealthy as we did. We have a moral obligation to continue in our just cause, and we would bring more than shame on ourselves if we don't. We will not thrive in a world where our leadership and ideals are absent. We wouldn't deserve to." See: https://medium.com/@ SenatorJohnMcCain/remarks-at-the-2017-liberty-medal-ceremony-8d69751a5ac1,   accessed December 5, 2017.

[21]   President Trump's rhetoric and policies have been very anti-immigrant though he claims otherwise. Some of his earliest executive orders included a "travel ban," deportation of undocumented immigrants and convicted permanent residents. He also revoked the Deferred Action for Childhood Arrivals (DACA) provisions put in place by his predecessor to protect from deportation persons who were brought into the United States as minors and have lived there all their lives. Other Republican law makers have shown anti-immigrant bias through their comments. Take for example the incendiary tweets from Steve King, congressman from Iowa: "Wilders understands that culture and demographics are our destiny. We can't restore our civilization with somebody else's babies." https://t.co/4nxLipafWO— Steve King (@SteveKingIA) March 12, 2017.

Uzo, a sixty-five-year-old retired nurse who often spends the winter months in Nigeria, her country of birth, told me she was so angered and saddened by what happened in Charlottesville. "It is worrisome what is going on," she said, "ICE[22] is going around looking for people to deport." At the time of my interview, she was preparing to travel to Nigeria to help with an orphanage she has been supporting financially for twenty years. Sark, a seventy-two-year-old man from Ghana, who in 2016 voted for Donald Trump to become president, told me how disappointed he was. On his last trip to Ghana, an amount of 28,000 dollars he had on him was seized by the US customs agents because he failed to fill the necessary disclosure forms at the airport. Part of the money, he explained, was from friends who asked him to give to their family members in Ghana.

African Transnationals and Civic Responsibility

The growing presence of African immigrants in cities and towns in North America and Europe has been noted by many scholars.[23] According to the 2018 World Migration Report issued by the International Organization for Migration (IOM), there were about 2 million immigrants from Africa living in Northern America in 2015. This is out of a total of 16 million residents outside of Africa—in Europe, Asia and North America.[24] African immigrants in the United States are made up of women, men, and children from various countries in Africa. They come with different cultural and religious beliefs and practices which they live by and try to pass on to their children. They are also varied in terms of legal statuses—undocumented, visa holders, permanent residents, and citizens. Like other post-1965 immigrants, they resist any pressure to completely cut ties with their home countries. As evident from my interviews with some of them presented in the previous section, they maintain highly transnational lifestyles and networks. "Transnationalism," as Steven Vetrivel defines it, is a "sustained cross-border relationships, patterns of exchange, affiliations and social formations spanning nation states."[25]

---

[22]   ICE is acronym for Immigration and Custom Enforcement. It is a branch of the US Department of Homeland Security.
[23]   See Paul Stoller, *Money Has No Smell: The Africanization of New York* (2002), Rogaia Abusharaf, *Wanderings, Sudanese Migrants and Exiles in North America*, Jacob Olupona and Regina Gemingnani, *Africa Immigrant Religions in America* (2007), Jehu J. Hanciles, *Beyond Christendom, Globalization, African Migration and the Transformation of the West* (2008), Moses O. Biney, *From Africa to America: Religion and Adaptation Among Ghanaian Immigrants in New York* (New York: NYU Press, 2011); and Mark R. Gornik, *Word Made Global: Stories of African Christianity in New York* (2011).
[24]   Of those migrants living outside of Africa, 9 million were in Europe, 4 million in Asia and 2 million in Northern America. *World Migration Report 2018*, 45.
[25]   Steven Vertovec, *Transnationalism* (Oxon and New York: Routledge, 2009), 2.

The immigrants often shuttle personally and through proxies between their "host" and "home" countries and are simultaneously immersed in the affairs of both.[26] Some have multiple "home" countries. Take for instance, Charles who was born in the UK to Nigerian parents. He moved to the United States when he was 18 years and has lived here for the last 20 years. Though currently a US citizen, he has maintained close contact with family and friends in the UK and Nigeria. Ami is also an American citizen born to Ghanaian parents. Her current spouse, Fred is from Jamaica. They have homes in Ghana and Jamaica in addition to the residence here in New Jersey. They travel back and forth between these multiple places. Among other things, these examples raise questions about citizenship and its relationship to civic responsibilities such as "What does it truly mean to be a global citizen? To what extent can one's civic responsibilities then extend beyond the borders of one's country of residence? What is the relationship between our civic responsibility and our moral responsibility toward the world?"

As indicated earlier, African immigrants in North America are essentially transnationals. The mindset of some is that they are global citizens. Many believe their rights and civic responsibilities derive from their membership of the world rather than from a nation. "Doing good to others is what humans are required to do, irrespective of where they are," Steve, a seventy-year-old Ghanaian man who gave money toward a youth empowerment project in Ethiopia once told me. Depending on their legal statuses, many play varying economic, political and social roles in multiple places at the same time. They put down roots in the United States, where they live, work, and have a family, perform their civic duties and as much as possible, also participate in the civic and economic lives of their countries of birth and any other nation where they have roots. There are some limitations however. The most crucial is the issue of disenfranchisement. Some African countries, such as Ghana currently disallow their nationals resident abroad and who have other forms of citizenship to vote or be voted for in national elections.[27] Generally, therefore, naturalizing as US citizens curtails some of the rights and responsibilities of these Africans in their home countries.

---

[26] Helpful publications on the transnational life styles and networks of African immigrants include: Afe Adogame and James V. Spickard, eds., *Religion Crossing Boundaries: Transnational Religious and Social Dynamics in Africa and the New African Diaspora*; Frieder Ludwig and J. Kwabena Asamoah-Gyadu's edited volume *African Christian Presence in the West: New Immigrant Congregations and Transnational Networks in North America and Europe*; Moses O. Biney, "Transnational Religious Networks: From Africa to America and back to Africa" in *Christianities in Migration: The Global Perspective*, ed. Elaine Padilla and Peter C. Phan (Palgrave Macmillan, US: December 2015).

[27] I know of a case where a naturalized American citizen had to relocate to Ghana and renounce his American citizenship before he could run for public office.

Nonetheless, African residents in North America, particularly those with American and Canadian citizenship, strive individually and collectively through institutions such as churches, mosques, regional, township associations, etc. Typically, their involvement in their home countries takes three main forms (a) charitable giving—financial, goods and services, (b) advisement—lobbying, advocacy, and (c) leadership—serving as traditional rulers, community leaders, family heads, etc. Religion, both in terms of beliefs as well as institutions, play important roles in the facilitation of these.

Religious Participation

A typical feature of African immigrants in North America is their religious participation. In several American cities and towns, they have founded churches, mosques, and temples which cater to their spiritual, social, and cultural needs and that of their children and grandchildren. The majority of African immigrants in North America adhere to Christianity though there is also a sizeable number of Muslims and African indigenous religious worshippers. All forms of African Christian congregations are present in the United States—Mainline Protestant Churches, Roman Catholics, African Independent Churches such as Aladura, Cherubim and Seraphim, and Pentecostals/Charismatics.

Andrew F. Walls, the renowned historian and mission theologian, has compared the new African migration to Europe and North America to the "Abrahamic" form of migration.[28] He writes:

> It is the three-dimensional aspect of the Abrahamic migration that raises particular important issues. In the Biblical model, Abraham himself responds to the hope of a better future but experiences little of the promised blessings himself. His descendants eventually receive the land; but the fullest meaning and purpose of Abraham's migration, in response to the divine call, is that others receive benefit; ultimately all families of the earth are blessed.[29]

This model in some ways describes accurately the hope and aspiration of African immigrants in North America. Like Abraham, many of them acknowledge the presence and power of God in their travels and sojourn in North America. They hope for and work very hard toward a better future for themselves and their descendants. It is for this reason they migrated in the first place. Kwame Boateng, a male nurse who works two jobs at two different hospitals told me:

---

[28] Andrew F. Walls, "Towards a Theology of Migration." In *African Christian Presence in the West: New Immigrant Congregations and Transnational Networks in North America and Europe*, ed. Frieder Ludwig and J. Asamoah Gyadu (Trenton: Africa World Press, 2011, 407–17).

[29] Walls, "Towards a Theology of Migration," 415.

I didn't come here to watch the sea. I'm here to secure a better future. Even if I don't get everything I want, I'm sure my children will have life easier.

This hope in a better, even blissful, future is not merely wishful thinking. For many, it is a hope stemming from their strong faith in God. "God's providence abounds for those who believe in him and patiently wait for him to act," yelled Grace, a young lady from Cameroun, at me one day I complained about the many challenges I was facing at the time. In my pastoral ministry with African immigrants or in my research, I have often heard variations of this assurance from many other African immigrants. These congregations serve as communities of faith for African Christians in the diaspora, providing spaces and opportunities for networking, and for the maintenance, reproduction, and transmission of African religious beliefs and cultural values.

In their book, *Pews, Prayers and Participation: Religion and Civic Responsibility in America*, Corwin E Smidt and others postulate that religion plays a crucial role in the enhancement of civic responsibility. They are right when they argue that the importance of religion, in this context, lies in the fact that it "helps generate and maintain behaviors, capacities, dispositions, that we identify as component parts of civic responsibility." [30] This is true about African immigrants in America. Their congregations and other religious institutions serve as conduits for civic engagement in four main ways.

1. Spiritual and Social Capital

Elsewhere, I have indicated that through worship and community life, African immigrant religious congregations provide their members the opportunity to strike a balance between the adjustment needed to succeed in America and contribute to the strength of the society and the preservation of their cultures and identities.[31] This means that the congregations provide spiritual and social capital which help immigrants to execute their civic responsibilities. In the face of increased opprobrium against immigrants and refugees, faith communities provide the spiritual and social support needed to help them live and act with both exilic and civic consciousness. Through sermons and Bible studies, members are encouraged to be charitable, selfless, just, and law-abiding. I have heard sermons preached from different pulpits during my research on the theme of "Caring for One's Neighbor" based on the story of the "The Parable of the Good Samaritan" in Luke 10: 25–37 and Cain's question, "Am I my brother's keeper?" in Genesis 4:9. Such sermons reinforced by words of hymns, songs, and prayers serve as important catalysts for spiritual and moral belief and practice that shape one's

---

[30]   Corwin E. Smidt et al., *Pews, Prayers, & Participation*, 208
[31]   Moses O. Biney, *From Africa to America: Religion and Adaptation Among Ghanaian Immigrants in New York* (New York: NYU Press, 2011), 3-4.

character toward civic responsibility. Aside from spiritual and moral teachings, the congregations offer members opportunities for direct service both in the United States and their home countries. It must be mentioned here that these congregations, like most of their members, have transnational networks.

2. Charitable Giving and Social Development Programs

Literature on African Diaspora mention "remittances" as one of the most important contributions of immigrants toward the development of their home countries. In many cases, the remittances are seen in monetary terms and calculated as percentage of GDP.[32] I have intentionally used the expression charitable giving here to cover every form of giving—money, goods and services, and to reflect the mindset of religious institutions and nonprofit organizations. Many churches founded by recent African immigrants in the United States see themselves as doing global rather than local mission. The whole world, they believe, is their mission field. Some of the congregations also operate as "franchises" of the home denomination. Examples include Presbyterian Church of Ghana (PCG) congregations and Redeemed Church of God in Christ (RCGC) headquartered in Nigeria. These and other such congregations often send funds and other resources for "mission projects" to the parent denominations. These are generally less so among the nonaffiliated congregations. I recall my conversation with the Senior Pastor of the Pan African Church of God in Christ in the Bronx. He was emphatic that a key reason they are interested in building congregations in the United States and countries in Africa was to be able to send aid from America to the needy places in Africa. They also sent money as scholarships and tuition for some children and provided money to pay for medical care. Other churches and faith-based organizations deal directly with social problems and needs of whole communities. The United Ghanaian Community Church in Wyncote, PA for instance provides water for selected villages in Ghana through its Borehole Project.

Worthy of mention is the work of Fountain of Life Ministries (hereafter FOLM), a fellowship of over one hundred churches in various cities and towns in Kenya, Uganda, Tanzania, and Burundi.[33] FOLM, according to its general overseer, Bishop Armstrong, seeks donations and raises funds to support poverty alleviation and social development programs in the nations mentioned earlier.

---

[32]   Read, Aderanti Adepoju, ed., *International Migration: Within, to and from Africa in a Globalized World* (Legon-Accra, Ghana: Sub- Saharan Publishers, 2010), 141–68.

[33]   His website www.amstrongchiggeh.org states that the fellowship has over one hundred and fifty churches in Kenya, Uganda, Tanzania, and Burundi. As Presiding Bishop and General Overseer, Bishop Armstrong has over 140 ministers serving with him in these three countries. He also assists two other fellowships of churches in Malawi and Democratic Republic of Congo.

3. Advisement and Advocacy

In addition to direct financial and material contributions, African immigrants' churches in North America provide various forms of business, scientific politcal, and civic advisement to institutions and ministries on the African continent. This is sometimes in collaboration with other professional associations. Together with these professional groups they organize seminars and conferences around the needs of specific cultural areas or institutions in Africa. They also raise funds for development projects in these communities. Additionally, these congregations and groups sometimes advocate for or against issues of concern.

4. Direct Leadership

African royals and professional residents in North America, like their counterparts in other diasporas, offer direct leadership and various forms of assistance to institutions in their home countries elsewhere. These institutions include the traditional(indigenous) political systems, modern political government, social and religious institutions. Some of them like Eric Manu and Charles Wesley Mumbere, the two kings mentioned at the beginning of this paper, relocate to their respective home countries while others who exercise their leadership from here in North America return periodically.

CONCLUSION

The overall goal of this chapter is to disabuse minds that immigrants are only "takers" who participate less than the native-born in the exercise of civic responsibilities. I have attempted to do so by (a) exploring the meaning of "civic responsibility" as generally understood in North America, particularly the United States, and its implications for post-1965 African immigrants' resident there and (b) showcased in a limited way the transnational life of these African immigrants and how that influences their manner of fulfilling their civic responsibilities.

In the United States, African immigrants participate in civic duties of all kinds. They, at the bare minimum, pay taxes. But more than that, some serve as council men and women on community and school boards, are called for jury duty, and vote in elections. Others serve in the military, police force, FBI, and other government agencies. Yet, they are treated as second-class citizens notwithstanding the fact that many are naturalized citizens. This has grown worse since the 2016 election. However, in the face of partial social acceptance and sometimes outright rejection, they live their lives as citizens of the world, people who extend their responsibilities beyond the borders of their countries of residence. Through the support system of religious congregations, they forge transnational networks which facilitate civic engagement in their countries of origin and interest.

There are a few lessons to be learned here. First, that, it is possible and in fact desirable to have a more global and multi-directional understanding of civic and social responsibility, and an understanding that is informed by global and transnational concerns as well as the citizenship of a nation. Second, though Christianity cannot absolve itself completely from the evils of the world, it can serve as an important vehicle for mobilizing people and resources for the greater good of all. We live in a world that is torn between ideas of globalism and nationalism; a world where racism, white supremacy and bigotry is on the rise; a world where many are displaced through violence and war; a world where extreme poverty exists amid opulence; and a world where the foreigner-immigrants and refugees are not very welcome.

Several years ago, the Rev. Dr. Martin Luther King Jr. called the world "The World House."[34] Comparing humanity to a family that have inherited a house they must live in together, he argued that "all inhabitants of the globe are neighbors." For that reason, we must all help to solve the world's problems which include racism, poverty, economic inequality, and war.

BIBLIOGRAPHY:

Adogame, Afe and James V. Spickard, eds. *Religion Crossing Boundaries: Transnational Religious and Social Dynamics and the New African Diaspora*. Leiden: Brill, 2010.

Biney, Moses O. *From Africa to America: Religion and Adaptation among African Immigrants in the United States*. New York: New York University Press, 2011.

———. "Singing the Lord's Song in the Strange Land: Spirituality, Communality and Identity in a Ghanaian Immigrant Congregation." *In African Immigrant Religions in America*, edited by Jacob K. Olupona and Regina Gemignani. New York: New York University Press, 2007.

---

[34]   Martin Luther King Jr. "Where Do We Go from Here?" in *A Testament of Hope: The Essential Writings and Speeches of Martin Luther King Jr.*, ed. James M. Washington (New York, NY: Harper Collins Publishers 1986), 617-33.

Ebaugh, Helen Rose and Janet Saltzman Chafetz, eds. *Religion Across Borders: Transnational Immigrant Networks*. Walnut Creek: AltaMira Press, 2002.

Eck, Diana. *A New Religious America: How a 'Christian Country' Has Become the World's Most Religiously Diverse Nation*. New York: HarperCollins Publishers, 2002.

Falge, Christiane. "Transnational Nuer Churches: Bringing Development to the Homeland and Morals to the US." In *African Christian Presence in the West: New Immigrant Congregations and Transnational Networks in North America and Europe*, edited by Frieder Ludwig and J. Kwabena Asamoah-Gyadu. Trenton, NJ: Africa World Press 2011.

Foley, Michael W. and Dean R. Hoge. *Religion and the New Immigrants: How Faith Communities Form our Newest Citizens*. New York: Oxford University Press, 2007.

Gornik, Mark R. *Word Made Global: Stories of African Christianity in New York City*. Grand Rapids, Michigan: William B. Eerdmans Publishing Company, 2011.

Ludwig, Frieder and J. Kwabena Asamoah-Gyadu, eds. *African Christian Presence in the West: New Immigrant Congregations and Transnational Networks in North America and Europe*. Trenton, NJ: Africa World Press, 2011.

Robertson, Roland. *Globalization, Social Theory and Global Culture*. Thousand Oaks, CA: Sage Publications Ltd, 1992.

Smith, Michael Peter and Luis Eduardo Guarnizo, eds. *Transnationalism from Below*. New Brunswick NJ: Transaction, 1998.

Washington, James M., ed. *A Testament of Hope: The Essential Writings and Speeches of Martin Luther King Jr*. New York, NY: HarperCollins Publishers, 2003.

Wuthnow, Robert and Stephen Offutt. "Transnational Religious Connections." *Sociology of Religion*, 69, no.2 (2008): 209–32.

PART II

MIGRANTS' EXPERIENCES AND RELIGIOUS DISCOURSE

CHAPTER 4

MIGRATING THEOPOLITICS: THE EFFECT OF UNDOCUMENTED PARISHIONERS ON THE PASTORAL THEOLOGY OF LATIN AMERICAN EVANGELICALS IN THE UNITED STATES

João Chaves

INTRODUCTION

An overwhelming number of American evangelicals voted for Donald Trump in the 2016 presidential election. Trump's rhetoric of tough immigration policies did not change the stance of most American evangelicals; in fact, some evidence suggest that it may have strengthened the group's support for his campaign. The theopolitical[1] anxieties of American evangelicals, however, were not limited to the US context as different iterations of such imagination attained global reach through the agency of evangelical missionaries. Historically, Latin American evangelicals affiliated to several denominations internalized the often-conservative political tendencies of American evangelical missionaries, and despite the qualified indigenous contextualization of missionary tendencies, the American evangelical conservative imagination was effectively disseminated among significant groups in the region. Evangelical denominations such as the Southern Baptist Convention—the largest Protestant denomination in the United States—sent missionaries to Latin America and helped maintain

---

[1] For the purpose of this chapter, the term "theopolitical" is used to name the intersection of theological and theologically-informed political stances that has generally characterized US evangelicalism. For examples of this intersection, see Matthew Avery Sutton, *American Apocalypse: A History of Modern Evangelicalism* (Cambridge, Massachusetts: Belknap Press, 2014); Molly Worthen, *Apostles of Reason: The Crisis of Authority in American Evangelicalism* (New York: Oxford University Press, 2013); and Lydia Bean, *The Politics of Evangelical Identity: Local Churches and Partisan Divides in the United States and Canada*, (Princeton: Princeton University Press, 2014).

denominational identity and practice through their continuous control of institutions of cultural output, such as seminaries, universities, publication houses, and denominational periodicals.[2] Such environments ensured that, both theologically and politically, there is an affinity between American evangelicalism and Latin American evangelicalism that characterizes the identity of both groups. Among Brazilian Baptists, leaders who migrate from Latin America to pastor churches in the United States, therefore, are very often ideologically close to American evangelicals when they leave their native countries. The reality of immigrant, Latin American churches in the United States, however, challenges central aspects of such conservatism. At the center of the challenges presented to Latin American pastors in the United States is the need for a theological apparatus that responds to their immigrant context.

The last few years have seen several theologies of migration and theologically informed calls for Christians to advocate for immigration reform that gesture toward the need for a theology of the new immigrants. As the issue of US immigration policy became highly contentious since the administration of George W. Bush, a number of books attempting to respond biblically and theologically—from a wide spectrum of Christian perspectives—to the tensions generated by the perceived injustices of the American immigration system were published.[3] The majority of these works represent theological reflections produced by academics for the consumption of academics or highly educated

---

[2]   In the case of Brazilian Baptists, both major seminaries, the North Brazil Baptist Theological Seminary and the South Brazil Baptist Theological Seminary as well as the major publication of the denomination, the *Jornal Batista*, and the denominational publication house has been historically controlled by Southern Baptist missionaries and/or their native supporters. For details, see Joao B. Chaves, "Disrespecting Borders for Jesus, Power, and Cash: Southern Baptist Missions, The New Immigration, and the Churches of the Brazilian Diaspora." PhD thesis, Baylor University, 2017; Fávio Marconi Lemos Monteiro, "Radicalism in Pernambuco: A Study of the Relationship Between Nationals and Southern Baptist Missionaries in the Brazilian Baptist Struggle for Autonomy." Masters thesis, Baylor University, 1991; and Mário Ribeiro Martins, "O Radicalismo Batista Brasileiro." Masters thesis, Seminário Teológico Batista do Norte do Brasil, 1972.

[3]   For examples, see James K. Hoffmeier, *The Immigration Crisis: Immigrants, Aliens, and the Bible* (Wheaton, Ill: Crossway, 2009); Matthew Soerens, Jenny Hwang Yang, and Leith Anderson, *Welcoming the Stranger: Justice, Compassion & Truth in the Immigration Debate* (Downers Grove, Ill: IVP Books, 2009); Kristin E. Heyer, *Kinship Across Borders: A Christian Ethic of Immigration* (Washington, D.C: Georgetown University Press, 2012); Steven Talmage et al., *Bishops on the Border: Pastoral Responses to Immigration* (New York: Morehouse, 2013); Daniel Carroll, *Christians at the Border: Immigration, the Church, and the Bible* (Grand Rapids: Brazos Press, 2013); E. Padilla and P. Phan, eds., *Contemporary Issues of Migration and Theology* (New York: Palgrave Macmillan, 2013); E. Padilla and P. Phan, eds., *Theology of Migration in the Abrahamic Religions* (New York, NY: Palgrave Macmillan, 2014); Elaine Padilla and Peter C. Phan, eds., *Christianities in Migration: The Global Perspective*, Christianities of the World (New York: Palgrave Macmillan, 2016); Mark R. Amstutz, *Just Immigration: American Policy in Christian Perspective* (Grand Rapids, Michigan: Eerdmans, 2017).

clerics. The religious convictions and practices of most immigrant Christians themselves, however, remain largely unexplored in terms of their theology of migration. Except for immigrants who belong to the intellectual and clerical establishment in the US—which is not a representative group—the theopolitical convictions of the common immigrant remains mostly neglected. In other words, scholarly works focused mostly on producing theologies for immigrants, not on documenting immigrants' theology.

This chapter represents an exception to the general scholarly production on the connection between theology and US immigration as it focuses on documenting theological commitments of immigrants rather than producing theology for the potential benefit of immigrants. More specifically, this chapter explores how the challenges posed by undocumented parishioners push Latin American pastors and denominational leaders in the United States to revise their theopolitical conservatism. I will look primarily at Brazuca[4] Baptists and will explore the ways in which Brazuca Baptist pastors and denominational workers in the United States change after migrating. In order to pastor faith communities comprised of primarily migrant parishioners, Brazuca Baptist pastors often change their stance on theology, American immigration policy, and political tendency because of their exposure to the conundrums created by the presence of undocumented parishioners.[5] The challenge of undocumented presence, therefore, deeply affects the dynamics of immigrant churches in terms of leadership ideology and, given the influence of these leaders in their respective communities, it informs the public witness of evangelical immigrants.

---

[4]   Among Brazilian immigrants in the United States, the term *Brazuca* is used to refer to Brazilian immigrants in the U.S. and/or Brazilian-Americans. This term was used in a number of books dealing with Brazilians in the U.S. For examples, see José Victor Bicalho, *Yes, Eu Sou Brazuca Ou A Vida Do Imigrante Brasileiro Nos Estados Unidos Da América* (Governador Valadares: Fundação Serviços de Educação e Cultura, 1989); Annie McNeil Gibson, *Post-Katrina Brazucas: Brazilian Immigrants in New Orleans* (New Orleans: University of New Orleans Press, 2012); and Jouët-Pastré, Clémence, and Leticia J. Braga, eds., *Becoming Brazuca: Brazilian Immigration to the United States* (Cambridge: David Rockefeller Center for Latin American Studies, 2008).
[5]   For the purposes of this chapter, I will focus on interviews and ethnographic work. Over the course of the last three years, I have conducted twenty-three such interviews. Among the interviewees, twenty were or are pastors of Brazuca Baptist churches, one is a founding leader of a West Coast church, and two are US-born denominational workers whose careers were partially invested in work among Brazilians. I also observed services in eleven Brazuca Baptist churches located in the states of Florida, New York, Connecticut, New Jersey, Massachusetts, California, Texas, and Maryland. In addition, I have participated in two annual meetings of the Fellowship of Brazilian Baptist Pastors in North America and one Annual Meeting of Brazilian Religious Leaders in North America. Although I have not drawn any explicit data from my own experiences as a worker in Brazuca Baptist communities, the three years I spent planting and helping lead a Brazuca Baptist church in Florida, gave me additional insight into the migration dynamics negotiated in these communities.

Brazuca Baptist Churches and Undocumented Immigrants

Undocumented immigrants have a central place in Brazuca Baptist churches. Although most Brazuca Baptist pastors are documented, most Brazuca Baptist parishioners are not, and the sheer presence of undocumented immigrants in some Brazuca Baptist churches is so great that it accounts for the reason for their existence.[6] The issues raised by the overwhelming presence of undocumented parishioners generate a moral tension for Brazuca pastors. Whereas Paul Freston noted this tension in relation to Brazuca Protestants in general, his comments are particularly applicable to Brazuca Baptists. In their Brazuca Baptist communities, the members are forced to adapt social conservatism that typifies Brazilian Protestantism in order to cope with so many of their members being outside of the law.[7] No formal theological system can fully articulate the theological reasoning that legitimizes Brazuca Baptist beliefs and practices regarding the presence of undocumented parishioners. However, one can attempt to account for the fundamental anxieties behind the rudimentary theological dispositions of Brazuca Baptists who are pushed to make theological concessions to their otherwise socially conservative tendencies. Freston helps in this regard as he points out that a rudimentary theology of the undocumented includes arguments such as: God created a world without borders; Jesus was an illegal immigrant in Egypt; Jews are ordered to treat the aliens well; and the United States is a land of immigrants.[8] But behind these explicit theological apologies, there is a more fundamental and more practical feeling: that there is something within the law itself that is deeply immoral and that United States immigration law is fundamentally damaging to the humanity of undocumented brothers and sisters.

As Kara Cebulko argued, undocumented status changes the role of the church in immigrant life,[9] given that the church often becomes a place that gives people a measure of protection from the struggles of undocumented living. Church life, however, is also changed in the process as legally documented pastors arrive to lead these churches, armed with religious visas and theopolitical tendencies heavily informed by US evangelicalism, and are confronted by

6 My ethnographic research and interviews reveal the dynamics and demographics of Brazuca Baptist churches. For further information regarding Brazilian Baptists in the United States, see Joao B. Chaves, "Disrespecting Borders for Jesus, Power, and Cash: Southern Baptist Missions, The New Immigration, and the Churches of the Brazilian Diaspora." PhD thesis, Baylor University, 2017.

7 Paul Freston, "The Religious Field Among Brazilians in the United States," in *Becoming Brazuca: Brazilian Immigration to the United States*, ed. Clémence Jouët-Pastré and Leticia J. Braga (Cambridge: Harvard University Press, 2008), 264.

8 Freston, "The Religious Field Among Brazilians in the United States," 265.

9 Kara B. Cebulko, *Documented, Undocumented, and Something Else: The Incorporation of Children of Brazilian Immigrants* (El Paso: Lfb Scholarly Pub Llc, 2013), 8.

the reality that these churches are backed by money earned by undocumented workers and that they can neither ignore their members' narratives of migrant experiences nor side with the system that oppresses them.[10]

Though the adaptation of Brazuca Baptist pastors' theopolitical conservatism to the reality of undocumented immigration is by no means seamless or automatic, the existential, ministerial, and financial price of non-adaptation is too great for them to bear. The testimonies of influential Brazuca Baptist pastors in regard to this crisis of documentation reveal the tension created by their moralistic tendency, pointed out by Freston, and the reality of United States immigration dynamics. Two longtime pastors in the United States, for example, shared similar stories that include their experience of seeking the opinion of immigration agents to cope with the existential conflict connected to their harboring of undocumented immigrants. Cases such as these illustrate that the conflictive nature of pastoring undocumented parishioners is considerable and, at least in some instances, Brazuca Baptist pastors received pastoral lessons from United States immigration officials—who told them to worry about pastoring and let immigration agents worry about law enforcement.

Given the importance of undocumented members in immigrant churches, most of these faith communities legitimize the presence of undocumented immigration either directly or indirectly through practices that include: prayers for people crossing the border, testimonies of successful border-crossing or successful obtainment of tourist visas (that will be overstayed), setting up living and employment arrangements for incoming migrants, and establishing programs that help parishioners navigate the new country more effectively.[11] A pastor provided an example that illustrates this form of influence: "If someone calls saying 'I want to go to the United States' there is no discouragement. Most leaders would say: 'Here is good. You will be undocumented but almost everyone here is illegal anyway. Come and join us.'"[12] There are Brazuca Baptist pastors who state that their churches are neutral in regard to their role in the

---

[10]   My time working with the Order of Brazilian Baptist Pastors in North America convinced me that a small number of Brazuca Baptist pastors are themselves undocumented. Given their small number, however, I did not include them in my data collection process.

[11]   Annie McNeil Gibson, *Post-Katrina Brazucas: Brazilian Immigrants in New Orleans* (New Orleans: University of New Orleans Press, 2012), 224. Gibson also noticed this dynamic in Brazilian Pentecostal churches in New Orleans. She argued that churches not only justify illegal migration, but also that going to church functions as an additional practice that legitimizes the migration experience.

[12]   All interviews were conducted in Portuguese and translated into English by the author. In addition, the identities of the interviewees were omitted for their and their communities' protection; therefore, transcribed portions of the interviews will not be footnoted. Due to the sensitivity of the material, references that could help identifying communities that cater to undocumented individuals were also omitted.

decision of immigrants to migrate. They, however, also engage in the same legitimizing practices that characterize Brazuca Baptist churches in general.

Brazuca Baptist churches engage in initiatives that create a safety net that transcends common avenues of socioeconomic relief. Sometimes these initiatives for immigrant assistance manifest themselves transnationally in ways that ensure an easier migration experience. Churches have also developed programs to address, in proactive ways, the lack of immigration papers by sponsoring clinics and seminars about immigration laws, applying for religious visas for leaders of the church whom the community wants to hire officially, or partnering with businesses and educational institutions that could help immigrant members change their visa status. The issue of undocumented status, then, has prompted such churches to facilitate a transition to legal immigration status whenever possible.

Pastoral Responses to the Challenge of Undocumented Parishioners

Brazuca Baptist pastors are aware of the fact that their pastoral practices—which sometimes include transnational advertising—inform undocumented immigration and activity and have developed diverse ways of rationalizing their potential role in migration dynamics or admitting and coping with the situation. One of the pastors who, as mentioned above, called immigration officials to ask them for guidance and who advertises his Brazuca church in Brazil mentioned:

> When I advertise my church in Brazil, I am indeed attracting migrants, but I am not saying: "come as an undocumented immigrant" . . . because it is very hard for an undocumented person to live in this country without a driver's license—especially in my state, which does not give drivers' licenses to undocumented immigrants—but people come anyway. And now, the number of people coming from Brazil is as large as it was during the peak of Brazilian migration between 2000 and 2003. [...] I believe in that (Bible) verse that says: "The earth is the Lord's, and everything in it, and all who live in it." I do not believe in borders. I believe that God puts us in places and opens the doors for us to live in them.

The migration dynamics in which this pastor is involved informed the development of a theology of borderlessness that allowed him not only to legitimize his potential role in the decisions of people who migrate, but also to sanctify it. He went from seeking border agents to disregarding borders all together.

Likewise, Edvar Gimenes, who pastored a church in the southern United States, described his experiences of trying to cope with his role on legitimizing, and being supported by, undocumented migrants. Gimenes had a column in the *Jornal Batista*—the flagship publication of the Brazilian Baptist Convention—that he used to write about various ethical and theological subjects. When he left Brazil to pastor a church in the United States, he continued to contribute to the publication. In 2003, the year Gimenes arrived in the United States, the *Jornal Batista* published three pieces written by him that documented the progression of his thought on the morality of undocumented immigration and his pastoral position in regard to undocumented immigrants. The first time he wrote about the issue, Gimenes provided objective observations about undocumented immigrants, saying they were hard workers who lived well financially but whose insecurity in terms of immigration papers caused great anxiety, mostly because they could not visit their family members in Brazil.[13]

After he had spent more time pastoring a community that served a great number of undocumented immigrants, Gimenes's account was much more personal:

> It hurts me every time I listen to the cries of the sons and daughters of undocumented immigrants who came to the United States when they were still very little, without knowing what awaited them. They studied until they finished high school and then, even though they were exemplary students and are totally integrated into North American life, they must endure the profound sadness of being denied access to the university for not being recognized as citizens. Waiting for the North American government to act altruistically, looking to benefit the immigrants or the poor in the planet, is naïve because the ethic that rules the world is the ethic of convenience, even when those who occupy positions of leadership, such as President Bush, advertise themselves as practicing Christians.[14]

Later, Gimenes extended his solidarity to include undocumented immigrants in general, thus going beyond undocumented children. Gimenes told the Brazilian audience of his meditations, during his walks in Florida streets. He said that on a hot morning, he passed by a street made with interlocking brick pavers—a work very commonly done by Brazilian undocumented immigrants—and that this street reminded him of a leader in his church who worked under harsh conditions. Gimenes reflected: "I was then reminded that, as pastor, I live from the tithes and offerings dedicated to God that are given by

---

[13]   Edvar Gimenes de Oliveira, "Welcome to America: Sem Documentos," *O Jornal Batista* CIII, no.34 (2003), 11.
[14]   Edvar Gimenes de Oliveira, "Dores de Um Brasileiro," *O Jornal Batista* CIII, no.42 (2003), 11.

people who, like this leader, work hard."[15] The title of the *Jornal Batista* column in which Gimenes tells this story is suggestive: "Solitary Walk and Paradigm Shift." It was then, it seems, that Gimenes realized the full implications of the fact that for Brazuca Baptist pastors, it is impossible to separate the idea of a calling to minister to Brazucas from the fact that such a calling is inevitably a call to side with undocumented bodies in their daily struggles.

The presence of undocumented bodies also challenge Brazuca pastors to implement an incarnational practice.[16] One pastor, for instance, created a form of incarnational practice that had the daily struggles of the undocumented as a model. He said:

> The form that I have found to deal with . . . [the struggles of undocumented members] is to live with them as if I was not legal myself; to feel their pain; to share their struggles; to fight their fight. So when I do this I minimize the suffering they feel, I feel they feel loved, that there is someone who worries about them and wants their best. When I get close to them they see that the people, if they have patience and perseverance, have opportunity. So this is the form that I have found to minimize this issue here.

It is unclear what this pastor meant by living "as if I was not legal myself." Does he not hand over his driver's license to a police officer at a traffic stop or his immigration-related paperwork in an ICE raid? How about the existential insecurity so commonly felt by the undocumented immigrants living under an antagonistic empire? The point here is, however, that pastors at times have been so involved in their relationship with their undocumented members that they have regarded their condition as something they should imitate to be able to offer more appropriate pastoral care.

A pastor who has formal training in theology and in psychology, often pondered the effects of undocumented living in his pastoral texts in his church's bulletin—directed to the membership of the church he pastored in the East Coast. In March of 2000, he wrote down his reflections in a pastoral letter entitled *The Immigrant's Emotional Health* in which he said:

> Self-esteem seems to be the great source of immigrants' emotional problems. Although all work is dignified, in general the immigrant works in areas where those who belong to the land do not want to work, such as cleaning, construction, and other related activities. Some people can work for years in these areas without apparent issues. Most, however, stay because they have no

---

15   Edvar Gimenes de Oliveira, "Caminhada Solitária E Mudança de Paradigmas," *O Jornal Batista* CIII, no.44 (2003), 11.

16   By "incarnational practice," for the purposes of this chapter, I mean the initiative by Brazuca Baptist pastors to adapt a number of their pastoral practices to the specific needs and lifestyles of their undocumented parishioners.

other option. They lack language skills, documents of legal residence, or even courage to begin to study. As a result, dissatisfaction begins to take over the heart. The feeling could not be different from one that takes the color out of life. For those who have a healthy space for social living, things are better. In the last decade Brazilian immigrants formed churches. They have a very important role in the preservation of the culture and in the maintenance of the Brazilian identity. The less charged with prejudices and more open to laughter and community life—without leaving the Bible aside—the more important for the emotional health of its members a church becomes. The church, because of the opportunity it gives for individuals to take up roles and feel useful, acts in the strengthening of their self-esteem, a function that, in and of itself, is already a great service to the community.

This pastor understands the church as helping undocumented immigrants endure the daily struggles of their lives in the United States by providing a space for meaningful activity. He wrote to the *Jornal Batista* arguing that in an immigrant context it is more important to have churches that function as "therapeutic communities" than churches that focus strongly on abstract doctrinal matters.[17]

This pastor's approach to the conundrum presented by undocumented bodies, however, went beyond concerns about emotional health. His migration experience, as that of other Brazuca Baptist leaders, opened his eyes to broader migrant motifs in the Bible. In his *Jornal Batista* article entitled "Abraham: An Immigrant Who Succeeded," he said, "I want to highlight aspects of Abraham the immigrant, bringing them into harmony with situations experienced by other immigrants, particularly us, Brazilians living in other lands."[18] He went on to say that Abraham, not unlike most Brazilian Baptist immigrants left his own land, had problems with Egyptian "immigration," and had to work very hard in a strange land.[19]

After this pastor read an article written by famous liberation theologian Gustavo Gutiérrez—an author not commonly appreciated among average Brazilian Baptists—he began to apply liberationist insights to his pastoral anxieties. He wrote:

> Yesterday I was reading an article written by Gustavo Gutiérrez about liberation theology in which he analyzed the trajectory of the movement since its inception. Among a number of challenging things, the text calls us to act in a liberative fashion in all occasions of our walk in the world. This means

---

[17]   Josias Bezerra, "Opressão Num Contexto de Imigrantes," *Jornal Batista* XCX, no.48 (2000), 11.

[18]   Josias Bezerra, "Abraão: Um Imigrante Que Deu Certo," *Jornal Batista* XCX, no.26 (2000), 13.

[19]   Bezerra, "Abraão: Um Imigrante Que Deu Certo."

that Christian practice must always come with the most absolute respect for the human being and must compel us to act with the intention of liberating humans from any form of oppression to which they may be subjugated. [...] In the church, acting in a liberative way is, among other things, fostering a (collective) conscience of dignity and value in the members of the community; practicing tolerance toward the deviants and avoiding any moves, in gestures or verbally, that diminish the other.[20]

In addition, the issue of undocumented workers fit the pastor's broad application of Dietrich Bonhoeffer's ethics, in which, according to his interpretation of the German theologian, issues of right and wrong—and consequently legality and illegality—had to be measured according to specific contextual dynamics. For him:

No one should expect, therefore, that God's will is readily systematized in a body of rules that comes to us from the top down or the inside out. No! God's will is born out of relationship with Christ, out of hearing him in intimacy, and it manifests itself as an answer, given in Jesus, to the stimulus of a specific situation.[21]

Thus, this pastor applied the insights of famous theologians such as Gustavo Gutiérrez and Dietrich Bonhoeffer as articulations that helped him cope with the tension caused by undocumented parishioners. Although his language and theological dialogue partners may be idiosyncratic, his anxieties ably encapsulate the much broader general spirit of Brazuca Baptist leadership.

When it comes to the presence of undocumented pastors, however, most Brazuca Baptist pastors tend to be against their role as ministers who live without legal immigration papers. Although the overwhelming majority of Brazuca Baptist pastors are permanent residents or United States citizens, some still live in the country without legal statuses. The situations of the pastors who are against undocumented pastors, however, are complicated at times by their own migration experiences. The business meeting of a Brazuca Baptist church in New England reveals such complexity. In a crisis that was created by the issue of preaching by undocumented pastors, the church minutes registered a heated exchange between the pastor and the members:

The pastor also talked about his position about an illegal pastor, questioning the ability of such an individual to go up to the pulpit to preach. The pastor said that during the week two people approached him questioning him and

---

20   Josias Bezerra, "Ecos de Libertação," *Folha Da Primeira*, April 3, 2000, 1. Bezerra re-printed the same article in the *Folha da Primeira* issue of July 9, 2002.

21   Josias Bezerra, "A Vontade de Deus Na Ética Cristã de Bonhoeffer," *Folha Da Primeira*, July 2, 2002, 1.

saying: "you were also an illegal and you were deported!" The pastor then explained that he came with a student visa (he had a visa) and he was deported because he changed universities without communicating, but only because he did not know that when moving from one university to another he would have to communicate [this to] the immigration office. Also, he said he was not yet a pastor when this happened, affirming once again that he is still adamant in his position, thinking that it is wrong for a pastor to minister if he is undocumented.

But the issue of documentation of ministers, in that same church, did not affect the legitimation of the immigration status of members in general. The minutes of the church's meeting show an interaction between an undocumented member and the same pastor who was adamantly against undocumented ministers. It reads: "Brother José questions the pastor about the illegality of members: 'What would be the right thing to do? Getting in the plane and leaving?' The pastor responded justifying that the brothers escape from Brazil because of the economy, and escaping is normal."

As this example illustrates, even the condemnation of the undocumented status of the very small number of Brazuca Baptist pastors often comes with the accompanying legitimation of the undocumented status of everyone else. Another East Coast pastor, now retired, made this dynamic even more explicit. In his church, he said, "(Being undocumented) did not change anything, nothing. I did not pay attention to this, I did not ask who was documented or not. I was against undocumented pastors, this I was against. But any other person was not a problem for me."

Conclusion

The implications of the moral, theological, and practical negotiations experienced by Brazuca Baptist churches because of the presence of undocumented parishioners are manifold. First, the sheer numbers of undocumented immigrants in most of these church communities accounts for their financial feasibility. Second, the social conservatism generally associated with the theology of Brazuca Baptist pastors—who were educated in Brazilian Baptist seminaries that taught a translated form of Southern Baptist theology—is negotiated in the US context due to this reality. That is the case especially in regard to immigration policies—which involves a negotiation of the meaning of obedience to the law. However, Brazuca Baptist pastoral disposition is also pushed beyond policy issues as the migrant experiences of parishioners become a central pastoral and communal concern. Third, Brazuca Baptist churches legitimize undocumented living in several ways, such as through prayer, testimonies, church advertisement, and pastoral practice, and they use those same practices to encourage migration. Finally, the presence of undocumented bodies has shaped the social initiatives of Brazuca Baptist churches, prompting them to direct their attention and resources toward various activities that aim at alleviating immigrant adjustment and protecting immigrants as much as possible. The current US administration's toughening of anti-immigration regulation strengthened the self-understanding of Brazuca Baptist churches as protectors of immigrants (some of them even put their tax-exempt status at risk by asking publicly the documented members in their communities to vote for Hillary Clinton because of the immigration issue), and the fact that the election of Donald Trump coincided with one of the biggest economic crisis in the contemporary history of Brazil means that the effect of the anti-immigration rhetoric and policies of Trump's administration may not discourage Brazilian immigration significantly. As a matter of fact, pastors are verbally reporting an increase in the numbers of Brazilian immigrants arriving in the United States due to the deepening economic crisis affecting Brazil since 2016. How the Trump administration's immigration policies will affect Brazuca Baptist development is yet to be seen, and one must not forget that economic and political developments in Brazil are also part of the migration equation.

The experiences of Brazuca Baptist pastors reveal that in the context of churches whose membership is largely comprised of undocumented immigrants, an incarnational theology and practice that claims to love the human being and God simultaneously may understand as antagonistic the relationship between justice and the current US immigration law. This disposition is not only consistent with Christian theology, but also allows Brazuca Baptist pastors to embrace the undocumented immigrants while negotiating central aspects of their modus operandi.

BIBLIOGRAPHY:

Amstutz, Mark R. *Just Immigration: American Policy in Christian Perspective.* Grand Rapids, MI: Eerdmans, 2017.

Bean, Lydia. *The Politics of Evangelical Identity: Local Churches and Partisan Divides in the United States and Canada.* Princeton: Princeton University Press, 2014.

Bezerra, Josias. "A Vontade de Deus Na Ética Cristã de Bonhoeffer." *Folha Da Primeira.* July 2, 2002.

———. "Abraão: Um Imigrante Que Deu Certo." *Jornal Batista* XCX, no.26 (2000): 13.

———. "Opressão Num Contexto de Imigrantes." *Jornal Batista* XCX, no.48 (2000): 11.

Bicalho, José Victor. *Yes, Eu Sou Brazuca Ou A Vida Do Imigrante Brasileiro Nos Estados Unidos Da América*. Governador Valadares: Fundação Serviços de Educação e Cultura, 1989.

Carroll, Daniel. *Christians at the Border: Immigration, the Church, and the Bible*. Grand Rapids, MI: Brazos Press, 2013.

Cebulko, Kara B. *Documented, Undocumented, and Something Else: The Incorporation of Children of Brazilian Immigrants*. El Paso: Lfb Scholarly Pub Llc, 2013.

Chaves, Joao B. "Disrespecting Borders for Jesus, Power, and Cash: Southern Baptist Missions, The New Immigration, and the Churches of the Brazilian Diaspora." PhD thesis, Baylor University, 2017.

Freston, Paul. "The Religious Field Among Brazilians in the United States." In *Becoming Brazuca: Brazilian Immigration to the United States*, edited by Clémence Jouët-Pastré and Leticia J. Braga, 255–68. Cambridge: Harvard University Press, 2008.

Gibson, Annie McNeil. *Post-Katrina Brazucas: Brazilian Immigrants in New Orleans*. New Orleans: University of New Orleans Press, 2012.

Heyer, Kristin E. *Kinship Across Borders: A Christian Ethic of Immigration*. Washington, D.C: Georgetown University Press, 2012.

Hoffmeier, James K. *The Immigration Crisis: Immigrants, Aliens, and the Bible*. Wheaton, IL: Crossway, 2009.

Jouët-Pastré, Clémence, and Leticia J. Braga, eds. *Becoming Brazuca: Brazilian Immigration to the United States*. Cambridge, MA: David Rockefeller Center for Latin American Studies, 2008.

Martins, Mário Ribeiro. "O Radicalismo Batista Brasileiro." Masters' thesis, Seminário Teológico Batista do Norte do Brasil, 1972.

Monteiro, Fávio Marconi Lemos. "Radicalism in Pernambuco: A Study of the Relationship Between Nationals and Southern Baptist Missionaries in the Brazilian Baptist Struggle for Autonomy." Masters' thesis, Baylor University, 1991.

Oliveira, Edvar Gimenes de. "Caminhada Solitária e Mudança de Paradigmas." *O Jornal Batista* CIII, no.44 (2003): 11.

———. "Dores de Um Brasileiro." *O Jornal Batista* CIII, no.42 (2003): 11.

———. "Welcom to America: Sem Documentos." *O Jornal Batista* CIII, no.34 (2003): 11.

Padilla, E., and P. Phan, eds. *Contemporary Issues of Migration and Theology*. New York: Palgrave Macmillan, 2013.

———, eds. *Theology of Migration in the Abrahamic Religions*. New York, NY: Palgrave Macmillan, 2014.

Padilla, Elaine, and Peter C. Phan, eds. *Christianities in Migration: The Global Perspective*. Christianities of the World. New York: Palgrave Macmillan, 2016.

Soerens, Matthew, Yang, Jenny Hwang, and Anderson, Leith. *Welcoming the Stranger: Justice, Compassion & Truth in the Immigration Debate*. Downers Grove, IL: IVP Books, 2009.

Sutton, Matthew Avery. *American Apocalypse: A History of Modern Evangelicalism*. Cambridge, MA: Belknap Press, 2014.

Talmage, Steven, Kirk Smith, Minerva Carcano, Mark Adams, and Gerald Kicanas. *Bishops on the Border: Pastoral Responses to Immigration*. New York: Morehouse, 2013.

Worthen, Molly. *Apostles of Reason: The Crisis of Authority in American Evangelicalism*. New York: Oxford University Press, 2013.

CHAPTER 5

DISPLACED CONTINUITY:
JUCHE, CHRISTIANITY, AND SUBJECTIVITY
OF NORTH KOREAN MIGRANTS

Shalon Park

While the border between the two Koreas appears an insurmountable obstacle, the number of North Koreans migrating to South Korea has grown drastically in the past twenty years.[1] As of 2018, there are nearly thirty-two thousand North Korean migrants residing in South Korea.[2] As with the numerical growth of migrants, the discourse surrounding North Korean migrants has also expanded, varying from issues of terminology (i.e., defectors, refugees, the new settlers) to the affairs of immigration policy and the migrants' settlement.[3]

On almost every level, the lives of migrants intertwine closely with Christianity. It is common to see North Korean migrants on South Korean television shows or in churches, where they are invited to give testimonies about their conversion and their experiences in North Korea. Moreover, the astonishing statistic that "80-90 percent of North Korean migrants identified themselves as Christian when they arrive in South Korea and around 70 percent continued to rely on church services after they arrive"[4] demands a critical discussion on the relationship of North Korean migrant lives to Christianity.

---

[1] Tara O., *The Collapse of North Korea: Challenges, Planning and Geopolitics of Unification* (London: Palgrave Macmillan, 2016), 102.

[2] Ministry of Unification, "Statistics." Accessed October 2018. http://www.unikorea.go.kr/unikorea/business/statistics

[3] Cf. Sung Kyung Kim,"'Defector,' 'Refugee,' or 'Migrant'? North Korean Settlers in South Korea's Changing Social Discourse." *North Korean Review* (2012): 94–110. http://www.jstor.org/stable/43910315.

[4] Jin-Heon Jung, *Migration and Religion in East Asia: North Korean Migrants' Evangelical Encounters* (New York: Palgrave Macmillan, 2015), 1.

Beneath the discourse lies the issue of representation, based on a presupposed connection between the migrants' subjectivity to the political aspirations of the Democratic People's Republic of Korea. The act of border-crossing is often represented as a change of migrants' political aspirations, a shift from a form of irrationality toward rationality. While the recent scholarship shows that migrants' motives for border-crossing vary from their "spatial perception, intimate human network of relatives, and sense of familiarity with language, feelings and emotions for place and people,"[5] the dominant discourse remains the stereotypical media representation of North Koreans as the yet-to-be-freed political subjects. The implications of such representation are far-reaching, especially when conflated with the narrative of conversion.

This chapter interrogates the discursive framing of migrants' conversion to Christianity as their political aspiration for freedom. By examining the interconnection between the representation of North Korea as a religious entity and the logic of assimilation projected on migrants, I problematize the notion that the North Korean migrants' status as internally displaced people determines their subjectivity. Delineating limitations of the narrative, which posits Christianity as a medium for North Korean migrants' transition from being subjugated by North Korean ideology to becoming free subjects, I call for a new conceptualization for migrants' agency.

"INTERNALLY DISPLACED" LOGIC OF ASSIMILATION

North Korean migrants have been situated in a unique position ever since South Korean government enacted the "Act for the Protection and Resettlement Support for the Residents" in 1997.[6] The migrants, whose journey typically involves crossing multiple national borders, are immediately sent to *Taesongkongsa* upon their arrival at the South Korean border. Here, "national intelligence agents interrogate each person in order to determine fake or unqualified migrants (e.g., spies, criminals, or Korean-Chinese) from the real migrants."[7] Those who pass this investigation are classified as "internally displaced persons" who originally belonged to South Korea.[8] Categorized as potential South Korean citizens, the migrants are sent to *Hanawon* (House of Unity), a South Korean government settlement center run by the Ministry of

[5]   Sung Kyung Kim, "Mobile North Korean Women and their Places in the Sino-North Korea Borderland." *Asian Anthropology,* 15, no.2 (2016): 116–31. https://doi.org/10.1080/168 3478X.2016.1215540

[6]   United Nations High Commissioner for Refugees. "Republic of Korea: Protection of Defecting North Korean Residents and Support of Their Settlement Act, 1997," accessed November 9, 2017, Refworld, www.refworld.org/docid/3ae6b4ef28.html.

[7]   Jung, *Migration and Religion in East Asia,* 87.

[8]   Jung, *Migration and Religion in East Asia,* 103.

Unification.[9] At *Hanawon*, migrants go through a three-month long compulsory settlement program, which provides "education, vocational training, psychological counseling, and physical examinations."[10] After these processes, North Korean migrants receive social security numbers and South Korean citizenship, without being given the option to maintain their original citizenship. They are perceived as de facto defectors, who have chosen their political side and now are willing to assimilate into South Korean society.

Christianity plays a significant role in the process of migrants' settlement. As Jin-Heon Jung points out in his book *Migration and Religion in East Asia,* South Korean churches are "second only to the state in providing various services to facilitate migrants' integration into the South Korean capitalist system."[11] Through various forms of humanitarian aid, the experiences of North Korean migrants are "directly and indirectly entangled with Christian missionary networks, discourses, and identity politics."[12] The intricate power dynamics between North and South Koreans that result from this structure lead to a conception that the migrants' aspirations and motives for migration correspond to their political positioning.

Assimilation appears as the logic that underlies such a conception, as a way of framing the migrants as internally displaced subjects who strive to assimilate to the new society through the means of Christian conversion. For example, Jin-Heon Jung argues that North Korean migrants' encounter with Christianity signifies "socio-economic assimilation to South Korean capitalist ways of working and behaving."[13] Jin-Heon Jung juxtaposes "anticommunism in the South and anti-imperialism in the North" as oppositional causes for "the project of political-religious differentiation entailed in both South Korean and North Korean subject making."[14] For him, Christianity is the "primary force and vehicle for the North and South Korean participants acting in a heterogeneous figured world—an imaginary condition that simulates the future of a unified Korea."[15] Christianity in this framework is a medium for change of aspiration, which necessitates the re-politicization of North Korean subjects.

9   Jung, *Migration and Religion in East Asia,* 82.
10   Ahlam Lee, *North Korean Defectors In a New and Competitive Society: Issues and Challenges In Resettlement, Adjustment, and the Learning Process* (Lanham: Lexington Books, 2016), 54.
11   Jung, *Migration and Religion in East Asia,* 3. See also, Marie-Orange Rivé-Lasan, "Korean Christian Churches, the ibuk ch'ulsin Minority and the Perception of the North." *Journal of Korean Religions* (2013), 123–46. https://www.jstor.org/stable/23943357
12   Jung, *Migration and Religion in East Asia,* 134.
13   Jung, *Migration and Religion in East Asia,* 21. See also, Jin-Heon Jung, "The Religious-Political Aspirations of North Korean Migrants and Protestant Churches in Seoul." *Journal of Korean Religions* (2016), 123–48. https://www.jstor.org/stable/24892380
14   Jung, *Migration and Religion in East Asia,* 10.
15   Jung, *Migration and Religion in East Asia,* 98.

The migrants' conversion to Christianity is "a cultural passage and process" for changing of political aspirations.[16] The migrants' conversion to Christianity for him is "both an interior transformation from Juche to Christianity and a physical *relocation* from the North to the South."[17] As Jin-Heon Jung's conclusion shows: "North Korean migrants become largely re-politicized and empowered to realize a 'meaningful' state of being and becoming, in evangelical terms, and in future-oriented national aspirations."[18]

Yet, the question of what really changes in the migrants' conversion process arises. More specifically, what is involved in the process of migrants' realization of their pre-conversion state as one of scarcity, and of Christianity as a "meaningful state of being and becoming"? The conflation of the migrants' political situatedness with the migrants' aspiration also engenders another assumption—namely, that the migrants necessarily desired to arrive at South Korea in the first place and that they wish to continue to reside in the new society.

Counterexamples exist as ethnographic lacunae which put Jin-Heon Jung's framework into question: the often disregarded voices of the migrants' demand for repatriation. While not the story of the majority, the vexing cases of North Korean migrants' voluntary demand for repatriation surface in the media. A story of Kwon Chol-Nam and his ongoing struggle for repatriation, presented by *The New York Times* article, "North Korean Defector, 'Treated Like Dirt' in South, Fights to Return," shows one side of the complex realities of North Korean migrants. Kwon Chol-Nam's legal demand for his return, and his quest for other North Korean voluntary cases of repatriation, tell us that the North Korean migrants' "internally displaced" status is not always an indication for their crossing of the seemingly irreversible border, whether on political, social, or legal grounds. As Kwon Chol-Nam expresses: "I will go back to the North and hold a news conference there to tell the truth about what the life was like in the South . . . . I am a citizen of Democratic People's Republic of Korea."[19] Similarly, Son Jung-Hun, another North Korean migrant, claims in his interview with the *Guardian*:

> The South Korean media portray us as people who want to be seen as a victimized minority with a sense of entitlement . . . . The government here won't accept how difficult it is for defectors to adapt to life in a free-market economy,

---

[16]   Jung, *Migration and Religion in East Asia,* 125.

[17]   Jin-Heon Jung, *Free to Be: North Korean migrants and the South Korean Evangelical Church*. Diss. University of Illinois at Urbana-Champaign, 2010, 46. [Emphasis mine].

[18]   Jin-Heon Jung, "The Religious-Political Aspirations of North Korean Migrants and Protestant Churches in Seoul," 142.

[19]   Sang-hun Choe. "North Korean Defector, 'Treated Like Dirt' in South, Fights to Return." *The New York Times*, August 5, 2017, www.nytimes.com/2017/08/05/world/asia/north-korea-defector-south-korea.html.

and for that we are treated with contempt. By going public with my desire to defect again [to North Korea] I hope to send a message about how badly South Korea treats defectors . . . . If I don't do everything by the book, what hope is there for the other defectors I know who want to go back to North Korea?[20]

The cases of migrants' demand for repatriation initializes the abovementioned assumptions concerning the migrants' relocation of political aspiration. As Sung Kyung Kim points out, researchers constantly run into the accounts of "those who decide not to migrate or to return to their homeland even though it does not provide the same economic opportunities as foreign countries," which cannot be easily explained.[21] Such stories appear troublesome, if assimilation is a working frame for interpreting migrants' religiosity. The migrants' determination for repatriation makes us wonder how Christian conversion can ever co-exist with the cases when the migrants' political identification with the North seems rather reaffirmed than re-politicized.

The juxtaposition of the "old" and "new" political aspirations of migrants, consequently, confines the migrants' religiosity to the ideological structure of the two states. On a discursive level, this framework works in conjunction with the projected aspiration of the Southerners' regarding the Northern migrants, particularly with those of anticommunist Protestants. The political slogan of "exterminate communism" may work side by side with the Protestant right's rhetoric of conversion: exterminate communism out of the migrants' bodies in every possible semiotic form. Theodore Hughes articulates how this ideological tension prevails in the South:

> The South Korean developmentalist state of the 1960s and 1970s aimed to elide domestic class conflict and "exterminate communism" (*myolgong*). The latter phrase reveals the biopolitics (and necropolitics) of the south's sovereign claim over the north, which is included as part of the ethnonational body even as it is othered as communist. The north becomes one form of what Achille Mbembe has called a "death-world," the site of a population to be exterminated and given life at the same time. The division of the peninsula, and South Korea's developmentalist state claim to sovereignty over it, is thus marked by racialization on two levels: the assumption of the homogeneous ethnonation

---

[20]   Justin McCurry, "The Defector Who Wants to Go Back to North Korea." *The Guardian*. Guardian News and Media, April 22, 2014. Web. May 16, 2017. https://www.theguardian.com/world/2014/apr/22/defector-wants-to-go-back-north-korea

[21]   Sung Kyung Kim, "Mobile North Korean Women and their Places in the Sino-North Korea Borderland." *Asian Anthropology,* 15, no.2 (2016), 116–31. https://doi.org/10.1080/1683478X.2016.1215540

(*minjok*)—that which is to be given life—and the figuring of the communist as radical other—that which is to be put to death.[22]

The discourse of assimilation locates the migrants' subjectivity as the ethnically related yet politically othered, a differentiation to be amended through religious identification. The cases of migrants who demand repatriation to the "death-world," or any other accounts of the migrants' expression of political loyalty to North Korea, reads as a story signifying the danger and naiveté of migrants. The discourse of the Other is fused with the general representation of North Korean migrants in South Korea, as Jin-Heon Jung shows in his ethnography:

> The construction of biases among South Koreans against the Northerners as lazy, violent, ungrateful toward their Southern helpers, selfish, good at lying, opportunistic, and so on, are often attributed to the embodiments of souls brainwashed by Juche (self-reliance) ideology or Kimilsungism; the North Korean official ruling philosophy that accentuates collective national self-independence from foreign influences.[23]

This results in the Protestant effort to bring about integration for migrants with the new society. The migrants are perceived as the people group who desire change, regardless of the degree of change. Yet, as Afe Adogame points out, such a view on migrants leads to "the invention of varied paradigms of integration such as multiculturalism, assimilation and emancipation at the expense of their real *modus operandi* or signification in concrete terms."[24] To what degree, or in what meaningful way, do North Korean migrants relate to their new religious affiliation? Furthermore, how can we conceptualize a discourse on the migrants' conversion that does not necessitate re-politicization of North Korean aspiration at the expense of the migrants' pre-conversion state? In order to understand this more fully, let us turn to Juche, the North Korean ruling ideology, which has a profound connection to the North Korean terms of subjectivity. The next section, pointing to Juche as a significant feature that constructs North Korean subjectivity, examines the ways in which the discursive turning of Juche into a distorted form of religion affects the representation of the migrants as the subjects to be rectified.

---

[22] Theodore Hughes, "Return to the Colonial Present: Ch'oe In-hun's Cold War Pan-Asianism." *Positions: East Asia Cultures Critique* 19, no.1 (2011), 109–31. https://doi.org/10.1215/10679847-2010-026

[23] Jin H. Jung, *Free to Be,* 136.

[24] Afe Adogame, *The African Christian Diaspora: New Currents and Emerging Trends in World Christianity*, (New York: Bloomsbury Academic, 2013), 133. Emphasis mine.

Juche and Christianity

Juche means, "master (*ju*) and body (*che*)," and its idea "insists on self-determination and self-reliance."[25] In the Juche idea, "man is the master of the world and of his own destiny."[26] Juche has been a central feature for understanding what constructs North Korean nationhood ever since Kim Il-Sung publicized its idea as an official state ethos in 1955.[27] In his speech to the "Korean Workers' Party Propaganda and Agitation Department," Kim Il-Sung introduced the principle of self-reliance as the central concept of Juche. Juche articulates North Korea's anti-colonial and anti-imperial origin, which historically has been "growing out of a half century of Japanese colonial rule and another half century of continuous confrontation with a hegemonic United States and a more powerful South Korea."[28]

On a conceptual level, Juche is a ground for the distinctively North Korean ethos for anti-imperialism. As Charles K. Armstrong remarks, "North Korea has defied all 'imperial logics' since the Korean War began," and its principle of "self-reliance was a common aspiration among postcolonial nations striving for independence."[29] The implementation of Juche has been reconfigured since the Korean War, as Armstrong points out, changed in its expressions from Marxist-Leninist socialism to a form of familism with "'Confucian' resonances of filial piety."[30] This distinctive development of familism has been conceptualized as the biopolitical structure of the inseparable relationship between the state and the citizens.

While Juche's structure can be at best compared with other forms of political organicism—such as the nineteenth-century German organicism or the early twentieth-century Japanese national body theory *kokutai*, the current discourse on Juche tends to treat Juche as a *sui generis* category of religion with all its historicity put aside. For example, Hyang-Jin Jung in her 2013 article, "Jucheism as an Apotheosis of the Family," pays attention to "North Koreans'

---

[25]   Sonia Ryang, *North Korea: Toward a Better Understanding,* (Lanham, MD: Lexington Books, 2009), 60.

[26]   Kim Il-Sung, *Selected Works,* Volume 8, Foreign Languages Publishing House, 1996, 454.

[27]   Jae-Jung Suh, "Introduction: Making Sense of North Korea: Institutionalizing Juche at the Nexus of Self and Other," *Journal of Korean Studies* 12, no.1 (2007): 1–13. http://muse.jhu.edu/article/416551

[28]   Bruce Cumings, *North Korea: Another Country,* (New York: New Press, 2004), 76.

[29]   Charles K. Armstrong, *Tyranny of the Weak: North Korea and the World, 1950-1992,* (Ithaca: Cornell University Press, 2013), 53.

[30]   Charles K. Armstrong, "Familism, Socialism and Political Religion in North Korea," *Totalitarian Movements and Political Religions* 6, no.3 (2005): 383. https://doi.org/10.1080/14690760500317743

love for their founding leader,"[31] maintaining that the North Korean migrants' "love for the leader was not lacking in religiosity . . . . Just as a Christian or a believer in any religion would project his or her fantasies onto the divinity, a believer in Jucheism would likely do so as well."[32] Similarly, Shin Eun-Hee describes Juche as an "indigenous national religion."[33] Shin finds religious elements of Juche in that it exhibits doctrinal, ritual, and priestly features that are commonly observable in other institutionalized religions, thus concluding, "[North Koreans] believe in him [Kim Il-Sung] as 'Father,' in the sense of being the national provider, healer, and even savior."[34] Furthermore, Lim Jae-Cheon in his *Leader Symbols and Personality Cult in North Korea*, terms Juche as a "personality cult."[35] Lim is not hesitant to turn the biopolitical structure of Juche and its Confucian element of familism into a deviant form of religion, to which its citizens are blindly subjected.

This discursive move—the conflation of Juche with a category of religion—consequently reduces historical and sociopolitical aspects of the North Korean subjects into a form of irrationality. In turn, the North Korean migrants' political aspirations based on the principle of Juche are relegated to a deviant domain of religion. Merged with the conversion narrative, such a tendency constructs a dichotomy between Christianity—a civilized religious ground for freedom compatible with the ideals of liberal citizens, and Juche—a deviant form of religion that threatens migrants' subjectivity.[36] Within this construction, Juche becomes the "religious" category from which North Korean migrants must depart in the process of their conversion to Christianity.

One may ask the question once raised by Talal Asad, concerning "why particular elements of 'religion' as a concept should be pieced out as definitive" in this case.[37] More importantly, we should pay attention to the implications from such a discourse. According to this framework, Juche becomes dehistoricized; North Korea's historical anti-imperial ethos from the Korean War become irrelevant, and its nationalist conceptualization of family symbols gets treated

---

31   Hyang-Jin Jung, "Jucheism as an Apotheosis of the Family: The Case of the Arirang Festival," *Journal of Korean Religions* (2013): 93–122. https://www.jstor.org/stable/23943356

32   Jung, "Jucheism as an Apotheosis of the Family," 109.

33   Eun Hee Shin, "The Sociopolitical organism: The Religious Dimensions of Juche Philosophy." *Religions of Korea in Practice* (2007), 518–519.

34   Shin, "The Sociopolitical organism," 517.

35   Jae-Cheon Lim, *Leader Symbols and Personality Cult in North Korea: The Leader State.* (London: Routledge, 2015), 4–5.

36   See discussions on religion and civility from the introduction of Timothy Fitzgerald, *Discourse on Civility and Barbarity: A Critical History of Religion and Related Categories* (Oxford: New York, Oxford University Press, 2007).

37   Talal Asad, *Formations of the Secular: Christianity, Islam, Modernity,* (Stanford: Stanford University Press, 2003, 189).

as an unprecedented system that is incomparable to other forms of nationalism. To speak of Juche as a religion under the guise of politics seems to imply that North Korean migrants' veneration of the Dear Leader and affinity to the North Korean state are due to their lack of reflexivity. The political aspirations of North Koreans are only understood in terms of a deviant religiosity, a personality cult, to which North Korean citizens are subjected.[38] North Korean migrants remain as the perpetual Other, whose misplaced religiosity is to be rectified.

Meaning-making Migrants

If Christianity does not necessarily function as a corrective medium for the Juche-minded migrants, then how can we conceptualize Christianity for understanding North Korean migrants' religiosity and agency? One must be attentive to the hints of continuity in the migrants' stories, to their critical responses to, and to their resourceful utilization or recalibration of, religion. In the context of South Korean representation of North Korean migrants, Juche may be hidden, occluded by the South Korean assumption of Christianity as the corrective to North Korean nationhood. Yet, with a closer look, Christianity possibly can be postulated as a point of contact for the migrants' reevaluation of their understanding of subjectivity *through* Juche.

One can observe from North Korean migrants' conversion narratives that their reflection on Juche is far from romantic. The common narrative form among North Korean migrants, often a sharp critique on Juche, is made in their conversion stories.[39] Juche becomes the source of reflexivity through which the migrants rethink their own subjectivity in relation to the state: the individual-state relationship that constructs "duality of subject," as described by Suzy Kim.[40] As she points out, Juche's subjectivity, based on the concept that "mastery is contingent upon the survival of the political and the social, that is, the nation-state and its leader," [41] creates a dissonance of "what it means to be a person of this world as both a product and a producer."[42] Kim Woon-Ju, a North Korean migrant, expresses this dissonance through reflecting on Juche in comparison to Christianity. For Kim Woon-Ju:

---

[38]   Lim, *Leader Symbols and Personality Cult In North Korea,* 4.

[39]   Cf. Jin-Heon Jung's chapter "Conversion to Be: The Christian Encounters of North Korean Migrants in Late Cold War Korea" in *Atheist Secularism and Its Discontents: A Comparative Study of Religion and Communism In Eurasia,* ed. Tam T. T. Ngo and Justine B Quijada (Houndmills, Basingstoke Hampshire; New York, NY: Palgrave Macmillan, 2015), 200.

[40]   Suzy Kim, "(Dis)Orienting North Korea," Critical Asian Studies 42:3 (2010): 481–95. https://doi.org/10.1080/14672715.2010.507397

[41]   Kim, "(Dis)Orienting North Korea," 494.

[42]   Kim, "(Dis)Orienting North Korea."

> Juche communicates the idea that the masses are the master of everything, and that its foundation is in fact that we are the master of ourselves. Its deep contradiction lies in its reality, that Dear leader is the only master and the rest of the people are slaves. By classifying people into different classes, Juche contradictorily regards people outside those class groups as non-humans. Therefore, there is no substance to Juche . . . . Juche from a distance might look like the system of Christianity, but in fact, it is closer to Japanese imperial worship.[43]

For him, North Korean subjectivity is contingent upon the Dear Leader, and this consequently creates a class-oriented society, which in fact, contradicts the true meaning of Juche. Juche loses its "substance," and thus is degraded as something comparable to imperial worship.

One migrant calls venerating Kim Il-Sung idolatrous, because it contradicts Juche's original meaning of self-reliance: "Kimilsungism is an idol. It taught me that I cannot live without *syurong* [i.e. Dear Leader]. This is contradiction to self-reliance of the Juche ideology."[44] Another convert says in his interview, "I learned that someone wrote the Bible to deceive people. That was not true. On the contrary, I came to realize that the Juche ideology of Kim Il Sung eliminated people's self-reliance."[45] Juche becomes an empty object of faith when migrants realize that it "eliminates" their subjectivity. Juche, in its dissonant duality of subject, loses its "substance," and thus no longer functions as the foundation for migrants' subjectivity.

Another migrant convert points to the inconsistencies of Juche in the class-driven structure of North Korea, in the unequal distribution of privilege:

> I lived in Pyongyang with all privileges. I think, the elites know that the Juche ideology is inconsistent. They pretend to show loyalty to Kim Jong Il and believe in the Juche ideology due to their social interest and benefits. One day I had a question, why do a small number of the privileged elites live in plenty?[46]

In such a case, disillusionment with North Korea comes from the migrant's realization of the inconsistent implementation of Juche. For the migrant, Juche's inconsistency and the North Korean authorities' manipulative use of its ideology fails to bring about the ideal society that promises equality.

---

43 Woon-Ju Kim, "Association of the North Korean Defectors." *Talbookja-Dongjihwae*, N.p., July 29, 2007. Web. May 16, 2017. Translation mine.
44 See Young Sub Song, "Socio-cultural Factors Influencing the Conversion to Christianity among North Korean Refugees in South Korea," ProQuest Dissertations Publishing (Trinity International University, 2011), 103.
45 Song, "Socio-cultural Factors," 109.
46 Here I use the anonymous interviews of North Korean migrants conducted by Young Sub Song. Cf. Song, "Socio-cultural Factors," 108.

For some, Juche is an obstacle for conversion to Christianity, not necessarily because conversion entails the transferring of the object of faith, but because Juche is based on a materialist worldview which has no room for a supernatural being. As one migrant convert expresses:

> When I look back to the point of conversion to Christianity, a major obstacle was the indoctrination of the Juche ideology inculcated in my thoughts. North Korea is a communist country that rejects Christianity. I could not believe in God because I grew up within a materialistic worldview when I was young. So I did not understand that God exists, that is, God created this world and Jesus was resurrected from the dead.[47]

In this case, the migrant regards Juche to be something antithetical to religion that entails belief in a supernatural being. In the same way, an expression from a different migrant turns the equation of Juche and Christianity: "I thought that the Juche ideology conflicted with Christianity. These have different masters."[48] Juche and Christianity are contradictory because Juche is based on materialism, whereas Christianity requires belief in a supernatural being. As one migrant says: "Evolution is the unifying principle of all life. Man is purely a physical or biological creature. Man, through the use of scientific reason, will solve his own problems. It was difficult to believe that God exists."[49] Many migrants reflect Kim Il-Sung's teachings on religion that "religion is a reactionary and unscientific outlook on the world. If people start to follow religion, their class consciousness will be paralyzed and their enthusiasm for revolution will disappear."[50]

Christianity for them becomes a resource for migrants to reevaluate where the "substance" of Juche subjectivity is located. For some, Christianity appears as a positive point of contact. As one migrant says: "I have thought that Christianity had an influence on Kim Il-Sung's life. The reason is that there are so many similarities between Christianity and the Juche ideology. For example, Jesus felt compassion at [sic] seeing the crowds. Likewise, Kim Il-Sung loved Korean people and lived for them."[51] The substance of Juche is found in the leader's care for the masses, wherein North Koreans' political subjectivity is ideally located. Similarly, another migrant says: "I thought the story of Kim Il-Sung is similar to the Bible story. Just as Jesus came to the marginalized, so Kim

---

[47]   Song, "Socio-cultural Factors," 88.
[48]   Song, "Socio-cultural Factors," 94.
[49]   Song, "Socio-cultural Factors," 96.
[50]   Institute for Unification Education, Ministry of Unification (South Korea), "Understanding North Korea: Totalitarian dictatorship, Highly centralized economies, Grand Socialist Family," Giljabi Media, 2015, 387.
[51]   Song, "Socio-cultural Factors," 102.

Il Sung showed his attention to the common people."[52] The story of Jesus, his compassion and care for the marginalized, becomes a resource for redefining the true meaning of Juche, a glimpse of which some migrants seem to have seen in Kim Il-Sung's character.

In negative terms, similarities between Juche and Christianity are not necessarily found in their supernatural character, but in their coercive implementation, which suppresses migrants' subjectivity. As Jin-Heon Jung in his ethnography finds that some migrants are "surprised at the fact that Christian elements and the church system are more similar to each other and not that different from the ways of North Korean Kimilsungism and social management system."[53] One migrant compares the repressive regime to Christianity:

> I thought that there were many good words in the Bible. However, I felt an aversion to Christianity when I listened to the sermon. I felt that the pastor was so greedy of his authority when he preached the sermon. I thought, what is the difference between this and the compuls[ory] education in North Korea?[54]

For him, the North Korean oligarchy is similar to Christianity because of their imperious implementation. The migrant expresses aversion to Juche and Christianity, because he perceives neither as affirming his freedom. Comparing Juche and Christianity, rather on the terms of structural than religious, the migrant chooses to reject both. The migrant's concern is in the affirmation of his subjectivity, rather than assimilating from one form of aspiration to another. What seems to be hiding in our plain sight of representing the migrants' conversion, then, is the migrants' self-reflexivity on subjectivity through both Juche and Christianity. Thus, Christianity can be seen as a reflexive point for the migrants' reevaluation of what falsifies their subjectivity, which in some cases found a failed attempt of the North Korean regime to care for them, or in any form of coercive powers that they encounter.[55]

CONCLUSION

At the core of the misconception exists the problem of representing North Korea as a historically inexplicable and thus irrational and demonic entity. As noted by Bruce Cumings at the height of the military tension between the Trump administration and North Korea, what is "infuriating is Washington's implacable refusal ever to investigate our 72-year history of conflict with the

---

[52] Jung, *Free to Be,* 102.
[53] Jung, *Free to Be,* 11.
[54] Ibid.
[55] Cf. Ju H. J. Han, "Beyond Safe Haven: A Critique of Christian Custody of North Korean Migrants in China." *Critical Asian Studies* 45, no.4 (2013), 533–60. https://doi.org/10.1080/14672715.2013.851153

North; all of our media appear to live in an eternal present, with each new crisis treated as *sui generis*."[56] Cumings' remarks capture the underlying problem of representation when it comes to understanding the circumstances from which North Korean migrants are coming. North Korea, removed from its historical context, surfaces in the media as a solely irrational entity, a deviant and fanatic political body frozen in time.

Yet, historicity cannot be easily exterminated, and religious conversion does not easily occlude the passage of one's political aspiration. Such representation of North Korea often translates into the view in which North Korean migrants exercise their agency through religious conversion. The migrants' conversion to Christianity often has been interpreted as signifying their relocation of aspiration as a whole, whether processual or instant. Located in the process of assimilation, the migrants are seen as unsettled, and thus as not yet having reached the destination of their religious journey.

We see the expressions of migrants that point to a continuity of migrants' aspirations from the pre-conversion state, whether it occurs through forms of the migrants' critical assessment of Juche or Christianity, work one way or another to affirm their subjectivity. Change may occur, even in a form of political affiliation, yet this process is reflexive in the migrants' conversion process. Migrants critically engage with Juche for self-formation, in searching for the political and ethical grounds for self-reliance.

From this angle, North Korean migrants' conversion to Christianity can be seen as a means of self-reflexivity through examining a false notion of subjectivity. Through the active engagement of their own terms of subjectivity through Juche, migrants contradict false notions of subjectivity. In their conversion, the distinctive understanding of North Korean migrants' subjectivity is not dissolved in, or assimilated to, the South Korean ideals of freedom.

Besides the cases of migrants' demand for repatriation, this also may explain the growing number of North Korean migrants who strongly identify themselves beyond the confinement of citizenship. In broader terms, the migrants' conversion to Christianity may be an indication of their reaffirmation of North Korean identity, or the source for their disillusionment with either North or South. Migrants' notions of Juche, inseparable from their formation of aspirations, remains as a resource for reaffirming their distinctive subjectivity in the post-conversion state. Christianity, then, may not be an end point of assimilation that migrants have to reach, but the context for migrants' self-reflexivity.

---

[56]   Bruce Cumings, "This Is What's Really Behind North Korea's Nuclear Provocations." *The Nation*, March 23, 2017, https://www.thenation.com/article/this-is-whats-really-behind-north-koreas-nuclear-provocations/

BIBLIOGRAPHY:

Adogame, Afe. *The African Christian Diaspora: New Currents and Emerging Trends in World Christianity*. New York: Bloomsbury Academic, 2013.

Armstrong, Charles K. *Tyranny of the Weak: North Korea and the World, 1950-1992*. Ithaca: Cornell University Press, 2013.

Armstrong, Charles K. "Familism, Socialism and Political Religion in North Korea." *Totalitarian Movements and Political Religions* 6, no.3 (2005). 383–94. https://doi.org/10.1080/14690760500317743

Asad, Talal. *Formations of the Secular: Christianity, Islam, Modernity*. Stanford, CA: Stanford University Press, 2003.

Cumings, Bruce. *North Korea: Another Country*. New York: New Press, 2004.

———. "This Is What's Really Behind North Korea's Nuclear Provocations." *The Nation*, March 23, 2017. Accessed on November 9, 2017. www.thenation.com/article/this-is-whats-really-behind-north-koreas-nuclear-provocations/.

Fitzgerald, Timothy. *Discourse on Civility and Barbarity: A Critical History of Religion and Related Categories*. Oxford, New York: Oxford University Press, 2007.

Han, Ju Hui Judy. "Beyond Safe Haven: A Critique of Christian Custody of North Korean Migrants in China." *Critical Asian Studies* 45, no.4 (2013). 533–60. https://doi.org/10.1080/14672715.2013.851153

Hughes, Theodore. "Return to the Colonial Present: Ch'oe In-hun's Cold War Pan-Asianism." *Positions: East Asia Cultures Critique* 19, no.1 (2011): 109–131. https://doi.org/10.1215/10679847-2010-026

Institute for Unification Education, Ministry of Unification (South Korea), "Understanding North Korea: Totalitarian Dictatorship, Highly Centralized Economies, Grand Socialist Family," Giljabi Media, 2015.

Jung, Jin-Heon. *Free to Be: North Korean Migrants and the South Korean Evangelical Church*. Diss., University of Illinois at Urbana-Champaign, 2010.

Jung, Jin-Heon. *Migration and Religion in East Asia: North Korean Migrants' Evangelical Encounters*. New York: Palgrave Macmillan, 2015.

Jung, Jin-Heon. "The Religious-political Aspirations of North Korean Migrants and Protestant Churches in Seoul." *Journal of Korean Religions* (2016): 123–48. https://www.jstor.org/stable/24892380

Jung, Hyang Jin. "Jucheism as an Apotheosis of the Family: The Case of the Arirang Festival." *Journal of Korean Religions* (2013): 93–122. https://www.jstor.org/stable/23943356

Lee, Ahlam. *North Korean Defectors In a New and Competitive Society: Issues and Challenges In Resettlement, Adjustment, and the Learning Process*. Lanham: Lexington Books, 2016.

Lim, Jae-Cheon. *Leader Symbols and Personality Cult In North Korea: The Leader State,* Abingdon, Oxon; NY : Routledge, 2015.

Il-Sung, Kim. *Selected Works,* Volume 8, Foreign Languages Publishing House, 1996.

Kim, Sung Kyung. "'Defector,' 'Refugee,' or 'Migrant'? North Korean Settlers in South Korea's Changing Social Discourse." *North Korean Review* (2012): 94–110. http://www.jstor.org/stable/43910315.

Kim, Sung K. "Mobile North Korean Women and their Places in the Sino-North Korea Borderland." *Asian Anthropology,* vol. 15, no.2 (2016): 116–31. https://doi.org/10.1080/1683478X.2016.1215540

Kim, Suzy, "(Dis)Orienting North Korea," *Critical Asian Studies* 42, no.3 (2010): 481–95. https://doi.org/10.1080/14672715.2010.507397

Kim, Woon-Ju. "Association of the North Korean Defectors." Talbookja-Dongjihwae, N.p., July 29, 2007. Accessed November 9, 2017.

McCurry, Justin. "The Defector Who Wants to Go Back to North Korea." *The Guardian.* Guardian News and Media, April 22, 2014. Accessed November 9, 2017. https://www.theguardian.com/world/2014/apr/22/defector-wants-to-go-back-north-korea

Ngo, Tam, and Justine Quijada, eds. *Atheist Secularism and Its Discontents: A Comparative Study of Religion and Communism in Eurasia.* New York: Springer, 2015.

O, Tara. *The Collapse of North Korea: Challenges, Planning and Geopolitics of Unification.* London: Palgrave Macmillan, 2016.

Rivé-Lasan, Marie-Orange. "Korean Christian Churches, the ibuk ch'ulsin Minority and the Perception of the North." *Journal of Korean Religions* (2013): 123–46. https://www.jstor.org/stable/23943357

Republic of Korea: Protection of Defecting North Korean Residents and Support of Their Settlement Act, 1997, July 14, 1997. Accessed November 9, 2017. Available at: http://www.refworld.org/docid/3ae6b4ef28.html

Ryang, Sonia. *North Korea: Toward a Better Understanding.* Lanham, MD: Lexington Books, 2009.

Sang-hun, Choe. "North Korean Defector, 'Treated Like Dirt' in South, Fights to Return." *The New York Times* (August 5, 2017). Accessed November 9, 2017. www.nytimes.com/2017/08/05/world/asia/north-korea-defector-south-korea.html

Shin, Eun Hee. "The Sociopolitical Organism: The Religious Dimensions of Juche Philosophy." *Religions of Korea in Practice* (2007): 517–33.

Song, Young Sub. "Socio-cultural Factors Influencing the Conversion to Christianity among North Korean Refugees in South Korea." *ProQuest Dissertations Publishing*, Trinity International University, 2011.

Suh, Jae-Jung. "Introduction: Making Sense of North Korea: Institutionalizing Juche at the Nexus of Self and Other." *Journal of Korean Studies* 12, no.1 (2007): 1–13. http://muse.jhu.edu/article/416551

United Nations High Commissioner for Refugees. "Republic of Korea: Protection of Defecting North Korean Residents and Support of Their Settlement Act, 1997." Accessed November 9, 2017. Refworld, www.refworld.org/docid/3ae6b4ef28.html

CHAPTER 6

IDENTITY, RELIGION, AND RESISTANCE OF RUSSIAN PEOPLE IN BRAZIL

Sonia Maria de Freitas

Introduction

Russian immigration to Brazil is complex for several reasons. Standing astride the European and Asian continents, Russia has the largest territory in the world and features an ethnic diversity which includes over 132 languages. Also, references to Russian immigration are scarce in the literature, which has until now focused mostly on the study of numerically expressive waves of immigrants to Brazil, such as the Italian, Portuguese, Japanese, and Syrian-Lebanese. Except for studies on famed figures from the Russian community, there has been academic silence about Russian immigrants in Brazil.[1]

Thus, the research which gave birth to this chapter[2] is a milestone, as it brings to light elements of Russian immigration to Brazil through oral testimonies from the protagonists themselves. Such accounts paint a portrait of the Russian community in Brazil, documenting singularities of its main

---

[1]   There may be a political motive behind that silence: Russians were stigmatized for coming from a country which had turned communist to another which was avowedly anti-communist when the military dictatorship was instated in 1964. Toward the end of the 1980s, the collapse of the Soviet Union and the end of the dictatorship in Brazil intensified the integration of this group of immigrants into diverse social spaces of the Brazilian society and strengthened their organization as a community.

[2]   The text presented here stems from a research I conducted with the Russian community in the city of São Paulo, as a contribution to the development of the collection of the Immigration Museum of São Paulo. Tamara Kalinin, director of the Nadejda Cultural Center, collaborated with me in the field work. Subsequently, I expanded that research as I worked on my doctoral dissertation "Falam os Imigrantes: Memória e Diversidade Cultural em São Paulo," presented at the School of Philosophy, Letters, and Human Sciences of the University of São Paulo (FFLCH/ USP) in 2001.

immigration flows, the different historical moments they relate to, and the mechanisms for preserving their traditions and culture.

BETWEEN REVOLUTIONS AND WARS: THE SEARCH FOR A HOME IN BRAZIL

In general, the Russian immigration to Brazil can be divided into three periods: (1) Pre-Bolshevik, up to 1917; (2) between 1917 and 1945 (from the revolution to World War II), and; (3) from 1945 on (postwar era). The first two periods coincided with a huge influx of immigrants to Brazil. Between 1881 and 1941, Brazil received 2,897,545 individuals, the fourth largest contingent of immigrants in that period in the Americas, with the United States, Canada, and Argentina being the American countries that recorded a higher number of immigrants during the same period.[3]

Immigrants in general came mainly to the state of São Paulo to meet the demands of coffee farming, a booming industry at the time. The then-province of São Paulo became their main point of arrival, especially after 1881, due to the Brazilian policy of subsidizing immigration. The subsidy included free ship or train fares, and the construction of hostels for housing and orienting new immigrant arrivals. Between 1887 and 1936, upto 2,847,687 immigrants set foot on São Paulo soil, of which 1,610,648 came spontaneously, while 1,127,039 people were subsidized.[4]

In 1888, the state built a *Hospedaria de Imigrantes* (migrant hostel) in the city of São Paulo, with the capacity to host 3,000 immigrants. In its first decade of operation, the administration of the hostel was administered by the Society for the Promotion of Immigration, being reassigned later to the Department of Colonization and Immigration at the State of São Paulo's Secretariat of Agriculture.

Many immigrants admitted into that hostel were sent to the twenty-five state-sponsored colonial settlements established between 1877 and 1894 in the countryside of São Paulo state. In addition to working on coffee farms, Russian immigrants established themselves in these settlements, where they purchased small plots of land.[5]

The documental archives of the old hostel reveal that, in 1907, Russian immigrants owned plots in the Nova Odessa settlement. Established through

---

[3]   *Boletim do Departamento de Imigração e Colonização.* São Paulo. Secretaria de Agricultura, Indústria e Comércio. N. 5, dez. 1950, 139–40.

[4]   Secretaria da Agricultura do Estado de São Paulo, *Boletim da Diretoria de Terras, Colonização e Imigração.* São Paulo: Secretaria da Agricultura. Ano 1, n. 1, 35 e 36, 1937.

[5]   *Boletim do Departamento de Colonização e Imigração.* São Paulo. N. 3. Mar. 1941.

decree number 1,286 on May 24, 1905, this settlement was donated to a large number of Russian immigrants. That same year witnessed new arrivals of Russian families through the Port of Santos. However, since those immigrants were not farmers, they "left the settlement in search of jobs in the cities. By the end of 1905, few families remained in the settlement."[6] I also identified the presence of Russian immigrants in the Pariquerassú (1861), São Bernardo (1877), Sabaúna (1889), Quiririm (1890), Piagui (1892), Campos Sales (1897), and Nova Europa (1907) settlements.[7]

The liturgical changes and the greater tolerance in uses and customs that stemmed from the 1905–1906 renewal movement in the Russian Orthodox Church altered the profile of Russian immigrants in Brazil.[8] From that year onward, one notices the arrival of the Old Believers or *Staroveri*, whom I will discuss later. In 1909, a group of Russian immigrants arrived in Rio Grande do Sul, the southernmost Brazilian state. According to the Brazilian Institute of Geography and Statistics (IBGE), 19,525 individuals had been admitted into the country through that port by 1912. In that state, they founded the municipality of Campina das Missões. Their presence was also recorded in the cities of Porto Alegre, Santa Rosa, and Passo Fundo.[9]

According to the Gregorian calendar, March 2017 marked the centenary of the Russian Revolution, the string of historical events that culminated with the end of the Romanov dynasty (1613–1917) and the execution of Czar Nicholas II and his family by a Bolshevik firing squad. Between 1918 and 1925, Russian migration was therefore motivated by the effects of the revolution, especially

<hr>

6 Anastassia Bytsenko, *Imigração da Rússia para o Brasil: Visões do Paraíso e do Império (1905-1914), (*Master's Thesis. School of Philosophy, Letters, and Human Sciences of the University of São Paulo, São Paulo, 2006), 36.

7 Cf. Archives of the State of São Paulo. *Núcleos Coloniais*, accessed on August 23, 2018, http://www.arquivoestado.sp.gov.br/site/acervo/repositorio_digital/nucleos_coloniais

8 About the Russian Orthodox Church and its impact on Russian immigration see: Ruseishvili, Svetlana, "Ser russo em São Paulo: os imigrantes russos e a (re)formulação de identidade após a Revolução de 1917," Doctoral dissertation. São Paulo: FFLCH/USP. 2016, accessed August 24, 2018, http://www.teses.usp.br/teses/disponiveis/8/8132/tde-13022017-124015/pt-br. php; Vorobieff, Alexandre, "Identidade e memória da comunidade russa na cidade de São Paulo," Master's thesis. Geography Department at FFLCH/USP. 2006.

About the history of the Russian Church in Exile see: *I.M. Andreev,* "Brief Overview of the History of the Russian Church from the Revolution to Our Day," *Jordanville, 1952*; and Second All-Diaspora Council [Sobor] of the Russian Orthodox Church Abroad, accessed August 22, 2018, http://www.synod.com/synod/engdocuments/enhis_2vsezarsobor.html

Various articles on the history of the Russian Orthodox Church in Exile are available at http://www.synod.com/synod/engdocuments/articles.html, accessed on August 20, 2018.

Jacinto Anatólio Zabolotsky, *A Imigração Russa para o Rio Grande do Sul: Os Longos Caminhos da Esperança*. (Campina das Missões, Brazil: Martins Livreiro, 1998), 15.

9 Jacinto Anatólio Zabolotsky, *A Imigração Russa para o Rio Grande do Sul: Os Longos Caminhos da Esperança*. (Campina das Missões, Brazil: Martins Livreiro, 1998), 15.

the civil war, the establishment of a communist regime, and the formation of the Union of Soviet Socialist Republics (USSR). The Russian dispersion took place through some major routes: the Baltic countries, the islands of Lemnos, Gallipoli (on the Aegean Sea), and China.

Despite the fact that this is a theme regularly addressed in academic circles, and that some soon-to-be-published studies on this topic are promising,[10] the importance of that event has not yet generated much interest among Brazilian publishers, and many research gaps still persist.[11]

There are records of the presence of Russian immigrants in São Paulo in the 1920s.[12] Most of them ended up on coffee farms or settlements in the "paulista" countryside.[13] Back then, the state of São Paulo recruited workers in Europe to meet the needs of its coffee-based economy. As experience in working in crop fields was required, many Russians concealed their education or professional qualifications, pretending they were farmers to be given a free ticket to come to Brazil, as reported by Ivan Solomca, an immigrant of the day.[14]

According to Demétrio Coev, there were many Slavic immigrant colonies in the Alta Sorocabana region, between the municipalities of Quatá and Varpa. In the Nova Esperança and Feiticeiro colonies there were only Bulgarians, while in Presidente Epitácio, Russians were predominant. By contrast, the colonies of Nova Bessarábia, Aurora, Regente Feijó, and Balisa received both Russians and Bulgarians. To counter the competition from the Baptist churches, the

[10]   Works recently launched in Brazil: *História Cultural da Rússia (Natasha's Dance)*, by Orlando Figes, and *A Verdade sobre a Tragédia dos Romanov*, by Marc Ferro, *Reconstruindo Lenin* (Tamáz Krausz), *O Ciclo do Totalitarismo*, by Ruy Fausto, and *A Cortina de Ferro*, by Anne Applebaun. However, according to Marcelo Godoy, classical works about the Russian revolution remain unavailable in Brazilian bookstores, such as those by Alexander Rabinowitch (*The Bolsheviks Come to Power* and *Bolsheviks in Power*), Sheila Fitzpatrick (*A Spy in the Archives*) and Oleg Khlevniuk (*The History of the Gulag, from Collectivization to the Great Terror*). Cf. Marcelo Godoy, Revolução Russa completa centenário sem historiografia ser traduzida, in O Estado de São Paulo, accessed on August 25, 2018, https://alias.estadao.com.br/noticias/geral,revolucao-russa-completa-centenario-sem-historiografia-ser-traduzida,70001702656

[11]   For more on the events that changed the course of Russian history, one can consult the political writings of Lenin (1870–1924) and Leon Trotsky (1879–1940) – both Bolshevik leaders – as well as the critical and historical study by Edmund Wilson, *To the Finland Station: A Study in the Writing and Acting of History* (New York, NY: NYRB, 2003). It is also worth mentioning John Reed's *Ten Days that Shook the World* (New York, NY: Boni & Liveright, 1919), an account in which John Reed deals with the events leading to the 1917 revolution, and also Alexandr Solzhenitsyn's account in *The Gulag Archipelago: An Experiment in Literary Investigation* (New York: Haper & Row, 1985), which relied on testimonies from 227 forced labor camp survivors under Joseph Stalin's rule.

[12]   Zabolostsky, *A Imigração Russa para o Rio Grande do Sul*, 15.

[13]   *Paulista* means that which is pertinent to the state of São Paulo.

[14]   Excerpt from interview by the author in June, 1996. A child to Russian parents, immigrant Ivan Solomca was born in Bessarabia in 1908. He came to Brazil in 1926 to avoid being conscripted into the army of the Romanian government which ruled the region.

Russian Orthodox Church of São Paulo built a small church in Balisa. A priest visited that church twice a year to perform weddings, christenings, and to celebrate the Eucharist. Immigrants coming to that region would get off a train in Martinópolis, where someone would meet them. Then they would go on horseback to the colony.[15]

A number of Russians arrived in São Paulo onboard the French ships *Aquitaine* and *Provence*. The first ship left from Marseille and berthed at the Port of Santos on July 12, 1921, with 422 Russians. A total of 651 Russians boarded the second steamship at the Port of Ajaccio (on the island of Corsica), one passenger got on in Provence, 39 Spaniards at the harbor of Gibraltar, and arrived in Santos on August 2, 1921.[16] Most passengers were Russian Imperial Army and White Army officers and their families, led by Colonel Vassily Faesy, General Staff officer of the Russian Imperial Army.[17] It is assumed that many of those immigrants settled down in the city of São Paulo.

Despite the prominent position of the state of São Paulo in the hosting of Russian immigrants, the whole country witnessed remarkable stories of Russian immigration at that time. In the early 1930s, a group of Russian families crossed the Syrian desert of Palmyra and Pakistan on foot until they reached India, where they boarded a ship bound for Brazil. They were sent to Três Bocas, where the city of Londrina would later be founded. In Três Bocas, Russian immigrants settled on land owned by the Terra Norte Company of Paraná, which appointed the Russian employee Vladimir Revensky to welcome them. Between 1930 and 1935, the Company sold thirty-two plots to immigrants of Russian origin.[18]

As that decade came to a close, Russian Revolution refugees could be found in many countries such as Yugoslavia, France, China, Bulgaria, Poland, Estonia, Germany, and the then-Czechoslovakia, with a larger concentration among the first three countries. Seeking to redeem their identity, they built churches,

---

[15] Interview by the author with Pastor Demétrio Coev from the Baptist Church on February 15, 1996. He devoted his life to evangelizing the Bessarabian Bulgarian colonies in both the countryside and the capital city.

[16] According to the testimony of Father Constantino Bussyguin, the passenger list of each steamship can be found in the archives of the Immigration Museum. From those lists, Father Constantino identified the following Russian immigrants (with their numbers on the list) on the ships: (a) on the *Aquitaine*: 156 - Pierre Bartchevsky, 191- Frontzkievitch - Jean, Cleopatra (both buried in the cathedral crypt), Victor and Arianda, 206 - Alexandre Razgouliaeff, 256 - Gregorio Ivanoff, 267 - Efrem Poliakoff, 289 - Gleb Arsky; and (b) on the *Provence*: Faezy family, Nicolai Dakhoff, Alexandre Sekirko (buried in the crypt). Interview by the author with Father Constantino Bussyguin, on June 12, 2001.

[17] Colonel Faesy played an active role in the building of St. Nicholas Orthodox Cathedral in the city of São Paulo. He was 44 when he arrived in Santos with his wife and two children.

[18] See Boni, Paulo César. *A História do Norte de Londrina com a Fotografia*, accessed August 14, 2017, http://www.unicentro.br/rbhm/ed04/dossie/09.pdf

schools, and cultural organizations. The immigrants who came to Brazil back then were children of lawyers, business owners, engineers, judges, professors, and Russian army officials. That was the case for Andre Vechniakoff, the son of a Czarist general who fled the Bolshevik Revolution.[19]

The World War II (1939–1945) changed the European map, and again the course of the Russian people, and marked the third flow of Russian immigration in Brazil. Among those established in Yugoslavia, the hope that Germans would defeat the Soviet Union fed the dream of return to their homeland. Soviet soldiers were made prisoners, and many civilians were taken to forced labor camps in Germany. Immigrant Maria Zotz said that she spent two months in Mauthausen, where

> conditions were awful. At night, when you needed to go to the restroom, you walked out of the dormitory and the lights from the lookout towers immediately followed the prisoners along to the restroom. When you returned the lights would follow you back so you could not run away. I was assigned to work at a cable factory, and my father was also sent to forced labor. He dug ditches; and as for my mother, because she was over 50, she remained free, not being forced to work. But she had to come to the camp to receive her food stamp, so that she could buy food.[20]

The conditions in Europe after the conflict prevented many people from going back to their home countries. Between 1947 and 1951, one could notice a large outward migratory movement made up of refugees and people displaced by the war who could not return or who refused to go back to their home countries, especially those incorporated by the Soviet Union.[21]

In an effort not to make their relationships with the Soviet government worse, the Allied occupation forces (England, France and the United States) set up camps for displaced persons in the countries under their

---

[19]   Interview by the author in August, 1994. Andre Vechniakoff was born in Saint Petersburg in 1902 and came to Brazil in 1926. Before fleeing, he served in the Red Army for one year in northern Russia.

[20]   Interview by the author in June, 1996. Maria Zotz was born in Ivanica, Yugoslavia on May 10, 1948.

[21]   Those refugees/displaced persons were mainly Russian, Polish, Ukrainian, Romanian, Czech, Yugoslavian, Lithuanian and Bulgarian. Addressing that issue, Hélio Lobo distinguishes between displaced persons and refugees by arguing that "the former left their countries spontaneously because of political problems while the latter were driven out forcefully. In the case referred to here, the majority was made up of displaced people, thousands of men and women brought for labor servitude." See Hélio Lobo, "O Drama dos Deslocados," *Boletim do Departamento de Imigração e Colonização*. São Paulo, 5 (1950): 88–97.

administration (Germany, Austria, Italy and Greece).[22] The United Nations Relief & Rehabilitation Administration (UNRAA)—and, subsequently, the International Refugee Organization (IRO)—played a key role in the process of relocating those populations, using migration to other countries as its main strategy.[23] Several countries entered into agreements to select and receive those groups.

At that time, the Russian influx into Brazil was also increased by those who left China in the early 1950s because of the Chinese Revolution.[24] The significant presence of Russians in that country was related to the building of the Trans-Siberian Railway. By the mid-nineteenth century, the Sino-Russian borders had been redefined, allowing for constant movements of populations between the two countries. One of the largest populational movements across the border took place in 1896, when the construction of the railway stretched from Harbin in China to Vladivostok in easternmost Russia began. Due to the arrival of technicians and workers with their families, the Russian community in Harbin grew so large that it became known as the "Russian City." Because of the Bolshevik Revolution, civilians and army members also settled down in that Chinese municipality.

Without either Chinese or Russian documents, these stateless people were placed under the responsibility of the Intergovernmental Committee for European Migration (ICEM)[25] in 1952, leaving then for the United States, Canada, Australia, Argentina, and Brazil—countries that welcomed them at

---

[22]   See Odair da Cruz Paiva. "Migrações Internacionais Pós Segunda Guerra Mundial: A Influência dos Estados Unidos no Controle e Gestão dos Deslocamentos Populacionais nas Décadas de 1940 a 1960." *Anais do XIX Encontro Regional de História: Poder, Violência e Exclusão*, ANPUH–USP, São Paulo, September 8–12, 2008. http://www.anpuhsp.org.br/sp/downloads/CD%20XIX/index.html.

[23]   See *Boletim do Departamento de Imigração e Colonização*. São Paulo, n. 5, 91, Dec. 1950. See also *Revista de Imigração e Colonização*, 1950. Before the end of the war, they set up the Intergovernmental Committee on Refugees; and in 1943 the United Nations Relief and Rehabilitation Administration (UNRRA) was established, being tasked with repatriating or relocating thousands of people who were in European camps. In 1947, that organization was replaced by the International Refugee Organization (IRO), which operated until 1951. In 1950, the UN established the Office of the United Nations High Commissioner for Refugees (UNHCR). The UNHCR has helped thousands of people and has been awarded two Nobel Prizes for its humanitarian work. Accessed August 1, 2017, http://www.unhcr.org

[24]   With the victory of the Communist Party in the Chinese Civil War, Mao Zedong proclaimed the People's Republic of China in 1949. In 1950, the Sino-Soviet Treaty of Friendship, Alliance, and Mutual Assistance was signed, lasting until 1960.

[25]   The Intergovernmental Committee for European Migration (ICEM) was founded in 1951 administered by the United States and was joined by 14 countries, including Brazil. The name ICEM was changed to International Organization for Migration (IOM), the main intergovernmental organization devoted to migration, working in partnership with other organizations and the civil society to respond to migration challenges. Accessed August 1, 2017, https://www.iom.int

that time. In the case of Brazil, between 1955 and 1962 (the year when the last group arrived), those immigrants traveled from Harbin to Hong Kong by train, where they got on ships that made stops in Singapore and South African harbors before crossing the Atlantic to Rio de Janeiro. For Katharina Neverovsky, the trip was beautiful:

> We crossed the Atlantic after the war after all that horror. Just imagine the sea, blue skies, no bombing, regular food. For me those were the best vacations after five long years of war, suffering and horror. Because with bombings every day, we didn't have tomorrow; we just had today.[26]

As soon as the immigrants disembarked in Brazil, they were all sent to the migrant hostel on Ilha das Flores, Guanabara Bay, where they were kept in quarantine, and then taken by train to São Paulo.[27] Katharina Neverovsky remembers that

> three, four, or five people were placed together in a small room. And there we waited for six weeks to see if any disease or epidemic was detected. As nothing happened, they prepared our documents. Then we got the entry visa, a real document, because we entered the country legally.[28]

At that time, the migrant hostel premises in São Paulo were being used by the Air Force Technical School (from 1943 to 1951). Provisional lodging was set up then in coffee warehouses, which came to be known later as the Campo Limpo Paulista Hostel, just some kilometers away from the state capital. Magda Petroff describes it:

> The families were separated by hanging blankets, and we were in the middle. At night we heard arguments, displays of jealousy, and children crying. My mother was young too, so we didn't bother with it. We thought we were very lucky because we arrived on firm land, and we were going to start life again.[29]

According to the Department of Immigration of the Ministry of Labor, Industry and Commerce, Brazil received 22,009 Russians who escaped from forced repatriation and from the Chinese Revolution. Of that total, 51 percent ended up in São Paulo because of the greater job opportunities in its growing industrial park. The others settled down in the states of Paraná, Rio Grande do Sul, Federal District, Goiás, Santa Catarina, Rio de Janeiro, Minas Gerais, and Bahia. However, the data does not represent the total numbers of all who got

---

26 Interview by the author in 1996. Katharina Neverovsky was born in St. Petersburg in 1921.
27 One group went to the city of Porto Alegre in the beginning of 1949.
28 Interview by the author on July 3, 1996.
29 Interview by the author in 1996.

in, since many Russian immigrants omitted their origins for fear of deportation to the USSR.[30]

The Russian wave of immigration to Brazil in the postwar period was mainly comprised of a highly skilled and intentionally chosen labor force. As of 1946, we note an increasing entry of qualified professional groups, a trend which occurred hand in hand with the transformation of the industrial and urban economy into the backbone of the development-based policy implemented by the administrations of presidents Getúlio Vargas (1951–1954) and Juscelino Kubitschek (1956–1961).[31] Katharina Neverovsky remembers that

> Dr. Azambuja, the Brazilian consul, came in with a sheet of paper in his hand, and chose a quota of specialized engineers. That was the case for my husband, a certified chemical engineer. We had to come to São Paulo, an industrial city.[32]

In São Paulo, the Service of Immigration and Colonization (1939–1946), and later the Department of Immigration and Colonization (1946–1968), which also coordinated the works of the Fund for Immigration and Colonization, sent Russian immigrants and refugees to perform urban and rural activities. The arrival of these technicians enhanced several industrial plants, such as BASF, Volkswagen, Arno, COSIPA (São Paulo's Steel Company), and Estrela Toy Factory both in the state capital and in the Greater São Paulo area.

The natural difficulties of adapting were overcome through community organization, mainly through charities and churches. One of the emblematic cases is the São Paulo Philanthropic Society, founded on September 9, 1946 to aid World War II victims—the elderly of Slavic origin and their descendants. Its first head office was located on Aleixo Street, in the Vila Mariana district, in a building donated by Alexander Razgulalev. Later, in the mid-1960s, with the support of the World Council of Churches and the United Nations Commissariat on Immigration, they built two other units: the first located on Washington Luiz Avenue, and the second, named Lar São Nicolau (Saint Nicholas Home), on 203 Cafezais street, according to Igor Schnee, the president of the Society.

---

[30]   See "Boletim do Departamento de Imigração e Colonização," *Revista de Imigração e Colonização*, São Paulo, 5 (1950): 91.

[31]   The policy served as an incentive to base industries, construction of roads, and hydroelectric power stations. The car industry developed mainly in the region known as the São Paulo ABC; and the construction industry went hand in hand with urban growth. The industrial development also made it possible to set up tool and appliance factories. The Russian immigrants worked in the automobile industry, a booming industry at that time; they built Brasília, the new capital city of Brazil, and opened up many new highways through the country. Among these skilled laborers there were some women who also broke ground in the country, and headed large teams, not common work for them at that time.

[32]   Excerpt from interview by the author in 1996.

Identity and Resistance through Faith: The Orthodox Face of immigration

Religion is one of the main identity bonds of a culture, and preserving its practices makes those who left their countries feel a little more at home in the new place. It was no different for the mostly Orthodox Russian immigrants in Brazil. The origins of the Orthodox Church date back a thousand years to the Christian communities of the old Byzantine Empire, which recognized the primacy of the Ecumenical Patriarchate of Constantinople since the East–West Schism or the Great Schism of 1054, when they broke away from the Roman Apostolic Church.[33]

In general, Russian immigrants settled in Brazil clustered together in communities of Old Believers and around parishes of the Russian Orthodox Church in Exile. In São Paulo, six churches were built in the city, in places with large concentrations of Russian immigrants, such as some neighborhoods in the central zone, in the East Side (Vila Alpina, Vila Zelina, and Vila Bela), and on the South Side (Moema and Pedreira). The strong presence of these two groups indicates that the religious question permeated the whole emigration process, and it was doubtlessly one of the mechanisms for the renegotiation of identity in the country of destination.

Known for being strict, Orthodox rites were the object of a Council held in the mid-sixteenth century that came to be known as *Stoglav* or the Council of One Hundred Chapters, in which the original Greek precepts were endorsed. In 1652 and 1653, Patriarch Nikon implemented reforms which were not accepted by the more conservative members, and the dissidents became known as Old Ritualists (*Staro-obriadtsi*), or more commonly, Old Believers (*Staroveri*).[34]

The first general census of the Russian Empire in 1897 counted 2,204,596 Old Believers.[35] Despite being persecuted by Czars and the communist regime established in 1917,[36] there are currently, according to the Ministry of Justice, 336 religious organizations of Old Believers registered in Russia. Most of them

---

[33]   See Gilberto Cotrim. *História Global Brasil e Geral* (São Paulo: Saraiva, 2008).

[34]   See *Information Sheet on the Old Rite*. Accessed September 10, 2017, http://www.synaxis. info/old-rite/0_ oldbelief/instructional_eng/information_sheet.html

[35]   The data of the First General Census of the Russian Empire (1897) was published in N.A. Troynitskogo, "The Total Body of the Empire's First General Census of Population Development Results Produced by 28 January 1897," St. Petersburg, 1905. (Table XII. Population by religions). *Demoscope Weekly*. Institute of Demography of the National Research University –School of Economics. Accessed September 13, 2017, http://demoscope.ru/weekly/ssp/rus_rel_ 97.php?reg=0

[36]   BBC Brazil. "A Família que Viveu Isolada na Sibéria por 42 anos sem Saber da 2ª Guerra Mundial e da Viagem à Lua", Jan. 22, 2017. Accessed September 12, 2017, http://www.bbc.com/ portuguese/internacional-38711257

are concentrated in the Nizhny Novgorod region. They are also present in Moscow, Saint Petersburg, Novosibirsk, Yekaterinburg, and Kazan. There are large communities in the Baltic countries, Belarus, Ukraine, Poland, Bulgaria, Moldova, and Italy. Also, there are significant groups in Australia, the United States, Bolivia, Chile, Argentina, Uruguay, and Brazil.[37]

The Old Believers who came to Brazil established themselves as small farmers, cultivating the land in a communal system in the states of Paraná, Mato Grosso, and Tocantins. The Santa Cruz and Montividiu settlements are located in the region of Ponta Grossa, Paraná state. Today, there are 150 families living on 40,000 hectares of land in the Primavera do Leste settlement, in Mato Grosso. In the Campos Lindos settlement, in the state of Tocantins, soybean production stands out. Agriculture is the main activity in these complexes which have kept up with the modernization of techniques and farming machinery.

The first three colonies mentioned above are located in places with difficult access and are extremely closed because they still face prejudice. They preserve their Orthodox beliefs, maintaining rites, customs, and traditions practiced in the nineteenth century. Their schools teach Greek and Russian, the latter being their main language. Marriages occur among people who follow the Orthodox liturgy, even if they come from other colonies in Brazil or in other countries. Men wear long beards and a belt tied above the hip. Women wear long dresses, and married women are identified by wearing headscarves. They are devoted to their families, help in farming activities, sew their own clothes, and make handicrafts.

There is also a considerable presence of Old Believers in the city of São Paulo, which makes it the main urban expression of this immigrant community. Built in 1929 by a group of approximately 300 *Staroveri*, the Russian Orthodox Old-Rite Church is located on Junquilhos Street, in the Vila Alpina district. The records of the church include the first wedding held in 1934 by priest Simião Ribakovas, who held the priesthood of that church until his death in 1969.

Nastácia Kozmekim is the daughter of Russian immigrants who guides religious practices in this church, an activity also carried out by her mother for ten years after the death of Father Simião. After her mother's death in 1984, Nadeja, the priest's daughter, took over and remained in the administration until 1997. According to Nastácia, Old Believers are so called because they have

---

[37]   Maria Bachmakova. "Como os Velhos Crentes Mantêm suas Tradições no Mundo Moderno", November 22, 2014. Accessed September 10, 2017, https://br.rbth.com/sociedade/2014/11/22/como_os_ velhos_crentes_mantem_suas_tradicoes_no_mundo_moderno_28363

not modernized since the birth of their religion. The Emperor, Peter the Great thought Russians were too archaic and strict. Nastácia's mother used to say Peter the Great was so obsessed with westernizing Russia that those who didn't want to convert were not allowed to use their chimneys in the winter. They were mistreated, persecuted, and killed, but they didn't back down.[38] Nastácia argues that Russian immigrants were very austere and that it was necessary to tone down the strictness of rituals:

> We shortened the length of the Mass, the Sunday Mass, because people felt tired. Can you imagine starting a Mass that goes on for 4 or 5 hours as in the past, when it lasted the whole night? It's absurd! God does not want this sacrifice of us.

São Paulo also is the headquarters of the Brazilian Diocese of the Orthodox Church in Exile. To understand the relevance of that fact, it is important to note that in 1657, the Russian Patriarchate became independent from the Patriarchate of Constantinople. Abolished in 1721, the Russian Patriarchate was reorganized in 1917. After the revolution, a group of Orthodox bishops took refuge in Constantinople,[39] and in 1920 they went to Yugoslavia at the invitation of the Serbian Patriarch and the Royal Government of Yugoslavia. There, the Russian Orthodox Church in Exile was structured with the purpose of attending to the large number of believers exiled by the revolution, lasting until the end of World War II and the establishment of the communist regime in the country. It was then transferred to Germany, remaining in Munich until 1951, and then to New York City, United States, taking the name Russian Orthodox Church in Exile. In the United States, they built a monastery and a seminary in Jordanville, acccording to Orthodox Bishop Gregório.[40]

The year 1935 marked the foundation of the Brazilian Diocese of the Russian Orthodox Church, with the arrival of Bishop Theodosius in the city of São Paulo at the request of the Saint Nicholas parish to the Episcopal Council

---

[38]   Excerpt from interview by the author on October 2, 1999. Peter the Great (1689–1725) wanted to Europeanize the country, and established Saint Petersburg as the capital. He instituted reforms in the Church and subjugated it to the rule of the State, replacing the Patriarch with a Holy Synod (1721) presided over by the Czar (Caesaropapism). He also outlawed "old customs," such as wearing beards or traditional garments. Furthermore, he founded the Saint Petersburg Academy of Sciences (1725) and several higher education schools, on top of hiring foreign technicians, artisans and artists. See Hermann Kinder and Wener Hilgemann, *Atlas Histórico Mundial: de la Revolucion Francesa a Nuestros Dias* (Espanha: Istmo, 1977), 291.

[39]   Alexandre Vorobieff, *Identidade e Memória da Comunidade Russa na Cidade de São Paulo*. Master's thesis in Human Geography, School of Philosophy, Letters, and Human Sciences of the University of São Paulo (USP), São Paulo, 2006.

[40]   Interview by the author on August 3, 2017.

of the Russian Orthodox Church in Exile. Bishop Gregório pointed out that the parish used to be much larger.[41]

The Most Holy Trinity Church was the first church built, erected between 1930 and 1931 in Vila Alpina on the initiative of Russian missionary Konstantino Izratsoff.[42] The second religious building was the Saint Nicholas Cathedral, erected between 1938 and 1939 on Tamandaré Street, in the Liberdade neighborhood. According to Father Constantino Bussyguin,

> The first building was the Church of the Most Holy Trinity in Vila Alpina, and the second one was our cathedral of 1938–1939. It took nine months of construction between the laying of the foundation stone and consecration; but as a parish, ours is the oldest. The first Russian Orthodox priest came to Brazil, if I am not mistaken, in 1922 or 1923. [His name was] Father Michail Kliarowsky. He came from Estonia, and stayed for a few years in Brazil, and then left for Paraguay. At the time, as there wasn't a church, the Russian community, before this Father Michail came . . . used the Antiochian Orthodox Church, located on Basílio Jafet Street, in the 25 de Março area.[43]

Subsequently, the Church of Saint Seraphim of Sarov (1949), in Carapicuíba, and the Church of Saint Sergius of Radonezh (1952), in Moema, São Paulo, were built, along with the Church of Our Lady of Protection (1962), in Vila Zelina, São Paulo, which is being renovated very slowly due to lack of financial resources.

Orthodox and Russian are not synonymous, but a large proportion of the immigrants and their descendants up to the third generation in São Paulo are adherents of the Orthodox Church. We also noted that many of the interviewed Russian immigrants preserve traditions and defend the monarchy. This trend was observed not only among Russian immigrants in Brazil and their

---

[41]   Interview by the author on August 3, 2017.

[42]   Father Konstantino Izratsoff was married to the daughter of a wealthy Dutch family and came to South America in the late nineteenth century. He was, for some time, the diplomatic representative of the Russian Empire in Argentina, where he built the magnificent Orthodox Church of Buenos Aires, raising funds with society and with the Russian Imperial family in Moscow, with the support of the Russian Orthodox Church.

[43]   Interview by the author with Father Constantino Bussyguin (St. Nicholas Cathedral) on June 12, 2001. As for the Antiochian Orthodox Church, few people know of its existence because it is hidden in the hall of a commercial building. One of the priests of the Antiochian community spoke Russian because he studied in Russia so he could provide masses for the community. When Father Michail arrived, masses continued to be given there, and, later, they rented a hall on Itobi Street. Actually, the Orthodox Church of the Annunciation of Our Lady, opened in 1905, with donations made by Arab merchants in the region, was probably the first one erected in Brazil. In order to be financially independent, its dome was cut off in the 1930s, and a commercial building was erected on top of it. The rental income enables the church's financial independence. Accessed July 31, 2017, https://menteplural.wordpress.com/2014/12/13/entre-lojas-e-camelos-o-discreto-oasis-da- 25-de-marco/

descendents. "For faith, Czar, and Fatherland" was a popular motto before the Bolshevik Revolution. Curiously enough, the current coat of arms of the Russian Federation (adopted in 1993) derives from the old Russian Empire, with a figure of an eagle grasping a scepter and an orb, traditional symbols of the divine authority of the Czars. When the Soviet regime ended, over 10,000 churches were reopened; churches and monasteries were restored and rebuilt. The last Russian Czar, Nicholas II, and his family were canonized on August 19, 2000. For the then Father George Petrenko, now Bishop Gregório for South America,

> There are traditional people, people who fight for the return of a monarchical regime, which is considered by the Church and the Russian people to be the only system of government blessed by God.

In 2007, the Russian Orthodox Church of Moscow and the Russian Orthodox Church in Exile (headquartered in New York) were reunited with the encouragement of President Vladimir Putin, putting an end to eight decades of schism.[44] However, in Brazil, only three parishes accepted the unification, along with the Argentina and South America Diocese, which aligned itself with the Moscow Patriarchate: the Annunciation of Our Lady of Sorrows, in São Paulo; Saint Zenaide, in Rio de Janeiro; and Saint Sergius of Radonezh, in Porto Alegre. Elsewhere in the world, many parishes did not agree with the unification and remained attached to the Orthodox Church in Exile. According to Father Constantino Bussyguin,

> In reality, it was not a union, but a way of morally and materially snatching what existed outside Russia which had been formed and nurtured for decades; and suddenly it lost its spiritual value. . . . Moments of history were either distorted or simply ignored.[45]

About 70 percent of the parishes adhered to that unification; however, Father Constantino points out that

> Many of the priests didn't join because they wanted to. They did it either out of obedience to their Bishop or for fear of losing their positions. Many had been in the parish with their families for 10, 20 years. . . . In South America,

---

[44] See G1 Globo, "Reunificada, Igreja Ortodoxa Russa vira a página da era soviética," accessed July 31, 2017, https://glo.bo/2LAiZkn. At that time, the head of the Orthodox Church in Exile and the Patriarch of Moscow and all Russia signed the canonical communion act at the Cathedral of Christ the Savior, in the Russian capital. According to Father Constantino Bussyguin, the reunification was premature. This process started in 2003 during a meeting in the United States, when the issue of reunification was brought forward, and many who had opposed reunification flipped and began to defend it. According to him, the movement was headed by Metropolitan Hilarion of New York.

[45] Interview by the author with Father Constantino Bussyguin on June 12, 2001.

one group accepted it and the other didn't. Some parishes in the United States, Canada, Australia have both groups today. In Europe, most joined the unification. But some didn't: a convent located one hour from Paris (the parish in Lyon), two monasteries in England, in London; they are small but exist and have their religious life. Interestingly, in Russia we already had parishes that did not accept the Patriarchate and came under the Church in Exile. And suddenly they see themselves in a situation in which they have to switch back to the Patriarchate. Some accepted it, some didn't. And the Russian Orthodox Church in Exile ended up breaking apart. But, unfortunately, that what existed until 2003, which had its strength, a representation, doesn't exist anymore. [46]

Regardless of the new direction of the Orthodox Church, the references and testimonies that underlie this article demonstrate that professing their religion was a way for Russian immigrants to maintain their roots and rebuild their identity on foreign land. In the case of Brazil, the strangeness and difficulty of the language and customs led to the formation of more isolated groups, which are real cultural portraits of Russia throughout the ages. In the state of São Paulo, the integration process was greater probably because of its consolidated structure for the absorption of immigrants.

BIBLIOGRAPHY:

Bachmakova, Maria. "Como os Velhos Crentes mantêm suas tradições no mundo moderno." Accessed September 10, 2017. https://br.rbth.com/sociedade/2014/11/22/como_os_velhos_crentes_mantem_suas_tradicoes_no_mundo_moderno_28363

Baeninger, Rosana and Claudio Dedecca (eds.). *Processos Migratórios no Estado de São Paulo*. Campinas: Nepo/Unicamp, 2013. Accessed July 30, 2017. http://www.nepo.unicamp.br/publicacoes/livros/colecaosp/VOLUME_10.pdf

Boni, Paulo César. "A História de Sorte de Londrina com a Fotografia." Accessed August 13, 2017. http://www.unicentro.br/rbhm/ed04/dossie/09.pdf

---

[46] Interview by the author with Father Constantino Bussyguin on August 9, 2017. Speaking about the future of the Russian Orthodox Church in Exile and the formation of new priests at the Jordanville seminary in the United States, Father Constantino stresses the closeness to the Greeks who still use the old Julian calendar, which maintains the traditions and seminaries both in Greece and in the United States.

Bytsenko, Anastassia. *Imigração da Rússia para o Brasil: Visões do Paraíso e do Império. (1905–1914)*. Master's thesis, University of São Paulo (USP), São Paulo, 2006.

Cotrim, Gilberto. *História Global Brasil e Geral*. São Paulo: Saraiva, 2008.

Folha de São Paulo. "Europa do Leste: Império Acorda e Luta Contra a Decadência." Caderno Especial, March 10, 1990.

Freitas, Sonia M. "Os Caminhos Russos no Brasil." *Jornal da Tarde*, Caderno de Sábado, Nov. 2, 1996.

———. *Falam os Imigrantes: Memória e Diversidade Cultural em São Paulo*. Doctoral Dissertation, School of Philosophy, Letters and Human Sciences, University of São Paulo (USP), São Paulo, 2001.

———. *História Oral: possibilidades e procedimentos*. 2nd ed. São Paulo: Humanitas, 2006.

Godoy, Marcelo. "Revolução Russa Completa Centenário sem Historiografia ser Traduzida." *O Estado de São Paulo*, March 17, 2017.

Kinder, Hermann and Wener Hilgemann. *Atlas Histórico Mundial: De la Revolucion Francesa a Nuestros Dias*. Madrid, Spain: Istmo, 1977.

Magalinski, Jan. *Igreja Ortodoxa Russa: Exílio e Fé em Goiânia*. Goiânia, Brazil: Gráfica e Editora Vieira Ltda., 2005.

Paiva, Odair da Cruz. "Desafios da Informatização de Documentos sobre a Imigração Pós-II Guerra Mundial para São Paulo." *Revista Patrimônio e Memoria*, UNESP/FCLAs/CEDAP, v.4, n.1, 2008.

———. "Migrações Internacionais Pós Segunda Guerra Mundial: A Influência dos EUA no Controle e Gestão dos Deslocamentos Populacionais nas Décadas de 1940 a 1960." *Annals of the 19th Regional History Meeting: Power, Violence and Exclusion*. ANPUH–USP, São Paulo, September 8–12, 2008.

Paiva, Odair da Cruz e Célia Sakurai. "Migrações Internacionais, Geopolítica e Desenvolvimento Econômico (1947–1980)." *Annals of the National Association for Graduate Studies and Research in Social Sciences (ANPOCS)*, 2004.

Reed, John. *Os Dez Dias que Abalaram o Mundo*. São Paulo: Global Editora, 1978.

Soljenitsin, Alexandre. *O Arquipélago Gulag*. São Paulo: Círculo do Livro, 1975.

Tolstoi, Leon. *O Reino de Deus Está em Vós*. São Paulo: Rosa dos Tempos, 1994.

Tompson, Paul, *A Voz do Passado: História Oral*. São Paulo: Paz e Terra, 1992.

Tincq, Henri, "Igreja Ortodoxa Russa Canoniza último Czar," *Folha de São Paulo*, Caderno Mundo, São Paulo, August 7, 2017.

Troynitskogo, N.A.. *The Total Body of the Empire's First General Census of Population Development Results Produced by 28 January 1897*. Accessed September 13, 2017. http://demoscope.ru/ weekly/ssp/rus_rel_ 97.php?reg=0

Vassilnenko, Angelina. *As Rotas dos Imigrantes Russos em sua Viagem para o Brasil.* 5th *Brazilian Conference on Immigration and Integration*, São Paulo, March 17–21, 1986.

Vorobieff, Alexandre. *Identidade e Memória da Comunidade Russa na Cidade de São Paulo.* Master's thesis, School of Philosophy, Letters and Human Sciences, University of São Paulo (USP), São Paulo, 2006.

Zabolotsky, Jacinto Anatólio. *A Imigração Russa para o Rio Grande do Sul: Os Longos Caminhos da Esperança.* Campina das Missões, 1998.

Websites:

BBC Brasil. "A família que viveu isolada na Sibéria por 42 anos sem saber da 2ª Guerra Mundial e da viagem à Lua", Jan. 22, 2017. Accessed September 12, 2017. http://www.bbc.com/portuguese/internacional-38711257

G1 GLOBO. *"Reunificada, Igreja Ortodoxa Russa vira a página da era soviética."* Accessed July 31, 2017. https://glo.bo/2LAiZkn.

Information Sheet on the Old Rite. Accessed September 10, 2017. http://www.synaxis.info/oldrite/0_oldbelief/instructional_eng/information_sheet.html

"O cisma dos Velhos Crentes." Accessed June 20, 2017. https://www.ecclesia.com.br/biblioteca/igreja_ortodoxa/a_igreja_ortodoxa_historia16.html

"História do Município de Lucélia." Accessed July 24, 2017. http://www.camaralucelia.sp.gov.br/index2.php?pag=T1RVPU9EZz1PV0k9T1RrPU9UUT0=&&id=3

https://www.fatheralexander.org/page23.htm. Accessed August 1, 2017.

CHAPTER 7

WHEN WOMEN LEAVE: EXAMINING THE INTERSECTION OF FAMILY, FAITH AND PERSONAL DEVELOPMENT IN THE LIVES OF AFRO-CARIBBEAN WOMEN IN NEW YORK CITY

Janice A. McLean-Farrell

Human mobility or migration is a central element in the history of the world. From ancient to most recent history, people have moved from one place to another and sought to adapt to their new environment. Much could be said about the complex and multi-layered reasons that fostered this movement be it voluntary/involuntary, economic/self-actualization, push/pull, national/international, permanent/temporary, etc. In contemporary times however, the discussions about these reasons especially within the public sphere have, at times, taken on a pernicious tone. Within "xenophobic" framings of the migration phenomena, the people who move are often classified as "criminals," the "under developed" sending countries are labeled deficient and thus unable to provide for its citizens, and the "resource rich" receiving countries are positioned as needing to protect their borders/culture/ "nationhood" from those who will exploit these resources by becoming increasingly "fortress-like." This particular "framing" of migration gives very little room to uncovering the policies (historical, economic, political, spiritual and socio-cultural, etc.) that continue to drive migration locally and globally or the "triple win," i.e., the fundamental benefits migration produces within cities and nation states (sending and receiving) and among the migrants themselves.

When contemporary migration is placed under the microscope, a face with feminine features comes into view. As migration scholars and others study the increasing feminization of migration, much attention is given to the following issues: invisibility of women within traditional studies on the migration project; the impact of the woman's departure on the rest of the family, especially on her children; the high concentration of female migrants in service industries that offer limited job advancement or benefits and expose many women to exploitative and/or abusive practices; the psychological and emotional burden female migrants grapple with as they strive to create a better future for their families and themselves; etc.[1] Oftentimes, due to the focus of the enquiry into the abovementioned issues, the complexity that undergirds the feminization of migration is not given adequate attention.[2] For the women who are central to this field of study, all aspects of their lives are integrated and seemingly "compartmentalized" components which influence and are influenced by each other. Using the intersection of family, faith and personal development as my areas of enquiry, I will investigate how Afro-Caribbean females' lives are being shaped in the diaspora. What is the singular and summative impact of these issues within the women's lives? What changes, and what remains the same in the female migrant's understanding of self? How are the expressions of Afro-Caribbean faith in New York City and the Caribbean shaped by these women's lives? Utilizing ethnographic research conducted among Afro-Caribbean women in New York City, I will seek to interrogate the above questions above.[3] By broadening the scope of enquiry to include the above mentioned issues— family, faith, and personal development, this study will provide us with a more representative portrayal of what an integrated life is like for Afro-Caribbean women in New York City.

Prior to delving into the roles that family, faith, and personal development play in shaping an integrated life among Afro-Caribbean women in New York City, it is necessary to provide a brief overview about migration in the Caribbean and the current movement to the United States. As I have argued

---

[1]   Rhacel Salazar Parreñas, *Children of Global Migration: Transnational families and Gendered Woes* (Stanford: Stanford University Press, 2005); Monica Boyd and Elizabeth M Grieco, *Women and Migration: Incorporating Gender into International Migration Theory*, 2003. accessed December 9, 2018, https://www.migrationpolicy.org/article/women-and-migration-incorporating-gender-international-migration-theory; Paola Bonizzoni, "Immigrant Working Mothers Reconciling Work and Childcare: The Experience of Latin American and Eastern European Women in Milan," *Social Politics: International Studies in Gender, State & Society* 21, no.2 (2014): 194–217; Patricia R. Pessar. "Engendering Migration Studies. The Case of New Immigrants in the United States." *American Behavioral Scientist* 42, no.4 (1999): 577–600.

[2]   See Livia Elisa Ortensi, "Engendering the Fertility/Migration Nexus: The Role of Women's Migratory Patterns in the Analysis of Fertility after Migration," *Demographic Research*, Vol.32 (2015): 1435–1468; Sabrina Marchetti, and Alessandra Venturini, "Mothers and Grandmothers on the Move: Labour Mobility and the Household Strategies of Moldovan and Ukrainian Migrant Women in Italy," *International Migration* 52, no.5, (2014), 111–26.

[3]   This fieldwork was conducted in the spring of 2007 and December 2017. The names of the respondents have been changed to pseudonyms to protect their identities.

elsewhere, "the majority of studies conducted on Caribbean and West Indian migration have used an economic approach to explain why migration takes place."[4] Framed within a functionalist and historical-structural framework, Caribbean international migration is normally perceived to be a classic example of the equilibrium theory, i.e., the movement of labor from an area of surplus to a region of demand. As I stated, this uni-dimensional approach does not do justice to the complexity that accompanies the immigration phenomena.[5] In order to provide a more nuanced approach to the migration phenomena, in this chapter I will briefly discuss the history of migration within the Caribbean region, the economic system and America's regional hegemony, how they created some of the "push/pull" factors that continue to systematically plague the region, and finally, the exercise of agency by migrants and the way their movement fosters a culture of migration.

CARIBBEAN MIGRATION HISTORY

The Caribbean region and the associated cultures, languages, societies, and people are all products of external migration.[6] There were the ancestors of the native peoples who moved from Asia to America at the point where the Bering Strait now divides the two continents and later their descendants who moved slowly throughout the Caribbean islands as they "adapted to changing environmental conditions and developed distinctive lifestyles and languages."[7] With the inauguration of the colonial period marked by the coming of the Spaniards in 1492, migration to and within the region became diversified as Europeans, African slaves, Indians, Jews, Syrians, and Chinese peoples "made" these islands their home.[8] As a result, it is fair to say that migration is an integral feature within the very DNA of Caribbean life.

ECONOMICS

As Portes and Grosfoguel so aptly state, while the "language and religion of colonizers [were] different, the economic system they imposed throughout

---

[4]   McLean-Farrell, *West Indian Pentecostals: Living their Faith in New York and London* (New York: Bloomsbury, 2016), 47.

[5]   Janice McLean-Farrell, *West Indian Pentecostals* 45–60; Elizabeth M. Thomas-Hope, *Explanation in Caribbean Migration* (London: Macmillan Press Ltd, 1992).

[6]   With the exception of the native peoples, all the other peoples were part of the creation of an artificial society focused on enriching European metropoles and exploiting the natural and human resources to fund such ventures. See: McLean-Farrell, *West Indian Pentecostals*, 16–35; Orlando Patterson, *The Sociology of Slavery* (London: Macgibbon & Kee, 1967), 9.

[7]   Philip Sherlock and Hazel Bennett, *The Story of the Jamaican People* (Kingston: Ian Randle, 1998), 42

[8]   While I will not elaborate on this topic in this chapter, it is imperative to highlight that for the slaves and the Chinese and Indians who arrived under the indentured servitude schemes, attention needs to be given to interrogating their agency in actually making these islands their home.

the region [was] the same."[9] This was primarily mono-agricultural and operated with a closed economic system.[10] Within this scheme, the islands provided their European colonizers with the tropical products they required, and were the necessary outlets for their export goods.[11] While this economic structure "made many Europeans wealthy, [it] devastated the island society social[ly] and economic[ally]."[12] For "built within [it] was an unhealthy dependence upon the beneficent and favorable external markets for both economic growth and progress."[13] For the former British colonies where sugar reigned supreme, the years following the abolition of slavery in 1834 initiated a series of events that were calamitous for local economies. First, the popularity of campaigns encouraging the non-consumption of West Indian sugar, the growth of competitors (Cuba, Brazil, the United States), the loss of "free" labor (no more slaves), and the passage of the Sugar Duties Act in 1846, combined to produce the eventual loss of the islands' monopoly on the global sugar market. Second, the floundering economies were further buffeted in the 1880s by the introduction and growth of beet sugar within the global market, serious outbreaks of cane diseases (the borer and blast stains), natural disasters (hurricanes), and the depression of world sugar prices. The result was crippling, evidenced in the foreclosure of sugar estates, economic hardship for the associated industries (peasant farming, local entrepreneur ventures, etc.), and a period marked by high population growth, un/under-employment, and limited economic advancement. These three economic features continue to systematically plague the region in the twentieth century and beyond.[14] While various measures were implemented to diversify the various islands' economy (Jamaica – bauxite, Trinidad – oil, etc.), and negate their economic isolation through organizations like the Caribbean Community (Caricom),[15] the foundation of the dependence on external economic beneficence nurtured during the colonial period remained. These relationships however were "far from being wholly beneficial to the region, for they tend[ed] inevitably to give rise to uneven development patterns, to the

---

[9]   Alejandro Portes and Ramón Grosfoguel, "Migration and Ethnic Communities," *The Annals of the American Academy of Political and Social Science*, Vol. 533, Trends in U. S.-Caribbean Relations (May, 1994), 50.

[10]   Within the British colony, the mono-agricultural crop upon which the economy was oriented was sugar.

[11]   Selwyn H. H. Carrington, *The Sugar Industry and the Abolition of the Slave Trade, 1775-1810* (Gainesville: University of Florida Press, 2002), 13.

[12]   Portes and Grosfoguel, "Migration and Ethnic Communities," 50.

[13]   McLean-Farrell, *West Indian Pentecostals,* 50.

[14]   David Watts, *The West Indies: Patterns of Development, Culture and Environmental Change since 1492,* (New York: Cambridge University Press, 1994 [1987]), 518–23.

[15]   Caricom is a grouping of twenty Caribbean nations to promote economic integration, foreign policy coordination, human and social development and security.

detriment of many."[16] On the one hand, there was the preservation of high-cost production patterns that allocated limited room for experimenting with agricultural diversification, while on the other, there was the growth of a trend away from the land—namely through emigration (regional and/or international), or youth seeking prestigious white-collar jobs in the developed areas of the island, i.e., rural to urban migration.[17] In the latter half of the twentieth century, the white-collar job has been augmented to also include various service jobs within the tourism industry.[18]

AMERICA'S REGIONAL HEGEMONY

West Indian migration to the United States and specifically New York is not new. According to Portes and Grosfoguel, "Jamaicans and other West Indians had been coming to New York in some numbers since the late 1880s."[19] What the post-1965 migration reveals however are the effects of a dramatic reorientation of the islands from their former European colonizers to the United States, and America's dominance and hegemony within the region. Beginning in the mid-1880s, America began to implement a new interpretation of the Monroe Doctrine articulated by Theodore Roosevelt that endued the United States with international policing authority. America had the authority to intervene in any country or national situation that warranted policing. Within the region however, it meant that "Caribbean itself was to become America's closed sea, . . . [where] as assistant Secretary of State Loomis stated in 1904: 'no picture of the future is complete which does not contemplate and comprehend the United States as the dominant power in the Caribbean Sea.'"[20] America's dominance was exerted on two primary fronts—politically through direct intervention in the island national states and economically through its huge foreign investment

---

16   Watts, *The West Indies,* 523.

17   Watts, *The West Indies,* 523.

18   For a glimpse into the manner the mega-industry of tourism affects the people and economies of the Caribbean see: Polly Pattullo, *Last Resorts: The Cost of Tourism in the Caribbean,* (New York: Monthly Review Press, 2005).

19   Portes and Grosfoguel, "Migration and Ethnic Communities," 55.

20   Eric Williams, "American Capitalism and Caribbean Economy," in *Caribbean Freedom: Economy and Society from Emancipation to Present,* ed. Hilary Beckles and Verene Shepherd (Kingston: Ian Randle Publishers Limited, 1993), 342.

in various industries and "infrastructural projects such as the canal in Panama and railroads in Central America and Cuba."[21]

Within the region, these economic investments accelerated the growth in export agriculture in certain countries and provided the means to complete certain infrastructural projects. These developments also generated increased demands for unskilled labor—the majority of which was provided by the West Indian workers. Throughout the rest of the twentieth century, this US-influenced regional migration pattern was augmented to also include migration to the US mainland. This ranged from temporary visas for farm workers,[22] to permanent visas for certain skilled professionals like nurses and teachers. Indelibly linked with America's political and economic dominance was its cultural hegemony within the region. This "mean[t] that the images Caribbean people [saw daily] on their screens [were] not largely of their own societies but glamourized or sensationalized images of the métropole [the U.S.]. [As such], events in the métropole [were] therefore allowed to dominate the informal public agenda."[23]

AGENCY AND A CULTURE OF MIGRATION

There is no denying the significant role that economics and labor redistribution play within the migration process. However, they are not the only influencers—the agency migrants exhibit is also critical. Set within the context of the struggle to improve the conditions of their lives, the decision by the newly emancipated slaves to leave the plantation and seek other means of employment—either on their own land or on another island—was a part of an emerging "social conscience concerning their own affairs."[24] In actualizing their agency, potential migrants would access the factors influencing their lives and act according to what was deemed most beneficial for them and their families. The trajectories of their movements were diverse, encompassing intra-island, regional

---

[21]   Ransford W. Palmer, *Pilgrims from the Sun: West Indian Migration to America* (New York: Twayne Publishers, 1995). America's economic dominance was further solidified in two specific ways: "through the implementation of the Caribbean Basin Initiative (CBI); and the adjustment measures imposed on several islands by the International Monetary Fund (IMF), the World Bank, and the US agency for International Development (USAID)." These measures served to continue the region's enduring dependence on an external nation for its economic vitality and growth. See McLean-Farrell, *West Indian Pentecostals*, 54.

[22]   These temporary workers worked for the Florida Sugar Plantations and other East Coast growers. See Portes and Grosfoguel, "Migration and Ethnic Communities," 55.

[23]   Shaheed Mohammed, "Migration and The Family In The Caribbean," *Caribbean Quarterly*, 44, no.3/4, (Sept/Dec. 1998): 112.

[24]   Shirley C. Gordon, *Our Cause for His Glory: Christianisation and Emancipation in Jamaica* (Kingston: The Press of the University of the West Indies, 1998), 99.

and international relocation.[25] Within families and communities throughout the Caribbean, these relocations eventually fostered a culture of migration. Constructed from experiences of past migration, these narratives—individual and collective—"served to link family members [and communities] across generational and national boundaries, while also facilitating the process whereby each 'subsequent' generation is 'socialized in a way of life and livelihood conditioned by migration.'"[26] When the respondents who participated in this research were asked where they heard stories about America in their island homes, they stated that they originated from either a relative or from members within their community. What was noteworthy was that that narration of the migration experience was not necessarily verbal or articulated by the individual who migrated. Instead it was revealed in the American consumer goods now accessible to the migrant's family, the accompanying status they gained within the community, and stories told about those who had migrated, i.e., "gaan to foreign."[27]

FAMILY, FAITH AND PERSONAL DEVELOPMENT IN SHAPING AN INTEGRATED LIFE AMONG AFRO-CARIBBEAN WOMEN IN NEW YORK CITY

Having discussed some of the complexities driving the migration process and its accompanying culture throughout the Caribbean region, I will now turn my attention to the roles family, faith, and personal development play in shaping the lives of Afro-Caribbean women who migrate.

Family

For my female respondents, their "family" included members of their biological family (parents, siblings, cousins, and other extended family members), very close friends, their partners and his relatives, and members of their church. The influence of this diverse group is twofold—enabling migration and supporting adaptation. Examples of this duality of function played by this diverse "family" will be given below. The enablement of the migration process took the form of sponsorship (for a visit or to live on a permanent basis), "sending" them away

---

[25]   Following emancipation, regional migration was normally temporary and predominantly male in its demographic. See McLean-Farrell, *West Indian Pentecostals*, 51–2. For information about female regional migration, see Paula L. Aymer, *Uprooted Women: Migrant Domestics in the Caribbean* (Westport: Praeger Publishers, 1997).

[26]   McLean-Farrell, *West Indian Pentecostals*, 57; Thomas-Hope, "Caribbean Migration," 194; Monica Boyd, "Family and Personal Networks in International Migration: Recent Developments and New Agendas," *International Migration Review* 23, no.3 (1989): 642–3.

[27]   For a discussion on remittances, "barrel children" and the influences of these narratives upon families and communities see, McLean-Farrell, *West Indian Pentecostals*, 57–8, 74–6. The expression "gaan to foreign" is the Patois term for "gone to foreign."

for health reasons, or encouragement to migrate as a means of taking a break from a difficult situation and possibly starting life over. As one places each type of "enablement" under the microscope, some distinctive stories emerge. There is Mary[28] who is the fourth of eleven children of her parents. She describes her childhood as being on the hard side because her father was the only adult working in her family. This dynamic created various financial struggles resulting in her missing out on various educational opportunities. Her initial visit to New York was made possible by an invitation from her ex-boyfriend's family. After a six-month stay, she returned home. Her father encouraged her to return to the United States, and she did. Unlike Mary, Susan's move to the United States was permanent from the beginning having arrived on a spousal visa. She and her husband were from the same community and prior to marriage knew each other but did not have any close relations. He relocated to New York and got married. Following the death of his first wife, he visited Susan's community in Jamaica, where a permanent relationship was initiated. Upon his return to New York, he completed the relevant documents that would allow her to legally migrate to the United States. Once these documents were approved, she relocated to New York and they got married.[29]

Jane's relocation to the United States was unusual in that it was the result of an emergency family intervention—i.e., her uncles "shipping" her off to live with her aunt in New York. Following her father's death when she was sixteen, her uncles became her surrogate fathers. Just prior to her relocation, she had been involved in four car accidents with her boyfriend. In an effort to prevent their niece, a.k.a., surrogate daughter, from being killed by this young man, they sent her to the United States. While she stated that she was reluctant to come to the United States primarily because of her boyfriend, she had no say in the matter. The power and authority to make the decision concerning her wellbeing were a part of the responsibility of her "fathers."[30] Diane on the other hand had an established life in her home country prior to migrating to New York. She owned a house and had a job that paid well. For her, coming to the United States was supposed to provide a break from a difficult personal situation. For some of these women and my other respondents, their move to the United

---

[28]   As stated earlier, pseudonyms will be used to protect the identities of the women who participated in this study.

[29]   In Afro-Caribbean nomenclature, this entire process is summarized in one phrase—her husband filed for her. This statement gives little attention to the cost, logistics (medical check-up, interview at the United States embassy in Jamaica, etc.) and time that normally accompanies this process.

[30]   Interview with first-generation female, Spring 2007.

States was also accompanied by a sense of adventure, i.e., having their own experience of going to "the land of opportunity."[31]

Along with enabling migration, family members also facilitated the adaptation processes of my respondents. For most of my respondents their first "home" in this new country was with a family member. For Jane who lived with her aunt, this period was one of much support. While Mary's initial stay was marked by some exclusion from her ex-boyfriend's family, upon her return to New York—since she was the only member of her family living in the United States—she assumed the position of welcoming and assisting her relatives as they adapted to the life in New York. For Diane however, the year she and her son lived with her brother gave rise to a situation that almost severed that familial relationship. While she was intentional in raising her son in a manner like how she was raised, her brother's three children were not. In fact, one of her nephews would regularly "terrorize" her son—"he made his life a living hell, [he] treated him terribly."[32] This recurring behavior between her nephew and son resulted in two decisions—one, to send her son to live with her best friend in Florida and second, to contact her aunt in Jamaica to solicit her advice on the situation and possible next steps. In the end, Diane moved to Florida for a year before eventually returning to New York.

Diane's example also highlights a seminal issue in the lives of Afro-Caribbean women in New York—raising children. While my respondents who had children either migrated with them or gave birth to them in New York, the dynamics of migrating and leaving one's children behind in the home country—child minding—remains a seminal feature in the migration practices within the Caribbean.[33] For Diane and other respondents, it was important to rear their children in a manner similar to how they were raised. This included being respectful of others—especially one's elders—not misbehaving, i.e., being obedient and listening to one's parent, working hard in school, etc. In her

---

[31] A similar image that many immigrants have of the U.S. and of New York is that of a "promised land." See McLean-Farrell, *West Indian Pentecostals*, 59–60.

[32] Interview with first-generation female, December 2017.

[33] This dynamic is a feature of my life and the lives of many Afro-Caribbean immigrants. The making of a transnational family and caring for this family has given rise to diverse lifestyles including that of barrel children. See McLean-Farrell, *West Indian Pentecostals*, 1–2; 75–6. On the psychological issues accompanying the reunification of immigrant families, see Cerola Suárez-Orozco, Irina L.G. Todorova, and Josephine Louie, "Making Up For Lost Time: The Experience of Separation and Reunification Among Immigrant Families," *Family Process*, 41, issue 4 (2002): 625–643; Andrea Smith, Richard N. Lalonde, and Simone Johnson, "Serial Migration and Its Implications for the Parent-Child Relationship: A Retrospective Analysis of the Experiences of the Children of Caribbean Immigrants," *Cultural Diversity and Ethnic Minority Psychology, 10*, no.2 (2004): 107–22; Carola Suárez-Orozco, Hee Jin Bang, and Ha Yeon Kim, "I Felt Like My Heart Was Staying Behind: Psychological Implications of Family Separations & Reunifications for Immigrant Youth," *Journal of Adolescent Research*, 26, issue 2 (2010): 222–57.

interview, Diane talked at length about her son and his "model behavior." From birth he had not given her any cause to "regret getting pregnant with him" and in school he was described as the model student, one who made the teachers reflect with admiration on who were his parents and how they had raised such a son.[34] As I have also argued in *West Indian Pentecostals*, however, raising children in this new context can also mean finding the delicate balance between navigating, embracing and/or muting facets of American and Caribbean culture, where a hybrid system is developed within each family where best practices from both cultures are brought to bear in raising one's children.[35] For Jane and Diane, there was a period when they had to send their children to live with a "family member" either in the country of origin or another state. While this iteration of "child minding" is different from that associated with children who are left behind due to migration, depending on the length of separation it could also generate feelings of abandonment, unfavorably impact children's behavior and self-esteem, and could sometimes result in permanent rifts in the parent–child relationship.[36] It should be noted that in each circumstance, the decision to send one's child away was not taken lightly and was made to create an environment deemed to be the healthiest for the child.[37]

Faith

Religion, and the Christian faith, is an essential part of life in the Caribbean.[38] In fact, within the West Indies, it has been the regular practice to send one's children to church on Sundays even if the parents do not attend church. Given this reality, it was not surprising to learn that most of my informants grew up in a Christian home and attended church regularly as children. While their church attendance and Christianity in the home and at school play a significant

---

[34]   Interview with first-generation female, December 2017.

[35]   McLean-Farrell, *West Indian Pentecostals*, 4, 128.

[36]   See Smith et. Al., "Serial Migration and Its Implications for the Parent-Child Relationship," 107–22.

[37]   Interview with first-generation female, December 2017 (getting her son out of an unhealthy living situation where he was being terrorized); Interview with first-generation female, April 2007 (a diagnosis of medical issues that would seriously impact the care she could provide for her daughter). In both of these scenarios, there would also be the expectation of providing some kind of financial support to the family member who was taking care of the child.

[38]   The importance of religion in civic and social life is seen in the teaching of religious education within the school curriculum, and the presence of devotions within the educational day; opening various civic events with an invocation; and presence of the speech invoking God's guidance in the national anthems of several islands, including Jamaica, Trinidad and Tobago and Barbados. Most display of religion's influence was Jamaica's Prime Minister Andrew Holness's endorsement and participation in the National Day of Fasting, Prayer and Repentance organized by the Jamaica Umbrella Group of Churches. See Ainsworth Morris, "PM Joins Hundreds in Prayer for the Nation," *Jamaica Information Service*, December 4, 2017, accessed December 2017, http://jis.gov.jm/pm-joins-hundreds-prayer-nation/.

role in their formative years, this did not prevent them from "leaving" the church during their teenage and early adult years. This time outside of committed Christian fellowship involved leaving their parental home and making their own decisions, sometimes this also meant behaving in ways that they were taught were prohibited, i.e., backsliding. In many cases, this backsliding meant engaging in sex outside of marriage and possibly becoming pregnant, and/or living with one's significant other without being married. According to my informants, living in a "backslidden" state did not negate their belief in God or prevent them from praying, reading scripture, or attending crusades. According to Mary, while outside of committed Christian fellowship she became pregnant. She stated, "during [my] pregnancy things did not work out and it took a toll on me." During that time, she did not have a constant support system since her sister and cousin who lived with her were employed in babysitting jobs that required that they live in during the week and only come home on weekends. To deal with the pressure resulting from her pregnancy, Mary would attend open crusades[39] after work to "feed her spiritual life and to keep her faith intact." It is in this context that she remembered the Christian foundation she had and "got her life back on track with God."[40]

While a recommitment to their faith due to a crisis scenario is also present in the lives of some of my other informants, this in no way diminishes that commitment. In fact, God saving her from a situation that could have killed her, has made Jane very committed in her relationship with Jesus and has resulted in her growth to become a pillar or key leader in the church as well as a "mother" to the congregants.[41] In these two roles, she exerts tremendous influence on how things function in the church while making sure that fellow congregants have access to multiple resources—spiritual (prayer, home visits, advice, etc.), social (employment, housing, etc.), legal (immigration, notary public), etc.[42] It is worth noting that in Susan's case, her faith and lifestyle as a Christian woman in her community played a significant role in the relationship that resulted in her marriage and relocation to New York. For while there may have been marriageable women at his church in New York, her husband was intentional about returning to his community and finding a "particular" Christian woman to marry—a particularity that Susan clearly exhibited.

---

[39]   This is an evangelistic service that is held outside.
[40]   Interview with first-generation female, December 2017.
[41]   Jane's role as a "mother" to congregation members was affirmed by her exhibiting particular normally behavior associated with a mother-figure, namely: nurture, discipline, support, guidance, possible financial provision, etc.
[42]   Interview with first-generation female, April 2007.

Personal Development

The primary way in which these Afro-Caribbean women sought their own personal development was through education. In large part, this was a result of them recognizing very early in their adaptation process that it was "not as easy [to get a job] as [they] thought or how people make it out to be." Because of the delay in finding jobs, many informants pursued courses of study for their General Educational Development (GED) and other courses.[43] These qualifications enabled them to secure employment in various service sectors. For those who were in the United States without the proper immigration papers, finding a suitable employment took on additional difficulty. However, because they came to the United States prior to September 11, 2001, they were able to take certain courses like the GED, and thus secure positions of employment even with their unauthorized immigration status. This pathway to gaining educational qualifications and securing employment became increasingly challenging for unauthorized immigrants after September 11. It is necessary to note however that these women's personal development was not limited to gaining qualifications to secure a job. For Jane, obtaining various ministerial, chaplaincy, and notary public qualifications has allowed her to serve members of her church and the wider community more effectively. As a result, she is one of the primary persons congregation members contact whenever they require assistance—spiritual, personal, legal, etc. When I was conducting my research on her congregation, I had to get her permission as one of the main gatekeepers/leaders in the congregation prior to proceeding with my study. Another dimension associated with the informants' personal development is the way their employment in the United States placed them in a position where they were key in providing financial support for their family—in the United States and back in their country of origin. In the cases where the women were married, this meant that they were actively involved in many of the decision-making processes in the family.[44] Another area where the women were engaged in their personal development is in living their daily lives. From their daily experiences, these women gained invaluable knowledge of how to navigate life in a global city. This knowledge became vital social capital that was then shared with others (family members, church brothers and sisters, their children, etc.) to instruct them as they too learned what life is really like in the "land of opportunity."

[43] In New York City the GED no longer exists and has been replaced with the High School Equivalency Diploma (HSED).

[44] This activity would also produce a shift in power and dynamics in the family, with the woman gaining power and the man losing some. Exactly how that would be played out would depend on the spouses and the decision they would make for their families. In terms of the family in the country of origin, the person in New York may gain more influence and voice in family decisions as a result of the support they render to the family's welfare.

An Understanding of Oneself

For the Afro-Caribbean women I interviewed, their understanding of themselves is a composite of influence of their families, faith, personal development, and their experience of life in New York. There is a clear awareness of their connection to others, first and foremost their family but also those with whom they worship and share their lives. For all my respondents, their faith enables them to perceive themselves as God's daughters, assists them to reinterpret and redeem their past especially their "mistakes," and provides them with a framework to navigate life in New York. Therefore, regardless of the difficulty and challenges they encounter, they are assured that "God has a plan for [their] lives." They are also able to see with new clarity the blessings that have grown from their perceived missteps, be it character and strength or the child she had in her "backslidden" state who now sponsors her to get her green card and the legality that accompanies this change in immigration status. As they grow in their personal development as Afro-Caribbean women, the informants have drawn on the traditions and values of their country and brought it to bear on the cosmopolitan, global context in which they currently live. In the process, there is an amalgamation where the host and home cultures are brought into dialogue and thus exert certain influences (positive and negative) upon each other and the lives of these women.

CONCLUSION

Much has been written in recent decades about the feminization of migration. In most of these studies, attention has been given to the impact of the woman's departure on the rest of the family, especially on her children, the high concentration of female migrants in service industries, the psychological and emotion burden female migrants grapple with as they strive to create a better future for their families and themselves, etc. Often, because of the primary focus of the above mentioned enquiry, adequate attention is not given to the complexity that accompanies the feminization of migration. In taking a more integrative approach, I have sought to illustrate how the intersections of family, faith, and personal development shaped Afro-Caribbean female life in the diaspora. Framed as an understanding of oneself, we can see how each of these three areas—family, faith, and personal development—interplay and shape the lives of these women. However, as I have shown, this process does not happen in a vacuum, but draws upon both the traditions and values of the country of origin and the women's lived experiences in the host country. Only as we bring all these factors together can we broaden the scope of enquiry to include multiple relevant issues, and thus gain a more representative portrayal of what the integrated life for Afro-Caribbean women truly looks like in New York City.

BIBLIOGRAPHY:

Aymer, Paula L. *Uprooted Women: Migrant Domestics in the Caribbean*. Westport: Praeger Publishers, 1997.

Bonizzoni, Paola. "Immigrant Working Mothers Reconciling Work and Childcare: The Experience of Latin American and Eastern European Women in Milan," *Social Politics: International Studies in Gender, State & Society* 21, no.2 (2014): 194–217.

Boyd, Monica. "Family and Personal Networks in International Migration: Recent Developments and New Agendas." *International Migration Review* 23, no.3 (1989): 638–70.

Boyd, Monica, and Elizabeth M Grieco. *Women and Migration: Incorporating Gender into International Migration Theory,* 2003. Accessed December 9, 2018. https://www.migrationpolicy.org/article/women-and-migration-incorporating-gender-international-migration-theory

Carrington, Selwyn H. H. *The Sugar Industry and the Abolition of the Slave Trade, 1775-1810*. Gainesville: University of Florida Press, 2002.

Gordon, Shirley C. *Our Cause for His Glory: Christianisation and Emancipation in Jamaica*. Kingston: The Press of the University of the West Indies, 1998.

Marchetti, Sabrina, and Alessandra Venturini. "Mothers and Grandmothers on the Move: Labour Mobility and the Household Strategies of Moldovan and Ukrainian Migrant Women in Italy." *International Migration* 52, no.5, (2014): 111–26.

McLean-Farrell, Janice. *West Indian Pentecostals: Living their faith in New York and London*. New York: Bloomsbury, 2016.

Mohammed, Shaheed. "Migration and the Family in the Caribbean." *Caribbean Quarterly* 44, no.3/4 (Sept/Dec. 1998). 105–21.

Morris, Ainsworth. "PM Joins Hundreds in Prayer for the Nation." *Jamaica Information Service*, December 4, 2017. Accessed December 2017. https://jis.gov.jm/pm-joins-hundreds-prayer-nation/.

Ortensi, Livia Elisa. "Engendering the Fertility/Migration Nexus The Role of Women's Migratory Patterns in the Analysis of Fertility after Migration," *Demographic Research*, 32 (2015): 1435–68.

Palmer, Ransford W. *Pilgrims from the Sun: West Indian Migration to America*. New York: Twayne Publishers, 1995.

Parreñas, Rhacel Salazar. *Children of Global Migration: Transnational Families and Gendered Woes*. Stanford: Stanford University Press, 2005.

Patterson, Orlando. *The Sociology of Slavery*. London: Macgibbon & Kee, 1967.

Pattullo, Polly. *Last Resorts: The Cost of Tourism in the Caribbean*. New York: Monthly Review Press, 2005.

Pessar, Patricia R. "Engendering Migration Studies. The Case of New Immigrants in the United States." *American Behavioral Scientist* 42, no.4 (1999): 577–600.

Portes, Alejandro, and Ramón Grosfoguel. "Migration and Ethnic Communities." *The Annals of the American Academy of Political and Social Science* 533, Trends in U. S.-Caribbean Relations (May, 1994): 48–69.

Sherlock, Philip, and Hazel Bennett. *The Story of the Jamaican People*. Kingston: Ian Randle Publishers, 1998.

Smith, Andrea, Richard N. Lalonde, and Simone Johnson. "Serial Migration and Its Implications for the Parent-Child Relationship: A Retrospective Analysis of the Experiences of the Children of Caribbean Immigrants." *Cultural Diversity and Ethnic Minority Psychology* 10, no.2 (2004): 107–22.

Suárez-Orozco, Cerola, Irina L.G. Todorova, and Josephine Louie. "Making Up for Lost Time: The Experience of Separation and Reunification Among Immigrant Families." *Family Process* 41, 4 (2002): 625–43.

Suárez-Orozco, Carola, Hee Jin Bang, and Ha Yeon Kim. "I Felt Like My Heart Was Staying Behind: Psychological Implications of Family Separations & Reunifications for Immigrant Youth." *Journal of Adolescent Research* 26, 2 (2010): 222–57.

Thomas-Hope, Elizabeth M. *Explanation in Caribbean Migration*. London: Macmillan Press Ltd, 1992.

Watts, David. *The West Indies: Patterns of Development, Culture and Environmental Change since 1492*. New York: Cambridge University Press, 1994 [1987].

Williams, Eric. "American Capitalism and Caribbean Economy." In *Caribbean Freedom: Economy and Society from Emancipation to Present*, edited by Hilary Beckles and Verene Shepherd. Kingston: Ian Randle Publishers Limited, 1993.

PART III

PART III

MIGRANTS' NARRATIVES AS THEOLOGY

CHAPTER 8

STORIED PEOPLE:
THE INTERGENERATIONAL POWER OF
STORY IN THE LIVES OF IMMIGRANTS

Christine J. Hong

INTRODUCTION: THE STORY OF WOORI

My maternal grandmother and grandfather escaped to what is now known as North Korea on one of the last boats traveling south. Together, they packed up whatever they could carry and with one of my young uncles holding my grandfather's hand and my other uncle, a six-month-old infant, strapped to my grandmother's back, they hurried toward the harbor hoping against hope that they would find room onboard. My infant uncle died on that journey. He suffocated on my grandmother's back from the hot press of the desperate crowd. My grandmother did not realize he had died until they were onboard. The boat was teeming with people and it immediately began to sink. My grandmother once described the scene to me saying, "We looked like ants swarming a piece of fruit. You couldn't distinguish one body from another." People were hanging off the boat's exterior and pushing others overboard trying to survive. Others, frantic to keep the boat from sinking, demanded my grandparents throw the body of their infant into the sea, along with others who were sick or injured, so that the boat would stay afloat. My grandmother wrapped my uncle's body in her skirt, clutched him against her, and carried him to their new home in the south. In that way, they remained together, separated by death but not by an impassible border. He traveled with them, if only in body. My grandparents left everyone behind, their parents, siblings, aunts, uncles, cousins, and friends. They would never again see their family or home. In the wake of so much loss, they were not about to leave the body of their youngest son behind. For my family, into the next two generations, my infant uncle would become the most significant symbol of what my grandparents had clung to and lost, their biggest sacrifice and the price of war.

Growing up and listening to the story of my grandparent's escape and the many other painful stories in our shared family narrative, I learned about my identity and its connectional nature. I was not alone. I learned to define myself in relationship to the joy, grief, and pain that emerged from these narratives and within the contextual power of *woori*[1] or the "us" of what it meant to be a Korean person in diaspora. These stories, and the tenor of the voices that told these stories grounded me. I began to see myself by extension in the places and people I had never seen or met. I knew who I was and who I wanted to become because of how I was directly connected to the stories shared with me by my family as well as others in my Korean American community. As a second-generation Korean American, born in Los Angeles, these stories connected me directly to my motherland, to the Korean peninsula and to the Korean people. Sitting at the feet of my elders, I felt claimed by a tradition and story larger than my own, a narrative more expansive than what I had been allowed as a non-white person in the United States. As a liminal and bicultural person who often experiences life in North America as betwixt and between, these connections, facilitated through story, anchored me in a transnational sense of home, particularly in seasons of my life where I felt invisible or essentialized in an American cultural context that constantly measured me as deficient against the yardstick of whiteness.

Immigrants and refugees who cross borders and those who are crossed by borders, carry with them stories and histories that sustain and affirm their human dignity in new and hostile lands even when they can bring little else. Their memories and stories, and the potential for the cocreation of new stories and the intergenerational reinterpretation of stories is invaluable during what can be the trauma of settling in a new place. These memories and stories contribute to the fostering and nurturing of entire generations of people past the point of immigration, migration, and displacement, while acting as a form of resistance to the often white, colonist, and Western lenses through which native and indigenous stories are filtered and diminished.

This chapter explores the significance of stories among immigrant, migrant, and otherwise displaced communities. It focuses on the importance of

---

[1]   "Woori" is a Korean word that is used to describe a collective "we." It is used in both the personal and familial realm and the political sphere. Korean people will commonly refer to the Republic of Korea as *woori nah-rah*, or "our Nation" rather than as South Korea. The possessive term emerges out of the collective mindset of the Korean people which is opposed to individualism, particularly when it is counter to the good of the whole. *Woori* also carries with it, a feeling of collective responsibility for what is being claimed.

intergenerational story formation and sharing as a form of resilience, resistance, and survival in the midst of human movement and other migratory legacies. The stories of the first generation of migrants and immigrants are often the only connections that younger diasporic generations have to their motherlands and even mother tongues. These shared stories shape and form entire generations culturally, communally, and spiritually, carrying with them lessons, warnings, and a thousand hopes. Sometimes the stories that are birthed in immigration and migration change as they are told and shared, becoming imbued with new meanings for new generations; they are stories and memories that become living co-formed histories. My identity, spiritual, religious, and theological formations are irevoccably bound up in the stories of my family and the legacies of joy and pain inherited within them. These stories were not written down but shared through story. These stories were fleshed out to me over years and decades by my grandparents and parents as fragments and details, released from the vise of pain and silence little by little. Drawing on these oral storytelling traditions and theologies of Asian and Asian American peoples, the chapter will explore the importance of intergenerational story formation and storytelling as a means of keeping histories, cultures, and spiritual practices intact for the sake of hope, survival, and intergenerational connection in a new homeland.

STORIES IN TRANSMISSION

For immigrants, stories and storytelling are vehicles for the transmission of what is important from one generation to the next. Stories and how they are shared teach and inform. They shape communal and individual identity, pass on familial and cultural traditions and heritage, preserve language, and form faith and spiritual values. Storytelling encompasses folk stories, stories of lived experiences, and stories that are created. When told intergenerationally, stories impart significant messages from the immigrant and migrant generation to those who are growing up in a different time and context. The transmission of stories is more than about stagnant preservation and survival. In the North American context, storytelling is in its essence about the cultivation and deepening of personhood and peoplehood, often over and against a national white supremacist narrative that seeks to diminish any foreign affiliations or transnationally constructed identities, including and especially of immigrants, migrants, and refugees. Stories facilitate the building up of personhood and peoplehood in an inhospitable land and against all odds.

However, intergenerational story transmission is not without its tensions and complications. It is not as simple as children wanting to docilely sit and listen to nostalgic tales. The second generation, or the American born generation, may not initially want to hear stories about homeland or the things that they consider gone and past in the midst of what could be considered developmental crises. For instance, children and adolescents of immigrant, migrant, refugee families often find the roles between themselves and their caretakers reversed.[2] Children and adolescents learn language and soft culture more quickly than their parents because of public education. Attending school helps them grow wider, multiracial social networks than their caretakers, and they are able to learn English primarily through immersion.[3] In early elementary, my parents asked me to help them read mail, make phone calls, and pay bills. I learned to read in kindergarten and distinctly remember my frustration at not being able to learn quickly enough. Not only was I impatient to read books on my own, the weight of necessity drove me. I needed to learn to read so that I could translate for my parents, help them read and understand the news, and help them with their mail. In many ways, I had to grow up quickly and take on roles and responsibilities traditionally reserved for parents and guardians. I visited hospitals with my parents and grandparents as a child and an adolescent, translating for them with health care practitioners. I learned early on that my caretakers were dependent on me to get through their day-to-day realities.

While living in an Asian and Latinx part of Los Angeles, I watched as other children of immigrants and migrants also lived into role reversals. Simultaneously, dominant culture people discounted, diminished, and tore down our parents as we helplessly watched. The adults in our lives, who had made the greatest sacrifices for the collective good, were dependent on us, the second generation, for survival. The more quickly the second generation acculturated, the more quickly we could assist our parents who visibly struggled and depended on us. This diminishment of the first generation in the eyes of the second generation via larger North American culture and society causes deep distress in the psychological development of children and adolescents.[4] Children and adolescents learn that they are unable to count on their caretakers for protection and must instead find ways to protect their parents. I remember being devastated by the emotional tension I felt when helping my parents and grandparents. I was both proud that they could lean on me and I was worried

---

[2]   Barbara W.K. Yee, Jenny Su, Su Yeong Kim, and Loriena Yancura. "Asian American Pacific Islander Families." In *Asian American Psychology: Current Perspectives*, eds. Nita Tewari and Alvin N. Alvarez (New York: Psychology Press, 2009), 3023.

[3]   Hirokazu Yoshikawa, Niobe Way. "From Peers to Policy: How Broader Social Contexts Influence the Adaptation of Children and Youth in Immigrant Families." In *Beyond The Family: Contexts of Immigrant Children's Development*. eds. Hirokazu Yoshikawa, Niobe Way (San Francisco: Jossey-Bass, 2008), 3–4.

[4]   Barbara W.K. Yee, Jenny Su, Su Yeong Kim, and Loriena Yancura. "Asian American Pacific Islander Families." In *Asian American Psychology: Current Perspectives*, eds. Nita Tewari and Alvin N. Alvarez (New York: Psychology Press, 2009), 302–3.

that I would fail them. I lay awake at night grieved and concerned about their safety every time I witnessed them face racism and discrimination and I was angry at them for letting me see them become so small, therefore making me feel even smaller. For those of us in the second generation, as acculturation accelerated, the more quickly many of us began to lose touch with our home culture and languages, having now to operate out of two different value systems, two different vocabularies, and two distinct and often oppositional cultures. In cases like these, how does one generation impart storified personhood and peoplehood to a generation that is experiencing the reverberations of immigration and migration in a completely different and disruptive way? How does the immigrant generation retain and regain their authority as elders and storytellers in the eyes of a generation that is losing touch with their home languages while simultaneously learning to negotiate survival and thriving?

LANGUAGE AND CULTURE

Children and adolescents who experience role reversals at home and the diminishment of their caretakers in the public sphere, need to hear and learn the memories of the immigrant and migrant generations through shared story in order to feel reconnected with their caretakers and a larger kin-group and community. In the midst of the isolating experience of immigration and migration, transmitted stories help children of immigrants and migrants course correct children and adolescent's relationships with their caretakers and with themselves. Instead of watching their loved ones suffer in inhospitable spaces, transmitted and shared narratives help the second generation to witness their parents and guardians as once again empowered and vibrant. As the immigrant and migrant generation bring to life what was lost through shared story, they are able to cultivate collective memory in their children. The story of immigration and migration become a collective story of *woori*, or us. Through the sharing of story, immigrants are able to return to their ancestral homes[5], their ancestral selves and in a sense, take their children with them.

There are two levels to the significance of language and cultural transmission. First, whether the stories are memories or fiction, the ways in which they are shared impart the perspective of the teller. Just as when multiple eye-witness accounts are recounted, the stories are different, a memory when recounted reveals the perspective of what is important to the teller. Second, the stories are embodied. My maternal grandfather when talking about how he built his own business after he had been internally displaced always glowed with pride.

---

[5]   Jane Iwamura. "Ancestral Returns," in *Off the Menu: Asian and Asian North American Women's Religion and Theology,* eds. Rita Nakashima Brock et. al. (Louisville: Westminster John Knox Press, 2007), 112.

When my mother told me the same stories about how her family had started over with nothing, she held the embers of the same spark of life in her eyes and voice. She may have been wearied from holding down multiple jobs, but when she reminded us of the memories she had of her homeland, of her parents, her family, the *Ki* or the collective familial energy swelled back into her demeanor and voice. The pride and strength she exhibited rebuilt her before my very eyes. She was no longer an immigrant woman who I had witnessed berated for not speaking English by a stranger in the grocery store, she was a woman deeply grounded in the words she chose and the culture that had formed those words. It was from that demeanor, spark, and form of those words that I felt connected, not only to my mother or the memories she shared but to an entire culture and an entire collective experience of a people. When I began to see her once again empowered, it was contagious, I began to see myself as powerful too.

Language, culture, and how they are embodied becomes increasingly difficult to transmit in diaspora. I spend copious amounts of time speaking Korean to my third-generation Korean American son. At two and a half, he primarily uses English to communicate with his father and I, and when we respond in Korean he understands but chooses not to respond in Korean just yet. Interacting with him, I feel the echoes of my own parent's frustration at trying to transmit language to me. For immigrant, migrant, and refugee parents, the transmission of language is more than about another lexicon, it is about the transmission of the stories behind the words, the feeling behind *how* they say *what* they say. The expression of an entire people is embedded in their words, the things and places important to them, the values they carry, and the experiences they share. For instance, in English we sometimes say that birds sing, in Korean we say, *seh-gah oohn-dah*, or birds cry. As a people who have endured multiple periods of colonization and war, continuing today to be under US military occupation and the triggering of nuclear war at any moment, our words express a collective sorrow. The Korean word for this collective pain is called *han*, it is woven into the way we see and describe the world around us.

Jennifer Cho coined the phrase mel-*han*-choly as the feeling of unfinished mourning behind Korean people's collective grief, often expressed through the Korean language. Cho argues that the mel-*han*-coly of the Korean people and the Korean language is a form of resistance to the oppressive nature of the official global history of the Korean Peninsula.[6] A history that is forever tied to the division of land and people via American intervention and military occupation. Official US history recollects this period as salvific for the Korean people through the strategic implementation of American military aid while

6   Jennifer Cho, "Mel-*han*-cholia as Political Practice in Thersa Hak Kyung Cha's Dictee," *Meridians: Feminism, Race, Transnationalism* 11, no.1, (2011): 38–9.

for many Korean and Korean American people, it is a period of sadness where the Japanese occupation was traded for an American one. Retaining Korean mel-*han*-choly through language transmission to diasporic generations is a form of resistance to remind ourselves that we are not yet free, that we are not done grieving for what we have lost.

Teresa Hak Kyung Cha, in her seminal autobiographical work, *Dictee*, writes about diasporic peoples, particularly women, as those who have internalized subjugated knowledge.[7] One could understand this as knowledge that subjugates the *woori*-ness of Korean lament to a history filtered through the lens of American exceptionalism, and the knowledge of self, subjugated through the filter of the model minority myth via white supremacist constructs. To resist subjugation in diasporic spaces requires the liveliness of language and all the history and *han* that it carries to continue to flourish. As long as language and lexicon grounded in peoplehood continues to erupt out of generations in diaspora, minoritized people are better able to resist the subjugation and colonization of their minds and tongues by those that desire their erasure. For a Korean American child or adolescent, to understand why a bird might cry rather than sing signifies an imbedded cultural and historical understanding of mel-*han*-coly and what it means to be part of the Korean culture and narrative.

Despite each generation's best efforts, language can unfortunately be lost over time as generations of immigrants and migrants settle into a new land and culture. Sometimes this occurs through coercive force and at other times it is from the impact of physical distance. For indigenous people in North America, the conscription of their children and adolescents into religious boarding schools enforced the loss of language and culture in inhumane ways.[8] For many immigrants, after they depart from their homeland, the evolution of language stalls. The home culture no longer affects the way they speak or what they say and how language has formed thus far is fossilized through the process of separation from homeland. For instance, contemporary colloquial Korean is often mixed with words from different languages, abbreviations, and slang that immigrants do not recognize. My cousins are forever telling me that my Korean, though fluent, sounds like my grandmothers', meaning I inherited the words and perspectives of a bygone era. When my parents visit their homeland now, their peers say the same things about them, their way of speaking is like an artifact from the past, indicating for others that they do not quite belong. The meaning and perspective embedded in languages also get buried over time. The transmission of stories is one way to keep the memories from a particular era,

---

[7]   Teresa Hak Kyung Cha, *Dictee* (Berkeley: University of California Press, 2001).

[8]   Eric Hanson, "The Residential School System," *Indigenous Foundations,* accessed August 22, 2018. http://indigenousfoundations.arts.ubc.ca/the_residential_school_system/

strung together by those very words, alive and whole, even as conversational language changes or disappears. Keeping those memories alive sustains immigrants, keeps them grounded in their culture and reminds them of their human dignity, even as they experience downward mobility and loss of status during immigration.

RELIGION AND VALUES

Stories shared across generations in immigrant families carry within them religious significance and value. My research with Korean American youth explored how Korean folktales and biblical stories in Korean immigrant Christian households were ways of transmitting both Christian values and cultural values about identity and gender, particularly with Korean American girls.[9] Research among Canadian Arab immigrant families also reveals how storytelling is a vehicle for the cultivation of both Islamic and cultural values among children and adolescents.[10] Research on the development of children and youth of immigrant, migrant, and refugee communities has shown that the transmission of religio-cultural beliefs and values works to bolster their self-esteem and resiliency in the face of experiences of discrimination and erasure.[11] The more children and adolescents of immigrant communities feel grounded in their communities, particularly in communities of faith, the more they are able to internalize a healthy counter-narrative to the damaging messages of North Amerian anti-immigrant and anti-refugee sentiments they are inundated with on a daily basis.

Storytelling is also an act of profound religio-cultural meaning making. Religious stories told in immigrant communities, particularly around rites and rituals, help to make theological meaning and significance out of the lived experiences of daily immigrant life and experiences. In the Korean immigrant church, Easter Sunday is overshadowed by the poignancy of Good Friday. Churches celebrate Easter but is viscerally embodied in the story of Good Friday. The rituals congregations create and share during Good Friday often reflect the pain and suffering of crossing borders. A church I once pastored set up a series of doors in the sanctuary. The doors signified crossing boundaries and borders in one's life as Christ did in his death. People wept as they opened and shut the various doors, thinking of homes and relationships lost through the Korean war and subsequent immigration. Storytelling brings together the past and the present, bridging the way communities experienced their values

---

9   Christine J. Hong. *Identity, Youth, and Gender in the Korean American Church* (New York: Palgrave MacMillan, 2015).

10   Lynda M. Ashbourne and Mohammed Baobaid, "Parent-Adolescent Storytelling in Canadian-Arabic Immigrant Families (Part 2): A Narrative Analysis of Adolescents' Stories Told to Parents," *The Qualitative Report* 19, no.60 (2014): 1–18.

11   Ashbourne, "Parent-Adolescent Storytelling in Canadian-Arabic Immigrant Families," 3.

and religious commitments of the motherland to the collective reconstruction of those values and religious commitments in the new homeland.[12] Systematic theologians and first-wave Asian American theologians, Sang Hyun Lee and Joung Young Lee, both discuss the saliency of the biblical exodus narrative. As Korean immigrants and theologians, they embraced the narrative, not as a story of exile but of sojourning. They see the Korean American experience as being pilgrims in a foreign land, aliens that are never fully accepted, and a people who are wandering in wilderness yet with a call upon their lives to bravely venture into new places seeking God's presence.[13]

For first-wave Asian Americans, yellow peril,[14] anti-Asian legislation, and discrimination, was a daily reality. In today's North American political climate, new immigrants, migrants, and refugees are once again bombarded with dehumanizing messages, including the threat of deportation for those who are undocumented. The impact of dehumanizing messaging, policies and legislation around immigrants, migrants, and refugees affects the entire family system. Studies of children and adolescents of undocumented parents have found slower cognitive development in children beginning at 24 months due to the ramifications of social exclusion, economic hardship, lack of social support, and increased parental psychological distress.[15] Undocumented parents often do not seek out necessary social support, legal counsel, or kinship groups for fear of being detained or deported. Children learn secrecy and silence for fear of losing their parents. In the midst of these high stress lived realities, it is important for religious immigrant communities that experience themselves as aliens and in exile to believe and internalize a message of divine purpose, guidance, and protection undergirding their experiences of displacement, particularly in the face of feelings of isolation, separation from homeland, and the detrimental experiences of bigotry, hostility, and impending loss. Connecting family and community stories to religious ones creates new sacred stories, and transmitting them to children and adolescents is a sacral way of weaving the new liminal

---

[12]   Jane Iwamura. "Ancestral Returns," in *Off the Menu: Asian and Asian North American Women's Religion and Theology,* eds. Rita Nakashima Brock et. al. (Louisville: Westminster John Knox Press, 2007), 108.

[13]   Sang Hyun Lee, "Asian American Theology in Immigrant Perspective: Called to be Pilgrims," in *Korean American Ministry,* eds. Sang Hyun Lee and John V. Moore (Louisville: General Assembly Council, Presbyterian Church, 1993), 52.

[14]   Yellow Peril is a racist term that refers to xenophobia white Americans and Europeans have felt toward Asians and Asian Americans. This fear dehumanizes Asians and Asian Americans making it justifiable in the eyes of perpetrators to incite violence against them.

[15]   M. Brinton Lykes, Kalina M. Brabeck, and Christina J. Hunter, "Exploring Parent-child Communication in the Context of Threat: Immigrant Families Facing Detention and Deportation in Post-9/11 USA," *Routledge Community, Work, and Family* 16, no.2 (2013): 126.

experiences of the betwixt and between generations into the tapestry of larger narrative of immigration and migration in the face of fear and trauma.

The Dissonance between Stories

If you have ever played telephone, you know that what you whisper directly into the ear of the person next to you is usually completely distorted by the time it reaches the person at the end of the telephone chain. We say and share one thing but what our neighbor hears is slightly different or drastically different! As in the game, dissonance between stories occurs in different forms. Here, I outline three forms of dissonance between the stories we tell across generations, creative liminal dissonance, the dissonance produced through silence, and the dissonance between what is directly transmitted by the community and the stories produced by colonial and dominant culture perspectives.

The first form of dissonance is creative liminal. The stories shared between the immigrant and second generation shift and change in their retellings. They are actively re-negotiated between generational transmission. One could say that the danger of story transmission between the immigrant generation and the second generation is that alternate meanings might be mapped over the stories of the first generation. Dissonance between stories transmitted between generations is present but not necessarily to the detriment of the story itself. This dissonance and mapping can be a liminally creative space that inculcates a deeper understanding of self and community between generations. When we consider why immigrant communities share stories between generations, it is often to teach not only what has happened but what they have overcome, and what they will collectively continue to overcome together. The second generation and those beyond them need to see themselves in these stories. They need to eventually lay claim to the stories they have heard, retelling and reshaping them in their own words, in a new language, and through bicultural lenses.

When I share the stories of my grandparents and parents in writing, as I do here in this chapter, I do so in the English language. As mentioned previously, there is a cultural essence to how words are shaped and how they describe our world. When retelling stories in a foreign tongue, the story reshapes itself. It does not change the meaning of the story or erase the original sentiments but it instead adds to the narrative's complexity. The retelling of the first generation's stories through the eyes of the second generation adds another layer and perspective that creates new meanings for new experiences of displacement. When I reflect on my grandparent's experience of being internally displaced people, their stories hold a different significance for me than they do for them or even for my mother. Their stories and my retelling of them helps me see and connect to a genealogy of resilience and faith. Their strength is my strength, their sorrow, my sorrow. Their stories and the act of retelling their stories connects me to the collective *han* of both my family's personal losses and sacrifices, and the cultural and national lament of an entire people. As the hope of reunification on Korean Penninsula once again blossoms through renewed and progressing peace talks, I feel a sense of renewed hope as well. It is through this hope that I reflect on the sacrifices of those who have gone before me and experience my own empowerment as a second-generation Korean American. Weaving my perspective into the stories of my elders reminds me that even with continental difference, language barriers, cultural and contextual misunderstandings, we in fact do belong to one another, even across space and time.

A second form of dissonance between stories is created when communities choose silence or modulated disclosure[16] as their narrative. For many immigrants there are some stories, some experiences and realities that are too painful to verbalize, and too traumatic to share with their children. For Korean Americans, these are the stories from the 38th parallel. In my own family, we didn't know how to talk about the people who had been left behind, wives, children, parents. How do you speak of someone who may or may not be alive? One way is to never speak of them at all. For many Issei and Nissei Japanese Americans who were interned, the pain of their collective and individual dehumanization was too great to share with the Sansei and Gosei generations.[17] Though some did not speak of their experiences at all, others used modulated disclosure. For instance, Sansei report that some in the Nissei generation would choose to refer to chronological time as "before camp and after camp," without reference to what happened in between, thereby creating dissonance.[18] Dissonance occurs when the second and third generation do in fact know what happened but they hear it through whispers and read about it through textbooks. In the United States, these are textbooks that retell histories from imperial and colonist perspectives if they retell them at all. In the worst case, these stories go untold in both displaced communities and the public narrative. Silence, though understandable and sometimes necessary for survival, creates a dissonance that results in feelings of disconnection and isolation between generations. Russell Jeung in his book *Faithful Generations* retells the story of a Japanese American congregation that, though they might not have shared some of their most painful stories, found ways to nurture intergenerational

---

16 Modulated disclosure refers to the sharing of traumatic narratives with children and adolescents in disconnected snippets rather than as a whole.

17 Nobu Miyoshi, "Identity Crisis of the Sansei and the American Concentration Camp," *Pacific Citizen*, December 19–26, 1980: 41–55.

18 Donna K. Nagata, *Legacy of Injustice: Exploring the Cross-Generational Impact of the Japanese American Internment* (New York: Plenum, 1993), 26–35.

connection through an annual bazaar that celebrated their shared culture. As the Nisei generation aged and were unable to continue running the annual bazaar, the Sansei generation took up the tradition, continuing the legacy of embodied narrative sharing. Through shared activities like cooking up teriyaki chicken, they shared the narratives of everyday life.[19] These practices of embodied cultural storytelling, though different from verbally retelling painful histories, knit generations together across even necessary silence and the void it produces, to continue to thrive in their lives together.

A third form of dissonance occurs when the children of immigrants, migrants, and refugees hear first-person narratives about homeland and a colonial or imperial one in the public sphere. JoAnn D'Alisera in her study of Sierra Leonian refugee families discovered that while children and adolescents heard their parents and grandparents describe the land and people of Sierra Leone as vibrant and beautiful, at school and in the media children and adolescents heard a completely alternative narrative. This alternative described Sierra Leone and its people as the "heart of darkness," starving, disease ridden, and without resources. These disparate representations created a dissonance in their understanding of homeland, their understandings of their caretakers, and their own identities.[20] Which narrative should they claim? What was the risk of claiming the edifying narrative over the ugly one? Would claiming the anti-imperial narrative isolate them further from communities beyond the American Sierra Leonian community?

When I hear the dehumanizing tropes around North Korea and South Korea emerging once again from the United States, the constant threat of impending war, and the caricature of an entire people as brainwashed, uneducated, and disposable, I cringe and remember what it felt like to feel pulled in multiple directions as a child. As a young person, I was constantly asked whether or not I think war with North Korea is imminent and which side I am on, American or Korean. I am now answering these same queries as an adult. Then and now, the disparity between what I know about North Korea from the stories my family has told me and what the United States government and public opinion says disturbs me. My grandparent's stories, particularly my grandmother's stories about her beloved little brother whom she left behind, the stories about village life, and her descriptions of the beauty of the land, the trees and mountains, are what hold salience and significance for me. Those are the words and stories

---

[19]   Russell Jeung, *Faithful Generations: Race and New Asian American Churches* (New Brunswick: Rutgers University, 2005), 139.

[20]   JoAnn D'Alisera, "Images of a Wounded Homeland: Sierra Leonean Children and the New Heart of Darkness," in *Across Generations: Immigrant Families in America,* ed. Nancy Foner (New York: New York University Press, 2009), 114–30.

embedded in my identity and in my soul. Those cords of connection formed in childhood are now so strong that the disparaging narratives emerging from the American public sphere no longer cast a shadow of doubt over my understanding of self and community. It instead affirms in me the profound connection to peoplehood that my grandmother helped cultivate and nurture in me. Because of her and others in my family, the people of North Korea are still my people, they are my family and kin, utterly human in my eyes, flesh, and blood. In cases where the second generation is exposed to injurious and conflicting narratives about homeland, self, and community, the firsthand narratives of the first generation are significant and need to be constantly retold. This is necessary not only to provide a counter narrative to a destructive and colonial one, but to edify the personhood of children and adolescents who are quickly identified with the stereotypes that emerge from the distressing narratives of other nations and people produced through the auspices of American exceptionalism.

CONCLUSION: STORYING OUR COMMUNITIES WITH SPECTERS IN THE ROOM

The memories and stories of immigrants are filled with specters that continue to haunt the living. Ghosts of times, places, and people are no longer accessible except through the act of sharing stories. Communities of displaced people are knit together across generations, lands, and time with the resurrecting power of story. The specters never leave but cling to the words and bodies of those that call to them and claim them.

A constant specter in the lives of the Korean people is an active volcano on the Korean Peninsula called Baek-du-sahn. To the Korean people, Baek-du-sahn is a place of power and beauty, one of the most beautiful places on the peninsula. However, Baek-du-sahn sits on the border of North Korea and China. The restrictions around the 38th parallel make it difficult if not impossible for Korean people from the South to visit the mountain. It now exists for many as a memory only, and because of this, Baek-du-sahn has become sacred, perfect, and untouchable. It is a direct cultural loss to a people whose indigenous religions and contemporary ethos emphasizes connection to the land. Immigrants who have been separated from their homes, lands, and peoplehood carry with them memories of the places which hold meaning but are forever lost. The construction of sacred mythology around places and people who are lost and the transmission of these mythological stories to consecutive generations keeps the specters present among the people across scattered diasporas.

We story our communities even beyond the temporal human realm. We long to greet the specters that haunt us face to face without the many barriers and borders that have kept us apart. The narratives and stories transmitted by immigrants are not only heavily inundated with nostalgia and loss but also with ethereal and fantastic hope. My maternal grandmother, while she was alive, had a ritual of talking about heaven, or the afterlife, as a place that was merely next door, as if she could cross an invisible threshold at any moment and arrive there. She claimed heaven would call to her as she was going about her daily life, an invitation, and she would respond, "Not today. Another day, perhaps." She spoke of heaven as someone who had already been there, as someone who was already a citizen of heaven and was only sojourning on this temporal plane. As a woman who had always felt internally displaced, even on the Korean peninsula, the earth indeed did not feel like home, likewise her natal home was now an unattainable reality, and heaven was the only destination left where her two worlds and two homes would converge. Heaven was the place where she would indeed smile at her little brother again. The place where she would see her parents' faces again, the place where she would hold her baby, breathing and healthy, once again. It was the place where she would finally reunite with all the people she had lost over time. What a comfort to know it was just next door, after all.

Stories and the specters that haunt us are in the marrow of our bones, all of our formations and creations. Who would we be without a story to share or remember? Where would we be as religious people without our sacred stories, textual and not, as the basis for how and what we believe about ourselves, God, and the world? For those who are minoritized through experiences of immigration, migration, and other forms of displacement, story facilitates intergenerational, co-ethnic, and co-racial kinship and solidarity. Through story, parents pass on a shared language, teach cultural values, and bring to life people and places through the lenses of insiders to their children. Through the act of sharing narratives and reviving memories, caretakers are restored as resilient and capable in the eyes of their children and grandchildren in the wake of constant societal dehumanization. The transmission of story through mother tongues and new languages build bridges between generations toward the nurturing of whole peoplehood, an embodied act of resistance against the subjugation and erasure of identities and histories. For ethnic communities and within racial groups in the United States, the telling of stories affirms human dignity in a society that seeks to destroy it via white supremacist systems and policies. The dissonance produced by stories challenges the way we hold onto interpretative and experiential particularity and lifts them up to nuance and enrich the stories we tell across places and generations.[21] The power of story in the lives of immigrants lies in its embodied nature. We *are* the stories we are told and the stories we retell; words and expressions are like colorful ribbons wrapped around our bodies connecting us to one another, to the specters, and to the many who will come after us.

Bibliography:

Ashbourne, Lynda M. and Mohammed Baobaid, "Parent-Adolescent Storytelling in Canadian-Arabic Immigrant Families (Part 2): A Narrative Analysis of Adolescents' Stories Told to Parents." *The Qualitative Report*, 19, no.60, (2014): 1–18.

Cha, Teresa Hak Kyung. *Dictee*. Berkeley: University of California Press, 2001.

Cho, Jennifer. "Mel-*han*-cholia as Political Practice in Thersa Hak Kyung Cha's Dictee." *Meridians: Feminism, Race, Transnationalism*, 11, no.1 (2011): 38–9.

D'Alisera, JoAnn. "Images of a Wounded Homeland: Sierra Leonean Children and the New Heart of Darkness," in *Across Generations: Immigrant Families in America,* edited by Nancy Foner, 114–30. New York: New York University Press, 2009.

Hanson, Eric. "The Residential School System." *Indigenous Foundations*. Accessed August 22, 2018. http://indigenousfoundations.arts.ubc.ca/the_residential_school_system/.

Hong, Christine J. *Identity, Youth, and Gender in the Korean American Church*. New York: Palgrave MacMillan, 2015.

Iwamura, Jane. "Ancestral Returns." In *Off the Menu: Asian and Asian North American Women's Religion and Theology,* edited by Rita Nakashima Brock et. al. Louisville: Westminster John Knox Press, 2007.

Lee, Sang Hyun. "Asian American Theology in Immigrant Perspective: Called to be Pilgrims," in *Korean American Ministry*, edited by Sang Hyun Lee and John V. Moore. 52, Louisville: General Assembly Council, Presbyterian Church, 1993.

---

[21]   Henry W. Morisada Rietz. "Living Past: A Hapa Identifying with the Exodus, the Exile, and the Internment," in *Ways of Being Ways of Reading: Asian American Biblical Interpretation*, eds. Mary F. Foskett and Jeffery Kah-Jin Kuan (St. Louis, Mo.: Chalice Press, 2006), 194–97.

Lykes, M. Brinton, Kalina M. Brabeck, and Christina J. Hunter. "Exploring Parent-Child Communication in the Context of Threat: Immigrant Families Facing Detention and Deportation in post-9/11 USA," *Routledge Community, Work, and Family*, 16, no.2 (2013): 126.

Miyoshi, Nobu. "Identity Crisis of the Sansei and the American Concentration Camp." *Pacific Citizen*, December 19, no.26 (1980): 41–55.

Nagata, Donna K. *Legacy of Injustice: Exploring the Cross-Generational Impact of the Japanese American Internment*. New York: Plenum, 1993.

Rietz, Henry W. Morisada. "Living Past: A Hapa Identifying with the Exodus, the Exile, and the Internment." In *Ways of Being Ways of Reading: Asian American Biblical Interpretation*, edited by Mary F. Foskett and Jeffery Kah-Jin Kuan, 194–92. St. Louis, Mo: Chalice Press, 2006.

Jeung, Russell. *Faithful Generations: Race and New Asian American Churches*. New Brunswick: Rutgers University, 2005.

Yee, Barbara W.K., Jenny Su, Su Yeong Kim, and Loriena Yancura. "Asian American Pacific Islander Families." In *Asian American Psychology: Current Perspectives*, edited by Nita Tewari and Alvin N. Alvarez. 302–3. New York: Psychology Press, 2009.

Yoshikawa, Hirokazu and Niobe Way. "From Peers to Policy: How Broader Social Contexts Influence the Adaptation of Children and Youth in Immigrant Families." In *Beyond The Family: Contexts of Immigrant Children's Development*, edited by Hirokazu Yoshikawa and Niobe Way. San Francisco: Jossey-Bass, 2008.

CHAPTER 9

"SPEAK TO ME LORD": SEEKING GOD'S INTERVENTION IN TIMES OF DURESS AMONG CAMEROONIAN MIGRANTS IN CAPE TOWN[1]

Henrietta M. Nyamnjoh

INTRODUCTION

Aaron and Pat's story

In December 2016, Aaron's wife (Pat) collapsed as a result of a stroke. She was rushed to the hospital and doctors marvelled at the fact that she survived at all, considering the alarming increase in her blood pressure (BP). She was hospitalized for three months and had to undergo speech therapy and relearn to walk after she was discharged from the hospital with a partial left paralysis on the arm and leg. She went to the hospital weekly for physiotherapy. As of the time of this publication, she had travelled to Cameroon to continue treatment and be assisted by family due to lack of finances. Given that Aaron and his spouse are entrepreneurs in the informal economy, their business took a nosedive during Pat's illness. During her stay in the hospital and after having been discharged, they sought out various men/women of God for prayers. While in the hospital, only her pastors paid her a visit as no member of her community was allowed to visit her, fearing she has been bewitched. Aaron joined a prayer warrior group that is engaged in battlefield of spiritual warfare prayers and, starting at midnight, he would pray with her on the phone from home daily. He believed that witches are very active starting at midnight, hence his aim was to pray against his spouse's devourers. Throughout Pat's illness, Aaron believed that "God was testing his faith to take them to a better place and would change

---

1   The research project this article draws from was funded by the African Humanities Program (AHP) Postdoctoral Fellowship of the American Council of Learned Societies.

their tests into testimonies."[2] When I paid them a visit, Aaron narrated how he had sought help from various pastors who would come to pray for Pat at home and expressed his belief that it is thanks to prayers that she is still alive. Looking at Pat and looking up to the sky, Aaron said, "Speak to me Lord, tell me how to handle the situation." Aaron wanted direction from God on where to find healing for his wife. Quoting the Bible (from the book of Jas 1:2–4), Aaron notes that his "growth in faith is also made possible by difficulties." The Bible says that "whenever you face trials of many kinds, because you know that the testing of your faith produces perseverance. Let perseverance finish its work so that you may be mature and complete, not lacking anything." Aaron believes that trials will reveal whether his faith is genuine and will strengthen and mature him. It is for this reason that he stopped his family in Cameroon from consulting any diviner to seek the cause of Pat's illness or ask for treatment because it may delay her healing.

Acknowledging the help received from the many pastors, Aaron maintains that their relationship with God through the different men/women God puts on their path to pray with them is the "strength that fuels our hearts," and he concludes by saying a short prayer; "Thank You, God, for being with us in our trials, and for helping us to grow through difficult circumstances."[3]

Aaron's story speaks to the notion of health and divine healing that is at the fore of Pentecostal religious life in Africa, bringing communities of suffering together and ushering supernatural power in the gathered community.[4] Conversely, it speaks to the notion of increased faith and closeness to God to make meaning of such challenges. Despite these trials, there is hope and perseverance because the afflictions are seen to be temporal; it is a way of God communicating with them or wanting them to come close to Him.

Against this backdrop, this chapter focuses on the challenges and insecurities that some migrants face in the host countries and explore the ways in which they seek solutions to these challenges by turning to Pentecostal churches for divine healing and prayers.

While the study of religion and Pentecostalism has witnessed heightened attention from the nexus of religion and migration, and appropriation of

---

2   Conversation with Aaron, Cape Town, December 1, 2017.
3   Conversation with Aaron, Cape Town, December 12, 2017.
4   Ogbu Kalu, *African Pentecostalism: An Introduction*, (Oxford ; New York: Oxford University Press, 2008).

media technologies,[5] there is still a paucity in studies focusing on trans-local and transnational religious mobilities and the search for healing—physical, emotional, psycho-social and spiritual healing by migrants within Pentecostal churches.[6] Moreover, when scholarship does pay attention, empirical evidence is drawn from African migrants in the diaspora or how they seek spiritual blessings/prophecies to facilitate travels abroad.[7] Underscoring this inadequacy, the Late Ogbu Kalu[8] has shown how despite the new African immigrant religious communities and the religious pluralism catalysed by the dynamics of the new immigration processes, we are still left with a gap in knowing how migrants navigate and negotiate these processes—the Pentecostal dimension determined by African immigrant conditions, religious practices, and competing in a vibrant immigrant market, especially in their mobile search for healing.

In this chapter, I concentrate on the architectures of seeking healing from the perspective of inter-African cities—trans-locally and transnationally for migrants who can afford to travel to other African countries, especially Nigeria. I examine the mobile trans-local and transnational trajectories of Cameroonian migrants based in Cape Town in search of divine healing (physical, spiritual and psychosocial healing), the challenges they face in the host country, within various Pentecostal churches in South Africa. I explore trans-local/transnational activities of actors that reshape opportunities and structures at various geographical scales, from the most local to the most global.[9] This study therefore prioritizes mobilities and the people who engage in them to exemplify how

---

[5]   Henrietta Nyamnjoh, "Information and Communication Technology and Its Impact on Transnational Migration: The Case of Senegalese Boat Migrants," in *SideWays: Mobile Margins and the Dynamics of Communication in Africa*, ed. Mirjam de Bruijn (Mankon, Bamenda, Cameroon: Langaa, 2013), 159–77; Ogbu U. Kalu, "African Pentecostalism in Diaspora," *PentecoStudies: An Interdisciplinary Journal for Research on the Pentecostal and Charismatic Movements* 9, no.1 (2010): 9–34, https://doi.org/10.1558/ptcs.v9i1.9; Afeosemime U. Adogame and Cordula Weissköppel, eds., *Religion in the Context of African Migration* (Bayreuth: Eckhard Breitinger, 2005); Phillip Charles Lucas and Thomas Robbins, eds., *New Religious Movements in the 21ˢᵗ Century*, (New York: Routledge, 2004); Rosalind I. J. Hackett, "Charismatic/Pentecostal Appropriation of Media Technologies in Nigeria and Ghana," *Journal of Religion in Africa* 28, no.3 (1998): 258–277; R.I.J. Hackett and B.F. Soares, "Introduction: New Media and Religious Transformations in Africa," in *New Media and Religious Transformations in Africa*, ed. R.I.J. Hackett and B.F. Soares (Bloomington: Indiana University Press, 2015), 1–10.

[6]   Joseph Mensah, Christopher J. Williams, and Edna Aryee, "Gender, Power, and Religious Transnationalism among the African Diaspora in Canada," *African Geographical Review* 32, no.2 (2013): 151–71.

[7]   Adogame and Weissköppel, *Religion in the Context of African Migration*; R.A Van Dijk, "From Camp to Encompassment: Discourses of Transsubjectivity in the Ghanaian Pentecostal Diaspora," *Journal of Religion in Africa* XXVII, no.2 (1997): 135–59.

[8]   Kalu, "African Pentecostalism in Diaspora."

[9]   Nina Glick Schiller, Linda Basch, and Cristina Szanton Blanc, "From Immigrant to Transmigrant: Theorizing Transnational Migration." *Anthropological Quarterly*, 68 no.1, (1995). 48–63.

migrants' religious lives and the meaning-making of their daily lives are governed by mobilities. I seek to understand everyday mobile practices of health seeking migrants within Pentecostal churches as religious processes that define migrants' wellbeing. I argue that the search for healing is undergirded by mobility within churches, prayer cells, and crusades in pursuit of a man/woman of God who can prophesize good tidings and pray with migrants to cast away their challenges, problems, and restore healing and wholeness from their brokenness—a sense of wellbeing and security.

The use of trans-local mobility refers to migrants whose mobilities are within South Africa, while transnationalism refers to those who travel out of South Africa for healing. Such mobilities are dependent on the economic potential of migrants who may travel within South Africa, while others travel out of South Africa. The notions of trans-local and transnational Pentecostal religious mobilities widens our scope for the purpose of understanding and appreciating the rationale of migrants' movements and criss-crossing from one church to another. Similarly, this addition is important because it sheds light on migrants' adaptation strategies of the therapeutic role of religion in their lives, especially when they are away from home. The chapter is guided by the following question: to what extent does mobility within Pentecostal churches fulfil the quest for divine healing among Cameroonian migrants?

Following Brown, I opt for the term "divine healing" over other terms such as "spiritual healing" because it emphasizes healing by a supernatural force— God, and is holistic.[10] Divine healing is therefore all encompassing—holistic healing—and includes physical, spiritual, psycho-social and emotional healing, peace with God, fellow humans and the natural world. It also includes "full salvation"—forgiveness from sins, deliverance from demonic oppression and simply finding "the self" from emotional distress. Divine healing thus refers to restored "wholeness or well-being, which is characterized by obtaining an equilibrium or balance of mind, body, and spirit".[11] The pursuit of wholeness also extends to human flourishing that focuses on the image of salvation informed by

---

[10]   Candy Gunther Brown, ed., *Global Pentecostal and Charismatic Healing* (Oxford; New York: Oxford University Press, 2011), 4–5; Kalu, *African Pentecostalism*, 261.

[11]   A. Payne-Jackson, "Spiritual Illness and Healing: 'If the Lord Wills,'" in *Faith, Health, and Healing in African American Life*, eds. Stephanie Y. Mitchem and Emilie M. Townes (Westport: Praeger, 2008), 55; Candy Gunther Brown and C. Omenyo, eds., "New Wine in an Old Wine Bottle? Charismatic Healing in the Mainline Churches in Ghana," in *Global Pentecostal and Charismatic Healing*, 1st ed. (Oxford; New York: Oxford University Press, 2011), 236; Michael H. Cohen, *Healing at the Borderland of Medicine and Religion*, Studies in Social Medicine (Chapel Hill: University of North Carolina Press, 2006), 100.

upward mobility and personal success.[12] Flourishing or prosperity and wealth by the same token is derived from "inner peace, satisfaction, contentment and the maintenance of social networks".[13] Flourishing as such denotes material and immaterial wealth that together provide salvific wholeness. Pentecostalism offers these migrants a substitute community, providing new norms to confront their situation and to reclaim wholeness.[14] I refer to healings from the perspective of participants, removing the awkward necessity of using qualifications like "alleged" or "claimed."

In the sections that follow, I begin with an overview of who these migrants in question are. Next I look at mobility, insecurity, and religion, how insecurity and brokenness is fundamental in migrants' mobility to achieve religious healing and wholeness. It draws on Norris and Inglehart's theoretical underpinnings of insecurity.[15] This is closely followed by the methodological section. The last two sections introduce the empirical findings, starting with an in-depth exposé on trans-local, virtual and transnational mobilities, and how these various forms of mobilities are done interchangeably. The last section examines mobility in search of financial wealth and stability. Now I introduce the readers to the migrants whose stories are told here.

SETTING THE SCENE

Migration to South Africa (SA) blossomed in the aftermath of apartheid when the Cameroonian government lifted the ban on the migration of Cameroonians to SA. SA became an alternative destination for young Cameroonians who were fleeing the effects of the Structural Adjustment Programme (SAP)—unemployment, poverty, and the need for improved standard of living. SA as a destination was also as a result of Europe tightening its borders against African migrants. These are mainly economic migrants who come to South Africa with visitors' or study visas (with the intention of overstaying their visas), while others come in irregularly via Mozambique and are smuggled across the border by migration syndicates. Upon arrival, irrespective of their status and nature of arrival, they immediately file for asylum in order to extend their stay or have papers. For most, migration to SA was a springboard to further migration,

12   Ruth A. Marshall and André Corten, "Introduction," in *Between Babel and Pentecost: Transnational Pentecostalism in Africa and Latin America*, eds. André Corten and Ruth A. Marshall (Bloomington: Indiana University Press, 2001), 1–21.
13   Kalu, *African Pentecostalism*, 261.
14   Manuel A. Vásquez, "The Global Portability of Pneumatic Christianity: Comparing African and Latin American Pentecostalisms," *African Studies* 68, no.2 (August 2009): 273–86. https://doi.org/10.1080/00020180903109664
15   Pippa Norris and Ronald Inglehart, *Sacred and Secular: Religion And Politics Worldwide* (Cambridge; New York: Cambridge University Press, 2004).

but if they were unable to continue they stayed on. It is upon completion of a tertiary degree that they seek employment and a change in their status—from refugee to critical skills or migrate elsewhere.[16]

Upon arrival in Cape Town, SA, most migrants enter the informal economy as a way of making a living, while others stay in the professions they were pursuing in Cameroon such as panel beating, tailoring, hairdressing, restaurateur of ethnic food and carpentry.[17] Even at that, most did not expect life in Cape Town to be full of challenges, given the images that they have been fed by earlier migrants suggest that it is easier in SA to make money in the informal economy than in Cameroon. Worst still, they did not anticipate to be reduced to the margins of society and to have to struggle for visibility or experience high levels of xenophobia. Although newly arrived migrants are given start-ups by older migrants (family or hometown association), some could not reconcile their daily lives to the flashy lifestyles of visiting migrants when they were still at home.

Some compared their lifestyle in Cameroon to that in SA and decided to brave the disgrace to return home, while most carried on because they were the beacon of hope for their families. This also meant that for those who stayed on, it was the beginning of a life of struggle until when they are able to navigate the social ladder. These migrants live in ethnic enclaves in particular neighborhoods. Whereas migrants belonging to mainline churches would like to continue with the same faith, they soon discovered that it does not address their existential challenges and their inability to follow the Afrikaans accent. In the face of such dehumanizing circumstances, coupled with the challenges of having proper documentation, financial stress and other psycho-social trauma, most gravitated toward Pentecostal churches to make meaning of their situation and, perhaps, where they regained a sense of humanity. Beyond physical healing migrants wanted wholeness, or restoration from their brokenness. This is clearly stated by one of my informants:

> Can one live in this country as a migrant without God? We are living by His Grace! Life is really difficult here in South Africa that one just has to get close

---

16   Henrietta M. Nyamnjoh, "Navigating 'Ngunda'/'Adoro' and Negotiating Economic Uncertainty amongst Mobile Cameroonian Migrants in Cape Town (South Africa)," *Critical African Studies* 9, no.2 (2017): 241–60, https://doi.org/10.1080/21681392.2017.1340846.

17   Henrietta Nyamnjoh, "Penetrating the Unseen: The Role of Spiritual Practices in the Senegalese Boat Migration Process," in *The Public Face of African New Religious Movements in Diaspora: Imagining the 'Other'* (England: Ashgate, 2014), 191–213; Nyamnjoh, "Navigating 'Ngunda'/'Adoro' and Negotiating Economic Uncertainty amongst Mobile Cameroonian Migrants in Cape Town (South Africa)."

to God for protection and healing seeing the crime rate, xenophobia and diseases around.[18]

Given that "migration is one of the most important means of religious dissemination and migrants constitute the greatest means of spreading Christianity in Africa,"[19] it is therefore important to see religion as "being on the move," given that several Africans migrate with their religious ideologies and identities,[20] while in search of new religious identities to complement their existing religious identity. This is especially the case when they are confronted by insecurity and crisis.

Mobility, Insecurity, and Religion

Cathy is a nurse and came to Cape Town in 2002 for spousal reunion with a man she has never seen given the wedding arrangement was done between the two families. She was a staunch Catholic prior to joining the Pentecostal church. One month into the pregnancy of her second child in 2005, she realized one morning that she was bleeding slightly and was very frightened she would lose the baby. She went to the hospital but declined to be admitted under observation. Cathy explains further:

> The doctor said if it was brownish discharge it means that baby is dead inside, it's not going to be positive. I should be admitted so that, during the night if something happens they can just help me. So, I say no, I can't be admitted, there is nothing wrong with me, why must I have this situation? I've never done anything wrong. From the hospital I came straight to a family, that attends a Pentecostal church in Khayelitsha (township), and told the wife what happened. She said to me, there is a pastor from Nigeria in Khayelitsha, if I want to go with them, I should come because he will pray and this thing will finish. I believed immediately and I said, I have to start talking to God. Then I told God, if it is a vein that has a problem, please, You have to just connect that vein back to my child because my child must start getting oxygen, getting food, getting whatever the child needs to get. I was praying everyday. The following day, they took me to church, while there the pastor prayed for me in tongues

---

18   Conversation with my hairdresser, Cape Town, November 4, 2016.
19   Kalu, "African Pentecostalism in Diaspora."
20   A. Adogame, *The African Christian Diaspora: New Currents and Emerging Trends in World Christianity* (London; New York: Bloomsbury Publishing, 2013), Afe Adogame and Shobana Shankar, "Introduction: Exploring New Frontiers in Global Religious Dynamics"; in *Religion on the Move! New Dynamics of Religious Expansion in a Globalising World*, eds. Afe Adogame and Shobana Shankar, vol. 20 (Leiden: Brill, 2013), 1–20, https://www.euppublishing.com/doi/full/10.3366/swc.2014.0074; Peggy Levitt, "Religion on the Move: Mapping Global Cultural Production and Consumption," in *Religion on the Edge: De-Centering and Re-Centering the Sociology of Religion*, eds. Courtney Bender et al. (Oxford ; New York: Oxford University Press, 2013), 159–78; Nyamnjoh, "Information and Communication Technology and Its Impact on Transnational Migration: The Case of Senegalese Boat Migrants"; Kalu, *African Pentecostalism*.

and then he said "the child of God has run into her father's house, you have to go back!" when we finished, he asked people to come so he prays for them (*altar call*). So, I went up again, he prayed and then we left and came home. I had that belief that something should really happen here. The only thing I was worried now, what if I deliver and there's a problem with the ear or with the eyes. So, I was worried about those things, but I told God, that "please mend the artery, the vein, let my child get what she needs to get." I went for the first scan, it says she's a little girl and everything is normal. I was like, this is a dream. So, since then I started going, but not regularly, to that Pentecostal church and another one next to my house.[21]

Cathy's story illustrates the embeddedness of religion in human life, contrary to earlier studies by Anthony Wallace (1966) predicting the extinction of religion in the wake of globalization. Mobility and religion, therefore, are not mutually exclusive, but rather central to immigrants' everyday life in the host country as it appears fundamental to their daily existence and survival. As Kalu reiterates, "immigrant Christianity serves as a balm in the entire process, ranging from why and how immigrants come to their new countries, to how they cope in the new homeland . . . to prayers in immigrant churches for everyday survival needs such as working permits, employment"—religion is called upon in times of challenges, health crisis, and serves for networking and security.[22] This characterizes a high sense of mobility from one church to another to shop for renowned "men/women of God" believed to be wonderfully endowed with prophetic insights and divine healing and deliverance. It is precisely this gift of divine intervention, deliverance, and prophetic healing that Cathy was in search of to keep her pregnancy to full term. What informs the decision to seek healing from a particular man/woman of God? Do migrants find reprieve from their trans-local and transnational pilgrimages? As religious transmigrants,[23] they are gifted with agency that is capable of deciphering who they believe is blessed with healing and prophetic ministry, and what meaning they attribute to sermons, deliverance prowess of the pastors and "sermon

---

[21]   Interview with Cathy, Cape Town, April 27, 2017.

[22]   Nyamnjoh, "Penetrating the Unseen": The Role of Spiritual Practices in the Senegalese Boat Migration Process"; Adogame and Weissköppel, *Religion in the Context of African Migration*; Adogame, *The African Christian Diaspora: New Currents and Emerging Trends in World Christianity*; Afe Adogame, "Introduction: The Public Face of African New Religious Movements in Diaspora," in *The Public Face of African New Religious Movements in Diaspora: Imagining the 'Other'* (England: Ashgate, 2014), 1–28; Jacqueline Hagan and Helen Rose Ebaugh, "Calling upon the Sacred: Migrants' Use of Religion in the Migration Process," *International Migration Review* 37, no.4, (2003): 1145–62; Van Dijk, "From Camp to Encompassment: Discourses of Transsubjectivity in the Ghanaian Pentecostal Diaspora."

[23]   "Transmigrants are immigrants whose daily lives depend on multiple and constant interconnections across international borders and whose public identities are configured in relationship to more than one nation-state." (Glick-Schiller et al, 1995, 48).

infomercials"—business rhetorics in the selling of salvation by televangelists through business infomercials from religious sermon to entertaining infomercial that evoke the image of capitalism.[24] In other words, migrants are able to determine whether sermons are tainted with salesman rhetoric or political agenda, which coincide with capitalist propaganda, that ultimately contradict the foundations of the Christian doctrine and hinder the spread of Christianity to world cultures,[25] or a particular preacher is fake.

As transmigrants, they navigate and negotiate these life-world shifts from local to global articulation of religious transnationalism that zoom into the everyday life and bring to the fore its narratives, intrigues, energy and experiences, and the extent to which their ability to navigate and negotiate the local and the global gives them some degree of agency and security. In this respect, the concept of "emplacement" is useful in that it captures the betwixt and between of migrants' life-worlds, shedding light on how migrants engage with the global and the local religious movements, while providing a focus on embodied and situated presence.[26] What this highlights is the essential role of not only producing localities, but also embodied experiences as they are discursively imagined. Ideas, practices, images, and institutions (*of religious healing and deliverance*) are capable of spreading widely as elements of the globalist imagination as well as the networkings that forms part of their embodied experiences.[27] Inasmuch as Englund argues that localization is doubly disqualified to capture the contours of emplacement because placemaking as emplacement dissipates the local-global distinction,[28] while not discounting this perspective, I will concur with Kim Knott that in the case of religion and religious transmigrants, placemaking cannot be "separated from notions of embodiment and everyday practice, knowledge and discourse, and production and reproduction, and is an engaged and dynamic arena for religion no less than for other aspects of social and cultural life."[29] Trans-local and transnational religious mobilities encompass host and home countries and spread to various social fields and

---

[24]   Jordan Schonig, "The Trinity Broadcasting Network: Satellites Spreading More Than the Gospel" (Paper, 2006).

[25]   Schonig, "The Trinity Broadcasting Network."

[26]   David Garbin, "The Visibility and Invisibility of Migrant Faith in the City: Diaspora Religion and the Politics of Emplacement of Afro-Christian Churches," *Journal of Ethnic and Migration Studies* 39, no.5 (2013): 677–96; Harri Englund, "Ethnography after Globalism: Migration and Emplacement in Malawi," *American Ethnologist* 29, no.2 (2002): 261–86.

[27]   Englund, "Ethnography after Globalism: Migration and Emplacement in Malawi"; Kim Knott, "From Locality to Location and Back Again: A Spatial Journey in the Study of Religion," 39, no.2 (2009): 154–60.

[28]   Englund, "Ethnography after Globalism: Migration and Emplacement in Malawi," 268.

[29]   Knott, "From Locality to Location and Back Again: A Spatial Journey in the Study of Religion," 156.

nodal points that build multiple relations.[30] These connections are rooted in the religious networks that underpin the ability to link, interact, and intersect simultaneously with various churches and define individual and collective experiences in fulfilling their needs, especially when in despair.

This inter-relationality is best illustrated by Peggy Levitt in her 2003 study "You know Abraham was really the first immigrant . . ."[31] The mobility by migrants seeks to confirm the challenges and insecurities that characterize their trajectories. Religiosity and spirituality, it seems, provide a framework for migrants to understand the world and cope with their everyday lives and are deeply rooted in relationships across social fields and the community. It is against this backdrop that Cathy believed that going to the pastor in the township for divine intervention would secure the survival of her unborn child— "My baby started growing after some time, and I asked someone, can you see? Do I look pregnant? They say, yes. Then it was growing, growing and I was less worried."[32]

Mobilities in search of religious sanctuary and practices among most migrants are guided by insecurity. Following Norris and Inglehart, the basic tenet of insecurity theory is that migrants' turn toward religion is propelled by insecurities—insecurities shape and drive the demand for religion.[33] Such insecurities are visible among those who feel vulnerable or encounter personal risk, especially, those with health challenges, oppressed, psychosocially challenged, and unemployed migrants (local/international) who are more likely to turn to religion for security and network. Norris and Inglehart further suggest two forms of insecurity: ego-tropic and sociotropic—that pose a direct threat to individuals and family or to the community respectively.[34] This study focuses on both forms of insecurity, particularly health (physical/psychosocial). Related to ego-tropic insecurity, is physical healing and psychosocial wellbeing as migrants recognize the need to have legal documentation and survival in the host country. Physical healing ranging from various ailments such as cancer, hypertension, and inability to become pregnant, perception of witchcraft, and broken relationships that result in emotional distress are conditions for which deliverance and spiritual healing is sought.

---

[30]   Schiller, Basch, and Blanc, "From Immigrant to Transmigrant: Theorizing Transnational Migration," *Anthropological Quarterly*, 68 no.1 (1995). 48–63; Anthony Elliott and John Urry, *Mobile Lives* (London; New York, NY: Routledge, 2010).
[31]   Peggy Levitt, "'You Know, Abraham Was Really the First Immigrant': Religion and Transnational Migration," *International Migration Review* 37, no.3 (2003): 847–73.
[32]   Interview with Cathy, Cape Town, April 27, 2017.
[33]   Norris and Inglehart, *Sacred and Secular*.
[34]   Norris and Inglehart, *Sacred and Secular*.

Could psychosocial healing provide reassurance for those facing existential insecurity, the security of a higher power that will ensure that things will work out? Such beliefs, Norris and Inglehart argue, reduce stress, making people work toward coping with the problem and less anxious.[35] Insecurities, it seems, shape and drive the demand for religion and could explain the relevance of African Pentecostal churches for migrant/immigrant communities following their preaching and healing practices that assure them of better days ahead and of total healing. African Pentecostal churches seem increasingly relevant to migrant/immigrant communities following their acknowledgment of the reality of witchcraft and the organization of prayer and deliverance sessions of "spiritual warfare and permanent engagement with the figure of the demonic."[36] Whereas Marshall succinctly regards such a stance as the "anti-democratic side of the Pentecostal church,"[37] it is precisely for this reason that Pentecostal churches seem to appeal to migrants as opined by Sabar.[38] Hence, Maxwell's concept of "durawall" concisely echoes the notion of Pentecostal churches as a source of protection against hostility.[39] Looking at the mobilities embedded in the trans-local and transnational processes allows one to zoom into migrants' dynamic agency in which "religious trajectories intersect with religious biographies"[40] as they navigate and negotiate the various religious spaces.

René Devisch significantly shows how the search for healing is composed principally of those who are disconnected from their primary vital networks: migrants and other displaced persons and homeless youth.[41] Focusing on healing churches in Kinshasa, Devisch describes how healing churches have imagined and given concrete expression to a new existential reality and insecurity informed by their contextual life sphere. The healing churches serve "to re-channel people's discontent, loneliness and despair in the face of life's hardships into a community where divine energy binds, adapts together and where hopes and

35   Norris and Inglehart, *Sacred and Secular*.
36   Ruth Marshall, *Political Spiritualities: The Pentecostal Revolution in Nigeria* (Chicago; London: University of Chicago Press, 2009), 14; Kwamena Asamoah-Gyadu, *African Charismatics Current Developments within Independent: Indigenous Pentecostalism in Ghana* (Leiden; Boston: Brill, 2005); Birgit Meyer, "'Make a Complete Break with the Past.' Memory and Post-Colonial Modernity in Ghanaian Pentecostalist Discourse," *Journal of Religion in Africa* 28, no.3 (1998): 316–49, https://doi.org/10.2307/1581573.
37   Marshall, *Political Spiritualities*, 14.
38   Galia Sabar, "Witchcraft and Concepts of Evil amongst African Migrant Workers in Israel," *Canadian Journal of African Studies / Revue Canadienne Des Études Africaines* 44, no.1 (2010): 110–41.
39   David Maxwell, "The Durawall of Faith: Pentecostal Spirituality in Neo-Liberal Zimbabwe," *Journal of Religion in Africa* 35, no.1 (2005): 4–31.
40   Katrien Pype, S. van Wolputte and A. Melice, "The Interdependence of Mobility and Faith: An Introduction," *Canadian Journal of African Studies* 46, no.3 (2012): 361.
41   René Devisch, "'Pillaging Jesus': Healing Churches and the Villagisation of Kinshasa," *Journal of the International African Institute* 64, no.4 (1996): 556.

failures can be shared" by creating bonds that resemble kinship that is not solely tied to consanguinity. This is done through the process of "villagisation."[42]

Methodological Considerations

This study draws on qualitative research and a multi-sited ethnography that was conducted between 2016 and 2017 in Cape Town, South Africa, over ten months. The multi-sitedness of the study was informed by the mobilities of the informants that I accompanied to the different churches where they sought healing within Cape Town. Accompanying informants to a church is often after an interview or a conversation where I expressed the wish to go with them. They were always willing to invite me to join them when going to a new church or one that they have settled on that speaks to their needs. In this regard, I accompanied informants to six different churches and some of the churches were revisited either with different informants or with the same informant, especially when there was a guest pastor or a conference/crusade that runs for two or three days. Concerning those who sought healing trans-locally (Johannesburg and Pretoria) or transnationally (Nigeria and Cameroon), life histories and interviews were used to reconstruct their story upon their return. A total of eighteen migrants (twelve women and six men) were interviewed, and some were interviewed repeatedly, especially those who were constantly on the move. As such, the focus was on the migrants' mobilities to the different churches and their healing experiences in and out of Cape Town. The churches attended include Redeemed Church of Christ (Redeemed Tabernacle), Miracle Fire Ministries, Action Jesus Redeemer of All Nations, Christ Embassy, Omega Fire Ministries, and New World Save Ministry. My attendance was guided by non-participant observation and notes were taken copiously to capture the events. Further, attending prayer cells/Bible study sessions exposed the vulnerability of migrants in such tight-knit groups that are considered more as a family, showing how their hope for a "breakthrough" in life depends on realigning oneself closer to God. These cells/Bible study sessions give migrants the opportunity to share their problems and testimonies and collectively pray for one another by using passages from the Bible and listening to audio sermons of the pastors to illustrate and ease their fear. The things that stood out during these sessions were hope and conviction that they cannot be forsaken by God.

Long hours of interviews (open ended, in-depth, and semi-structured) gave informants the opportunity to narrate and map their religious trajectories, providing reasons that precipitated continuous mobilities and detailing when they reached the decision that they have found the "place." Relatedly, conversations

---

were important assets as they provided room for informants to bracket events and narrate them as they happened—gesturing and miming others present at the time of experiencing the phenomenon to convey absolute meaning to the experience as experienced by the subject. Knowledge of the experiences of others was known to some informants, hence informants introduced their friends whose experiences they felt could be useful to the research.

Attending services in the various Pentecostal churches frequented by my informants were watershed moments as I witnessed firsthand, the various healing practices that they went through and what they later made of their experiences. These services are often packed to capacity with members, friends, and virtual families and relatives who are represented by the photos sent from home. For each of these services, migrants and other congregants respond to the altar call of healing by lining up in front of the altar to be prayed for by the pastor and his spouse. The prayer sessions are often accompanied by gestures, shouts, and falling in trance as a sign of confronting and purging the evil spirits, cleansing, and healing, which are often very emotional.

FROM VIRTUAL TO TRANS-LOCAL TO TRANSNATIONAL MOBILITY

As shown by Rosalind Hackett, the appropriation of Information and Communication Technologies (ICTs) is a "tool of expansion, a reflection of globalizing aspirations, but it is also part of a calculated attempt to transform and Christianize popular culture so it is safe for consumption by 'born-again' Christians."[43] In order to stay connected with followers and disseminate their messages, Pentecostal churches have increasingly relied on ICTs to link congregations to its headquarters,[44] and to keep the transnational machinery afloat (crusades, conventions, and conferences). In other words, the success of Pentecostal churches is partly dependent on their appropriation of ICTs and the mobility of followers to attend events or in pursuit of a "powerful" pastor. The search for divine healing, deliverance, and prophecies that migrants hope

---

[43]   Hackett, "Charismatic/Pentecostal Appropriation of Media Technologies in Nigeria and Ghana," 258; Schonig, "The Trinity Broadcasting Network: Satellites Spreading More Than the Gospel."

[44]   Hackett, "Charismatic/Pentecostal Appropriation of Media Technologies in Nigeria and Ghana"; Afeosemime U. Adogame and James V. Spickard, "Introduction: Africa, the New African Diaspora, and Religious Transnationalism in a Global World," in *Religion Crossing Boundaries: Transnational Religious and Social Dynamics in Africa and the New African Diaspora*, ed. Afeosemime U. Adogame and James V. Spickard, Religion and the Social Order, v. 18 (Leiden, The Netherlands ; Boston: Brill, 2010), 1–28; Adogame, *The African Christian Diaspora: New Currents and Emerging Trends in World Christianity*; Nyamnjoh, "Penetrating the Unseen": The Role of Spiritual Practices in the Senegalese Boat Migration Process"; Kudzai Biri, "Migration, Transnationalism and the Shaping of Zimbabwean Pentecostal Spirituality," *African Diaspora* 7, no.1 (2014): 139–64, https://doi.org/10.1163/18725465-00701007; Hackett and Soares, "Introduction: New Media and Religious Transformations in Africa."

would change their life course has created opportunities for situations of exploitation.[45] There is a strong appeal among migrants to watch church services of televangelists on TV channels or permanently tune their TVs on one of the televangelists' channels. This is especially true of migrants who are "disconnected from their primary networks."[46]

With the addition of social media to the panoply of virtual resources, Pentecostals have appropriated social media within their respective congregations and tailored the medium as need be.[47] Receiving "the word" via social media is seen by migrants as uplifting. By way of illustration, I will draw on Mary's activities. Mary is a hairdresser and arrived in Cape Town in 2006. As a mainline Christian (protestant), she decided to continue with the same church. But due to language barrier (inability to understand the Afrikaans' English accent), and the thirst for the "word" she set out in search of a church that will give her spiritual healing and enrichment. Her search took her to three churches which she found spiritually wanting. She was finally invited by one of her clients to a crusade in Cape Town where Pastor Chris Oyakhilome would preside with other pastors. After the crusade she became an active member of Christ Embassy. She has created a phone directory with the mobile numbers of most of her clients and the messages sent are not limited to announce specials that are being offered at her salon, but she has gone further to send 'Rhapsody of Realities Daily Devotional' to most who do not mind receiving. Besides hair products that are displayed on sale, there are also DVDs of Pastor Chris' sermons, hardcopies of monthly Rhapsody and other religious materials on sale. The TV at the salon is permanently tuned to Love World television ministry.[48] As Mary maintains: "Every morning, I send Rhapsody of Reality for the day through WhatsApp to friends. I make sure every morning my phone sends the Rhapsody. You give your day a spiritual start, you see, just to heal and keep your spirit alive."[49]

Watching "healing/prayer crusades" and telecast services officiated by Pastor Chris from the "mother church," Church of Christ Embassy in Nigeria, or Pastor T.B. Joshua of SCOAN, and other televangelic TV stations, all echo the notion of flows of religions and religious healing, aided by communication technologies. Most informants admit that watching the healing and deliverance of someone on TV enable them to connect their faith to that person's

---

[45] Hackett and Soares, "Introduction: New Media and Religious Transformations in Africa."

[46] Devisch, "'Pillaging Jesus,'" 556.

[47] Henrietta M. Nyamnjoh, "'When Are You Going to Change Those Stones to Phones'? Appropriation of Social Media by Pentecostal Churches in Cape Town." (n.d.), (In Press).

[48] Love World television ministry is the TV channel of Christ Embassy – http://loveworld-televisionministry.org

[49] Conversation with Mary, Cape Town, March 14, 2015.

and could also receive healing. For others, simply following the preaching and teachings of the pastor via TV has impacted on their lives and caused them to rethink their understanding of the Bible and the word. This is the case with Grace who claimed to have begun her healing journey by watching programs on Love World television ministry[50] of Christ Embassy at a friend's house at her invitation. Grace joined her husband in Cape Town in 2008 and upon arrival enrolled at a university to study Food technology. She has since graduated with a first degree, is currently working and still pursuing further studies though on a part-time basis. Prior to watching Love World television channel at a friend's house, she was a committed member and a counsellor at Mountain of Fire Ministries church in Cape Town. She explains what programs she would go to watch daily at 8p.m.–10p.m.:

> My friend told me she called someone who installed for her Love World Satellite. She asked if I was interested to come and watch. So every evening I went there to watch, there was a program called "search the scriptures" that caught my attention. Every evening that program started at nine o'clock to half past nine. Pastor Chris was preaching from eight o' clock to half past eight and that program started at nine o'clock to half past nine. since she was next to me isn't clear as it could be either they watched the program together, seated next to each other or, the friend's house was next to her house. Every evening from eight o'clock to ten o'clock I would be there because after the program "search the scripture", Pastor Chris was preaching again. I had been so carried by the messages and the simplicity with which he presented the word. I learnt that Pastor Chris was coming to Johannesburg for a program called Night of Bliss. It was in 2011. So I wanted to go see him in person and see him preach live.[51]

For Grace, going to attend Night of Bliss was equally prompted by a desire to resolve a personal problem that she has been grappling with—inability to become pregnant. This was the moment to also seek healing—to attend the three-week healing school session. She explicates further:

> At that time I couldn't conceive (*become pregnant*), so I used that opportunity of going to Night of Bliss to attend the healing school. At the healing school they teach you mostly about the power of your mind, teach you what the Word of God says about healing. They will tell you it's God's will for you to be healed. There are different kinds of healing, it can be financial healing, spiritual healing or physical healing. They teach you about the different kinds of healing and how you can live in God's help because God's plan for you is that of healing. They will teach you different things about lifestyle that affect you, your health. Teaching you about the kind of foods you eat and how you prepare and all the

50 Interview with Cathy, Cape Town, April 27, 2017.
51 Interview with Grace, Cape Town, May 21, 2016.

different things. If you want to conceive (*become pregnant*), what lifestyle you should live.[52]

Grace's testimony is suggestive that healing in Christ Embassy is fashioned by Jesus's pedagogical manner of healing, that teaching can be linked to the wisdom traditions of Israel and exemplified by the use of short sayings that communicate familiar truths or observations about human experience.[53] These teachings convey a strong personal appeal, calling on people to learn from the actions of Jesus or abide by his teachings so that the work of God might be displayed in their lives (John 9:3).[54] The teachings undergirded in the word that Grace and other informants received from different Pentecostal churches I attended or the Rhapsody that Mary sends out daily suggest that the messages of these Pentecostals have a healing impact on them and "keep their spirit" alive. As Kwamena Asamoah-Gyadu aptly illustrates, the messages challenge listeners, and viewers of televised services by extension, to "rise above any difficult circumstances."[55] In other words, their teachings above all conscientize and empower Christians who feel helpless with tools to transform and overcome their difficult situation.[56] Grace confirms a perceptible change in her thinking barely a few days into the healing school sessions. She notes, "When I started healing school, after the third day I saw my life changing, my thinking, because you know when you always have this thing (*infertility*), you think, maybe, somebody is behind my inability to conceive." Grace's healing has come largely through the impartation of "words of knowledge".[57] A few months upon her return from the healing school, she became pregnant and gave birth to their first daughter in 2012. While she attributes her pregnancy to attending the healing school, she has not been able to become pregnant again. But this time she is emotionally prepared as it may simply be a matter of time.

Sickness often provides the occasion for people to draw closer to God and this was true of Ruth when she fell sick. Prior to her illness, she was a very buoyant young lady who was engaged in a thriving informal business with her spouse. However, when she fell sick her daily activities changed significantly and she was drawn closer to God as a result of that. Her attendance to church service and cell prayer meeting intensified. She joined warfare prayer groups who

---

[52]   Conversation with Jane, Cape Town, May 23, 2016.

[53]   Perkins, *Jesus as Teacher* (Cambridge England ; New York: Cambridge University Press, 1990).

[54]   Perkins, *Jesus as Teacher* , 24.

[55]   Kwamena Asamoah-Gyadu, "Anointing Through the Screen: Neo-Pentecostalism and Televised Christianity in Ghana," *Studies in World Christianity* 11, no.1 (2005): 13.

[56]   Jörg Stolz, "'All Things Are Possible': Towards a Sociological Explanation of Pentecostal Miracles and Healings," *Sociology of Religion* 72, no.4 (2011): 456–82.

[57]   Stolz, "'All Things Are Possible.'"

would pray for her or join her in midnight battle prayers at her home. When in church, she would go to the front during altar calls for those in need of healing prayers. Her quest for healing went beyond her regular church attendance, as she was invited by friends to go to their churches as well for special healing services or for crusades when there was a visiting pastor in town believed to have healing powers. When she became gravely sick, friends would bring pastors to pray with her. At home, her TV was permanently tuned to Emmanuel TV of Pastor T.B. Joshua. During televised healing services, she would put her hand on the TV and the other on her breast (as instructed by the pastor) to follow the healing prayers. Ruth's actions are an example of religious trans-local mobility and transnationality in search of wholeness. When Ruth's condition worsened she decided to travel to Nigeria to see Prophet T. B. Joshua of Synagogue Church of All Nation (SCOAN). Her sister, Jane,[58] narrates Ruth's experience:

> She travelled to Nigeria for divine healing and to see the man of God. While there, she was told by the man of God not to to have her breast operated and that she had been bewitched following her recent trip to Cameroon. He cautioned against surgery, saying that if she agreed to it she would not come out of the theater alive. She was prayed for and the man of God laid hands on her and gave her some anointed oil, holy water and anointed wrist band and wall stickers. But she returned to Cape Town. A few weeks later her condition deteriorated and she was hospitalized. For a second time she refused surgery and later developed a septic wound on her breast. Members of SCOAN in Cape Town and her warfare prayer group would often go to pray for her, while other friends invited their pastors to pray for her at the hospital as well. With no success to attain healing, Ruth died thinking that she had been bewitched as stated by the man of God.[59]

As seen in Ruth's case, not all who seek divine healing are cured, even after prayers by various pastors, trips to different churches, and two trips to Nigeria to see Prophet T.B. Joshua. How does the experience of the uncured affect their faith and that of those around them, especially, in this case, the faith of Ruth's sister and husband? It takes faith to realize that healing of some sort has been attained and it was this faith that gave strength to the family. According to her sister, Jane, when one pastor finally prophesied that "she will sleep" (die), he asked that if there were any friends that she had fallen out with, it was then the time to reconcile before she "sleeps." She took this opportunity to reconcile with her friends and also reconciled with those her spouse had fallen out with. When she died, her death was referred to as "reconciliation death."[60] As

---

58   I met Ruth when she was very sick. Information about her was narrated by her elder sister, Jane.
59   Conversation with Jane, Cape Town, May 23, 2016.
60   Conversation with Jane, Cape Town, October 8, 2016.

Asamoah-Gyadu puts it, "people may continue to live with disabilities . . . but God has his own way of helping such people to have holistic lifestyles—to have the grace to cope with disabilities itself constitutes a miracle that generates belief in the God of mission."[61] Although Ruth did not receive the desired healing, her personal testimony of reconciliation clearly establishes a relationship between faith and experience. Rather than focusing on the physical cure, her sister and friends focused on the "gift of faith and healing that achieved a transformative purpose" in their lives.[62] She was granted the strength to cope with the situation, and she was also given time to reconcile with her friends. Those around her drew strength from her courage to cope with her illness, her closeness to God, increased prayerfulness and her reconciliatory character as Jane noted, "my sister could pray even more than some pastors until you will not even know that she was sick. Because of my sister, a lot of people have given their life to Christ . . . even at her memorial service, three of her friends testified that their religious life today is thanks to my sister."[63] Similarly she was also consoled by the fact that neither Jesus nor the disciples healed all diseases that came their way, hence much as they were expecting wholeness, it came in other forms. While she died without having been physically healed from cancer, I posit that she received abundant "grace" to change her life, and the gift of faith toward spiritual healing—by making peace with death and reconciling with friends she had fallen out with over the years, given the urgency at which she called her friends by her bedside, as her sister testified: "She called all her friends one by one and even the one that had fallen out with her intimate friend and told them: 'you all should reconcile before I die.'" As Onyinah expounds, "sickness can draw people closer to God and increase in them obedience to God's will."[64] Healing thus becomes a process whereby the individual is restored to spiritual and mental health. It is however the grace of God that provides the strength. Her healing could be likened therefore to the epistle "by his wounds you have been healed" (1 Peter 2:24, NIV)—the strength not only to cope with her condition, but to be exemplary to others.

---

61   Kwamena Asamoah-Gyadu, "Faith, Healing and Missions: Reflections on a Consultative Process," *International Review of Missions* 93, no.370/71 (2004): 373; Asamoah-Gyadu, *African Charismatics: Current Developments within Independent Indigenous Pentecostalism in Ghana*, 195; Opoku Onyinah, "God's Grace, Healing and Suffering," *International Review of Missions* 95, no.376/377 (2006): 117–27.

62   Kalu, *African Pentecostalism*, 264.

63   Interview with Jane, Cape Town, October 8, 2016.

64   Onyinah, "God's Grace, Healing and Suffering," 125.

MITIGATING FINANCIAL FAILURE AND UNEMPLOYMENT: THE NEED FOR TRANSNATIONAL MOBILITY

While ill-health is often the cause of seeking healing, others seek healing from the difficulties faced in their everyday life. The mobile search for divine intervention is closely associated with whatever challenges that migrants go through and the belief that prayers/prophecy by the man of God will alleviate their plight. In Jonas's case, he needed healing from oppression—financial prosperity and the restoration of stability in his life. Jonas came to Cape Town in mid-2000 and in 2006, after having made some money working in the film industry, he decided to go back to Cameroon and set up his own business. He explains:

> After making money in South Africa, I decided to go back home because I wanted to go and establish and give back to my community and my people back home. I went back, it was not easy, it wasn't good, and it didn't really go the way I expected.
>
> After two and a half years (*in Cameroon*), I went back to South Africa because things really went bad and even the money that we had, was finished so I had to give up, I had to come back and when I came back I had six months of very bad experience, frustrated and disappointed. This was 2008/2009. I stayed at home without working . . . . I could not see myself going back to the film industry, reason being that I was so successful in the film industry and I made money and sold off my equipment when I was leaving and said I made enough in the film industry. So, seeing myself going back was a very big challenge. [65]

Having failed in his business and lacking the will to live, his last attempt and hope at jump-starting his life was to seek intervention from the man of God by travelling to Nigeria to visit SCOAN.

In response to my question of whether he saw that as a failure, he said:

> At that stage yes, it was a failure, for me, it was a failure. Life was not worth living anymore. I owed about 3 months house rent and the matter had to go to court. I was sent a paper to vacate the house and I didn't have food, I didn't have petrol money, I didn't have airtime, but I had to move. There are moments when you park your car and cry, you stay at home alone and you cry. You won't cry in front of your family but you cry everyday because you woke up in the morning and you barely know what is the next program, where to go, what to do. Because if they kicked me out of the house where was I going? There was no other place to go. At that stage of life my option was to go to Nigeria because I believed that my dream could come true knowing very well that I was not going to have money in Nigeria but I needed a divine intervention. So, I decided that if it's God's will, I will go to Nigeria, maybe the prophet will be able to

---

[65]   Interview with Jonas, Cape Town, May 1, 2017.

locate me and maybe prophesize that maybe my destiny still lies in Cameroon or the film industry but I need to know. I had to sell one of my cars to go to Nigeria because I didn't have any money. So, I went to Nigeria and spent about 5 days. I managed to go into the church just once because of the population and it happened on the last Sunday prior to my departure the next day. We prayed with Prophet T.B. Joshua, it was a mass prayer, it's not like I had the opportunity to see him in person, no. So, I had the mass prayer, the next day I travelled back but still believing that the fact I've been there my prayer had been answered. So, when I came back it was still not easy. At that point I contemplated suicide and went to the beach to drown. You know it was so painful when I thought about my beautiful boys, I thought about my family that I'd to leave behind. I asked myself the question "why can't I just take that disgrace?" I packed my bags, I knew that maybe my wife wouldn't want to follow me, and go home. But deep within, I trusted that my journey to Nigeria was not in vain. I went back to the film industry but was waiting to be called for an assignment. A week later I was called for work. I had about 6/7 days of commercial we were doing. When I started working, I began to make money again, R1200 per day (approx. 100 USD). After that job, we had to shoot a movie for 6 months for which I had to go out of the country. By the time I came back, I never remembered that I had problems before in my whole life. I believed God intervened at the right moment.[66]

Jonas's story underscores the inextricable link between migration, mobility, and insecurity and how such journeys are often viewed as the last hope to make meaningful changes in one's life. Many scholars have shown how migrants veered to these churches in search of prophecy that forms part of physical healing which migrants seek, to attain a higher spiritual level in order to enjoy success in whatever they do and avoid sickness and economic downturn.[67] It is perhaps in this respect that upon his return to Cape Town, and confronted by financial insecurity and unemployment, Jonas decided to sell his car and use the money to travel to Nigeria despite his financial challenges.

Jonas's belief in prophecy to relaunch his career is underpinned by hope and resilience: hope that he will receive divine intervention, that even though he has been "pushed to the wall, there is always a door around the corner to be opened,"[68] and resilience that by not losing hope, "you keep pushing until that door opens" as well as undertaking the journey when fully aware that he was

---

66   Interview with Jonas, Cape Town, May 1, 2017.
67   Van Dijk, "From Camp to Encompassment: Discourses of Transsubjectivity in the Ghanaian Pentecostal Diaspora"; Kalu, *African Pentecostalism*; Joseph Mensah, "Religious Transnationalism among Ghanaian Immigrants in Toronto: A Binary Logistic Regression Analysis," *The Candadian Geographer* 52, no.3 (2008): 309–30; Adogame, *The African Christian Diaspora: New Currents and Emerging Trends in World Christianity*.
68   See footnote 4 in Chapter 12.

not going to have money in Nigeria but was inspired by divine intervention. Conversely, Jonas's mobility is also influenced by Pentecostal religion's 'inventing and reconstructing the important theologies so that they can meet the practical needs created by immigrants' conditions,[69] as well as by Pentecostal churches that propagate themselves as "powerful and efficacious" in enabling people to be set free from the dangers and troubles of life.[70] But as Asamoah-Gyadu maintains, the "greatest virtue" of the "health and wealth" gospel of the Pentecostal churches lies in "the indomitable spirit that believers develop in the face of life's odds . . . . In essence, misfortune becomes only temporary."[71] Jonas corroborates Asamoah-Gyadu's thinking by confirming the temporality of his problems and how they were immediately forgotten once he was reabsorbed into the film industry.

CONCLUSION

This study has examined trans-local and transnational religious processes of migration in the search of physical healing from challenges emanating from migrants' everyday lives. The data presented in this study complement that of Meyer[72] and Yang & Ebaugh[73] in refuting secularization theories and a decline in religion, but also refining the latter by acknowledging the existence of secularization and the flipside of the influence to internal and external religious pluralism in the context of migration and mobility undergirded by existential insecurity. The challenges of being at the margins of society and of struggling to settle in, including migrants' everyday struggle to get by or acquire documentation, is significantly overwhelming and dehumanizing. As indicated by one of the informants above, their only way out is to get closer to God for solace.

As I have illustrated, Pentecostal churches have carved out a niche to attract immigrants with gospels of success, health, wealth, and wholeness, while the latter have sought refuge in those churches as places where they can turn to for healing, deliverance and divine intervention.[74] While some of them have sought and received healing, others have not. This however does not dampen their

---

[69]   Kalu, "African Pentecostalism in Diaspora," 180.

[70]   Emmanuel Y. Lartey, "'Of Formulae, Fear, and Faith: Current Issues of Concern for Pastoral Care in Africa,'" *Trinity Journal of Church and Theology* 10, no.1&2 (2001): 8.

[71]   Asamoah-Gyadu, *African Charismatics: Current Developments within Independent Indigenous Pentecostalism in Ghana*, 218.

[72]   Meyer, "'Make a Complete Break with the Past.' Memory and Post-Colonial Modernity in Ghanaian Pentecostalist Discourse."

[73]   Fenggang Yang and Helen Rose Ebaugh, "Transformations in New Immigrant Religions and Their Global Implications," *American Sociological Review* 66, no.2 (2001): 269–88, https://doi.org/10.2307/2657418.

[74]   Asamoah-Gyadu, "Anointing Through the Screen: Neo-Pentecostalism and Televised Christianity in Ghana," 13.

faith. In the cases studied in this chapter, interviewees felt that healing of some sort was received—the grace of perseverance to accept one's afflictions as well as a close connection with God was seen as miraculous healing. Furthermore, religion provides them with a sense of the self and a filial community, since everyone in church is referred to as "brother" or "sister," while the pastor and spouse are looked up to as "papa" and "mama." Migrants' mobilities, as we have seen, derive primarily from their search for an understanding of the fate of their health, as they seek for physical and spiritual healing. In addition, the evidence suggests that migrants are particularly attracted to Pentecostal spirituality as a means of seeking spiritual sanctity, and social and financial security. While the search for healing has caused a high traffic volume within Pentecostal churches in Cape Town and nationally, transnational trips are limited to those who can afford airfares to travel to Nigeria to visit, in particular, The Synagogue Church of all Nations, led by Prophet T.B. Joshua. These findings feed into the thesis statement that religious mobility and transnationalism are rife among migrant population as an effort to mitigate the challenges they face in the host country.

Bibliography:

Adogame, Afe. *The African Christian Diaspora: New Currents and Emerging Trends in World Christianity*. Bloomsbury Publishing, 2013.

———. "Introduction: The Public Face of African New Religious Movements in Diaspora." In *The Public Face of African New Religious Movements in Diaspora: Imagining the 'Other,'* 1–28. England: Ashgate, 2014.

Adogame, Afe, and Shobana Shankar. "Introduction: Exploring New Frontiers in Global Religious Dynamics." In *Religion on the Move! New Dynamics of Religious Expansion in a Globalising World*, edited by Afe Adogame and Shobana Shankar, 20:1–20. Leiden: Brill, 2013.

Adogame, Afeosemime U., and James V. Spickard. "Introduction: Africa, the New African Diaspora, and Religious Transnationalism in a Global World." In *Religion Crossing Boundaries: Transnational Religious and Social Dynamics in Africa and the New African Diaspora*, edited by Afeosemime U. Adogame and James V. Spickard, 1–28. Religion and the Social Order, 18. Leiden, The Netherlands; Boston: Brill, 2010.

Adogame, Afeosemime U., and Cordula Weissköppel, eds. *Religion in the Context of African Migration*. Bayreuth: Eckhard Breitinger, 2005.

Asamoah-Gyadu, Kwamena. *African Charismatics: Current Developments within Independent Indigenous Pentecostalism in Ghana*. Leiden; Boston: Brill, 2005.

———. "Anointing Through the Screen: Neo-Pentecostalism and Televised Christianity in Ghana." *Studies in World Christianity* 11, no.1 (2005): 9–28.

———. "Faith, Healing and Missions: Reflections on a Consultative Process." *International Review of Missions* 93, no.370/71 (2004): 372–78.

Biri, Kudzai. "Migration, Transnationalism and the Shaping of Zimbabwean Pentecostal Spirituality." *African Diaspora* 7, no.1 (2014): 139–64. https://doi.org/10.1163/18725465-00701007.

Brown, Candy Gunther, ed. *Global Pentecostal and Charismatic Healing*. Oxford; New York: Oxford University Press, 2011.

Brown, Candy Gunther, and C. Omenyo, eds. "New Wine in an Old Wine Bottle? Charismatic Healing in the Mainline Churches in Ghana." In *Global Pentecostal and Charismatic Healing*. 231–50. Oxford; New York: Oxford University Press, 2011.

Cohen, Michael H. *Healing at the Borderland of Medicine and Religion*. Studies in Social Medicine. Chapel Hill: University of North Carolina Press, 2006.

Devisch, René. "'Pillaging Jesus': Healing Churches and the Villagisation of Kinshasa." *Journal of the International African Institute* 64, no.4 (1996): 555–86.

Elliott, Anthony, and John Urry. *Mobile Lives*. London; New York, NY: Routledge, 2010.

Englund, Harri. "Ethnography after Globalism: Migration and Emplacement in Malawi." *American Ethnologist* 29, no.2 (2002): 261–86.

Garbin, David. "The Visibility and Invisibility of Migrant Faith in the City: Diaspora Religion and the Politics of Emplacement of Afro-Christian Churches." *Journal of Ethnic and Migration Studies* 39, no.5 (2013): 677–96.

Hackett, R.I.J., and B.F. Soares. "Introduction: New Media and Religious Transformations in Africa." In *New Media and Religious Transformations in Africa*, edited by R.I.J. Hackett and B.F. Soares, 1–10. Bloomington: Indiana University Press, 2015.

Hackett, Rosalind I. J. "Charismatic/Pentecostal Appropriation of Media Technologies in Nigeria and Ghana." *Journal of Religion in Africa* 28, no.3 (1998): 258–277.

Hagan, Jacqueline, and Helen Rose Ebaugh. "Calling upon the Sacred: Migrants' Use of Religion in the Migration Process." *International Migration Review* 37, no.4, (2003): 1145–62.

Kalu, Ogbu. *African Pentecostalism: An Introduction*. Oxford; New York: Oxford University Press, 2008.

Kalu, Ogbu U. "African Pentecostalism in Diaspora." *PentecoStudies: An Interdisciplinary Journal for Research on the Pentecostal and Charismatic Movements* 9, no.1 (2010): 9–34. https://doi.org/10.1558/ptcs.v9i1.9.

Knott, Kim. "From Locality to Location and Back Again: A Spatial Journey in the Study of Religion." 39, no.2 (2009): 154–60.

Lartey, Emmanuel Y. "'Of Formulae, Fear, and Faith: Current Issues of Concern for Pastoral Care in Africa.'" *Trinity Journal of Church and Theology* 10, no.1&2 (2001): 5–15.

Levitt, Peggy. "Religion on the Move: Mapping Global Cultural Production and Consumption." In *Religion on the Edge: De-Centering and Re-Centering the Sociology of Religion*, edited by Courtney Bender, Wendy Cadge, Peggy Levitt, and David Smilde, 159–78. Oxford; New York: Oxford University Press, 2013.

———. "'You Know, Abraham Was Really the First Immigrant': Religion and Transnational Migration." *International Migration Review* 37, no.3 (2003): 847–73.

Lucas, Phillip Charles, and Thomas Robbins, eds. *New Religious Movements in the 21ˢᵗ Century*. New York: Routledge, 2004.

Marshall, Ruth. *Political Spiritualities: The Pentecostal Revolution in Nigeria*. Chicago; London: University of Chicago Press, 2009.

Marshall, Ruth A., and André Corten. "Introduction." In *Between Babel and Pentecost: Transnational Pentecostalism in Africa and Latin America*, edited by André Corten and Ruth A. Marshall, 1–21. Bloomington: Indiana University Press, 2001.

Maxwell, David. "The Durawall of Faith: Pentecostal Spirituality in Neo-Liberal Zimbabwe." *Journal of Religion in Africa* 35, no.1 (2005): 4–31.

Mensah, Joseph. "Religious Transnationalism among Ghanaian Immigrants in Toronto: A Binary Logistic Regression Analysis." *The Canadian Geographer* 52, no.3 (2008): 309–30.

Mensah, Joseph, Christopher J. Williams, and Edna Aryee. "Gender, Power, and Religious Transnationalism among the African Diaspora in Canada." *African Geographical Review* 32, no.2 (2013): 151–71.

Meyer, Birgit. "'Make a Complete Break with the Past.' Memory and Post-Colonial Modernity in Ghanaian Pentecostalist Discourse." *Journal of Religion in Africa* 28, no.3 (1998): 316–49. https://doi.org/10.2307/1581573.

Norris, Pippa, and Ronald Inglehart. *Sacred and Secular: Religion And Politics Worldwide*. Cambridge/ New York: Cambridge University Press, 2004.

Nyamnjoh, Henrietta. "Information and Communication Technology and Its Impact on Transnational Migration: The Case of Senegalese Boat Migrants." In *SideWays: Mobile Margins and the Dynamics of Communication in Africa*, edited by Mirjam de Bruijn, 159–77. Mankon, Bamenda, Cameroon: Langaa, 2013.

———. "Penetrating the Unseen": The Role of Spiritual Practices in the Senegalese Boat Migration Process." In *The Public Face of African New Religious Movements in Diaspora: Imagining the 'Other,'* 191–213. England: Ashgate, 2014.

Nyamnjoh, Henrietta M. "Navigating 'Ngunda'/'Adoro' and Negotiating Economic Uncertainty amongst Mobile Cameroonian Migrants in Cape Town (South Africa)." *Critical African Studies* 9, no.2 (2017): 241–60. https://doi.org/1 0.1080/21681392.2017.1340846.

———. "'When Are You Going to Change Those Stones to Phones'? Appropriation of Social Media by Pentecostal Churches in Cape Town," n.d. (In Press).

Onyinah, Opoku. "God's Grace, Healing and Suffering." *International Review of Missions* 95, no.376/377 (2006): 117–27.

Payne-Jackson, A. "Spiritual Illness and Healing: 'If the Lord Wills.'" In *Faith, Health, and Healing in African American Life*, edited by Stephanie Y. Mitchem and Emilie M. Townes. Westport: Praeger, 2008.

Perkins. *Jesus as Teacher*. Cambridge, England; New York: Cambridge University Press, 1990.

Pype, Katrien, S. van Wolputte, and A. Melice. "The Interdependence of Mobility and Faith: An Introduction." *Canadian Journal of African Studies* 46, no.3 (2012): 355–65.

Schiller, Nina Glick, Linda Basch, and Cristina Szanton Blanc. "From Immigrant to Transmigrant: Theorizing Transnational Migration." *Anthropological Quarterly* 68, no.1 (1995): 48–63.

Schonig, Jordan. "The Trinity Broadcasting Network: Satellites Spreading More Than the Gospel." Paper. University of California - Irvine, 2006.

Stolz, Jörg. "'All Things Are Possible': Towards a Sociological Explanation of Pentecostal Miracles and Healings." *Sociology of Religion* 72, no.4 (2011): 456–82.

Van Dijk, R.A. "From Camp to Encompassment: Discourses of Transsubjectivity in the Ghanaian Pentecostal Diaspora." *Journal of Religion in Africa* XXVII, no.2 (1997): 135–59.

Vásquez, Manuel A. "The Global Portability of Pneumatic Christianity: Comparing African and Latin American Pentecostalisms." *African Studies* 68, no.2 (August 2009): 273–86. https://doi.org/10.1080/00020180903109664.

Yang, Fenggang, and Helen Rose Ebaugh. "Transformations in New Immigrant Religions and Their Global Implications." *American Sociological Review* 66, no.2 (2001): 269–88. https://doi.org/10.2307/2657418.

CHAPTER 10

FROM "NEIGHBOURHOOD" TO "PROXIMITY": AN OPPORTUNITY FOR HUMAN FULFILLMENT

Fabio Baggio

And now a lawyer stood up and, to test him, asked, "Master, what must I do to inherit eternal life?" He said to him, "What is written in the Law? What is your reading of it?" He replied, "You must love the Lord your God with all your heart, with all your soul, with all your strength, and with all your mind, and your neighbour as yourself." Jesus said to him, "You have answered right, do this and life is yours." But the man was anxious to justify himself and said to Jesus, "And who is my neighbour?" (Luke 10:25–29).

This text introduces the famous parable of the Good Samaritan, the starting point of the reflection I would like to propose as my contribution. Unfortunately, the English language does not do justice to the richness of the original Greek term πλησίον, which is the most usual translation of the Jewish word *rēa* in the LXX version of the Bible. Depending on the different contexts, *rēa* means "friend" or "companion" or "one similar to me" or "one of my kind" or simply "another." When connected to "respect" or "love," *rēa* usually means "the other of my kind who happens to be near to me."[1] The question of the lawyer—"And who is my neighbor?"—refers to a legalistic dispute concerning who should be considered a *rēa* to be loved, since it was generally assumed that the Jewish law—including the commandment of love—should apply only to members of the people of the covenant. "A man was going down from Jerusalem to Jericho" (Luke 10:30): not specifying the identity of the poor traveller to be

---

[1]   G. Johannes Botterweck, Helmer Ringgren, and Heinz-Josef Fabry, *Theological Dictionary of the Old Testament,* Vol.XIII, Annotated edition (Grand Rapids, Mich: Eerdmans, 2004).

loved, Jesus's answer enhances the scope of *rēa* by including all members of humankind.[2] And the final question at the end of the parable—"Which of these three do you think was a neighbor to the man who fell into the hands of robbers?" (Luke 10:36)—totally changes the perspective of the lawyer, since what really matters is not who is the *rēa* (one of my kind) to be loved, but who is able to be *rēa* (friend and companion) to the other in need.

From this perspective, it is possible to understand the difference between "neighborhood" and "proximity," which constitutes the core of my reflection. Neighborhood can be defined as the quality or state of being located near to one another. It does not imply any movement or active attitude. It simply refers to a geographical nearness—a passive status that one can even fail to acknowledge. Proximity, instead, can be defined as the quality or state of being close to one another. It entails a movement toward the other, a decision to get near, to be close, which opens up to genuine personal encounter and mutual concern. These are all active attitudes. Once this distinction is accepted, one can justly argue that only "proximity" can contribute to the fulfilment of the relational dimension that is innate to every human being as well as the foundation of fraternity: "A lively awareness of our relatedness helps us to look upon and to treat each person as a true sister or brother; without fraternity it is impossible to build a just society and a solid and lasting peace."[3]

In ordinary life, proximity translates into a series of positive attitudes toward the other. The first is the acknowledgment of the person's presence, meaning that we have to recognize the existence and situation of the other. The failure to acknowledge leads to indifference and rejection. This is the experience of the priest and Levite, who, after seeing the poor man, didn't acknowledge him, but "passed by on the other side" (Luke 10:31–32). But acknowledgment requires more than "seeing": one has to "look at," exactly as done by the Samaritan who came upon the poor traveller after the two holy men. The recognition of the situation of the man on his path—stripped, beaten, and half dead—leads the Samaritan to have compassion. And all the following positive attitudes are consequences of compassion: going to him, bandaging his wounds, pouring on oil and wine (cf. Luke 10:33–34a).

At this point, the compassionate attitude of the Good Samaritan would have sufficed to respond to the anxious lawyer. However, the parable continues

---

[2]   Giuseppe De Virgilio and Angela Gionti, *Le parabole di Gesù. Itinerari: esegetico-esistenziale; pedagogico-didattico* (Il Pozzo di Giacobbe, 2007); Gérard Rossé, *Il Vangelo di Luca: Commento esegetico e teologico* (Roma: Città nuova editrice, 206 AD).

[3]   Pope Francis, "Message for the World Day of Peace 2014," *Libreria Editrice Vaticana*, 2013, http://w2.vatican.va/content/francesco/en/messages/peace/documents/papa-francesco_20131208_messaggio-xlvii-giornata-mondiale-pace-2014.html.

with another series of actions: "Then he put him on his own animal, brought him to an inn, and took care of him" (Luke 10:34b). With an extraordinary sense of responsibility, the Samaritan decides to "take charge" of the poor man beyond the "first aid" offered on the road. The encounter with him changes his travel plans: he has to stop in order to take care of the unfortunate man. And aware of his personal limitations, the Samaritan is able to engage an unknown person in the care, assuming the cost of such engagement: "The next day he took out two denarii and gave them to the innkeeper. 'Take care of him,' he said, 'and on my return I will repay you for any additional expense'" (Luke 10:35).

All the good actions of the Samaritan are a "natural" consequence of his first decision to acknowledge the situation of the *rēa* (the other); the encounter with the latter changed his life and offered an opportunity of personal fulfilment that he recognized and took advantage of, so to become *rēa* (friend and companion) of the unfortunate traveller. Through his acknowledgment, the Samaritan passed from neighborhood to proximity, enriching his life with a new significant relationship generated by a random—or better, a providential—encounter. At the same time, the life of the poor man is also transformed and fulfilled by the encounter with the Samaritan, through an enriching experience of acknowledgment, compassion, and loving care.

To continue my reflection, I have selected four different stories of migration, which tell how the encounter with the "other" has been conducive to the transition from neighborhood to proximity. Migrants' and locals' narratives contextualize the parable of the Good Samaritan. I have selected the stories according to their relevance to the four verbs which, according to Pope Francis, summarize the pastoral response of the Catholic Church to the challenges posed by contemporary migration. In his address to the participants in the International Forum on Migration and Peace, in February 2017, the Holy Father underlines "the urgency for a coordinated and effective response to these challenges," and clarifies that such "shared response may be articulated by four verbs: to welcome, to protect, to promote and to integrate."[4]

The stories are located in four different regions of the world, showing that the experience of proximity is relevant in very different cultural settings.

WELCOMING: THE STORY OF OSCAR

> What is needed is a change of attitude, to overcome indifference and to counter fears with a generous approach of welcoming those who knock at our doors. For those who flee conflicts and terrible persecutions, often trapped within the

---

4   Pope Francis, "Address to Participants in the International Forum on 'Migration and Peace,'" *Libreria Editrice Vaticana*, 2017, http://w2.vatican.va/content/francesco/en/speeches/2017/february/documents/papa-francesco_20170221_forum-migrazioni-pace.html.

grip of criminal organisations who have no scruples, we need to open accessible and secure humanitarian channels.[5]

Welcoming is the first verb. It directly refers to the need to put fraternity before rejection, overcoming indifference and thus welcoming those who flee from suffering, poverty, and wars. The "culture of indifference" should be replaced with the "culture of encounter" "capable of bringing down all the walls which still divide the world . . . . Where there is a wall, there is a closed heart. We need bridges, not walls!"[6] Building bridges means also providing accessible and safe routes to migrants and asylum seekers.

In recent years, the dangers of the Mediterranean routes, taken by hundreds of thousands of migrants and refugees, have led to opportunities for proximity between rescued people and their rescuers. The story of Oscar tells about one of these experiences.[7]

On the night of October 7, 2015 the sea was very rough, but Oscar, a Spanish lifeguard, decided to deploy his watercraft to rescue the passengers of a small boat that was sinking a few miles off Lesbos. When he reached the spot, dozens of Syrian migrants had already drowned. The boat was overturned and many people were screaming in the water. Oscar saw a little girl who was struggling to stay afloat. Her mother was trying her best to support the child. The lifeguard decided to rescue the child first, since she was the one most in need of help. Running through the waves, he took her to the large vessel nearby and, after taking her life jacket off, he handed her over to his colleagues. Then Oscar went back to rescue the mother, but it was too late. All were drowned. While going back to the big boat, Oscar prayed for the life of the girl, who had been transferred to the shore for emergency medication. When everything was over the doctors told Oscar that, despite all their efforts, the child had died.

The next morning Oscar found a life jacket under his watercraft: it was the life jacket of the little girl he was unable to save. He immediately realized that it was not there by chance. It was there to stand as a sign of a tragedy to be reported to the world, a sign of something that should never happen again. It was there as a reminder of the moral duty we all share to save as many lives as possible in our earthly journey.

---

5   Francis, "Address to Participants in the International Forum on 'Migration and Peace.'"

6   Francis, "Message for the World Day of Peace 2014."

7   Francesca Caferri, "Migranti, ecco di chi era il giubbotto di salvataggio mostrato da Papa Francesco," Repubblica.it, June 7, 2016, https://www.repubblica.it/esteri/2016/06/07/news/migranti_giubbotto_salvataggio_bambina_siriana_papa-141471684/.

Oscar understood that the encounter with that child had permanently changed his life. He decided to leave his job in Spain and fully dedicate himself to rescuing migrants and refugees and sensitizing the world about their drama.

Moved by the words and example of Pope Francis, Oscar decided to give the Holy Father the life jacket of the poor girl during an audience in St. Peter's Square. The pontiff accepted the gift and passed it on to the Migrant and Refugee Section of the Dicastery for the Promotion of Integral Human Development. That life jacket is now the sign of the work of the Section.

Oscar still doesn't know the name of the little girl nor where she is buried. Nonetheless, the encounter with the unnamed child changed his life forever. Since then Oscar has rescued thousands of migrants and refugees, established the NGO Pro-Activa Open Arms, and received the Catalan of the Year Award for 2015.[8]

The similarities between the parable of the Good Samaritan and the story of Oscar are striking. The Spanish lifeguard acknowledged the presence of the little girl, had compassion, and went to her. He took care of her, lifted her up, put her on his own means of transportation and brought her to the other vessel, entrusting her to the care of others. Unlike the parable, we know the continuation of the story and in the case of Oscar it is not a happy ending. Nonetheless, that providential experience of proximity was instrumental for a deep shift in Oscar's life. He realized that his human fulfilment is saving others' lives, all anonymous as the poor traveller of the parable. In every migrant and refugee whom he is able to rescue, Oscar sees the unnamed child he was unable to save and, most often, he succeeds in changing the end of the story.

PROTECTING: THE STORY OF MOLLY

> Millions of migrant workers, male and female—and among these particularly men and women in irregular situations—of those exiled and seeking asylum, and of those who are victims of trafficking. Defending their inalienable rights, ensuring their fundamental freedoms and respecting their dignity are duties from which no one can be exempted.[9]

The ethical principle of the respect for human rights has been codified in the Universal Declaration of Human Rights, in two related covenants—the International Covenant on Civil and Political Rights and the International Covenant on Economic, Social and Cultural Rights—and a good number of

---

[8]   ACN, "Pro-Refugee Activist Wins 2015 Catalan of the Year Award," accessed December 2, 2017, http://www.catalannews.com/society-science/item/pro-refugee-activist-wins-2015-catalan-of-the-year-award, http://www.catalannews.com/society-science/item/pro-refugee-activist-wins-2015-catalan-of-the-year-award.

[9]   Francis, "Address to Participants in the International Forum on 'Migration and Peace.'"

international conventions. Such rights are not "assigned"; they are "recognized" with respect to every person equally and inalienably. Declarations, covenants, and conventions state the inalienability and inviolability of the rights that belong to every single human being according to the principle of non-discrimination. Every migrant is a human person and possesses all codified rights, which must be respected in every circumstance. Protecting migrants' inalienable rights is a moral imperative, which should be translated into fair juridical instruments at both the international and national levels.[10]

The ethical principle of the protection of human dignity reflects the special position of each human being within the universe. The social doctrine of the Church grounds such dignity on the creation of all human beings in the "image of God" (Gen 1:27). "'Protecting' has to do with our duty to recognize and defend the inviolable dignity of those who flee real dangers in search of asylum and security, and to prevent their being exploited. [...] God does not discriminate: 'The Lord watches over the foreigner and sustains the orphan and the widow.'"[11]

In 2008, Molly, a US building manager, was a young wife, studying and working, pregnant with her first child. Living in one of the apartments she was managing, Molly witnessed a mass exodus of tenants over several months due to a series of traumatic experiences within the complex: drug deals, domestic and child abuse, bedbug infestations, and even a case of suicide. The owners decided then to offer the apartments to refugee families from Iraq, Iran, and Bhutan.

Molly immediately anticipated harder times. However, her vision changed when she saw the faces of the first families that arrived in the complex. The apartments were very simple and outdated, but judging by the happiness and excitement of the newcomers, it was as if these were luxury hotel suites. In the next few days, Molly realized that the refugees had come with nothing. Moved by compassion, she prepared a list of basic house and personal goods and published it in the "Items Wanted" section of the local classified advertisements. The response was overwhelming and people willing to help more knocked Molly's door.

Being the building manager, Molly would enter their apartment frequently, listen to their terrible stories and assist in their slow process of healing. She was particularly moved by a two-year-old girl who had escaped from Iraq with her parents and a baby sister. She suffered from a post-traumatic stress disorder due to a car bomb that had exploded near her house. She often awoke at night

10   Francis, "Address to Participants in the International Forum on 'Migration and Peace.'"
11   Francis, "Message for the World Day of Peace 2018," *Libreria Editrice Vaticana*, 2017, http://w2.vatican.va/content/francesco/en/messages/peace/documents/papa-francesco_20171113_messaggio-51giornatamondiale-pace2018.html.

screaming with fear. Her parents were taking care of her with disarming patience. Their resilience, love, and happiness have been the foundation of Molly's hope in the moments of darkness that she too has had to face in recent years.[12]

Beyond her initial prejudice, Molly was able to acknowledge the presence of the refugee families and decided to pass from neighborhood to proximity. External circumstances had brought them together geographically in the vicinity, and this offered Molly the opportunity to get close and begin a real encounter with the newcomers. As the Good Samaritan, she was moved with compassion and chose to take care of them, providing them with what they needed. Just by being near to the traumatized girl, she contributed to her healing. Through her generous and sincere concern, Molly engaged other people in the care of the refugee families. The encounter with the young building manager provided the refugees a concrete opportunity to exercise their rights and restore their dignity. However benefits were mutual. The experience of proximity enriched Molly, fulfilling her relational dimension. The life lesson learned empowered Molly in terms of resilience and hope.

PROMOTING: THE STORY OF SUZANNE

> Promoting essentially means a determined effort to ensure that all migrants and refugees—as well as the communities which welcome them—are empowered to achieve their potential as human beings, in all the dimensions which constitute the humanity intended by the Creator.[13]

Personal and family development is an undeniable right of every human being. It must be guaranteed by ensuring the necessary conditions for its exercise, namely fair access to fundamental goods for all. The integral human development of migrants and refugees should be promoted in the countries of origin, transit and destination. "Development [...] must be guaranteed by ensuring the necessary conditions for its exercise, both in the individual and social context, providing fair access to fundamental goods for all people and offering the possibility of choice and growth."[14]

Most of the migrants and refugees are young, enterprising, and courageous, and ready to put their own lives at risk for a better future. They constitute a great potential for the transformation of the world, a providential opportunity

---

12 Molly Hogan, "Refugee Neighbors Changed My Life—On Common Ground," *Medium*, accessed December 2, 2017, https://medium.com/on-common-ground/nine-years-ago-i-ended-up-managing-an-apartment-complex-that-housed-refugees-who-would-now-be-6937b9c2a7bc.

13 Pope Francis, "Message for the 104th World Day of Migrants and Refugees 2018," *Libreria Editrice Vaticana*, 2017, http://w2.vatican.va/content/francesco/en/messages/migration/documents/papa-francesco_20170815_world-migrants-day-2018.html.

14 Francis, "Address to Participants in the International Forum on 'Migration and Peace.'"

for the development of all. The story of Suzanne tells of how migrants and refugees, when duly empowered and acknowledged, can make a difference in the world.[15]

Suzanne is a Malaysian lady, co-founder of the Picha Project, an enterprise that empowers marginalized groups in Malaysia through a sustainable food delivery and catering business. In 2016 Suzanne met Zaza, a Syrian chef who had to flee his country because of the war and had found refuge in Kuala Lumpur. Zaza had left everything in Syria. During his perilous travels he had almost lost his son, suffered cheating and abuse, and experienced homelessness and extreme poverty. Once his refugee status was confirmed, Zaza decided to join the Picha Project, and his industry, creativity, and dedication were outstanding. On Christmas, Zaza invited all his colleagues to dinner and didn't sleep for two nights in order to prepare the best food for them. He was well known for his generosity. He used to cook extra food for the driver, the cleaners, and the security guards. He frequently hosted homeless refugees in his house and gave them food. In February 2017, Zaza got sick and was admitted to the hospital. Despite his serious illness, he was always hopeful, making plans to distribute mandi rice for free to people around the mosque during the Ramadan period. Unfortunately Zaza never left the hospital and in May 2017, he passed away.

Suzanne was awarded the Chancellor's Gold Medal of the UCSI University three months later. At the convocation ceremony, she described Zaza as an inspirational model for all those who want to make a change.

The encounter between Zaza and Suzanne had been very meaningful for both. Zaza found an opportunity to unleash his potential and change his own story, that of his family and many other refugees. Suzanne was deeply inspired by this Syrian chef who taught her how to make great changes with very little. The passage from neighborhood to proximity was boosted by a simple dinner, where Suzanne was overwhelmed by the loving concern and selfless dedication of Zaza. The capacity of proximity of the Syrian chef was amazing, as shown by his connection with coworkers, the driver, the cleaners, the security guards, and the poor refugees. The story of Zaza and Suzanne presents a very interesting twist to the parable of Luke. The poor traveller, healed and empowered, becomes a Good Samaritan and inspires others to do the same.

INTEGRATING: THE STORY OF IAN

Integration, which is neither assimilation nor incorporation, is a two-way process, rooted essentially in the joint recognition of the other's cultural richness:

---

[15] Suzanne Ling, "The Refugee Who Changed My Life," Leaderonomics.com, September 1, 2017, https://leaderonomics.com/personal/refugee-changed-life.

it is not the superimposing of one culture over another, nor mutual isolation, with the insidious and dangerous risk of creating ghettoes. Concerning those who arrive and who are duty bound not to close themselves off from the culture and traditions of the receiving country, respecting above all its laws, the family dimension of the process of integration must not be overlooked.[16]

Integration, not to be confused with assimilation, is a process by which the contents of one's original culture are preserved and integrated with selected contents of another culture. Arising from international migration, integration is a two-way process. The local community is called to accept the cultural changes brought about by migrants, and the newly arrived are called to accept changes produced by their encounter with the host society. To be successful, this process entails the recognition of each other's cultural richness. With this as a goal, significant encounters with others should be promoted.[17]

Encounters with migrants and refugees offer special opportunities for intercultural enrichment. Meaningful relationships with others are necessary for one's own human fulfilment, because comparison with the identity of another helps one's own identity to become stronger and more clearly defined. Integration is an enriching process of intercultural dynamics that shape new community identities, each one of them being a step forward in the achievement of the plan of God for humankind. Integration "is a lengthy process that aims to shape societies and cultures, making them more and more a reflection of the multi-faceted gifts of God to human beings."[18]

Ian is an Australian businessman who serves as a volunteer with the Jesuit Social Service's English Language Support program in Sunshine. He learned of the program from a friend in the Rotary Club and decided to make use of his past experience in language teaching. On his first day of service at the Sunshine Library, Ian met his first two students: two brothers, asylum seekers on community detention. With their limited English they told their story to Ian. They had to flee from their country to survive, after experiencing torture and every kind of abuse. Their journey to Australia had been extremely long and full of hardship. Considering the confidential nature of such information, Ian felt honored by their trust.

As the weeks went by, the two brothers proved to be excellent learners, diligent in their homework and eager to do extra work. They would tell Ian about their little successes in adapting to the new environment. They were learning where to shop, how to book a check-up with the doctor, how to register at a

---

16   Francis, "Address to Participants in the International Forum on 'Migration and Peace.'"
17   Francis, "Address to Participants in the International Forum on 'Migration and Peace.'"
18   Francis, "Message for the 104th World Day of Migrants and Refugees 2018."

gym, and how to use the library and public transport. Upon being granted the proper documentation, one brother found a regular job while the other enrolled in a local university. Ian is convinced that while he gave his time and expertise to the two brothers, he received much more since he gained two friends.

The experience of encounter between Ian and the two brothers produced mutual benefits, since each side was able to enrich the other with their skills and life stories. With just a few English classes—but first and foremost with his welcoming attitude —Ian was able to pave the way for the brothers' integration into Australian society, providing helpful conditions for them to unleash their potential. The surprising trust of the two brothers enriched Ian's experience of friendship, adding to his meaningful relations. It is not that infrequent to meet asylum seekers and refugees in Australia and, like the Levite and priest of Luke's parable, Ian could have chosen to go on his way. Instead he accepted the invitation of his friend and acknowledged the presence of the two refugees. The encounter resulting from this acknowledgment marked the passage from neighborhood to proximity for all the people involved.

CONCLUSION

The stories of Oscar, Molly, Suzanne, and Ian are just a glimpse of hundreds of thousands of encounters between "locals" and newcomers that have deeply transformed the lives of all. Most such stories are untold and don't capture the attention of the media, which are too busy featuring stories of mistrust, fear, and cultural clashes. A substantially negative narrative on migration and the resulting perception of fear of the foreigner often obscures the opportunity offered by the presence of migrants and refugees to rediscover the supreme value of relationship, which God wanted as a distinctive trait of every human being and an essential condition to their fulfilment.

Instead, the stories that tell about outstretched hands, open doors, courageous rescues, generous hospitality, and meaningful friendships reveal how significant and beneficial is the passage from neighborhood to proximity for all people involved. In the parable of Luke, when the priest and Levite decided to pass by on the other side, they lost a great opportunity to "be more." The acknowledgment and care of the Samaritan was supremely beneficial to him, resulting in his personal growth.

Pope Francis's insistence on encouraging an authentic culture of encounter should be understood as part of his concern for promoting integral human development. Every meaningful encounter with the other is an opportunity to encounter the Other, God who is making himself present in the other, particularly in the needy (Matt 25:31–46).

The only way for individuals, families and societies to grow, the only way for the life of peoples to progress, is via the culture of encounter, a culture in which all have something good to give and all can receive something good in return. Others always have something to give me, if we know how to approach them in a spirit of openness and without prejudice.[19]

BIBLIOGRAPHY:

ACN. "Pro-Refugee Activist Wins 2015 Catalan of the Year Award." Accessed December 2, 2017. http://www.catalannews.com/society-science/item/pro-refugee-activist-wins-2015-catalan-of-the-year-award, http://www.catalannews.com/society-science/item/pro-refugee-activist-wins-2015-catalan-of-the-year-award.

Botterweck, G. Johannes, Helmer Ringgren, and Heinz-Josef Fabry. *Theological Dictionary of the Old Testament,* Vol.XIII. Annotated edition. Grand Rapids, Mich: Eerdmans, 2004.

Caferri, Francesca. "Migranti, ecco di chi era il giubbotto di salvataggio mostrato da Papa Francesco." Repubblica.it, June 7, 2016. https://www.repubblica.it/esteri/2016/06/07/news/migranti_giubbotto_salvataggio_bambina_siriana_papa-141471684/.

Pope Francis. "Address to Participants in the International Forum on 'Migration and Peace.'" *Libreria Editrice Vaticana*, 2017. http://w2.vatican.va/content/francesco/en/speeches/2017/february/documents/papa-francesco_20170221_forum-migrazioni-pace.html.

———. "Address to the Brazil's Leaders of Society." *Libreria Editrice Vaticana*, 2013. http://w2.vatican.va/content/francesco/en/speeches/2013/july/documents/papa-francesco_20130727_gmg-classe-dirigente-rio.html.

———. "Message for the 104th World Day of Migrants and Refugees 2018." *Libreria Editrice Vaticana*, 2017. http://w2.vatican.va/content/francesco/en/messages/migration/documents/papa-francesco_20170815_world-migrants-day-2018.html.

———. "Message for the World Day of Peace 2014." *Libreria Editrice Vaticana*, 2013. http://w2.vatican.va/content/francesco/en/messages/peace/documents/papa-francesco_20131208_messaggio-xlvii-giornata-mondiale-pace-2014.html.

---

[19]   Pope Francis, "Address to the Brazil's Leaders of Society," *Libreria Editrice Vaticana*, 2013, http://w2.vatican.va/content/francesco/en/speeches/2013/july/documents/papa-francesco_20130727_gmg-classe-dirigente-rio.html.

———. "Message for the World Day of Peace 2018." *Libreria Editrice Vaticana*, 2017. http://w2.vatican.va/content/francesco/en/messages/peace/documents/papa-francesco_20171113_messaggio-51giornatamondiale-pace2018.html.

Hogan, Molly. "Refugee Neighbors Changed My Life—On Common Ground," *Medium*. Accessed December 2, 2017. https://medium.com/on-common-ground/nine-years-ago-i-ended-up-managing-an-apartment-complex-that-housed-refugees-who-would-now-be-6937b9c2a7bc.

Ling, Suzanne. "The Refugee Who Changed My Life." Leaderonomics.com, September 1, 2017. https://leaderonomics.com/personal/refugee-changed-life.

Rossé, Gérard. *Il Vangelo di Luca: Commento esegetico e teologico*. Roma: Città nuova editrice, 206 AD.

Virgilio, Giuseppe De, and Angela Gionti. *Le parabole di Gesù. Itinerari: esegetico-esistenziale; pedagogico-didattico*. Il Pozzo di Giacobbe, 2007.

PART IV

MIGRATION, PUBLIC POLICY
AND CIVIL DISCOURSE:
THEOLOGICAL FORMULATIONS

CHAPTER 11

XENOPHILIA OR XENOPHOBIA:
TOWARD A THEOLOGY OF MIGRATION

Luis N. Rivera-Pagán

"I have Dutch, nigger, and English in me,

and either I'm nobody, or I'm a nation."

The Schooner 'Flight'
Derek Walcott[1]

"To survive the Borderlands

You must live sin fronteras

Be a crossroads."

Borderlands/La Frontera: The New Mestiza
Gloria Anzaldúa[2]

A HOMELESS MIGRANT ARAMEAN

The Bible's first confession of faith begins with a story of pilgrimage and migration: "A wandering Aramean was my ancestor; he went down into Egypt and lived there as an alien" (Deut 26:5). We might ask: Did that "wandering Aramean" and his children have the proper documents to reside in Egypt?

---

[1]   Derek Walcott, "The Schooner 'Flight,'" in his *Collected Poems, 1948-1984* (New York: Farrar, Straus and Giroux, 1986), 346.
[2]   Gloria Anzaldúa, *Borderlands/La Frontera: The New Mestiza* (San Francisco: Aunt Lute Books, 1999, orig. 1987), 217.

Were they "illegal aliens"? Did he and his children have the proper Egyptian social security credentials? Did they speak properly the Egyptian language?

We know at least that he and his children were strangers in the midst of a powerful empire, and that as such they were both exploited and feared. This is the fate of many immigrants. In their reduced circumstances they are usually compelled to perform the least prestigious and most strenuous kinds of menial work. Yet, at the same time they awaken the schizophrenic paranoia typical of empires, powerful and yet fearful of the stranger, of the "other," especially if that stranger resides within its frontiers and becomes populous. More than half a century ago, Franz Fanon brilliantly described the peculiar gaze of so many white French people at the growing presence of Black Africans and Caribbeans in their national midst.[3] Scorn and fear are entwined in that stare.

The biblical creedal story continues: "When the Egyptians treated us harshly and afflicted us, by imposing hard labor on us, we cried to the . . . God of our ancestors; the Lord heard our voice and saw our affliction . . . and our oppression" (Deut 26:6). So important was this story of migration, slavery, and liberation for the biblical people of Israel that it became the core of an annual liturgy of remembrance and gratitude. The already quoted statement of faith was to be solemnly recited every year in the thanksgiving liturgy of the harvest festival. It reenacted the wounded memory of the afflictions and humiliations suffered by an immigrant people, strangers in the midst of an empire; the recollection of their hard and arduous labor, of the contempt and disdain that is so frequently the fate of the stranger and foreigner who possesses a different skin pigmentation, language, religion, or culture. But it was also the memory of the events of liberation when God heard the dolorous cries of the suffering immigrants. And the remembrance of another kind of migration, in search of a land where they might live in freedom, peace, and righteousness, a land they might call theirs.

We might ask: Who today might be the wandering Arameans and what nation might represent Egypt these days, a strong but fearful empire?

DILEMMAS AND CHALLENGES OF MIGRATION

The Latino/Hispanic population has significantly increased in the United States. In 1975, little more than 11 million Hispanics made up just over 5 percent of the US inhabitants. Today they number approximately nearly 47 million, around 15 percent of the nation, its largest minority group. Recent projections estimate that by 2050 the Latino/Hispanic share of the US population might be between 26 percent and 32 percent. This demographic growth has become a

---

[3]   Franz Fanon, *Peau Noir, Masques Blancs* (Paris: Éditions du Seuil, 1952).

complex political and social debate for it highlights sensitive and crucial issues, like national identity and compliance with the law. It also threatens to unleash a new phase in the sad and long history of American racism and xenophobia,[4] one that, following the Sri Lankan novelist Ambalavaner Sivanandan, might be termed "xeno-racism."[5]

Two concerns have become important topics of public discourse:

1. What should be done regarding the growth of unauthorized migration? Possibly about a quarter of the Hispanic/Latino adults are unauthorized immigrants. For a society that prides itself of its law and order tradition, this represents a serious breach of its juridical structure.

2. What does this dramatic increase in the Latino/Hispanic population convey for the cultural and linguistic traditions of the United States, its mores and styles of collective self-identification?

Unfortunately, the conversation about these difficult issues takes place in an environment clouded by the gradual development of xenophobic attitudes. There are signs of an increasing hostile reaction to what the Mexican American writer Richard Rodríguez has termed "the browning of America."[6] One can clearly recognize this mind-set in the frequent use of the derogatory term "illegal alien." As if the illegality would define not a specific delinquency, but the entire being of the migrant. We all know the dire and sinister connotations that "alien" has in popular American culture, thanks in part to the sequence of four *Alien* (1979, 1986, 1992, and 1997) films with Sigourney Weaver fighting back atrocious creatures.[7]

Let me briefly mention some key elements of this emerging xenophobia:

1) The spread of fear regarding the so-called "broken borders," the possible proliferation of Global South epidemic diseases, and the alleged increase of criminal activities by undocumented immigrants.[8] A shadowy sinister specter is created in the minds of the public: the image of the intruder and threatening "other." These days that fateful specter is promoted by the president of the United States himself.

---

[4]   Pyong Gap Min, ed., *Encyclopedia of Racism in the United States* (3 vols.) (Westport, Conn.: Greenwood Press, 2005). A classic text on American nativism is John Higham, *Strangers in the Land: Patterns of American Nativism, 1860-1925* (New York: Atheneum, 1968).

[5]   As quoted in Susanna Snyder, *Asylum-Seeking, Migration and Church* (Farnham, Surrey, UK/Burlington, VT: Ashgate, 2012), 93.

[6]   Richard Rodríguez, *Brown: The Last Discovery of America* (New York: Viking, 2002).

[7]   See also Patrick J. Buchanan's book, with the inflammatory title, *State of Emergency: The Third World Invasion and Conquest of America* (New York: Thomas Dunne Books/St. Martin's Press, 2008).

[8]   David Leonhardt, "Truth, Fiction and Lou Dobbs," *The New York Times*, May 30 2007, C1.

2) The xenophobic stance intensifies the post 9/11 attitudes of fear and phobia regarding the strangers, those people who are here but who do not seem to belong here. Surveillance of immigration is now located under the Department of Homeland Security. This administrative merger links two basically unrelated problems: threat of terrorist activities and unauthorized migration.

3) Though US racism and xenophobia have had traditionally different targets—people with African ancestry the first (be they slaves or free citizens), marked by their dark skin pigmentation; foreign-born immigrants the second, distinguished by their particular language, religiosity, and collective memory—in the case of Latin American immigrants both nefarious prejudices converge and coalesce[9] (as was also the case with the nineteenth century Chinese indentured servants, which led to the infamous 1882 Chinese Exclusion Act).[10]

4) There has been a significant increase of anti-immigrants aggressive groups. According to a report by the Southern Poverty Law Center, "'nativist extremist groups'—organizations that go beyond mere advocacy of restrictive immigration policy to actually confront or harass suspected immigrants—jumped from 173 groups in 2008 to 309 in 2009. Virtually all of these vigilante groups have appeared since the spring of 2005."[11]

5) Proposals coming from the White House, Congress, states, and counties have tended to be excessively punitive. Some examples are:

   a. A projected wall along the Mexican border (compare it to Eph 2:14, "Christ . . . has broken down the dividing wall").

9   George M. Fredrickson, *Diverse Nations: Explorations in the History of Racial & Ethnic Pluralism* (Boulder & London: Paradigm Publishers, 2006).
10   Stuart Creighton Miller, *The Unwelcome Immigrant: The American Image of the Chinese, 1775-1882* (Berkeley: University of California Press, 1969).
11   Mark Potok, "Rage in the Right," *Intelligence Report*, Southern Poverty Law Center, Spring 2010, no.137, accessed in www.splcenter.org/get-informed/intelligence-report/browse-all-issues/2010/spring/rage-on-the-right.

b. The criminalization as felony not only of illegal immigration but also of any action by legal residents that might provide assistance to undocumented immigrants.[12]

c. Draconian legislation prescribing mandatory detention and deportation of non-citizens, even for alleged minor violations of law. Arizona's notorious and contentious Senate Bill 1070 is a prime example of this infamous trend. It has been followed by Alabama's even harsher anti-immigrants legislation (House Bill 56), soon to be cloned by other states.

d. Proposed legislation to curtail access to public services (health, education, police protection, legal services, drivers' licenses) by undocumented migrants.

e. Some prominent right-wing politicians have suggested the possibility of revising the first section of the fourteenth amendment of the US constitution.[13] Their purpose, apparently, is to deprive the children of immigrants of their constitutional right of citizenship. A campaign against the so-called "anchor babies" has been part and parcel of the most strident xenophobic campaign in years.

f. A significant intensification of raids, detentions, and deportations. This is transforming several migrant communities into a clandestine underclass of fear and dissimulation. Some legal scholars have even suggested that the United States is becoming a "deportation nation."[14] It brings to mind the infamous Mexican deportation program, authorized in 1929 by President Herbert Hoover. That program led, according to some scholars, to the forceful deportation

[12] This was one of the most controversial sections of the "Border Protection, Anti-terrorism, and Illegal Immigration Control Act of 2005" (H.R. 4437), a bill approved by Congress but not by the Senate. Several religious leaders expressed their objection to it. The Los Angeles Roman Catholic cardinal archbishop Roger Mahoney, in an article published March 22, 2006 in *The New York Times* under the title "Called by God to Help," asserted that "denying aid to a fellow human being violates a law with a higher authority than Congress—the law of God" and warned that the priests of his diocese might disobey the bill in case it would be finally approved.

[13] The first sentence of that section reads as follows: "All persons born or naturalized in the United States, and subject to the jurisdiction thereof, are citizens of the United States and of the State wherein they reside." The second sentence of that same first section has also become the center of attention of another key dispute in the US: whether its tenets of "due process of law" and "equal protection of the laws" preclude any legislative prohibition of gay marriage.

[14] Daniel Kanstroom, *Deportation Nation: Outsiders in American History* (Cambridge, MA: Harvard University Press, 2007).

195

of approximately one million people of Mexican descent, many of whom were, in fact, American citizens.[15]

g. Congress has been unable to approve the Development, Relief and Education for Alien Minors Act (DREAM Act), that would provide conditional permanent residency to certain deportable foreign-born students who graduate from US high schools, are of good moral character, were brought to the United States illegally as minors, and have been in the country continuously for at least five years prior to the bill's enactment, if they complete two years in the military or at an academic institution of higher learning.

The xenophobia and scapegoating of the "stranger in our midst" has resulted in the chaotic condition that now plagues the immigration system in the United States, judicially, politically, and socially. All recent attempts to enact a comprehensive immigration reform have floundered thanks to the resistance of influential sectors that have been able to propagate efficaciously fear of the "alien."[16] The increasing support that such phobic anxiety against the "outsiders" within the frontiers of the nation seems to enjoy among substantial sectors of the American public brings to mind Alexis de Tocqueville's astute critical observation: "I know no country in which there is so little true independence of mind and freedom of discussion as in America . . . . In America, the majority raises very formidable barriers to the liberty of opinion."[17]

FROM A CLASH OF CIVILIZATIONS TO A CLASH OF CULTURES

In this social context tending toward xenophobia and racism, the late Professor Samuel P. Huntington wrote some important texts about what he perceived as a Hispanic/Latino threat to the cultural and political integrity of the United States. Huntington was chairman of Harvard's Academy for International and Area Studies, and cofounder of the journal *Foreign Policy*. He was also the

---

[15]   Abraham Hoffman, *Unwanted Mexican Americans in the Great Depression: Repatriation Pressures, 1929-1939* (Tucson: University of Arizona Press, 1974); Francisco Balderrama and Raymond Rodríguez, *Decade of Betrayal: Mexican Repatriation in the 1930s* (Albuquerque: University of New Mexico Press, 2006).

[16]   Matthew Soerens and Jenny Hwang provide a succinct and precise summary of several failed attempts to enact a comprehensive immigration legislative and juridical reform in their book, *Welcoming the Stranger: Justice, Compassion & Truth in the Immigration Debate* (Downers Grove, IL: IVP Books, 2009), 138–58.

[17]   Alexis de Tocqueville, *Democracy in America* (London: Oxford University Press, 1959, orig. 1835/1840), 192.

intellectual father of the theory of the "clash of civilizations,"[18] with disastrous consequences for the foreign policies of George W. Bush presidency.

In 2004, Huntington published an extended article in *Foreign Policy*, titled "The Hispanic Challenge,"[19] followed by a lengthy book, *Who are We? The Challenges to America's National Identity*.[20] The former prophet of an unavoidable civilizational abyss and conflict between the West and the Rest (specially the Islamic nations) became the proclaiming apostle of an emerging nefarious cultural conflict inside the United States. Immersed in a dangerous clash of civilizations *ad extra*, this messenger of doom prognosticated that the United States is also entering into a grievous clash of cultures *ad intra*.

American national identity seems a very complex issue for it deals with an extremely intricate and highly diverse history. But Huntington has, surprisingly, a simple answer: The United States is mainly identified by its "Anglo-Protestant culture" and not only by its liberal republican democratic political creed. It has been, according to this historical reconstruction, a nation of settlers rather than immigrants. The first British pioneers transported not only their bodies, but also their fundamental cultural and religious viewpoints, what Huntington designates as "Anglo-Protestant culture." In the formation of this collective identity, Christian devotion—the Congregational pilgrims, the Protestantism of dissent, the Evangelical Awakenings—has been meaningful and crucial. This national identity has also been forged by a long history of wars against a succession of enemies (from the Native Americans to the Islamic jihadists). There is a certain romantic nostalgia in Huntington's thesis, an emphasis on the foundations of American culture and identity, in their continuities rather than their evolutions and transformations.

But the main objective of Huntington is to underline the uncertainties of the present trends regarding his nation's collective self-understanding. After the dissolution of the Soviet threat, he perceives a significant neglect of the American national identity. National identity seems to require the image of a dangerous adversary, what he terms the "perfect enemy." The prevailing trend is supposedly one of a notable decline and loss of intensity and salience of US awareness of national identity and loyalty.

Then, supposedly, emerges the sinister challenge of the Latin American migratory invasion. It is not similar to previous migratory waves. Its contiguity,

---

18   Samuel P. Huntington, "The Clash of Civilizations?" *Foreign Affairs*, Summer 1993, 72/3, 22–49; *The Clash of Civilizations and the Remaking of World Order* (New York: Simon & Schuster, 1996).

19   Samuel P. Huntington, "The Hispanic Challenge," *Foreign Policy*, no.141 (2004): 30-45.

20   Samuel P. Huntington, *Who Are We?: The Challenges to America's National Identity,* (New York: Simon & Schuster, 2004)

intensity, lack of education, territorial memory, constant return to the homeland, preservation of language, retention of homeland culture, national allegiance and citizenship, its distance to Anglo-Protestant culture, and its alleged absence of a Puritan work ethic makes it unique and unprecedented. This immigration constitutes, according to Huntington, "a major potential threat to the cultural and possibly political integrity of the United States."[21] This Harvard professor has discovered and named America's newest "perfect enemy," the Latin American immigrant!

Huntington's discomfiture is intense regarding the encroachment of Spanish in the American public life. He calls attention that now in some states more children are ominously christened José rather than Michael. This increasing public bilingualism threatens to fragment the US linguistic integrity. Linguistic bifurcation becomes a veritable menacing Godzilla. He neglects altogether the economic causes for the Latin American migration—its financial and social benefits both for the sending (remittances)[22] and the receiving nations (lower wages for manual jobs).[23] He does not seem to have any concern regarding the process whereby they become new *douloi* and *μέτοικοι*, helots at the margins of society, in a kind of social apartheid, cleaning stores, cooking meals, doing dishes, cutting grass, picking tomatoes and oranges, painting buildings, washing cars, staying out of the way.

Obfuscated by Huntington are the consequences of the present trend among metropolitan Global South diasporas toward holding dual citizenship. An increasing number of Latin American nations now recognize and promote double citizenship, a process that leads to multiple national and cultural loyalties and to what Huntington classifies, with a disdainful and pejorative tone, "ampersand peoples." Dual citizenship, he rightly recognizes, leads to dual national loyalties and identities. Huntington perceives this trend toward dual citizenship and national fidelity as a violation and disruption of the Oath of Allegiance and the Pledge of Allegiance, essential components of the secular liturgy in the acquisition of the United States citizenship.

---

[21]   Huntington, "The Hispanic Challenge," 33; Huntington, *Who are We?*, 243.

[22]   Dilip Ratha, "Dollars Without Borders: Can the Global Flow of Remittances Survive the Crisis?", *Foreign Affairs*, October 16, 2009, "[R]emittances are proving to be one of the more resilient pieces of the global economy in the downturn, and will likely play a large role in the economic development and recovery of many poor countries," http://www.foreignaffairs.com/articles/65448/dilip-ratha/dollars-without-borders.

[23]   This is a serious flaw in many ethnocentric critiques of immigration issues according to Francisco Javier Blázquez Ruiz, "Derechos humanos, inmigración, integración," in José A. Zamora (coord.), *Ciudadanía, multiculturalidad e inmigración* (Navarra, España: Editorial Verbo Divino, 2003), 86, 93.

He seems to suggest stricter policies regarding illegal migration, stronger measures to enforce cultural assimilation of the legal immigrants, and the rejection of dual citizenship. This perspective would not only be utterly archaic; it might also become the theoretical underground for a new wave of xenophobic white nativism.[24] The train has already left that outdated station. What is now required is a wider acceptance and enjoyment of multiple identities and loyalties and, if religious compassion truly matters, a deeper concern regarding the burdens and woes of displaced peoples. The time has come to prevail over the phobia of diversity and to learn how to appreciate and enjoy the dignity of difference.[25] For, as Dale Irvin has asserted, "the actual world that we are living in . . . is one of transnational migrations, hyphenated and hybrid identities, cultural conjunctions and disjunctions."[26]

Do the Latino/Hispanics truly represent "a major potential threat to the cultural and possibly political integrity of the United States," as Huntington has argued? Whether that is something to lament, denounce, or celebrate depends on the eyes of the beholder. Maybe, just maybe, it would not be such a negative historical outcome if the Latino immigrants prove in fact to be that dramatic and decisive "major potential threat to the cultural and political integrity of the United States."[27]

---

[24] A substantially more nuanced and intellectually complex analysis of the different aspects of immigration in the United States is provided by Alejandro Portes and Rubén G. Rumbaut, *Immigrant America: A Portrait* (third edition revised, expanded and updated) (Berkeley, CA: University of California Press, 2006).

[25] Jonathan Sacks, *The Dignity of Difference: How to Avoid the Clash of Civilizations* (London: Continuum, 2003).

[26] Dale Irvin, "The Church, the Urban and the Global: Mission in an Age of Global Cities," *International Bulletin of Missionary Research,*" 33, no.4 (October 2009), 181.

[27] Yet, at least Huntington recognizes the critical urgency of the substantial Latin American immigration for the cultural and political integrity of the United States. Cornel West, in another key text published in 2004, remains cloistered in the traditional White/Black American racial dichotomy and is unable to perceive the salience and perils of xenophobia and nativism as a chauvinistic reply to immigration. Cornel West, *Democracy Matters: Winning the Fight Against Imperialism* (New York: Penguin Press, 2004). Is there any possible conceptual manner of bridging the concerns of the African American ghettoes, struggling against color-coded racism, and the growing Latino/Hispanic barrios, facing an insidious cultural disdain? Both communities suffer from lack of recognition of their genuine human dignity, which should imply more than mere tolerance for their distinctive cultural traits, of socio-economic deprivation and political powerlessness. An always complex and difficult to achieve dialectics between cultural recognition and social-economic redistribution might be the key clue for solving this dilemma. Cf. Nancy Fraser and Axel Honneth, *Redistribution or Recognition? A Political-Philosophical Exchange* (London & New York: Verso, 2003). Ernesto Laclau and Chantal Mouffe emphasize this dialectics in the preface to the new edition of their famed text, *Hegemony and Socialist Strategy: Toward a Radical Democratic Politics*, 2nd ed. (London: Verso, 2001), xviii: "One of the central tenets of *Hegemony and Socialist Strategy* is the need to create a chain of equivalence among the various democratic struggles against subordination. . . to tackle issues of both 'redistribution' and 'recognition.'"

XENOPHILIA: TOWARD A BIBLICAL THEOLOGY OF MIGRATION

Migration and xenophobia are serious social quandaries. But they also convey urgent challenges to the ethical sensitivity of religious people and persons of good will. The first step we need to take is to perceive this issue from the perspective of the immigrants, to pay cordial (that is, deep from our hearts) attention to their stories of suffering, hope, courage, resistance, ingenuity, and, as so frequently happens in the wildernesses of the American Southwest, death.[28] Many of the unauthorized migrants have become *nobodies*, in the apt title of John Bowe's book, *Disposable People*, in Kevin Bales' poignant phrase, or as Zygmunt Bauman poignantly reminds us, *wasted lives*.[29] They are the Empire's new μέτοιχοι, *douloi*, modern servants. Their dire existential situation cannot be grasped without taking into consideration the upsurge in global inequalities in these times of unregulated international financial hegemony. For many human beings, the excruciating alternative is between misery in their third-world homeland and marginalization in the rich West/North, both fateful destinies intimately linked together.[30] The situation has painfully aggravated, with tens of thousands of children and teenagers fleeing poverty and violence from El Salvador, Honduras, Guatemala, or Mexico, daring to survive the gangs of human traffickers, the so-called "coyotes," to, at the end of that arduous and dangerous pilgrimage, face detention, contempt, and deportation in the southern frontier of the United States. Their dreadful situation has truly become a humanitarian crisis of epic dimensions.[31]

Will the Latino/Hispanics, during these early decades of the twenty-first century, become the new national scapegoats? Do they truly represent "a major

---

[28] See the poignant article by Jeremy Harding, "The Deaths Map," *London Review of Books*, 33, no.20, October 20, 2011: 7-13.

[29] John Bowe, *Nobodies: Modern American Slave Labor and the Dark Side of the New Global Economy* (New York: Random House, 2007); Kevin Bales, *Disposable People: New Slavery in the Global Economy* (Berkeley, CA: University of California Press, 2004); Zygmunt Bauman, *Wasted Lives: Modernity and Its Outcasts* (Cambridge: Polity, 2004).

[30] Branko Milanovic, "Global Inequality and the Global Inequality Extraction Ratio: The Story of the Past Two Centuries," (The World Bank, Development Research Group, Poverty and Inequality Group, September 2009); Peter Stalker, *Workers Without Frontiers: The Impact of Globalization on International Migration* (Geneva: International Labor Organization, 2000).

[31] Elizabeth Kennedy, *No Childhood Here: Why Central American Children are Leaving Their Homes* (Perspectives on Immigration: American Immigration Council, July 2014), accessed July 5, 2014, www.immigrationpolicy.org/sites/default/files/docs/no_childhood_here_why_central_american_children_are_fleeing_their_homes_final.pdf, *Mission to Central America: The Flight of Unaccompanied Children to the United States*, Report of the Committee on Migration of the United States Conference of Catholic Bishops, November 2013, accessed July 5, 2014, www.usccb.org/about/migration-policy/upload/Mission-To-Central-America-FINAL-2.pdf, and *Children in Danger: A Guide to the Humanitarian Challenge at the Border* (Immigration Policy Center, American Immigration Council, July 2014) accessed July 13, 2014, www.immigrationpolicy.org/special-reports/children-danger-guide-humanitarian-challenge-border.

potential threat to the cultural and political integrity of the United States"? This is a vital dilemma that the United States has up to now been unable to face and solve. We are not called, here and now, to solve it. But allow me, from my perspective as a Hispanic and Latin American Christian theologian, to offer some critical observations that might illuminate our way in this bewildering labyrinth.

We began this essay with the annual creedal and liturgical memory of a time when the people of Israel were aliens in the midst of an empire, a vulnerable community, socially exploited, and culturally scorned. It was the worst of times. It became also the best of times: the times of liberation and redemption from servitude. That memory shaped the sensitivity of the Hebrew nation regarding the strangers, the aliens, within Israel. Their vulnerability was a reminder of their own past helplessness as immigrants in Egypt, but also an ethical challenge to care for the foreigners inside Israel.[32]

Caring for the stranger became a key element of the Torah, the covenant of justice and righteousness between Yahweh and Israel. "When an alien resides with you in your land, you shall not oppress the alien. The alien who resides with you shall be to you as the citizen among you; you shall love the alien as yourself, for you were aliens in the land of Egypt: I am the Lord your God" (Lev 19:33f). "You shall not oppress a resident alien; you know the heart of an alien, for you were aliens in the land of Egypt" (Exod 23:9). "The Lord your God is God of gods . . . who executes justice to the orphan and the widow, and who loves the strangers, providing them food and clothing. You shall also love the stranger, for you were strangers in the land of Egypt" (Deut 10:17ff). "You shall not withhold the wages of poor and needy laborers, whether other Israelites or aliens who reside in your land in one of your towns . . . . You shall not deprive a resident alien . . . . Remember that you were a slave in Egypt and the Lord redeemed you from there" (Deut 24:14, 17–18). The twelve curses that, according to Deuteronomy 27, Moses instructs the Israelites to liturgically proclaim at their entrance to the promised land, include the trilogy of orphans, widows, and strangers as privileged recipients of collective solidarity and compassion: "Cursed be anyone who deprives the alien, the orphan, and the widow of justice" (Deut 27:19).

The prophets constantly chastised the ruling elites of Israel and Judah for their social injustice and their oppression of the vulnerable people. Who were those vulnerable persons? The poor, the widows, the orphans, and the foreigners. "The princes of Israel . . . have been bent on shedding blood . . . the alien

---

[32]   Cf. José E. Ramírez Kidd, *Alterity and Identity in Israel: The "ger" in the Old Testament* (Berlin: De Gruyter, 1999).

residing within you suffers extortion; the orphan and the widow are wronged in you" (Ezek 22:6f). After condemning with the harshest words possible the apathy and inertia of temple religiosity in Jerusalem, the prophet Jeremiah, in the name of God, commands the alternative: "Thus says the Lord: Act with justice and righteousness . . . . And do no wrong or violence to the alien, the orphan, and the widow" (Jer 7:6). He went on to reprove the king of Judah with harsh admonishing words: "Thus says the Lord: Act with justice and righteousness and deliver from the hand of the oppressor anyone who has been robbed. And do no wrong or violence to the alien, the orphan, and the widow . . . . If you do not heed these words, I swear by myself, says the Lord, that this house shall become a desolation" (Jer 22:3,5). The prophet paid a costly price for those daring admonitions.

The divine command to care for the stranger was the matrix of an ethics of hospitality. As evidence of his righteousness, Job affirms that "the stranger has not lodged in the street" for he always "opened the doors of my house" to board the foreigner (Job 31:32). It was the violation of the divinely sanctioned code of hospitality that led to the dreadful destruction of Sodom (Gen 19:1–25).[33] The perennial temptation is xenophobia. The divine command, enshrined in the Torah is xenophilia—the love for those whom we usually find very difficult to love: the strangers, the aliens, the foreign sojourners.[34]

The command to love the sojourners and resident foreigners in the land of Israel emerges from two foundations. One has already been mentioned—the Israelites had been sojourners and resident foreigners in a land not of theirs ("for you were strangers in the land of Egypt") and should, therefore, be sensitive to the complex existential stress of communities living in the midst of a nation whose dominant inhabitants speak a different language, venerate dissimilar deities, share distinct traditions, and commemorate different historical founding events. Love and respect toward the stranger and the foreigner is thus, in these biblical texts, construed as an essential dimension of Israel's national identity. It belongs to the essence and nature of the people of God.

A second source for the command of care toward the immigrant foreigner is that it corresponds to God's way of being and acting in history: "The Lord

---

[33] Sodom's transgression of the hospitality code was part of a culture of corruption and oppression, according to Ezekiel 16:49—"This was the guilt of your sister Sodom: she and her daughters had pride, excess of food, and prosperous ease, but did not aid the poor and needy." The homophobic construal of Sodom's sinfulness, which led to the term sodomy, is a later (mis) interpretation. Cf. Mark D. Jordan, *The Invention of Sodomy in Christian Theology* (Chicago: The University of Chicago Press, 1997).

[34] José Cervantes Gabarrón, "El inmigrante en las tradiciones bíblicas," in Zamora, *Ciudadanía, multiculturalidad e inmigración*, 262.

watches over the strangers" (Ps 146:9a),[35] "God . . . executes justice for the orphan and the widow and loves the strangers" (Deut 10:18). God takes sides in history, favoring the most vulnerable: the poor, the widows, the orphans, and the strangers. "I will be swift to bear witness. . . against those who oppress the hired workers in their wages, the widow, and the orphan, against those who thrust aside the alien, and do not fear me, says the Lord of hosts" (Mal 3:5). Solidarity with the marginalized and excluded corresponds to God's being and acting in history.

How comforting would it be to stop right here, with these fine biblical texts of xenophilia, of love for the stranger. But the Bible happens to be a disconcerting book. It contains a disturbing multiplicity of voices, a perplexing polyphony that frequently complicates our theological hermeneutics. Regarding many key ethical dilemmas, we find in the Bible often times not only different, but also conflictive, even contradictory perspectives. Too frequently we jump from our contemporary labyrinths into a darker and sinister scriptural maze.

In the Hebrew Bible, we also discover statements with a distinct and distasteful flavor of nationalist xenophobia. Leviticus 25 is usually read as the classic text for the liberation of the Israelites who have fallen into indebted servitude. Indeed, it is, as its famed tenth verse so eloquently manifests: "Proclaim liberty throughout all the land unto all the inhabitants thereof."[36] But it also contains a nefarious distinction: "As for the male and female slaves whom you may have, it is from the nations around you that you may acquire male and female slaves. You may also acquire them from among the aliens residing with you, and from their families . . . and they may be your property . . . . These you may treat as slaves" (Lev 25:44–46). And what about the terrifying fate imposed upon the foreign wives (and their children) in the epilogues of Ezra and Nehemiah? They are thrown away, exiled, as sources of impurity and contamination of the faith and culture of the people of God.[37] In the process of reconstructing Jerusalem, "Ezra and Nehemiah demonstrate the growing presence of xenophobia," as the Palestinian theologian Naim Ateek has highlighted.

---

35. This pericope deserves to be quoted in its entirety: "The Lord sets the prisoners free; the Lord opens the eyes of the blind. The Lord lifts up those who are bowed down; the Lord loves the righteous. The Lord watches over the strangers; he upholds the orphan and the widow, but the way of the wicked he brings to ruin" (Ps 146:8–9).

36. This text is inscribed in Philadelphia's Liberty Bell, a venerated US icon.

37. For a sharp critical analysis of the xenophobic and misogynist theology underlining Ezra and Nehemiah, see Elisabeth Cook Steicke, *La mujer como extranjera en Israel: Estudio exegético de Esdras 9-10* (San José, Costa Rica: Editorial SEBILA, 2011). Snyder contrasts what she terms "the ecology of fear," exemplified by the banishment of foreign wives (and their children) in Ezra and Nehemiah, with an "ecology of faith," as expressed in the stories of Ruth, a "Moabite woman," and the Syro-Phoenician mother that implores Jesus to heal her daughter. Susanna Snyder, *Asylum-Seeking, Migration and Church*, 139–94.

He immediately adds: "Ezra and Nehemiah demonstrate the beginning of the establishment of a religious tradition that leaned toward traditionalism, conservatism, exclusivity, and xenophobia."[38] Let us also not forget the atrocious rules of warfare that prescribes forced servitude or annihilation of the peoples encountered in Israel's route to the "promised land" (Deut 20:10–17). These all are, in Phyllis Trible's apt expression, "texts of terror."[39]

The problem with some evangelically oriented books like Matthew Soerens and Jenny Hwang's *Welcoming the Stranger* and M. Daniel Carroll R.'s *Christians at the Border: Immigration, the Church, and the Bible*[40] is that their hermeneutical strategy evades completely and intentionally those biblical texts that might have xenophobic connotations. Both books, for example, narrate the postexilic project of rebuilding Jerusalem, physically, culturally, and religiously, under Nehemiah,[41] but silence the expulsion of the foreign wives, an important part of that project (Ezra 9–10, Neh 13:23–31). The rejection of foreign wives in Ezra and Nehemiah does not seem too different from several modern anti-immigrants xenophobia: those foreign wives have a different linguistic, cultural, and religious legacy—"half of their children . . . could not speak the language of Judah, but spoke the language of various peoples. And I contended with them and cursed them and beat some of them and pulled out their hair" (Neh 13:24–25).

This conundrum is a constant irritating modus operandi of the Bible. We go to it searching for simple and clear solutions to our ethical enigmas, but it strikes back exacerbating our perplexity. Who said that the word of God is supposed to make things easier? But have I not forgotten something? This is an essay shared with fellow Protestant theologians, heirs of the sixteenth century Reformation. If something distinguishes that tradition, it is its christological emphasis. *Solus Christus* is one of the main tenets of the sixteenth century Reformation. What then about Christ and the stranger?

Clues to address Jesus's perspective regarding the socially despised other or stranger can be found in his attitude toward the Samaritans and in his dramatic and surprising eschatological parable on genuine discipleship and fidelity (Matt 25:31–46). Orthodox Jews despised Samaritans as possible sources of contamination and impurity. Yet Jesus did not have any inhibitions in conversing

---

38   Naim Stifan Ateek, *A Palestinian Christian Cry for Reconciliation* (Maryknoll, NY: Orbis Books, 2009), 132.

39   Phyllis Trible, *Texts of Terror: Literary-Feminist Readings of Biblical Narratives* (Philadelphia: Fortress Press, 1984).

40   Matthew Soerens & Jenny Yang (eds.). *Welcoming the Stranger: Justice, Compassion & Truth in the Immigration Debate* (Downers Grove, Illinois: IVP Books, 2018).

41   M. Daniel Carroll R., *Christians At the Border: Immigration, the Church, and the Bible*, (Grand Rapids, Mich.: Baker Academic), 2008.

amiably with a Samaritan woman of doubtful reputation, breaking down the exclusion barrier between Judeans and Samaritans (John 4:7–30). Of ten lepers once cleansed by Jesus, only one came to express his gratitude and reverence, and the Gospel narrative emphasizes that "he was a Samaritan" (Luke 17:11–19). Finally, in the famous parable to illustrate the meaning of the command "love your neighbor as yourself" (Luke 10:29–37)," Jesus contrasts the righteousness and solidarity of a Samaritan with the neglect and indifference of a priest and a Levite. The action of a traditionally despised Samaritan is thus exalted as a paradigm of love and solidarity to emulate.

The parable of the judgment of the nations, in the Gospel of Matthew (25:31–46), is pure vintage Jesus. It is a text whose connotations I refuse to reduce to a nowadays too common and constraining ecclesiastical confinement. Jesus disrupts, as he loved to do, the familiar criteria of ethical value and religious worthiness by distinguishing between human actions that sacramentally bespeaks divine love for the powerless and vulnerable from those that do not. Who are, according to Jesus, to be divinely blessed and inherit God's kingdom? Those who in their actions care for the hungry, thirsty, naked, sick, and incarcerated, in short, for the marginalized and vulnerable human beings. But also those who welcome the strangers, who provide them with hospitality; those who are able to overcome nationalistic exclusions, racism, and xenophobia and are daring enough to welcome and embrace the immigrant, the people in our midst who happen to be different in skin pigmentation, culture, language, and national origins. They belong to the powerless of the powerless, the poorest of the poor, in Frantz Fanon's famous terms, "the wretched of the earth," or, in Jesus's poetic language, "the least of these."[42]

Why? Here comes the shocking statement: because they are, in their powerlessness and vulnerability, the sacramental presence of Christ. "For I was hungry and you gave me food, I was thirsty and you gave me something to drink, I was a stranger [ξένοσ] and you welcomed me, I was naked and you gave me clothing, I was sick and you took care of me" (Matt 25:35). The vulnerable human beings turn out to be, in a mysterious way, the sacramental presence of Christ in our midst.[43] This sacramental presence of Christ becomes, for the first generations of Christian communities, the cornerstone of hospitality, *philoxenia*, toward those needy people who do not have a place to rest, a virtue insisted

---

[42]   See Clark Lyda and Jesse Lyda's moving documentary, *The Least of These* (2009).

[43]   Regarding Matthew 25:31–46, I am in accord with those scholars, like Cervantes Gabarrón ("El inmigrante en las tradiciones bíblicas", 273–75) who interpret "the least of these" as referring to the poor, dispossessed, marginalized and oppressed, and in disagreement with those who limit its denotation to Jesus' disciples, like M. Daniel Carroll R., *Christians at the Border*, 122–23.

upon by the apostle Paul (Rom 12:13).[44] When, in a powerful and imperial nation, like the United States of America, its citizens welcome and embrace the immigrant, who reside and work with or without some documents required by the powers that be, they are blessed, for they are welcoming and embracing Jesus Christ.[45]

The discriminatory distinction between citizens and aliens is therefore broken down. The author of the Epistle to the Ephesians is thus able to proclaim to human communities religiously scorned and socially marginalized: "So then you are no longer strangers and aliens, but you are citizens" (Eph 2:19). The author of that missive probably had in mind the peculiar vision of post exilic Israel developed by the prophet Ezekiel. Ezekiel emphasizes two differences between the post-exilic and the old Israel: the eradication of social injustice and oppression ("And my princes shall no longer oppress my people"—Ezek 45:8) and the elimination of the legal distinctions between citizens and aliens ("You shall allot it [the land] as an inheritance for yourselves and for the aliens who reside among you and have begotten children among you. They shall be to you as citizens of Israel; with you they shall be allotted an inheritance among the tribes of Israel. In whatever tribe aliens reside, there you shall assign them their inheritance, says the Lord God"—Ezek 47:21–23). This was not merely theological speculation. Ezekiel experienced himself the tragedy of being an immigrant. He was one of the countless Israelites who suffered forced deportation after the violent invasion of Israel by the Babylonian military forces. Exile and diaspora was the fate of the people of Yahweh and the source of Israel's sacred scriptures.[46]

AN ECUMENICAL, INTERNATIONAL AND INTERCULTURAL THEOLOGICAL PERSPECTIVE

We need to countervail the xenophobia that contaminates public discourse in the United States and other Western nations with an embracing,

---

[44] Peter Phan, "Migration in the Patristic Age," in *A Promised Land, A Perilous Journey: Theological Perspectives on Migration*, eds. Daniel G. Groody and Gioacchino Campese (Notre Dame, IN: University of Notre Dame Press, 2008), 35–61.
[45] There is an instance in which Jesus seems to exclude or marginalize strangers. When a woman, "Gentile, of Syrophoenician origin," implores from him healing for her daughter, Jesus declines. But her obstinate, clever, and hopeful response impresses him and leads him to praise her word of faith (Matt 15:21–28; Mark 7:24–30).
[46] Daniel L. Smith-Christopher, *A Biblical Theology of Exile* (Minneapolis: Fortress Press, 2002); James M. Scott, *Exile: A Conversation with N. T. Wright* (Downers Grove, IL: InterVarsity Press, 2017); René Kruger, *La diáspora: De experiencia traumática a paradigma eclesiológico* (Buenos Aires: ISEDET, 2008).

exclusion-rejecting, perspective of the stranger, the alien, the "other,"[47] one which I have named *xenophilia*, a concept that comprises hospitality, love, and care for the stranger. In times of increasing economic and political globalization, when in megalopolises like New York, Chicago, Dallas, or San Francisco many different cultures, languages, memories, and legacies converge,[48] *xenophilia* should be our duty and vocation, as a faith affirmation not only of our common humanity, but also of the ethical priority, in the eyes of God, of those vulnerable beings living in the shadows and margins of our societies.

There is a tendency among many public scholars and leaders to weave a discourse that deals with immigrants mainly or even exclusively as workers, whose labor might contribute or not to the economic welfare of the American citizens. This kind of public discourse tends to objectify and dehumanize the immigrants. Those immigrants are human beings, conceived and designed, according to the Christian tradition, in the image of God. They deserve to be fully recognized as such, both in the letter of the law and in the spirit of social praxis. Whatever the importance of the economic factors for the receiving nation (which usually, as in the case of the United States, happens to be an extremely rich country), from an ethical theological perspective, the main concern should be the existential well-being of the "least of these," of the most vulnerable and marginalized members of God's humanity, among them those who sojourn far away from their homeland, constantly scrutinized by the demeaning gaze of many native citizens.

One of the key concerns energizing and spreading the distrust against resident foreigners is fear of their possible consequences on national identity, understood as an already historically fixed essence. We have seen that anxiety in Samuel P. Huntington's assessment of the Latin American immigration as "a major potential threat to the cultural integrity of the United States." It is an apprehension that has spread all over the Western world, disseminating hostile attitudes toward already marginalized and disenfranchised communities of sojourners and strangers. These are perceived as sources of "cultural contamination." What is therein forgotten is, first, that national identities are historical constructs diachronically constituted by exchanges with peoples bearing different cultural heritages and, second, that cultural alterity, the social exchange with the "other," can and should be a source of renewal and enrichment of our own distinct national self-awareness. History has shown the sad consequences of xenophobic ethnocentrism. There have been too intimate links between

---

[47]   Cf. Miroslav Volf, *Exclusion and Embrace: A Theological Exploration of Identity, Otherness, and Reconciliation* (Nashville: Abingdon Press, 1996).

[48]   William Schweiker, *Theological Ethics and Global Dynamics in the Time of Many Worlds* (Malden, MA and Oxford: Blackwell, 2004).

xenophobia and genocide.[49] As Zygmunt Bauman has so aptly written, "Great crimes often start from great ideas . . . . Among this class of ideas, pride of place belongs to the vision of purity."[50]

The United States has a tendency to play the role of the Lone Ranger. Yet, migration and xenophobia are international problems, affecting most of the world community, and thus need to be understood and faced from a world-wide context.[51] The deportation of Roma people (Gypsies) in France and other European nations is an unfortunate sign of the times. Roma communities are expelled from nations where they are objects of scorn, contempt, and fear, to other nations where they have traditionally been mistreated, disdained, and marginalized. They are perennial national scapegoats, whose unfortunate fate has for too long been silenced.[52] It would also do good to compare the American situation with that prevailing in several European nations where, in the difficult and sometimes tense coexistence of citizens and immigrants resonate the his-torically complex conflicts between the Cross and the Crescent, for many of the foreigners happen to be Muslims, venerators of Allah, and thus subject to insidious kinds of xenophobia and discrimination.[53]

Migration is an international problem, a salient dimension of modern glo-balization.[54] Globalization implies not only the transfer of financial resources, products, and trade, but also the worldwide relocation of peoples, a transna-tionalization of labor migration, of human beings who take the difficult and frequently painful decision to leave their kith and kin in their search for a better future. We are in the midst, according to some scholars, of an "age of

---

[49]   Amin Maalouf, *In the Name of Identity: Violence and the Need to Belong* (New York: Arcade Publishing, 2000).

[50]   Zygmunt Bauman, *Postmodernity and Its Discontents* (Cambridge, UK: Polity Press, 1997), 5.

[51]   Malise Ruthven, "What Happened to the Arab Spring?," *The New York Review of Books* (July 10, 2014/Vol. LXI, No. 12), 74: "Of Qatar's population of 2.1 million, 85 percent are listed as 'foreign residents.' Many of these are construction workers from South Asia who work under poor conditions and suffer high casualty rates."

[52]   Cf. European Commission, "Roma in Europe: The Implementation of European Union Instruments and Policies for Roma Inclusion (Progress Report 2008-2010)" (Brussels, April 7, 2010) SEC (2010) 400 final.

[53]   Giovanni Sartori, *Pluralismo, multiculturalismo e estranei: saggio sulla società multietnica* (Milano: Rizzoli, 2000). Sartori perceives Islamist immigration as irreconcilable with, and thus nefarious for, Western democratic pluralism. His thesis is a sophisticated reconfiguration of the multisecular adversarial confrontation between Christian/Western (supposedly open, secular, and liberal) and Islamic/Eastern (allegedly closed, dogmatic and authoritarian) cultures, a new reen-actment of what Edward Said appropriately named "Orientalism."

[54]   A task to which not enough attention has been devoted is the advocacy for the signature and ratification by the wealthy and powerful nations of the 1990 "International Convention on the Protection of the Rights of All Migrant Workers and Members of Their Families," which en-tered into force on July 1, 2003.

migration."[55] Borders have become bridges, not only barriers. For, as Edward Said has written in the context of another very complex issue, "in time, who cannot suppose that the borders themselves will mean far less than the human contact taking place between people for whom differences animate more exchange rather than more hostility?"[56]

The intensification of global inequalities has made the issue of labor migration a crucial one.[57] It is a situation that requires rigorous analysis from: 1) a worldwide ecumenical horizon; 2) a deep understanding of the tensions and misunderstandings arising from the proximity of peoples with different traditions and cultural memories; 3) an ethical perspective that privileges the plight and afflictions of the most vulnerable, as "submerged and silenced voices of strangers need to be uncovered"[58]; and 4) for the Christian communities and churches, a solid theological matrix ecumenically conceived and designed.

The churches and Christian communities, therefore, need to address this issue from an international ecumenical and intercultural perspective.[59] The main concern is not and should not be exclusively our national society, but the entire fractured global order, for as Soerens and Hwang have neatly written: "Ultimately, the church must be a place of reconciliation in a broken world."[60] In an age where globalization prevails, there are social issues, migration being one of them, whose transnational complexities call for an international ecumenical dialogue and debate. As Susanna Snyder has so aptly written, "a transnational issue requires transnational responses and transnational, global networks such as churches could therefore be key international players."[61] One goal of that worldwide discursive process is the disruption of the increasing tendency of developed and wealthy countries to emphasize the protection of civil rights,

---

55 Stephen Castles and Mark J. Miller, *The Age of Migration: International Population Movements in the Modern World* (Fourth Edition/Revised and Updated) (New York and London: Guilford Press, 2009).

56 Edward W. Said, *The Question of Palestine* (New York: Vintage Books, 1992, 1976), 176.

57 Some scholars, for example, argue that the North American Free Trade Agreement, which came into force on January 1, 1994, created havoc in several segments of the Mexican economy and deprived of their livelihoods approximately 2.5 million small farmers and other workers dependent on the agricultural sector. The alternative for many of them was the stark choice between the clandestine and dangerous drug trafficking or paying the "coyotes" for the also clandestine and dangerous trek to the North. Ben Ehrenreich, "A Lucrative War," *The New York Review of Books*, 32, no.20, October 21, 2010: 15–8.

58 Susanna Snyder, *Asylum-Seeking, Migration and Church*, 31.

59 Raúl Fornet-Betancourt, ed., *Migration and Interculturality: Theological and Philosophical Challenges* (Aachen, Germany: Missionswissenschaftliches Institut Missio e.V., 2004); in *A Promised Land, A Perilous Journey*, eds. Daniel G. Groody and Gioacchino Campese, (Notre Dame, Ind.: University of Notre Dame Press, (2008), 243-70.

60 *Welcoming the Stranger*, 174.

61 *Asylum-Seeking, Migration and Church*, 205.

understood exclusively as the rights of *citizens*, vis-à-vis the diminishment of the recognition of the human rights of resident noncitizens.[62]

Pope Benedict XVI rightly reminded the global community, in his 2009 social encyclical *Caritas in Veritate*, of the urgent necessity to develop that kind of international and ecumenical perspective of migration:

> [M]igration . . . is a striking phenomenon because of the sheer numbers of people involved, the social, economic, political, cultural and religious problems it raises . . . . [We] are facing a social phenomenon of epoch-making proportions that requires bold, forward-looking policies of international cooperation . . . . We are all witnesses of the burden of suffering, the dislocation and the aspirations that accompany the flow of migrants . . . [T]hese laborers cannot be considered as a commodity or a mere workforce. They must not, therefore, be treated like any other factor of production. Every migrant is a human person who, as such, possesses fundamental, inalienable rights that must be respected by everyone and in every circumstance. (*Caritas in veritate*, 62)

Allow me to conclude, disrupting the English-only character of this essay, with some verses of the song *Extranjeros*, written by the Spanish songwriter Pedro Guerra, in the language of most undocumented immigrants arriving in North America.

> *Por ser como el aire su patria es el viento*
> *Por ser de la arena su patria es el sol*
> *Por ser extranjero su patria es el mundo*
> *Por ser como todos su patria es tu amor*
>
> *Recuerda una vez que fuimos así*
> *Los barcos y el mar, la fe y el adiós*
> *Ilegar a un lugar pidiendo vivir*
> *Huir de un lugar salvando el dolor.*

BIBLIOGRAPHY:

Anzaldúa, Gloria. *Borderlands/La Frontera: e New Mestiza*. San Francisco: Aunt Lute Books, 1999.

Ateek, Naim Stifan. *A Palestinian Christian Cry for Reconciliation*. Maryknoll, NY: Orbis, 2009.

---

[62] Fernando Oliván, *El extranjero y su sombra. Crítica del nacionalismo desde el derecho de extranjería* (Madrid: San Pablo, 1998).

Balderrama, Francisco, and Raymond Rodriguez. *Decade of Betrayal: Mexican Repatriation in the 1930s*. Albuquerque: University of New Mexico, 2006.

Bales, Kevin. *Disposable People: New Slavery in the Global Economy*. Berkeley, CA: University of California, 2004.

Bauman, Zygmunt. *Wasted Lives: Modernity and Its Outcasts*. Cambridge: Polity, 2004.

Bowe, John. *Nobodies: Modern American Slave Labor and the Dark Side of the New Global Economy*. New York: Random House, 2007.

Buchanan, Patrick. *State of Emergency: The Third World Invasion and Conquest of America*. New York: Thomas Dunne/St. Martin's Press, 2008.

Carroll R., and M. Daniel. *Christians at the Border: Immigration, the Church, and the Bible*. Grand Rapids, Michigan: Baker Books, 2008.

Cervantes Gabarrón, José. "El immigrante en las tradiciones bíblicas." *Ciudadanía, multiculturalidad eimmigración*. Edited by Jose A. Zamora. Aachen, Germany: Missionswissenschaftliches Institut Missio e.V., 2004.

Ehrenreich, Ben. "A Lucrative War." *The New York Review of Books*, 32, no.20, October 21, 2010: 15–8.

Fanon, Frantz. *Peau Noir, Masques Blancs*. Paris: Éditions du Seuil, 1952.

Fornet-Betancourt, Raúl, ed. *Migration and Interculturality: Theological and Philosophical Challenges*. Aachen, Germany: Missionswissenscha liches Institut Missio, 2004.

Fraser, Nancy, and Axel Honneth. *Redistribution or Recognition? A Political-Philosophical Exchange*. London; New York: Verso, 2003.

Fredrickson, George. *Diverse Nations: Explorations in the History of Racial & Ethnic Pluralism*. Boulder; London: Paradigm Publishers, 2006.

Harding, Jeremy. "The Deaths Map." *London Review of Books*, 33, no.20, October 20, 2011: 7-13.

Higham, John. *Strangers in the Land: Patterns of American Nativism*, 1860-1925. New York: Atheneum, 1968.

Hoffman, Abraham. *Unwanted Mexican Americans in the Great Depression: Repatriation Pressures, 1929-1939*. Tucson: University of Arizona, 1974.

Huntington, Samuel. "The Clash of Civilizations?" *Foreign Affairs*, 72, no.3 (Summer 1993): 22–49 .

———. *The Clash of Civilizations and the Remaking of World Order*. New York: Simon & Schuster, 1996.

———. "The Hispanic Challenge." *Foreign Policy*, March/April, 2004: 30–45.

———. *Who Are We? The Challenges to America's National Identity*. New York: Simon & Schuster, 2004.

Irvin, Dale. "The Church, the Urban and the Global: Mission in an Age of Global Cities." *International Bulletin of Missionary Research*, 33, no.4 (October 2009).

Jordan, Mark. *The Invention of Sodomy in Christian Theology*. Chicago: University of Chicago, 1997.

Kidd, José E. Ramírez. *Alterity and Identity in Israel: The "ger" in the Old Testament*. Berlin: De Gruyter, 1999.

Laclau, Ernesto, and Chantal Mouffe. *Hegemony and Socialist Strategy: Toward a Radical Democratic Politics*, 2nd ed. London; New York: Verso, 2001.

Leonhardt, David. "Truth, Fiction and Lou Dobbs." *The New York Times*, May 30, 2007.

Maalouf, Amin. *In the Name of Identity: Violence and the Need to Belong*. New York: Arcade, 2000.

Milanovic, Branko. *Global Inequality and the Global Inequality Extraction Ratio: The Story of the Past Two Centuries*. The World Bank, Development Research Group & Poverty and Inequality Group, September 2009.

Miller, Stuart Creighton. *The Unwelcome Immigrant: The American Image of the Chinese, 1775-1882*. Berkeley: University of California, 1969.

Oliván, Fernando. *El extranjero y su sombra. Crítica del nacionalismo desde el derecho de extranjería*. Madrid: San Pablo, 1998.

Phan, Peter. "Migration in the Patristic Age." In *A Promised Land, A Perilous Journey: Theological Perspectives on Migration*. Edited by Daniel G. Groody and Gioacchino Campese, eds. Notre Dame, Ind: University of Notre Dame Press, 2008.

Portes, Alejandro, and Rubén Rumbaut. *Immigrant America: A Portrait*. 3rd ed. Berkeley, CA: University of California Press, 2006.

Potok, Mark. "Rage in the Right." *Intelligence Report*. No. 137. Southern Poverty Law Center. Spring 2010.

Pyong, Gap Min, ed. *Encyclopedia of Racism in the United States* (3 vols.). Westport, CT: Greenwood Press, 2005.

Ratha, Dilip. "Dollars Without Borders: Can the Global Flow of Remittances Survive the Crisis?" *Foreign Affairs,* October 16, 2009.

Rodriguez, Richard. *Brown: The Last Discovery of America*. New York: Viking. 2002.

Ruiz, Francisco Javier Blázquez. "Derechos humanos, inmigración, integración", in José A. Zamora (coord.), *Ciudadanía, multiculturalidad e inmigración* (Navarra, España: Editorial Verbo Divino, 2003.

Sacks, Jonathan. *The Dignity of Difference: How to Avoid the Clash of Civilizations*. London: Continuum, 2003.

Said, Edward W. *The Questions of Palestine*. New York: Vintage Books, 1992, 1976.

Sartori, Giovanni. *Pluralism, multiculturalismo e estranei: saggio sulla societá multietnica*. Milano: Ruzzoli, 2000.

Schweiker, William. *Theological Ethics and Global Dynamics in the Time of Many Worlds*. Malden, MA; Oxford: Blackwell, 2004.

Secretariat-General European Commission (SEC). *Roma in Europe: The Implementation of European Union Instruments and Policies for Roma Inclusion*. Progress Report 2008–2010. April 7, 2010.

Soerens, Matthew, and Jenny Hwang. *Welcoming the Stranger: Justice, Compassion & Truth in the Immigration Debate*. Downers Grove, IL: InterVarsity, 2009.

Stalker, Peter. *Workers Without Frontiers: The Impact of Globalization on International Migration*. Geneva: International Labor Organization, 2000.

Steicke, Elisabeth Cook. *La mujer como extranjera en Israel: Estudio exegético de Esdras* 9-10. San José, Costa Rica: Editorial SEBILA, 2011.

Tocqueville, Alexis de. *Democracy in America*. London: Oxford University Press, 1959.

Trible, Phyllis. *Texts of Terror: Literary-Feminist Readings of Biblical Narratives*. Philadelphia: Fortress, 1984.

Volf, Miroslav. *Exclusion and Embrace: A Theological Exploration of Identity, Otherness, and Reconciliation*. Nashville: Abingdon, 1996.

Walcott, Derek. "The Schooner Flight." In *Collected Poems, 1948-1984*. New York: Farrar, Straus and Giroux, 1986.

West, Cornel. *Democracy Matters: Winning the Fight Against Imperialism*. New York: Penguin Press, 2004.

CHAPTER 12

A PEOPLE OF GOD WHO REMEMBERS: THEOLOGICAL REFLECTIONS ON A "REFUGEE CRISIS"

Gioacchino Campese

Dyonisis Arvanikatis is a Greek baker who makes 200 extra pounds of bread and pastries everyday to "break and give" them to the thousands of refugees and migrants who go through the small island of Kos (Greece) on their way from their countries of origin by the Mediterranean Sea to the heart of the European continent. As such, he is one of the thousand volunteers and common people in Europe who are responding with openness and generosity to the so-called "refugee crisis," a phrase that has become the customary definition of the most debated development of the phenomenon of human mobility on the continent. What stands out in his story is not so much the fact that he is a decent and good human being who helps his fellow human beings in need, but the reason why he does it: Dyonisis Arvanikatis remembers. He knows what it means to be a migrant, because when he was a teenager he followed his family from Greece to Australia. He understands the struggles migrants and refugees would have to go through to adapt to a new environment, to find housing and a job.[1]

This is the main reason why Mr. Arvanikatis, unknowingly, embodies the purpose of this chapter whose objective is to reflect on the central role of memory in the understanding of God in relation with migrants and refugees and, consequently, on the call to the people of God to remember their migratory past and act accordingly in the present in order to create a just and humane future. The geo-political context in which these theological reflections are rooted is the European continent, without ignoring that human mobility has

---

[1]   Dan Siegel and Jenny Yancey, "Bread for the Journey–The Greek Baker Who Remembers," accessed June 14, 2018, https://www.huffingtonpost.com/dan-siegel/bread-for-the-journey-the-greek-baker-who-remembers_b_8166242.html

always had global implications and that the plight of migrants and refugees is, today more than ever in human history, a prominent and controversial issue worldwide.

Mapping a "Refugee Crisis"

It is evidently impossible to draw a comprehensive map of the recent and substantial flows of migrants and refugees in Europe in a few paragraphs, but here it will suffice to offer some coordinates to grasp the magnitude of this reality. To sketch this map, it is essential to understand the nature of this "crisis" that is often misrepresented by mass and social media, among others. It might even be misleading to call it a crisis if we fail to grasp its deepest meanings.

First, what Europe is witnessing today is part of a human and historical phenomenon known as human mobility, which has accompanied humankind since its beginnings. It is surely an integral part of the history of the continent, from at least the migrations of the German tribes (the so-called "barbarian invasions") that contributed to the end of the Western Roman empire in the fourth century to the more recent "refugee crisis" caused partly by the implosion of Yugoslavia in the 1990s. An essential section of this history is represented by the migrations of millions of Europeans toward the rest of the world especially since the sixteenth century for different reasons, including colonialism. Second, in a globalized world, human mobility is not just an emergency or a humanitarian crisis, but it is also a structural element, a movement of persons and peoples that, for many reasons is to be expected, could be foreseen and, if there is the political will, can be properly managed. Third, to treat migration as if it were an emergency means to focus on the latest arrivals who have landed in Southern Europe, but at the same time it is to miss the largest part of the reality of migration in the continent that consists of millions of immigrants and their families who have been living for decades in the different European nations, contributing significantly to their wellbeing and welfare.[2] The reality of European migration includes also the presence of millions of European migrants who have been living for decades and even centuries now in Africa, the Americas, and Asia. Fourth, if it has not been possible until now to find a decent solution to the challenges posed by the most recent flows of migrants and refugees, it is not because of lack of means and resources. Instead, the situation is fundamentally the result of lack of unity and political will within the European Union (EU). Fifth, since human mobility is a global issue, it requires a global effort that goes

---

[2]   According to statistics provided by Eurostat, as of January 1, 2016 there were 35.1 million people born outside the European Union (EU) living in EU member states, accessed   June   14,   2018,   http://ec.europa.eu/eurostat/statistics-explained/index.php/ Migration_and_migrant_population_statistics.

beyond the good intentions of a few people and countries. Therefore, the endeavor by the United Nations to produce a global compact or agreement on safe, orderly and regular migration, and another on refugees by 2018 is to be applauded and, most importantly, supported.[3]

Many other factors could be added to this brief analysis to further support our argument that what is called "refugee crisis" is not essentially a humanitarian and emergency crisis, nor a capacity and resource crisis, but instead the warning light of major structural changes in Europe, whose peoples are struggling, among other things, with the values that have brought it to unity; with their historical memories, particularly their migrant past that is often and conveniently ignored; with their relative inability to invest in and pursue healthy processes of inclusion and integration of migrants and refugees that produce a genuine sense of belonging, and with a massive demographic decline. In the meantime, fear, and its implications and consequences, is becoming the common reaction of European peoples toward migrants and refugees. This is used as a powerful weapon by political actors and movements for personal and sectarian interests.[4] Fear cannot be underestimated nor censured, but it must be understood and faced head on. At the same time, it cannot be allowed to become the springboard of political and social choices that will decide the present and future of Europe. The success of nationalistic and xenophobic political movements all over the continent, and particularly in Poland, Hungary, Austria, Slovakia, and most recently Czech Republic and Sweden—countries whose governments often are led by representatives of such movements—shows lamentably a drift toward an anti-immigration stance that will breed more fragmentation and conflicts than integration, inclusion and harmony in Europe.

Focusing more specifically on the reality of refugees arriving by sea in Europe between 2014 and 2017, the total number according to UNHCR data is less than 2 million people. During the same period, 15,486 people have died or are missing in connection with these dangerous and sometimes lethal

---

[3]   As for its contribution to the global conversations and negotiations leading to these two global compacts, the Vatican Section on Migrants and Refugees (Dicastery for Promoting Integral Human Development) has presented 20 points of political and pastoral action based on the long standing experience and best practices of the Roman Catholic church with migrants and refugees, accessed June 14, 2018, https://migrants-refugees.va/20-action-points. Regrettably, on December 2, 2017 the US Mission to the United Nations has officially announced that it was quitting talks leading to these global compacts.

[4]   On the spread of the ideology of fear in Europe, see Paul Michael Zulehner, "L'Ideologia della Paura," *Regno Attualità* 20 (2017): 627–35. For an insightful theological analysis of the ecology of fear and the ecology of faith within society and church in the context of human mobility, see Susanna Snyder, *Asylum-Seeking, Migration and Church* (Surrey: Ashgate, 2012).

journeys.[5] It is important to underline that the European situation is just a segment of the global "crisis" of forced migration in the world today. Part of this larger phenomenon is, for example, the extremely precarious situation of the 647,000 Rohingya who had fled from Myanmar to Bangladesh since August 2017;[6] the 1.9 million people fleeing violence and unrest in the Democratic Republic of the Congo;[7] and the South Sudan's reality, which was dubbed as the "fastest growing refugee crisis" in 2016.[8] Many of these situations are relatively unknown partially because they do not receive the same media coverage given to the European "refugee crisis." Therefore, it is crucial to recognize the magnitude of forced migration around the world, of which only 16 percent interests Europe and other Western countries. In fact, contrary to media and political rhetoric that feed popular perceptions, refugees are not invading the European nations. In fact, 84 percent of forced migrants are hosted by developing countries, most often the nations neighboring those from which people are fleeing. To this we must add that most people escaping war, violence, and environmental disasters are internally displaced people, so they move from their places of origin to another within the borders of the same country.[9]

In order to face and manage this complex reality, a recovery of memory both as Europeans and Christian believers is urgently needed. It is in a certain sense ironic that in an age in which technology allows us to memorize an incredible amount of data and to access them with extraordinary speed in powerful computers, the issue of loss of memory must be addressed. Yet, we live in an age in which, despite our best efforts, there is a powerful inclination toward readily disregarding relevant portions of our history and identity as citizens and believers, especially when they challenge our established interpretations of human mobility and attitudes toward today's migrants and refugees. During his speech for the conferral of the Charlemagne Prize in 2016, Pope Francis, citing Elie Wiesel, affirmed that Europe needs a "memory transfusion" not only to avoid repeating the mistakes of the past, "but also to re-appropriate those experiences that enabled our peoples to surmount the crises of the past."[10] In other

---

[5]   For an update on the European situation, see http://www.unhcr.org/europe-emergency.html, accessed June 14, 2018.

[6]   See http://www.unhcr.org/rohingya-emergency.html, accessed June 14, 2018.

[7]   See http://www.unhcr.org/dr-congo-emergency.html, accessed June 14, 2018.

[8]   See http://www.unhcr.org/globaltrends2016/ and http://www.unhcr.org/south-sudan-emergency.html, accessed June 14, 2018.

[9]   For a detailed and updated presentation of forced migration today see UNHCR, *Global Trends. Forced Displacement in 2016*, accessed June 14, 2018, http://www.unhcr.org/globaltrends2016/.

[10]   Francis, "Address, Conferral of the Charlemagne Prize, May 6, 2016," accessed June 14, 2018, http://w2.vatican.va/content/francesco/en/speeches/2016/may/documents/papa-francesco_20160506_premio-carlo-magno.html.

words, using the terminology of sociologist Robert Bellah and his colleagues, European communities must become "communities of memory"[11] in which we recall and retell the stories of the past in all its complexity, which means to remember both the good and the painful events of the history that have contributed to the making of identities as citizens and religious adherents.

THE MEMORY OF GOD IS THE MEMORY OF THE VICTIMS

"After a long time, the king of Egypt died. The Israelites groaned under their slavery and cried out. Out of the slavery their cry for help rose up to God. God heard their groaning, and God remembered his covenant with Abraham, Isaac, and Jacob. God looked upon the Israelites, and God took notice of them." (Exod 2:23–25). This passage represents one of the several instances in which God is depicted in the Bible as the One who remembers his promises to people and intervenes to protect and guide them toward a situation of freedom and justice. God remembers Noah and all the animals that were on the ark and rescues them from the flood (Gen 8:1); God remembers Abraham and saves his kin, Lot from the destruction of Sodom and Gomorrah; God remembers Rachel and Hannah freeing them from their situation of infertility and shame (Gen 30:22; 1 Sam 1:19); and above all, God remembers the covenant made with Abraham, Isaac, and Jacob (Ps 105:9–10), a covenant recalled by both Mary (Luke 1:54–55) and Zechariah (Luke 1:72–73) on the occasion of the conception of Jesus and the birth of John. The Bible affirms that, ultimately, human beings live because God is mindful of them; on the contrary, absence of memory is the specific mark of the *sheol* (Ps 6:5), the reign of the dead. Memory is a question of life and death: in the theology of memory developed in Deuteronomy, to remember what God has done for Israel means life and well-being, while to forget God's loving actions means death (Deut 8:18–20).[12]

The act of remembering, therefore, is not just a marginal note, but a central theological category in that it states a fundamental characteristic of the God of Israel and Jesus Christ, a God who acts with compassion and mercy toward people. Those who believe in this God are supposed to remember the wonderful deeds that God has done for them, but also recognize the evil that they have committed. Here is where another dimension of God's memory is shown: God remembers people's infidelities and misdeeds, but despite this God will continue to maintain the promise made to their ancestors (Ezek 20:42–44); God

---

[11]   Robert N. Bellah et al., *Habits of the Heart: Individualism and Commitment in American Life* (Berkeley, CA: University of California Press, 1985).

[12]   On the subject of memory in the Bible see Federico Giuntoli, "Memoria/Memoriale," in *Temi Teologici della Bibbia*, eds. Romano Penna, Giacomo Perego and Gianfranco Ravasi (Cinisello Balsamo: San Paolo, 2010), 830–6; Stefano Bittasi, "Che Cosa Ricordare?," *Aggiornamenti Sociali* 7–8 (2014): 596–600.

will not act punishing them definitively according to their behavior but keep on showing them his steadfast love. The other dimension of God's memory, voiced by Exod 2:23–25, is its special sensibility to the cry and plight of powerless and troubled people, an aspect clearly embodied by Jesus's fellowship with the poor and the sinners, which caused the negative reactions of the religious elites represented by Pharisees and Scribes (Luke 15:1–7). Gustavo Gutiérrez makes this point by citing Bartolomé de Las Casas who wrote that "God has a very vivid and recent memory of the smallest and the most forgotten."[13] Daniel Groody, taking another small Mediterranean island such as Lampedusa as a springboard for his theological reflections on the refugees arriving in Europe, states that by remembering the "nobodies," God reveals their dignity as "somebodies" and in this process opens the way for the connection with and transformation of "everybody."[14] The intimate relationship between memory and the suffering of the others has been theologically explored particularly by Johann Baptist Metz who affirms that "God-talk is sensitive to suffering at its core." Metz builds his argument on a concept of global compassion not as a general empathic or philanthropic sentiment, but as an active remembrance of the suffering of others, a *memoria passionis* that does not focus just on Jesus's passion, but, following precisely Jesus's sensitivity to the suffering of the discarded and exploited, expands it to all human suffering whose authority is universal. In this context, the word of God becomes also a "dangerous memory," because it unveils the structures of violence and exclusion that exist in our world and forces Christians to a face-to-face encounter with the victims of unjust and innocent suffering.[15]

Among the vulnerable and suffering people remembered by God, a privileged place is given to migrants and refugees: "When an immigrant resides with you in your land, you shall not oppress the immigrant. The immigrant who resides with you shall be to you as the citizen among you; you shall love the immigrant as yourself, for you were immigrants in the land of Egypt: I am the Lord your God" (Lev 19:33–34; also Exod 22:21; Deut 10:19).[16] This passage that reminds an already settled people of Israel of its migratory past, is not consequential just from an ethical viewpoint, that is, as an injunction to Israel not to mistreat, but to actually love the immigrants in remembrance of its experience as foreign people in Egypt. As a matter of fact, the point of these verses

---

[13]   Gustavo Gutiérrez, "Memory and Prophecy," in *The Option for the Poor in Christian Theology*, ed. Daniel G. Groody (Notre Dame, IN: University of Notre Dame Press, 2007), 19. This quote is taken from the *Carta al Consejo de Indias* written by Bartolomè de las Casas in 1531.

[14]   See Daniel G. Groody, "Cup of Suffering, Chalice of Salvation: Refugees, Lampedusa, and the Eucharist," *Theological Studies* 78/4 (2017): 960–87.

[15]   Johann Baptist Metz, "Facing the World: A Theological and Biographical Inquiry," *Theological Studies* 75/1 (2014): 30.

[16]   I have changed on purpose the term "alien" used by the NRSV and adopted the term "immigrant," which represents also a legitimate translation of the Hebrew words *ger/gerim*.

is crucially theological and its message is: God remembered you when you were an immigrant and enslaved people in Egypt; God helped you when you were suffering as strangers in Egypt and God did it because it is God who protects the immigrant, the orphan, the widow (Deut 10:18; Ps 146: 9). To listen to the cry of the oppressed and the poor is a constitutive element of God's identity. To oppress the immigrants, therefore, would not only mean to deny one's identity and historical memory, but first to deny the God of Israel by choosing a different god. The affirmation "I am the Lord your God" at the end of this passage is like God's signature: I am the God who sides with powerless and exploited migrants just as I did with Israel in Egypt.[17]

The God who remembers exhorts Israel to remember its past and act accordingly: the Jews offering the first fruits of their harvest began their profession of faith in God by saying "A wandering Aramean was my ancestor ..." and continue telling the story of God's wonders and their concrete ethical implications for the Levite, the widow, the orphan and the immigrant (Deut 26:1–15); and Jesus asks his disciples to repeat the act of sharing the bread and the wine "in remembrance of me" (Luke 22:19; 1 Cor 11:23–25). We have purposefully portrayed right at the beginning of this chapter Mr. Arvanikatis' actions as "breaking and giving" bread (Matt 26:26; Mark 14:22; Luke 22:19) to displaced people mainly for two reasons: first, because it is an accurate picture of what this baker has been doing with refugees arriving in the island of Kos;[18] second, the sharing of the bread that he enacts everyday has some clear and essential eucharistic implications. It is a memorial since it does not simply remember a gesture from the past, but, most importantly, it makes present once again to the community of believers the essence of Jesus's life offered to the whole of humanity, particularly to the suffering and the vulnerable.[19]

A PEOPLE OF GOD WHO REMEMBERS

The God whose memory is focused on the people who are burdened by their lack of resources and most of all relational networks that could support them such as the orphan, the widow and the migrant, wants people to remember their own experience of vulnerability and migration. Christian communities, as communities of faith, must also be "communities of memory," because they cannot maintain their vital connection with God and their fellow human beings without remembering. Thus, the Father, in Jesus's name, entrusts the

---

[17] See Gianni Barbiero, "Lo Straniero nel Codice dell'Alleanza e nel Codice di Santità: tra Separazione e Accoglienza," in *Lo Straniero nella Bibbia. Aspetti Storici, Istituzionali e teologici*, XXXIII Settimana Biblica Nazionale, ed. Innocenzo Cardellini (Bologna: EDB, 1996), 47–52.

[18] Most of the pictures of Mr. Arvanikatis found in internet show him as he is breaking and distributing bread to refugees.

[19] Giuntoli, "Memoria/Memoriale," 834–6.

Holy Spirit with the task of reminding the disciples of all that Jesus said during his life (John 14:26). Listening attentively to the Spirit becomes, then, a fundamental responsibility for a community of memory that wants to follow in Jesus's steps.

The biblical passages that speak about God's relation with migrants are revealing of another crucial aspect of memory in the journey of faith: its active and practical dimensions. Gutiérrez explains it well: "Memory in the Bible goes beyond the conceptual; it points toward a conduct, a practice designed to transform reality. To remember is to have in mind, or care for, someone or something. One remembers in order to act. Without this, memory lacks meaning; it is limited to being a kind of intellectual gymnastics."[20] Listening to God's Spirit means to be reminded of one's past, a past defined by mobility—both in its Jewish roots (Lev 19:33–34) and in its Christian continuation (1 Pet 1:1; 2:11)—and also by God's wonders in favor of a people on the move. That memory must push people to action, to recognize and love fellow human beings that today are suffering because of migration. Listening to God's Spirit in the Jewish-Christian tradition means, in other words, to recognize that, ultimately, believers are migrants called to welcome and accompany other migrants.[21]

To become Christian communities of memory, implies to build up in societies, what Michael Nausner describes as, a "responsible culture of remembrance." This is a compelling and indispensable task for Europe today because without a healthy memory, Europeans will not be able to generate new and inclusive narratives about their national, cultural, and religious identities that function as an antidote against the waves of xenophobia and nationalism that we have been experiencing within the continent in the last decades.[22] At the beginning of an essay published in 1993, Frank Crüsemann lamented the failure of European Christianity in its reception of one of the central features of Old Testament teachings—the concern and protection of migrants and strangers, vis-à-vis the "terrifying" growth of nationalism. In particular, he observed that the catechism did not include the often repeated Old Testament

---

[20] Gutiérrez, "Memory and Prophecy," 19.

[21] See Christine Pohl, "Biblical Issues in Mission and Migration," *Missiology* 31/1 (2003): 5, who speaks of Christians as "strangers welcoming strangers."

[22] Michael Nausner, "Changing Identities, Changing Narratives: Can Theology Contribute to a New Cultural Imagination of Migration?," *International Journal for Religion and Transformation in Contemporary Society* 4 (2017): 236–9. See also Peter C. Phan, "'Always Remember Where You Came From'. An Ethics of Migrant Memory," in *Living With(out) Borders. Catholic Theological Ethics on the Migration of Peoples*, eds. Agnes M. Brazal and María Teresa Dávila (Maryknoll, NY: Orbis Books, 2016), 173–86. Phan in this essay focuses on why, what and how migrants themselves should remember.

commands about the rights of strangers.[23] The fact that after 25 years, we are still complaining about the same issues increases the urgency of the appeal to develop a "responsible culture of remembrance." This is a vital task in a time in which politicians and also a few church leaders use the defense of Christian identity against the "invasion" of foreigners, and particularly Muslim migrants and refugees, as an excuse to justify and promote an exclusive and at times violent nationalism that has nothing to do with the radical and gentle demands of Christian faith rooted in our biblical traditions.

It is precisely the partial failure to teach and transmit in the Christian communities a consistent ethics of hospitality, welcoming and inclusion, that reveals the "refugee crisis" as a missionary/pastoral and theological crisis.[24] Despite remaining the most committed and effective non-governmental organizations in this field and, in many cases, being at the forefront of the processes of welcoming and integration in their respective contexts,[25] the churches are detecting at the grassroots alarming levels of fear and hostility, which indicate a certain degree of inability to deal with the social, cultural, religious, and demographic transformations that are taking place in Europe. The famous appeal by Pope Francis "to parishes, religious communities, monasteries and shrines throughout Europe, that they express the Gospel in a concrete way and host a refugee family"[26] has been heard only partially and sometimes only minimally. From a mission viewpoint, it is enough to say that Europeans appear readier to think of themselves as "the missionaries" who go to the Global South to evangelize, and less suited and prepared to deal with the people from the Global South arriving and living in their own countries. The idea and the experience of being on the receiving side of mission or, even better, to "mission with" rather than "mission to," has still to take root in European churches. It is also a theological crisis simply because, despite the efforts of a minority of scholars who

---

[23]   Frank Crüsemann, "'You Know the Heart of a Stranger' (Exodus 23.9). A Recollection of the Torah in the Face of New Nationalism and Xenophobia," in *Migrants and Refugees*, eds. Dietmar Mieth and Lisa Sowle Cahill (London: SCM Press, 1993), 95–7.

[24]   This point has been conveyed in more detail in Gioacchino Campese, "The Irruption of the Migrants in the 21st Century: A Challenge for Contemporary Theology," *Journal of Catholic Social Thought* 14/1 (2017): 9–27.

[25]   See for instance the talk given by Bishop Nunzio Galantino, general secretary of the Italian Catholic Bishops' Conference, at the presentation of the annual report of the Centro Astalli, the Italian branch of the Jesuit Refugee Service, on April 11, 2017, "Una Solidarietà Competente. Una Chiesa che si Spende in Prima Persona senza Ignorare la Complessità del Fenomeno," *Regno Attualità* 8 (2017): 195–9.

[26]   Francis, Angelus, September 6, 2015, accessed June 14, 2018, http://w2.vatican.va/content/francesco/en/angelus/2015/documents/papa-francesco_angelus_20150906.html.

are writing on the phenomenon of human mobility,[27] mainstream Christian theology in Europe has still to come to terms with the centrality of migration issues from a practical and systematic perspective.

In conclusion, among the many assignments of a people of God who remembers, I would like to underline three: First, to confess the sin of forgetfulness regarding the past as nations and churches. It is not to be forgotten, for example, how the churches themselves have been persecuting people from the fifteenth to the seventeenth century and how in the name of the Christian God, millions of Protestants, Catholics, Jews, Muslims were expelled from their places of origin to purify communities from "heretics" and "pagans."[28] At the same time, the migration of millions of Europeans who did not leave just as migrants and refugees, but also as colonizers and conquerors, must be remembered.[29] Second, Europeans must take responsibility for what has been happening in the last decades in the continent in terms of human mobility. In other words, they cannot pretend to be innocent vis-à-vis the economic inequalities, the armed conflicts, and the environmental imbalances that are pushing millions of people toward their shores. Referring to the current "refugee crisis," Nausner rightly observes: "I interpret this situation not so much as a sudden crisis that has erupted due to a war, but as an expression of years, decades, and centuries of colonial rule, unjust economic relations, and cultural imperialism."[30] Third, communities must find creative and imaginative ways to pass on their cultural, national, and Christian migratory memories to the next generations. To develop a "responsible culture of remembrance" means to build up healthy and truthful traditions (from the Latin term *tradere*, which means precisely to deliver). Here comes to mind the passage in Joshua 4:1–7 in which the twelve tribes of Israel set up stones in remembrance of their crossing of the Jordan so that when their children may ask in the future: "What do those stones mean to you?," their meaning will be explained to them.[31] So what are the stones that Europeans are going to set up as a memorial of their identity as a pilgrim

---

[27]   Among the most recent essays that work out a theological and ethical reflection starting from the current European situation, in addition to the writings by Groody, Nausner and Campese, see Anna Rowlands, "After Lesvos and Lampedusa: The European 'Crisis' and Its Challenge to Catholic Social Thought," *Journal of Catholic Social Thought* 14/1(2017): 63–85; Regina Polak, "Flight and Migration: *Signs of the Times* and *Loci Theologici*–A European Perspective," *Journal of Catholic Social Thought* 14/1 (2017): 105–21; Joshua Ralston, "Bearing Witness: Reframing Christian-Muslim Encounter in Light of the Refugee Crisis," *Theology Today* 74/1 (2017): 22–35.

[28]   See Nicholas Terpstra, *Religious Refugees in the Early Modern World. An Alternative History of the Reformation* (Cambridge UK: Cambridge University Press, 2015).

[29]   Conferenza Episcopale Ligure, "Migranti, Segno di Dio," *Regno Documenti* 11 (2017): 336–46, especially 338.

[30]   Nausner, "Changing Identities, Changing Narratives," 226.

[31]   On the meaning of this passage to understand the role and dynamics of collective memory, see Stefano Bittasi, "Memoria Collettiva" *Aggiornamenti Sociali* 9-10 (2011): 633–6.

people of God? What will be the visible markers that will allow persons and communities to narrate their cultural and Christian memories of migration? How are they going to transform these stones in liturgical events so that the next generations will re-experience migration not as a problem or a mark of shame, but as a defining quality of our journey as human beings and Christians?

In a global context characterized among other things by the manipulation of truth or post-truth, xenophobia and scapegoating of migrants and refugees, inequality and injustice, and the lack of care for the environment, to be faithful disciples of Jesus, people of a God who remembers, is going to be costly. As Kenneth Ross remarks, those who choose this path "are not likely to win any popularity contests."[32] It takes courage and faith to be a people of God who remembers, to swim against a tide that twists the truth and tells you to conveniently forget about your past experience as an oppressed stranger in the land of Egypt. The witness of Mr. Arvanikatis reminds us that costly as it may be, this represents also the "Joy of the Gospel," the *Evangelii gaudium*, to which all Christians are summoned.[33]

BIBLIOGRAPHY:

Barbiero, Gianni. "Lo Straniero nel Codice dell'Alleanza e nel Codice di Santità: tra Separazione e Accoglienza." In *Lo Straniero nella Bibbia. Aspetti Storici, Istituzionali e teologici*, XXXIII Settimana Biblica Nazionale, edited by Innocenzo Cardellini. 41–69, Bologna: EDB, 1996.

Bellah, Robert N. et al. *Habits of the Heart: Individualism and Commitment in American Life*. Berkeley CA: University of California Press, 1985.

Bittasi, Stefano. "Memoria Collettiva." *Aggiornamenti Sociali*, 9–10 (2011): 633–36.

Bittasi, Stefano. "Che Cosa Ricordare?" *Aggiornamenti Sociali*, 7–8 (2014): 596–600.

Campese, Gioacchino. "The Irruption of the Migrants in the 21st Century: A Challenge for Contemporary Theology." *Journal of Catholic Social Thought*, 14/1 (2017): 9–27.

[32] Kenneth R. Ross, "Brexit, Trump, and Christ's Call to Discipleship," *International Review of Mission* 106/2 (2017): 369–88 at 385.

[33] These concluding words have been inspired by Ross's mention at the end of his essay of the Apostolic Exhortation by Francis *Evangelii Gaudium*, Nov. 24, 2013, accessed June 14, 2018, http://w2.vatican.va/content/francesco/en/apost_exhortations/documents/papa-francesco_esortazione-ap_20131124_evangelii-gaudium.html. See Ross, "Brexit, Trump, and Christ's Call to Discipleship," 387–8.

Conferenza Episcopale Ligure. "Migranti, Segno di Dio," *Regno Documenti* 11 (2017): 336–46.

Crüsemann, Frank. "'You Know the Heart of a Stranger' (Exodus 23.9). A Recollection of the Torah in the Face of New Nationalism and Xenophobia," in *Migrants and Refugees*. edited by Dietmar Mieth and Lisa Sowle Cahill, 95-109. London: SCM Press, 1993.

Francis. "Apostolic Exhortation," *Evangelii Gaudium*, November 24, 2013, accessed June 14, 2018, http://w2.vatican.va/content/francesco/en/apost_exhortations/documents/papa-francesco_esortazione-ap_20131124_evangelii-gaudium.html

Francis. "Address, Conferral of the Charlemagne Prize," May 6, 2016, accessed June 14, 2018, http://w2.vatican.va/content/francesco/en/speeches/2016/may/documents/papa-francesco_20160506_premio-carlo-magno.html.

Galantino, Nunzio. "Una Solidarietà Competente. Una Chiesa che si Spende in Prima Personasenza Ignorare la Complessità del Fenomeno," *Regno Attualità* 8 (2017): 195–99.

Giuntoli, Federico. "Memoria/Memoriale." In *Temi Teologici della Bibbia*, edited by Romano Penna, Giacomo Perego and Gianfranco Ravasi, 830–36. Cinisello Balsamo: San Paolo, 2010.

Groody, Daniel G. "Cup of Suffering, Chalice of Salvation: Refugees, Lampedusa, and the Eucharist," *Theological Studies* 78/4 (2017): 960–87.

Gutiérrez, Gustavo. "Memory and Prophecy," in *The Option for the Poor in Christian Theology*, edited by Daniel G. Groody, 17–38. Notre Dame, IN: University of Notre Dame Press, 2007.

Metz, Johann Baptist. "Facing the World: A Theological and Biographical Inquiry," *Theological Studies* 75/1 (2014): 23–33.

Migrants and Refugees Section. *20 Pastoral Action Points–20 Action Points for the Global Compacts*. Accessed June 14, 2018. https://migrants-refugees.va/20-action-points.

Nausner, Michael. "Changing Identities, Changing Narratives: Can Theology Contribute to a New Cultural Imagination of Migration?," *International Journal for Religion and Transformation in Contemporary Society* 4 (2017): 226–51.

Phan, Peter C. "'Always Remember Where You Came From'. An Ethics of Migrant Memory." In *Living With(out) Borders. Catholic Theological Ethics on the Migration of Peoples*, edited by Agnes M. Brazal and María Teresa Dávila, 173–86. Maryknoll, NY: Orbis Books, 2016.

Pohl, Christine. "Biblical Issues in Mission and Migration," *Missiology* 31/1 (2003): 3–15.

Polak, Regina. "Flight and Migration: *Signs of the Times* and *Loci Theologici*–A European Perspective." *Journal of Catholic Social Thought* 14/1 (2017): 105–21.

Ralston, Joshua. "Bearing Witness: Reframing Christian-Muslim Encounter in Light of the Refugee Crisis." *Theology Today* 74/1 (2017): 22–35.

Ross, Kenneth R. "Brexit, Trump, and Christ's Call to Discipleship." *International Review of Mission* 106/2 (2017): 369–88.

Rowlands, Anna. "After Lesvos and Lampedusa: The European 'Crisis' and Its Challenge to Catholic Social Thought." *Journal of Catholic Social Thought* 14/1 (2017): 63–85.

Snyder, Susanna. *Asylum-Seeking, Migration and Church*. Surrey: Ashgate, 2012.

Terpstra, Nicholas. *Religious Refugees in the Early Modern World. An Alternative History of the Reformation*. Cambridge UK: Cambridge University Press, 2015.

UNHCR, *Global Trends. Forced Displacement in 2016*. Accessed June 14, 2018, http://www.unhcr.org/globaltrends2016/.

Zulehner, Paul Michael. "L'Ideologia della Paura." *Regno Attualità* 20 (2017): 627–35.

CHAPTER 13

CENTRAL AMERICAN MIGRATION AS THE WAY OF THE CROSS: IGNACIO ELLACURÍA'S NOTION OF THE "CRUCIFIED PEOPLES" FOR THEOLOGICAL REFRAMING OF THE MIGRANT EXPERIENCE

Francisco Pelaez-Diaz

Why is it important to reflect on the experience of millions of Central American and Mexican migrants to the United States from the perspective of their religious expressions? One of the reasons is because religion is at the center of the experience of migrating for many impoverished and displaced Latin Americans. Even though the journey is dangerous and difficult, they take the risk mostly because the conditions in their countries of origin are unbearable or plainly unpromising. Many times, religious expressions have been used as vehicles of denunciation and protest. At other times, they have served as havens and relief. Most times, they serve as a source of hope and encouragement. This chapter will focus on a particular Christian—and specifically Roman Catholic—expression, namely, the representation of the *via crucis* or the Way of the Cross that has been linked to the experience of migration. For migrants from Central America, the whole process of crossing Mexico occurs under precarious conditions due primarily to the lack of documents to gain authorized entry to Mexico and the United States, in addition to the extremely limited material and social resources available to them during their journey. The reenactment of the Way of the Cross, in this case, encompasses multiple functions, including the denouncement of violence, protest against abuses, the raising of awareness of the plight of the migrants, and even the possibility of crossing Mexico with the hope of crossing the US-Mexico border both in a physical way and also in a symbolic way.

Borders can be understood not only as physical lines dividing two nations, but more appropriately, as Thomas Nails has put it, they are "processes of 'social division'"[1] to control movement. This definition includes not only physical barriers—fences, walls, and checkpoints, which are material technologies designed to redirect social and material flows—but also seems to suggest that borders include all the social dynamics related to the goal of creating and maintaining social division. This definition helps to explain the condition of marginalization, abuse, discrimination and, in many cases, death that migrants experience. Therefore, the participation of the migrants in the reenactment of the Way of the Cross can be characterized as an attempt at breaking boundaries.

Although it is difficult to track exactly how the link between the reenactment of the Way of the Cross and the Central American migrant experience came about, its enactment reflects, among other aspects, a theological move that deserves attention. It seems to point to the notion of the crucified peoples that was crafted in El Salvador in the late 1970s by Oscar Romero and Ignacio Ellacuría. More than 35 years ago, this notion was born in a context of resistance to the violence and deadly repression fueled and in part orchestrated by the United States in El Salvador and in Central America, in general. It is now being reclaimed by migrants that are trying to reach US soil. As pointed above, this religious expression has become a vehicle of protest and denunciation of the brutal violence and poverty that has remained and worsened as a consequence of the continued intervention of the United States in this region. This chapter will try to clarify the link between the theological notion of the crucified peoples and the reenactment of the Way of the Cross of the Migrant.

The first part of this essay is devoted to exploring some of the current theories that explain the migration from Central America and Mexico to the United States. This part intends to provide a framework to understand the conditions in which a specific form of religious expression emerged, namely, the reenactment of the Way of the Cross of the Migrant. The second part will offer an account of Via Crucis (The Way of the Cross) and how it became utilized by activists and migrants to expose the conditions related to their journey and to try to make possible for the migrants to reach the United States. Finally, the third part will try to elucidate the connection between the theological notion of the crucified peoples and the reenactment of the Way of the Cross as performed by migrants, highlighting its purpose as a vehicle of protest.

CENTRAL AMERICAN MIGRATION TO THE UNITED STATES

The phenomenon of international migration has been amply documented and there are a number of theories that intend to provide an understanding of its

---

[1]   Thomas Nail, *Theory of the Border* (Oxford; New York: Oxford University Press, 2016), 2.

causes, characteristics, consequences and projections.[2] One of the distinct features of what some have called "the new face of international migration," referring to the latest big migration waves, is the great disparity between sending and receiving countries and the clear trend of poor people moving to wealthier societies.[3] However, economic disparities themselves do not fully explain the causes of international migration, particularly of the poor; rather there is a particular element that seems to be a determinant in the decision to migrate, namely, the perceived unbearable conditions in the migrants' countries of origin. As Douglas Massey puts it,

> International migration may require that economic conditions be perceived as insupportable—not simply inferior—in the country of origin [...] Migration typically has not ended with the equalization of wages, but with the attainment of bearable conditions of life in areas of origin, after which people find migration not worth the effort.[4]

The question is if the unbearable economic conditions is the only factor that put the most vulnerable people in certain Central American countries in the position to think that migrating is worth the risk? The answer to this question is extremely complex. Massey has clearly stated that it is practically impossible to fully understand contemporary migration based on a single theory, a conceptual model, a level of analysis, or even a single discipline. Accordingly, he suggests an approach that integrates different theories, levels of analysis, and assumptions.[5] In the following paragraphs, I will explain some of the most relevant factors involved in the increased migration from Central America to the United States.

The world systems theory[6] offers a good foundation for understanding the origin of Central American migration to the United States. This theory basically

---

2   See for example the comprehensive research led by Douglas Massey: Douglas S. Massey, Joaquín Arango, Hugo Graeme et al., *Worlds in Motion: Understanding International Migration at the End of the Millenium* (Oxford: Clarendon Press; Oxford University Press, 1998). See also Stephen Castles, *The Age of Migration: International Population Movements in the Modern World* (New York: Guilford Press, 1993).

3   Massey et al., *Worlds in Motion*, 7.

4   Massey et al., *Worlds in Motion*, 8–9.

5   Massey et al., 17. Massey analyzes the following theories: Neoclassical economics, the New Economics of Migration, Segmented Labor Market Theory, Historical-Structural Theory and World Systems, Social Capital Theory, and Cumulative Causation. See Massey et al., 17–59.

6   To learn more about this theory, see International Union for the Scientific Study of Population International Population Conference, ed., *International Population Conference, New Delhi 1989, 20–27 September, Congrès International de La Population, New Delhi 1989, 20–27 September* (Liège, Belgique: International Union for the Scientific Study of Population, 1989), 159–72; Alan B. Simmons, "World System-Linkages and International Migration: New Directions in Theory and Method, With an Application to Canada," September 6, 2011, http://yorkspace.library.yorku.ca/xmlui/handle/10315/9871.

suggests that the flows of international migrations have their origin in the socioeconomic disruptions and dislocations caused by the expansion of capitalist enterprises. This expansion concentrates on the use of land, raw materials, labor, and consumer markets. For example, in terms of land, capitalist farmers "seek to consolidate landholdings, mechanize production, introduce cash crops, and apply industrially produced inputs such as fertilizer, insecticides, and high-yield seeds."[7] This process causes a huge disruption in traditional systems and in the economic relationships of the countries where this is done.[8] This is exactly what happened in Central America from the moment the United States started its expansion in the continent as explained below.

The relationship between the United States and Mexico and Central America has been characterized as hegemonic since the mid-1800s,[9] starting with the issuing of the 1823 Monroe Doctrine. As Walter LaFeber explains,

> By the 1890s the influence of the U.S. in the region was growing rapidly through investments in banana and coffee plantations, railroads (to haul the bananas, not people), gold and silver mines, a little later, utilities and government securities.[10]

Basically, this hegemonic agenda has played a significant role in the dynamics of the political and economic life of Central America since then. In the anticommunist era, for example, the US policies and interventions led to violent and deadly results particularly in Nicaragua, El Salvador, and Guatemala. This period left millions of people displaced internally and externally. In the words of Maria Cristina García,

> A quarter of a million people died during the period 1974-96, and over one million people were internally displaced, forced to find refuge in other areas of their own countries. Many of those who survived the warfare and the human rights abuses chose temporary refuge in neighboring countries such as Costa Rica and Honduras, living anonymously as illegal immigrants or as documented refugees in government-run camps. When the camps filled up, or when their safety or economic survival was once again threatened, Nicaraguans, Salvadorans, and Guatemalans traveled further north, to Mexico, the United States, and Canada. Over two million of those who fled Central America during this period settled in these three countries.[11]

7   Massey et al., *Worlds in Motion*, 37.
8   Massey et al., *Worlds in Motion*, 36–37.
9   Lars Schoultz, *Beneath the United States: A History of U.S. Policy toward Latin America* (Cambridge, Mass.: Harvard University Press, 1998), xiii.
10 Walter LaFeber, *Inevitable Revolutions: The United States in Central America*, Expanded ed. (New York: W.W. Norton, 1984), 31.
11 María Cristina García, *Seeking Refuge: Central American Migration to Mexico, the United States, and Canada* (Berkeley: University of California Press, 2006), 1.

The US intervention in all these conflicts, in the form of military training, financial support to regimes that favored US interests, or directly guiding local elites to overthrow democratically elected leaders that represented a potential or actual threat to US interests, has been amply documented.[12] This strategy of direct or indirect intervention always implied economic interests, and it took different forms, the latest being the free trade agreements that were signed under the argument that they would help the development of the Latin American countries.[13] As part of these free trade agreements, many assembly plants were established in Mexico and Central America,[14] taking advantage of low wage rates. Two issues are closely linked to this fact. One is the fact that those low wages are usually barely enough to meet the needs of the worker's family.[15] The other one is the femininization of the workforce based on the demand of these assembly plants, which has created extremely disadvantageous and often times dangerous and fatal situations for many women.[16]

---

[12]   See LaFeber, *Inevitable Revolutions*. See also Schoultz, *Beneath the United States*. For Schoultz, "three interests have determined the content of United States policy toward Latin America: The need to protect U.S. security, the desire to accommodate the demands of U.S. domestic politics, and the drive to promote U.S. economic development." Schoultz, 367.

[13]   "Each generation's specific policies have changed with the times and the circumstances, as one year's fear of communist adventurism yields to next year's dismay over human rights violations, as the Big Stick transmutes into Dollar Diplomacy and the Good Neighborliness, as democracy and free trade vie for attention with the drug trafficking and immigration." Schoultz, *Beneath the United States*, 367.

[14]   The number of maquiladoras in Mexico grew from 1,920 in the 1990s to 5,055 in 2012. NAFTA was signed in 1994. Maquiladoras opened not only in Mexican states near the U.S.-Mexico border but also in the interior of the country. See Sławomir Dorocki and Paweł Brzegowy, "The Maquiladora Industry Impact on the Social and Economic Situation in Mexico in the Era of Globalization," in *Environmental and Socio-Economic Transformations in Developing Areas as the Effect of Globalization*, ed. Mirosław Wójtowicz and Anna Winiarczyk-Raźniak, Prace Monograficzne (Uniwersytet Pedagogiczny Im. Komisji Edukacji Narodowej w Krakowie) ; 699 (Kraków: Wydawnictwo Naukowe Uniwersytetu Pedagogicznego, 2014), 100, 102. In the case of Central America "Employment within export zones (EPZ), and free zones (FZ) [maquiladoras] increased more than 40 percent per year from 1990 to 1996." Jose Antonio Cordero, "Honduras: Recent Economic Performance" (Center for Economic and Policy Research, November 2009), 3, www.cepr.net.

[15]   Mateo Crossa, "Maquiladora Industry Wages in Central America Are Not Living Wages", accessed October 31, 2017, http://cepr.net/blogs/the-americas-blog/maquiladora-industry-wages-in-central-america-are-not-living-wages. See also Benjamin Hensler, "Global Wage Trends for Apparel Workers, 2001-2011" (Washington, DC: Center for American Progress, July, 2013), 8, https://www.americanprogress.org/wp-content/uploads/2013/07/RealWageStudy-3.pdf. For a summary of the history on Maquilas in El Salvador, see Jill Esbenshade, "The Process of Exporting Neo-Liberal Development: The Consequences of the Growth of EPZs in El Salvador", in *The Wages of Empire: Neoliberal Policies, Repression, and Women's Poverty*, ed. Amalia L. Cabezas, Ellen Reese, y Marguerite R. Waller, Transnational Feminist Studies (Boulder: Paradigm Publishers, 2007), 152–66.

[16]   For the case of Mexico, see Teresa Rodríguez, Diana Montané, and Lisa Pulitzer, *The Daughters of Juárez: A True Story of Serial Murder South of the Border* (New York: Atria Books, 2007).

There are other dynamics at play in the decision to migrate, such as the advantages and support derived from connections that migrants have with relatives, friends, and former neighbors who now reside in the United States. This phenomenon, often described through the framework provided by social capital theory, when applied to migration includes migrant networks. Migrant networks are defined as "sets of interpersonal ties that connect migrants, former migrants, and non-migrants in origin and destination areas through ties of kinship, friendship, and shared community origin. They increase the likelihood of international movement because they lower the costs and risks of movement and increase the expected net returns to migration."[17] What is important to note here is that the economic and social crisis in Guatemala, Nicaragua, and El Salvador was closely related to the implementation of certain economic policies and geopolitical interests that provoked different waves of migration in the past. The early migrants and their children are the ones who now represent a social capital for those who have migrated more recently. This is a cycle that scholars anticipate will continue. Therefore, it could be stated that the establishment of a certain economic model—one that benefits foreign interests and local oligarchies and that creates unbearable disruptions in Central American social and economic structures—is one of the main causes of migration from Central America to the United States.

There are a number of ramifications of these economic and political causes. One of the main ramifications is the violence experienced by Salvadorans, Hondurans, and Guatemalans, which is among the highest in the hemisphere.[18] This violence is being created primarily by street gangs such as the *Maras* whose origin can be traced to the violent episodes and civil wars in Central America in the 1980s and 1990s and the migration wave to the United States that occurred as a result in that period. They spread initially on the streets of Los Angeles, California, where Central American youths who came to the United States fleeing civil wars and violence in their countries of origin showed an unprecedented capacity for violence and cruelty, in some cases the product of the military training that they received from US Special Forces in El Salvador.[19] As a result of their involvement in this criminal activity, they were deported and sent back

17   Massey et al., *Worlds in Motion*, 43.
18   Joshua Partlow, "El Salvador Is on Pace to Become the Hemisphere's Most Deadly Nation," *The Washington Post*, May 17, 2015, http://www.washingtonpost.com/world/the_americas/el-salvador-is-on-pace-to-become-the-hemispheres-most-deadly-nation/2015/05/17/fc52e4b6-f74b-11e4-a47c-e56f4db884ed_story.html.
19   William C. Dunn, *The Gangs of Los Angeles* (New York: iUniverse, 2007), 217, quoted in Deborah Levenson-Estrada, *Adiós Niño: The Gangs of Guatemala City and the Politics of Death* (Durham; London: Duke University Press, 2013), 41.

to Central America in large numbers by 1996.[20] Upon their forced return to their home countries, which were still convulsed by the violence related to the political and social struggles, these youths implemented all the knowledge they acquired as gang members to survive in a very hostile environment, creating new gangs that overtime have become the main source of violence in the region.[21] This explains in large part why this kind of gang violence is so prevalent in Guatemala, Honduras, and El Salvador. Gangs are very versatile in their aims as Partlow explains: "Gangs have diverse criminal interests—drug trade, migrant trafficking, gun-running."[22] In Mexico, for example, gang members have created alliances with other criminal groups. This has been documented first by journalists: "The largest of these gangs, the *Mara Salvatrucha 13* and *Barrio 18*, have created alliances with the *Zetas* and the Gulf cartels that operate along the migrant routes. The cartels have bought off local police agents and immigration officials in many places, allowing drug trafficking, kidnapping and extortions operations to continue without prosecution."[23] This is only one of the multiple ramifications of the intervention of the United States in Central America in the past that extends its arms until the present, affecting Central American countries, and particularly children. This is what created the "crisis of unaccompanied children" since 2011.[24]

A statistical note seems to confirm that violence is playing a significant role in the migrations observed from El Salvador, Honduras, and Guatemala in recent years:

> The Center for Migration Studies of New York (CMS) found that the US undocumented population from Central America increased by 5 percent between 2010 and 2014, but decreased from Mexico by 9 percent (Warren 2016, 8,10). The US undocumented population from Central American nations other

---

[20]   "The expansion of MS-13 and 18th Street presence in Central America accelerated after the United States began deporting illegal immigrants, many with criminal convictions, back to the northern triangle region after the passage of the Illegal Immigrant Reform and Immigrant Responsibility Act (IIRIRA; P.L. 104–208) of 1996." Clare Ribando Seelke, "Gangs in Central America", Congressional Research Service, August 29, 2016, 3, https://fas.org/sgp/crs/row/RL34112.pdf.

[21]   Levenson-Estrada, *Adiós Niño*, 40–43. See also Frank de Waegh, "Unwilling Participants: The Coercion of Youth into Violent Criminal Groups in Central America's Northern Triangle" (Jesuit Conference of Canada and the United States, 2015), http://jesuits.org/Assets/Publications/File/Report_UnwillingParticipants_v4.pdf.

[22]   Partlow, "El Salvador is on Pace to Become the Hemisphere's Most Deadly Nation."

[23]   Martha Pskowski, "Viacrucis: Migrants Step out of Shadows into the Streets", *martha pskowski* (blog), accessed May 30, 2015, https://marthapskowski.wordpress.com/2014/06/06/viacrucis-migrants-step-out-of-shadows-into-the-streets/.

[24]   Adam Isacson, "Mexico's Other Border", 14–16, accessed June 2, 2015, http://www.wola.org/sites/default/files/Mexico%27s%20Other%20Border%20PDF.pdf. See also Peter J. Meyer et al., "Unaccompanied Children from Central America Foreign Policy Considerations," Congressional Research Service, April 11, 2016, https://fas.org/sgp/crs/homesec/R43702.pdf.

than the Northern Triangle states fell even more precipitously, by 17 percent for Nicaraguan nationals, for example, and 22 percent for South American nationals. Such a disparity suggests that irregular migration from the Northern Triangle is driven by more than just economic or family reunification motivations, but also by endemic violence.[25]

These facts are among the most important circumstances that are causing the migration of hundreds of thousands of Central Americans to the United States every year. The condition of violence has reached unbearable levels as most of the personal testimonies and stories show, and this fact is essential to understand why these migrants have chosen the reenactment of the Way of the Cross as the main form of protest, denunciation and also a vehicle of hope, which seems to be one of the core motivators to migrate. In what follows, the role of faith-based and non-profit organizations in the creation of the reenactment of the Way of the Cross of the Migrant will be explained.

THE WAY OF THE CROSS OF THE MIGRANT

The reenactment of the Way of the Cross is probably one of the most dramatic religious expressions within Christianity. In its more public version, it is mostly practiced within Latin American Roman Catholic Christianity. It consists of 14 stations in which various scenes of Jesus's last hours are remembered, including his trial and crucifixion. "The stations are characteristically used for prayer and devotion during Lent, and especially Good Friday, and it is common for pilgrims to carry life-size crosses along the way, as reenactment of the events of the passion."[26] In many Latin American countries, this reenactment takes place on the streets and attracts large multitudes. For example, around two million people gathered in 2015 to watch the 172nd anniversary celebration of the reenactment in Mexico City.[27]

The reenactment of the Way of the Cross of the Migrant has part of its origin in this established form. The other part seems to come from the work of a Roman Catholic order founded in Italy in 1887, known as The Missionaries of St. Charles, Scalabrinians.[28] This congregation that is devoted to help and

[25]   J. Kevin Appleby y Donald Kerwin, "International Migration Policy Report: Responsibility Sharing for Large Movements of Refugee and Migrants in Need of Protection" (New York, NY: Center for Migration Studies of New York (CMS), June, 2017), 84, http://cmsny.org/wp-content/uploads/2017/06/International-Migration-Policy-Report-2017-6.3.pdf.

[26]   George D. Chryssides y Margaret Z. Wilkins, *Christians in the Twenty-first Century* (Sheffield ; Oakville, CT: Equinox Pub, 2011), 36.

[27]   "El DF, listo para la 172 representación del viacrucis en Iztapalapa," La Jornada, accessed May 30, 2015, http://www.jornada.unam.mx/ultimas/2015/03/17/el-df-listo-para-la-172-representacion-del-viacrucis-en-iztapalapa-1545.html.

[28]   "Missionaries of St. Charles Scalabrinians," Missionaries of St. Charles Scalabrinians, accessed May 31, 2015, http://www.scalabrinians.org/website/index.html.

advocate for migrants around the world started its work in Mexico's borders in 1987 through *Las Casas del Migrante* [The Migrant Houses], which provide shelter, food, and a number of other services to migrants, including spiritual support and the promotion of human rights. The Scalabrinians opened a number of Migrant Houses in Mexico (Tijuana, Ciudad Juárez, Agua Prieta and Nuevo Laredo) and Guatemala (Tecún Umán and Guatemala City).[29] Through its *Centro de Pastoral Migratoria Scalabrini*, this religious order published in 1999 a booklet entitled *The Way of the Cross of the Migrant Jesus*.[30] This booklet contains Scripture readings, prayers, and reflections for each one of the 14 stations. It is basically an alternative way to reenact the Way of the Cross, taking into account the suffering and pain of the migrants and, seeking, at the same, to inspire hope in them. In the author's own words:

> Today Jesus walks the sorrowful journey of the migrant. For that reason we wish to celebrate this journey in solidarity with those people who leave their homes in search of the Promised Land of milk and honey (Exod 3:8), which is the reign of God that Jesus himself announces. This Way of the Cross is intended for all those communities and people who are living the difficult experience of migration, for those who work with migrants building a better world, a world without borders, and to those men and women who have opened their eyes to the harsh reality of this phenomenon and want to be challenged by it.[31]

Gioacchino Campese, the author of this booklet, is a professor of theology at the Scalabrini International Migration Institute and worked for seven years at the *Casa del Migrante* in Tijuana, Mexico. He has said that the most heartbreaking aspect of his work there was "to confront the tragic reality of thousands of migrant men, women, and children dying in the process of crossing the US–Mexico border. In many informal conversations, migrants described to me in vivid terms the ordeal of crossing the border throughout the mountains, the desert, or water channels."[32] In the introduction of the booklet, Campese explains his motivation to write this material: "The Way of the Cross of the Migrant Jesus was born as a celebration in front of the Cathedral of Tijuana (Mexico) during Lent 1999. Starting from our daily contact with the migrants

---

[29] "Casas del Migrante," Red Casas del Migrante, accessed May 31, 2015, http://www.migrante.com.mx/casas-del-migrante.html. See also Flor María Rigoni, "EL Norte se vuelve el Sur. 30 años de presencia scalibriniana en México" (Congregación de los Misioneros de San Carlos-Scalabrinianos. Provincia de San Juan Bautista, 2010), 41–64, http://www.migrante.com.mx/uploads/4/6/9/5/46959225/libro-flor-maria.pdf.

[30] Gioacchino Campese, *El Vía Crucis de Jesús Migrante = The Way of the Cross of the Migrant Jesus* (Liguori, Mo.: Libros Liguori, 2006).

[31] Campese, *El Vía Crucis de Jesús Migrante*, Location 96 of 673 (Kindle).

[32] Gioacchino Campese, "¿Cuántos Más? The Crucified Peoples at the U.S.-Mexico Border," in *A Promised Land, a Perilous Journey: Theological Perspectives on Migration*, ed. Daniel G. Groody and Gioacchino Campese (Notre Dame, IN: University of Notre Dame Press, 2008), 271.

in Casa del Migrante en Tijuana and in border region, we wanted to express through prayer the suffering and hope of the undocumented and the deported."[33] This booklet has apparently been used in many places and has contributed to a long-standing trend within Catholic and other Christian communities of utilizing the liturgical calendar to engage in activism in social justice issues related to migration. In fact, Sociologist Pierrette Hondagneu-Sotelo suggests that the strong critical feature of the work of the Scalabrinians who went to work at the US–Mexico border came from influences of Liberation Theology.

> Guided by the influence of . . . Liberation Theology, the mission work of the Scalabrinis along the U.S.-Mexico border extended to include more social change work. Scalabrinian Brother Gioacchino Campese, who worked at the Tijuana shelter for seven years, said that he believes "service and protest are two dimensions of the same mission." While committed to the offering of material and spiritual service, he also said, "Then there is another dimension, which is . . . the public dimension, the social dimension of the work of Casa del Migrante—which starts with events like Posada Sin Fronteras, Via Cruces [*sic*] del Migrante Jesus."[34]

This assessment of the influence of Liberation Theology seems to be accurate. In the particular case of the author of the liturgical resources prepared for the reenactment of the Way of the Cross of the Migrant Jesus, Gioacchino Campese has drawn his own reflection on migration issues from liberation theologians, Ignacio Ellacuría and Jon Sobrino. This connection will be briefly analyzed in the next section.

MIGRANTS AS CRUCIFIED PEOPLES

In his essay "¿Cuantos Más? [*sic*] The Crucified Peoples at the U.S.-Mexico Border,"[35] Campese explicitly says that two main sources inspired it: (1) on the one hand, the concept of the "crucified peoples" as coined and developed by Ignacio Ellacuría and Jon Sobrino respectively, and, on the other, (2) the cartoon by David Fitzsimmons that portrays a crucified migrant with the sign above his head that reads: "U.S. Border Policy." The background of this depiction is a hot day in the Arizona desert and the headline of the cartoon quotes a portion of Matthew 25:42: "I was thirsty and you gave me no drink: I was a stranger and ye took me not in"[36] In this piece, Campese offers a summary of the notion "crucified peoples" and how he sees the connection with the

---

[33]   Campese, *El Vía Crucis de Jesús Migrante*, Location 81 of 673 (Kindle).
[34]   Pierrette Hondagneu-Sotelo, Genelle Gaudinez, and Hector Lara, "Religious Reenactment on the Line. A Geneology of Political Religious Hybridity," in *Religion and Social Justice for Immigrants* (New Brunswick, N.J.: Rutgers University Press, 2007), 134.
[35]   Campese, "¿Cuantos Más? The Crucified Peoples at the U.S.-Mexico Border."
[36]   Campese, "¿Cuantos Más? The Crucified Peoples at the U.S.-Mexico Border," 273.

migrant experience, which constitutes one more step toward a theology of migration in his own work.[37] The notion of the crucified people was crafted originally in El Salvador in the late 1970s by Archbishop Oscar Arnulfo Romero, and was further developed by Spanish-Salvadoran Jesuit philosopher, theologian, priest and activist, Ignacio Ellacuría. Ellacuría defined the crucified people as "that collective body, which as the majority of humankind owes its situation of crucifixion to the way society is organized and maintained by a minority that exercises its dominion through a series of factors, which taken together and given their concrete impact within history, must be regarded as sin."[38] Regarding the relevance of the term "crucified people," Campese summarizes three functions of this metaphor. The first function of the crucified peoples is "to unmask the sin of the world and to expose its need for conversion, redemption, and renewal."[39] The second function is to illuminate historical reality, and to show "the ongoing presence of Jesus Christ in history."[40] The third function is to be "a principle of salvation," not only the object of salvation. The crucified peoples are a principle of salvation insofar as they make present in history the "Savior par excellence," the *Crucified*.[41] Here, Campese points out that with this theological move, Ellacuría highlights one of the basic aspects of salvation as understood in Christian theology, "that is, that salvation comes *desde abajo,* 'from below.'"[42]

This theological background explains the critical character of the reenactments of the Way of the Cross of the Migrant. It is not entirely clear how the liturgy written by Campese spread but there is evidence that at least since 2003, his leaflet was utilized, modified, and adapted in South America and Central

---

[37] See an earlier essay where Campese outlines the method and the main themes of a theology of migration: Flor Maria Rigoni and Gioacchino Campese, "Hacer teología desde el migrante: diario de un camino," *Center for Migration Studies special issues* 18, no.2 (March 2003): 181–203, https://doi.org/10.1111/j.2050-411X.2003.tb00322.x. And also a later essay on the same topic: Gioacchino Campese, "The Irruption of Migrants: Theology of Migration in the 21st Century," *Theological Studies* 73, no.1 (2012), 3–32, http://tsj.sagepub.com/content/73/1/3.short.

[38] Ignacio Ellacuría, "The Crucified People," in *Mysterium Liberationis: Fundamental Concepts of Liberation Theology* (Maryknoll, N.Y.: North Blackburn, Victoria, Australia: Orbis Books; CollinsDove, 1993), 590.

[39] Campese, "¿Cuántos Más? The Crucified Peoples at the U.S.-Mexico Border," 284. In the corresponding footnote 49, Campese offers the proper credit of these ideas: Kevin F. Burke, "The Crucified People as 'Light for the Nations': A Reflection on Ignacio Ellacuría," in *Rethinking Martyrdom*, ed. Teresa Okure, Jon Sobrino, and Felix Wilfred, Concilium, 2003/1 (London: SCM Press, 2003), 124–28.

[40] Campese, "¿Cuántos Más? The Crucified Peoples at the U.S.-Mexico Border," 284.

[41] Campese, "¿Cuántos Más? The Crucified Peoples at the U.S.-Mexico Border," 284–85.

[42] Campese, "¿Cuántos Más? The Crucified Peoples at the U.S.-Mexico Border," 285.

America.[43] Given the fact that Campese's liturgy seems to be the first one in Latin America linking the experience of the migrants with the *via crucis,* it is very likely that this liturgy was the inspiration for the reenactments that since 2011, have taken place every year as transnational caravans. In some cases, such reenactments involved crossing Mexico from Guatemala to the US–Mexico border. These reenactments, that took the form of caravans, were organized by a significant number of social actors who have worked for years as advocates and a network of care for the migrants.[44] The collective organizers of the first reenactment in 2011 were *"Paso a Paso Hacia la Paz"* [Step by Step Toward Peace], *"Nuestros Lazos de Sangre"* [Our Blood Linkage], *"Familia Latina Unida"* [United Latino Family], *"Movimiento Migrante Centroamericano"* [Central American Migrant Movement], *"Albergue Hermanos en el Camino"* [Shelter Brothers and Sisters on the Road] "Alianza Braceros del Norte," and "Albergue Hogar de la Misericordia."[45] Among the organizers of this reenactment, Father Alejandro Solalinde, who is the director of the migrant shelter, *"Hermanos del Camino"* in Ixtepec, Oaxaca, Mexico, stated in an interview the purpose of this reenactment: "The Via Crucis, which has become a caravan, attempts to shed a definite light on what is going on, and to let the Mexican government know about the many times that we have been stepped on or become the victims of extortion, thanks to criminals, public servants, police and immigration institutions—which are a den of corruption."[46] The caravan's motto "We, the migrants, are fed up!"[47] reflects the frustration expressed by Father Solalinde. The main demand was respect on the part of the Mexican authorities who consistently violated human rights and abused the migrants,

---

[43]   In Quito, Ecuador, a 2003 liturgy entitled "Via Crucis of the Migrant and Refugee Jesus" reproduced almost verbatim Campese's liturgy, see Comisión Ecuatoriana de Refugiados, "Via Crucis de Jesús migrante y refugiado," accessed July 20, 2015, https://dioscaminaconsupueblo. files.wordpress.com/2013/07/via-crucis-de-jesc3bas.pdf. In 2011, another liturgy that used extensive portions of Campese's leaflet, appeared in Guatemala indicating that it was based on the one from Ecuador, see "Via Crucis Del Jesus Migrante y Refugiado" (Centro de Formación y Espiritualidad CEBs Guatemala, 2011), https://dioscaminaconsupueblo.files.wordpress. com/2013/07/vc3a1crucis-de-jesus-migrante-y-refugiado.pdf.

[44]   Vargas Carrasco identified a hundred and twenty five social actors that help and support the migrants for the period between 2011 and 2015. Felipe de Jesús Vargas Carrasco, "El vía crucis del migrante: Demandas y membresía," *Trace. Procesos Mexicanos y Centroamericanos*, no.73 (January 2018): 127–29, http://trace.org.mx/index.php/trace/article/view/88.

[45]   "Migrantes centroamericanos escenifican el vía crucis que viven en México," Expansión (en alianza con CNN), April 20, 2011, https://expansion.mx/nacional/2011/04/20/ migrantes-centroamericanos-escenifican-el-via-crucis-que-viven-en-mexico.

[46]   "Protesting Migrants Recreate the 'Way of the Cross' Through Mexico", VICE News, accessed June 1, 2015, https://news.vice.com/article/ protesting-migrants-recreate-the-way-of-the-cross-through-mexico.

[47]   The original expression in Mexican Spanish is "¡Los migrantes estamos hasta la madre!" which is considered vulgar language. See "Migrantes centroamericanos escenifican el vía crucis que viven en México."

who additionally suffered extortion, kidnappings, assaults, and violent robbery committed by criminal individuals and groups.[48] This demand against Mexican authorities was brought up more intensely due to the lack of response to solve the massacre of 72 migrants in San Fernando, Tamaulipas (a northern Mexican state) in 2010. This *via crucis* seems to have been also inspired by other caravans for migrants' rights, such as the Caravan of Central American Mothers in Search for their Disappeared Children and a group of Honduran amputees who lost limbs on the train ride that they were hoping would take them to the northern border.[49] All of these initiatives seek to stop the violence and abuses, the extortions and the murders. Their constant demand is freedom to cross Mexico. The situation that Central American migrants face in their journey through Mexico is extremely dangerous. Without documents, migrants have to evade Mexican authorities to avoid deportation or extortion and most of the time they are victims of crime. As Pskowski has reported: "Boarding the train in Tabasco and southern Veracruz has become a matter of life and death. By February of this year [2014], every week or two news articles reported on migrants killed for not paying the 'quota.' The *maras*—Central American gangs who terrorize migrants throughout the country—demand that migrants hopping the train pay $100 each."[50] The undocumented condition of these migrants is directly related to the stringent and restrictive nature of the US immigration system. The four main categories under which the United States grants legal residency are: Family-based immigration, employment-based immigration, humanitarian-based immigration, and other, such as the diversity lottery. All these categories are very restricted and in some cases, the criteria are arbitrary or outdated. For these reasons, "there was never a 'line' for the vast majority of unauthorized immigrants. They do not have the necessary family relationships or employment connections to apply for legal entry, and very few qualify for refugee status. Those few who might have been eligible for visa would have to face years and even decades of waiting time."[51]

---

48   "Migrantes centroamericanos escenifican el vía crucis que viven en México."

49   "For years, the freight train collectively known as "The Beast" carried Central American migrants north through Mexico on their quest to reach the U.S. border, fleeing extreme poverty and violence in their home countries. Hundreds could be seen crammed on top of the cars, riding between them or clinging to ladders on the sides. It's easy to fall off the bumpy trains. Many who do are killed or lose limbs." Joseph Sorrentino, "How the U.S. 'Solved' the Central American Migrant Crisis," *In These Times*, May 12, 2015, http://inthesetimes.com/article/17916/how-the-u.s.-solved-the-central-american-migrant-crisis.

50   Pskowski, "Viacrucis."

51   "Breaking Down the Problems. What's Wrong with Our Immigration System?," Special Report (Washington, D.C.: Immigration Policy Center, October 2009), 5. https://www.americanimmigrationcouncil.org/sites/default/files/research/Problems_and_Solutions_2010.pdf.

Given the conditions to which migrants are subjected, it is not surprising that they have embraced and identified with the image of the crucified people. In the documentary *Viacrucis Migrante* (Migrant Crossing), one of the participants of the 2012 reenactment of the Way of the Cross appears, sanding the cross that was going to be used for the reenactment and shared his view on his participation in these terms: "This cross is very heavy, if I imagine that Jesus had to carry something that heavy on his back, not only is it heavy, there is the humiliation, the shouts, the lashes that he had to deal with. In this Easter season, I always think about it and I am reminded that we have hope that everything will turn out well."[52] This comment reflects not only the understanding of Jesus's passion as a comparable experience of suffering to that of the migrants, but also the hope that things "will turn out well."

Concluding Reflections

The notion of the crucified peoples was in Campese's mind when he wrote *The Way of the Cross of the Migrant Jesus,* which apparently became the starting point of a religious expression that has captured the essence of the experience of thousands of poor and marginalized Central American migrants. It is interesting to note that at the center of the notion of the crucified peoples is precisely its critical nature, which denounces the forces that cause death. That is exactly what the migrants themselves have embraced while participating in the reenactment of the Way of the Cross of the Migrant. These forces are not only the more recent violence but also the precarious economic conditions that Central American countries have experienced for decades. In the process of denouncing and protesting such violence and poverty, migrants are breaking the boundaries that have been designed to keep them from migrating and keep them marginalized. Despite all the efforts to stop and silence migrants, they have continued their struggle for life. A notion that started in Central America in the midst of extreme violence and repression has come back 35 years later in a context of violence and death to denounce the root causes of such death and suffering. As Friar Tomás, who is one of the organizers of the *via crucis* of the Migrant said: "We are making visible what for many years has been invisible . . . the death that our governments cause us, the economic system, which is the most responsible for forcing us to leave, which gives us death. We cannot continue to die. We have to transform this pathway of death into a pathway of life."[53]

---

52   *Viacrucis Migrante–Migrant Crossing*, Documentary (TIDE Hamburgs Communitysender und Ausbildungskanal, 2015), Minute 26, https://viacrucismigrante.com/en/.
53   Pskowski, "Viacrucis."

BIBLIOGRAPHY:

Appleby, J. Kevin, and Donald Kerwin. "International Migration Policy Report: Responsibility Sharing for Large Movements of Refugee and Migrants in Need of Protection." New York, NY: Center for Migration Studies of New York (CMS), June 2017. http://cmsny.org/wp-content/uploads/2017/06/International-Migration-Policy-Report-2017-6.3.pdf. "Breaking Down the Problems. What's Wrong with Our Immigration System?" Special Report. Washington, D.C.: Immigration Policy Center, October 2009. https://www.americanimmigrationcouncil.org/sites/default/files/research/Problems_and_Solutions_2010.pdf.

Burke, Kevin F. "The Crucified People as 'Light for the Nations': A Reflection on Ignacio Ellacuría." In *Rethinking Martyrdom*, edited by Teresa Okure, Jon Sobrino, and Felix Wilfred, 123–30. Concilium, 2003/1. London: SCM Press, 2003.

Campese, Gioacchino. "¿Cuántos Más? The Crucified Peoples at the U.S.-Mexico Border." In *A Promised Land, a Perilous Journey: Theological Perspectives on Migration*, edited by Daniel G. Groody and Gioacchino Campese, 271–98. Notre Dame, IN: University of Notre Dame Press, 2008.

———. *El Vía Crucis de Jesús Migrante = The Way of the Cross of the Migrant Jesus*. Liguori, MO: Libros Liguori, 2006.

———. "The Irruption of Migrants: Theology of Migration in the 21st Century." *Theological Studies* 73, no.1 (2012): 3–32. http://tsj.sagepub.com/content/73/1/3.short.

"Casas Del Migrante." Red Casas del Migrante. Accessed May 31, 2015. http://www.migrante.com.mx/casas-del-migrante.html.

Castles, Stephen. *The Age of Migration: International Population Movements in the Modern World*. New York: Guilford Press, 1993.

Chryssides, George D., and Margaret Z. Wilkins. *Christians in the Twenty-First Century*. Sheffield; Oakville, CT: Equinox Pub, 2011.

Comisión Ecuatoriana de Refugiados. "Via Crucis de Jesús migrante y refugiado." Accessed July 20, 2015. https://dioscaminaconsupueblo.files.wordpress.com/2013/07/via-crucis-de-jesc3bas.pdf.

Cordero, Jose Antonio. "Honduras: Recent Economic Performance." Center for Economic and Policy Research, November 2009. www.cepr.net.

Crossa, Mateo. "Maquiladora Industry Wages in Central America Are Not Living Wages." Accessed October 31, 2017. http://cepr.net/blogs/the-americas-blog/maquiladora-industry-wages-in-central-america-are-not-living-wages.

Dorocki, Sławomir, and Paweł Brzegowy. "The Maquiladora Industry Impact on the Social and Economic Situation in Mexico in the Era of Globalization." In *Environmental and Socio-Economic Transformations in Developing Areas as the Effect of Globalization*, edited by Mirosław Wójtowicz and

Anna Winiarczyk-Raźniak, 93–110. Prace Monograficzne (Uniwersytet Pedagogiczny Im. Komisji Edukacji Narodowej w Krakowie); 699. Kraków: Wydawnictwo Naukowe Uniwersytetu Pedagogicznego, 2014.

Dunn, William C. *The Gangs of Los Angeles*. New York: iUniverse, 2007.

"El DF, Listo Para La 172 Representación Del Viacrucis En Iztapalapa." La Jornada. Accessed May 30, 2015. http://www.jornada.unam.mx/ul-timas/2015/03/17/el-df-listo-para-la-172-representacion-del-viacru-cis-en-iztapalapa-1545.html.

Ellacuría, Ignacio. "The Crucified People." In *Mysterium Liberationis: Fundamental Concepts of Liberation Theology*, 580–603. Maryknoll, NY: North Blackburn, Victoria, Australia: Orbis Books; CollinsDove, 1993.

Esbenshade, Jill. "The Process of Exporting Neo-Liberal Development: The Consequences of the Growth of EPZs in El Salvador." In *The Wages of Empire: Neoliberal Policies, Repression, and Women's Poverty*, edited by Amalia L. Cabezas, Ellen Reese, and Marguerite R. Waller, 152–66. Transnational Feminist Studies. Boulder: Paradigm Publishers, 2007.

García, María Cristina. *Seeking Refuge: Central American Migration to Mexico, the United States, and Canada*. Berkeley: University of California Press, 2006.

Hensler, Benjamin. "Global Wage Trends for Apparel Workers, 2001-2011." Washington, DC: Center for American Progress, July 2013. https://www.americanprogress.org/wp-content/uploads/2013/07/RealWageStudy-3.pdf.

Hondagneu-Sotelo, Pierrette, Genelle Gaudinez, and Hector Lara. "Religious Reenactment on the Line. A Geneology of Political Religious Hybridity." In *Religion and Social Justice for Immigrants*, 122–40. New Brunswick, NJ: Rutgers University Press, 2007.

International Population Conference, International Union for the Scientific Study of Population, ed. *International Population Conference, New Delhi 1989, 20–27 September, Congrès International de La Population, New Delhi 1989, 20–27 September*. Liège, Belgique: International Union for the Scientific Study of Population, 1989.

Isacson, Adam. "Mexico's Other Border." Accessed June 2, 2015. http://www.wola.org/sites/default/files/Mexico%27s%20Other%20Border%20PDF.pdf.

LaFeber, Walter. *Inevitable Revolutions: The United States in Central America*. Expanded ed. New York: W.W. Norton, 1984.

Levenson-Estrada, Deborah. *Adiós Niño: The Gangs of Guatemala City and the Politics of Death*. Durham; London: Duke University Press, 2013.

Lorenz, Hauke. *Viacrucis Migrante—Migrant Crossing*. Documentary. TIDE Hamburgs Communitysender und Ausbildungskanal, 2015. https://viacrucismigrante.com/en/.

Massey, Douglas S, Joaquín Arango, Hugo Graeme, Kouaouci Ali, Adela Pellegrino, and J. Edward Taylor. *Worlds in Motion: Understanding International Migration at the End of the Millenium*. Oxford: Clarendon Press; Oxford University Press, 1998.

Meyer, Peter J., Rhoda Margesson, Clare Ribando Seelke, and Maureen Taft-Morales. "Unaccompanied Children from Central America Foreign Policy Considerations." Congressional Research Service, April 11, 2016. https://fas.org/sgp/crs/homesec/R43702.pdf.

"Migrantes centroamericanos escenifican el vía crucis que viven en México." Expansión (en alianza con CNN), April 20, 2011. https://expansion.mx/nacional/2011/04/20/migrantes-centroamericanos-escenifican-el-via-crucis-que-viven-en-mexico.

"Missionaries of St. Charles Scalabrinians." Missionaries of St. Charles Scalabrinians. Accessed May 31, 2015. http://www.scalabrinians.org/website/index.html.

Nail, Thomas. *Theory of the Border*. Oxford; New York: Oxford University Press, 2016.

Partlow, Joshua. "El Salvador Is on Pace to Become the Hemisphere's Most Deadly Nation." *The Washington Post*, May 17, 2015. http://www.washingtonpost.com/world/the_americas/el-salvador-is-on-pace-to-become-the-hemispheres-most-deadly-nation/2015/05/17/fc52e4b6-f74b-11e4-a47c-e56f4db884ed_story.html.

"Protesting Migrants Recreate the 'Way of the Cross' Through Mexico." VICE News. Accessed June 1, 2015. https://news.vice.com/article/protesting-migrants-recreate-the-way-of-the-cross-through-mexico.

Pskowski, Martha. "Viacrucis: Migrants Step out of Shadows into the Streets." *Martha Pskowski* (blog). Accessed May 30, 2015. https://marthapskowski.wordpress.com/2014/06/06/viacrucis-migrants-step-out-of-shadows-into-the-streets/.

Rigoni, Flor María. "EL Norte se vuelve el Sur. 30 años de presencia scalibriniana en Mexico." Congregación de los MIsioneros de San Carlos -Scalabrinianos. Provincia de San Juan Bautista, 2010. http://www.migrante.com.mx/uploads/4/6/9/5/46959225/libro-flor-maria.pdf.

Rigoni, Flor Maria, and Gioacchino Campese. "Hacer teología desde el migrante: diario de un camino." *Center for Migration Studies special issues* 18, no.2 (March 2003): 181–203. https://doi.org/10.1111/j.2050-411X.2003.tb00322.x.

Rodríguez, Teresa, Diana Montané, and Lisa Pulitzer. *The Daughters of Juárez: A True Story of Serial Murder South of the Border*. New York: Atria Books, 2007.

Schoultz, Lars. *Beneath the United States: A History of U.S. Policy toward Latin America*. Cambridge, Mass.: Harvard University Press, 1998.

Seelke, Clare Ribando. "Gangs in Central America." Congressional Research Service, August 29, 2016. https://fas.org/sgp/crs/row/RL34112.pdf.

Simmons, Alan B. "World System-Linkages and International Migration: New Directions in Theory and Method, With an Application to Canada," September 6, 2011. http://yorkspace.library.yorku.ca/xmlui/handle/10315/9871.

Sorrentino, Joseph. "How the U.S. 'Solved' the Central American Migrant Crisis." *In These Times*, May 12, 2015. http://inthesetimes.com/article/17916/how-the-u.s.-solved-the-central-american-migrant-crisis.

Vargas Carrasco, Felipe de Jesús. "El vía crucis del migrante: Demandas y membresía." *Trace. Procesos Mexicanos y Centroamericanos*, no.73 (January 2018): 117–33. http://trace.org.mx/index.php/trace/article/view/88.

"Via Crucis Del Jesus Migrante y Refugiado." Centro de Formación y Espiritualidad CEBs Guatemala, 2011. https://dioscaminaconsupueblo.files.wordpress.com/2013/07/vc3a1crucis-de-jesus-migrante-y-refugiado.pdf.

Waegh, Frank de. "Unwilling Participants: The Coercion of Youth into Violent Criminal Groups in Central America's Northern Triangle." Jesuit Conference of Canada and the United States, 2015. http://jesuits.org/Assets/Publications/File/Report_UnwillingParticipants_v4.pdf.

PART V

BRAZILIAN PENTECOSTALISM
AND MIGRATION:
TWO STORIES

CHAPTER 14

ZUMBI OF THE PENTECOSTALS: MIGRATIONS AND PENTECOSTAL MODULATIONS OBSERVED AT THE ZUMBI DOS PALMARES SETTLEMENT IN CAMPOS DOS GOYTACAZES

Fabio Py

INTRODUCTION

The goal of this chapter is to analyze how Pentecostalism is experienced at the Zumbi dos Palmares land reform settlement,[1] in Campos dos Goytacazes, a municipality located in the northern part of the Brazilian state of Rio de Janeiro. I will present accounts of two Pentecostal settlers who migrated to that region from different parts of Brazil and became involved in the struggle for the land in the late 1990s. I will pay particular attention to the different ways in which each of these individuals express their faith. In the process, I point to how lively and central religion has become over the years to the people living in these land settlements spread throughout Brazil as a result of the organizational work of the Movimento dos Trabalhadores Rurais Sem-Terra (MST), or the Landless Workers' Movement.[2] Religious expressions in the settlements are increasingly plural (that is, connection with Catholicism can no longer be assumed; instead,

---

[1] This is one of the thousands of land settlements or occupations in Brazil, where displaced people from rural areas, in the struggle to survive, come together, with organizational assistance of the Landless Workers Movement, known by its Portuguese initials MST, and organize in a given non-productive piece of land, often, underneath bamboos and black tarps, to fight for their right to land and to work.

[2] Eliane Domingues, "O Movimento dos Trabalhadores Rurais Sem Terra, Contestado e Canudos: algumas reflexões sobre religiosidade," *Memorandum*, 8 (2005): 38–51, accessed May 7, 2018, https://seer.ufmg.br/index.php/memorandum/article/view/10067; and Michael Lowy, *Cristianismo da Libertação* (São Paulo: Perseu-Abramo, 2017), 45–9.

this is increasingly a field dominated by evangelical denominations).[3] Such a change in the religious demographics of the settlements reflects the broader shift in the religious makeup of the Brazilian population, which has gradually drifted away from Catholicism toward evangelical, mainly Pentecostal denominations.[4]

As a result of this shift, there are new social and religious dilemmas. In this chapter, I will look at some of these dilemmas and examine how the newer evangelical/Pentecostal Brazilian faith has been made public in an environment as polarized as the Brazilian rural scene—still devoid of proper analysis and at the same time proportionately as violent as the urban environments in the country. More specifically, my intention is to enhance the understanding of how the migrants who are responsible for helping to develop the MST's settlements express themselves religiously. As for my methodology, I have chosen to examine the cases of two migrants who are part of the Zumbi dos Palmares settlement and who are linked to Pentecostal traditions.[5] The first one is Vicente,[6] now a member of the *Universal Church of the Kingdom of God* (IURD), who came to Northern Rio de Janeiro on a flatbed truck to work as a sugarcane harvester at local sugarcane mills. The second is the case of Paulo Poeta, who migrated from the state of Minas Gerais and who also helped in the construction of the settlement. He is presently a member of the Assemblies of God church.[7]

In order to deal with these two trajectories of Pentecostals that have undergone migrations to the countryside of Rio de Janeiro, I will first offer a brief overview of the land conflicts in the northern region of Rio de Janeiro, prior to discussing the Zumbi dos Palmares settlement, the largest in the North Fluminense region. Then, I will highlight the role which religion has exerted in

---

[3]   I have worked on this issue in Fábio Py and Marcos Pedlowski, "Atuação de religiosos luteranos na formação dos movimentos sociais rurais no Brasil," *Tempo*, Niterói 24/2, (2018): 232–50; Claudio Carvalhães and Fábio Py, "Liberation Theology in Brazil." *CrossCurrents*, 67 (2017): 157–79; Fábio Py, "Lutheran Rebellion in the Brazilian Countryside," *CrossCurrents*, 66 (2016): 252–66.

[4]   Gedeon Alencar, "Matriz Pentecostal Brasileira: Assembleia de Deus," *Revista Simpósio*, 10 (2008): 11–35.

[5]   Focusing on the case of Zumbi dos Palmares, we notice that the settled population is the outcome of two major Brazilian migration routes in the late twentieth century: (1) They are mostly northeasterners who have moved to the southeast states; and (2) also workers from the southern part of the neighbor state of Minas Gerais in search of work in the state of Rio de Janeiro. See Marcos Pedlowski, "Os Limites da Reforma Agrária Desassistida na Região Norte do Estado do Rio de Janeiro: Entre o Descaso do Estado e a Resistência dos Assentados," in *Desconstruindo o Latifúndio: A Saga da Reforma Agrária no Norte Fluminense*, eds. Marcos A. Pedlowski et al. (Rio de Janeiro: Apicuri, 2011), 119–36.

[6]   Vicente, an alias, interviewed by the author, November, 2017.

[7]   Paulo Poeta, interviewed by the author, December, 2017.

the formation and development of the MST. Finally, I will turn my attention to the specific cases of the two migrant settlers.

THE ORGANIZATION OF THE STRUGGLE IN RIO DE JANEIRO

The struggles for land and agrarian reform in Rio de Janeiro are directly linked to the agrarian conflicts taking place in other regions of Brazil. By the mid-twentieth century, land conflicts intensified due to the lack of state incentives for peasants. National policies that brought in imports and mechanized farming strongly affected the state of Rio de Janeiro. Paulo Alentejano[8] stresses that the municipalities around Rio de Janeiro city, which were experiencing a rapid process of urbanization, also had to deal with the "actions by big land development entrepreneurs and land squatters" who wiped out orange groves and small farms, replacing farming areas "with urban development or cattle raising."[9] This process led to a boom in urban population, the development of bedroom communities, and the construction of road, energy, and railroad systems that made the existence of those communities possible.[10]

On top of that, the government invested in factories, turning a predominantly agricultural area into a rural-urban confluence space attracting land speculation.[11] As the urbanization process intensified in the 1960s, there were armed conflicts between squatters and farmers, aided by the Federation of Associations of Farmers of Rio de Janeiro (FALERJ). Corruption was prevalent. It is worth noting that from the 1960s up to the mid-1980s, during the civil-military dictatorship installed in the country in1964, there was no land reform program. In the 1970s, according to Paulo Alentejano, the main rural conflicts took place in the region of the Bacia da Ilha Grande (Grand Island Basin) and on the coastal lowlands because of the construction of the Rio-Santos highway, which crossed the municipalities of Paraty and Angra dos Reis, "facilitating the implementation of major industrial projects while endorsing farms with slavery-like conditions."[12] In the 1980s, in the Rio de Janeiro lowlands, the conflict mostly involved "the unemployed population from poor peripheries, mostly from shantytowns, who, without other housing alternative, started squatting."[13] In the 1990s, the conflict moved to the northern part of

---

[8]   Paulo Roberto Alentejano, "Luta por Terra e Reforma Agrária no Rio de Janeiro," *Revista Fluminense de Geografia*, 1 (2002): 109–24.

[9]   Paulo Roberto Alentejano, "O Norte Fluminense, a Luta pela Terra e a Política de Reforma Agrária no Estado do Rio de Janeiro," in *Deconstrindo o Latifundio*, 19–55.

[10]   Alentejano, "O Norte Fluminense," 22.

[11]   Alentejano, "O Norte Fluminense," 23.

[12]   Alentejano, "Luta por Terra," 113.

[13]   In contrast to the way the conflict was shaped in previous years, which was mostly between those squatters who falsified documents to claim land possession and people who owned land but who lacked the documentation to prove legal ownership. See Alentejano, "Luta por Terra," 114.

Rio de Janeiro state. Campos dos Goytacazes, a municipality which, according to Nelia Ferraz Moreira Nunes,[14] was well-rooted in a colonial sugarcane oligarchy, saw its sugar-alcohol sector going bankrupt. Dozens of sugar and alcohol mills went out of business, and a considerable number of rural workers lost their jobs. As a result of this, a process of land occupation started. One example of this was the closing of the São João Mill Plant and the occupation that led to the formation of the Zumbi dos Palmares settlement.[15]

In 1997, with the direct participation of MST, the Zumbi dos Palmares[16] land reform settlement was formed. At the early negotiation stage conducted by INCRA,[17] five hundred fifty-nine families were given plots of land. Two hundred of those families were formed by former São João Sugar Mill workers. Besides the sugar mill workers, the MST activists "recruited residents from the shantytowns of Campos, Macaé, and São Francisco de Itabapoana municipalities."[18] Most residents of the settlement were migrants originally from the northeastern states of Brazil, people like Vicente, who came originally from the impoverished state of Alagoas.[19] The Zumbi dos Palmares settlement was portrayed "as a role model for the process of Land Reform during the presidency of Fernando Henrique Cardoso."[20] President Cardoso (FHC) himself acknowledged that no other land occupation project had taken place so quickly and

---

[14]   Neila Ferraz Moreira Nunes, "A Experiência Eleitoral em Campos dos Goytacazes (1870 - 1889): Frequência Eleitoral e Perfil da População Votante," *Dados* 46, 2 (2003): 151–65.

[15]   The bankruptcy of the São João Mill Plant came as a consequence of the federal government's cut of subsidies for the production of sugarcane and alcohol, which, among other things, made the payment of workers' salaries in the harvest seasons of 1995 and 1996 difficult. See Edward Dew, "Samba Revolucionário: A Revolta Agrária que Quase todo Mundo Apoia," in *Desconstruindo o Latifúndio: A Saga da Reforma Agrária no Norte Fluminense*, ed. M. Pedlowski, J. C. Oliveira, and K. A. Kury (Rio de Janeiro: Apicuri, 2011), 57–98.

[16]   The name of the rural settlement was given in honor of Zumbi dos Palmares, an important black leader in the history of Brazil. Zumbi organized the most important quilombo, a community of runaway enslaved Africans who freed themselves from the bonds of colonial power.

[17]   INCRA or "Instituto Nacional de Colonização e Reforma Agrária" ("National Institute of Colonization and Agrarian Reform") is a government agency created in 1970 to carry out agrarian reform, enable a national register of rural properties and administer the lands of the Union."

[18]   Ibid.

[19]   The base work for the settlement was developed by MST activists, who were relocated from the states of São Paulo and Paraná due to their previous experience with settlements at the Portal do Paranapanema region. These examples and others demonstrate that the base work of the MST activists was critical for the movement. As for the so-called monoculture oligarchy of Campos dos Goytacazes and its ties to political and economic power in the state of Rio de Janeiro, see the article by Walter Luiz Carneiro de Mattos Pereira, "Francisco Ferreira Saturnino Braga: Negócios e Fortuna em Campos dos Goytacazes", *História*, 31, no.2 (2012): 56–9. Highlighting the historical figure of Francisco Ferreira Saturnino Braga, De Mattos Pereira discusses the intricacies of the businesses and the political influence of plantation owners from the Vargas administration to the Brazilian civil-military dictatorship.

[20]   Pedlowski, "Os Limites", 130.

peacefully. As a result, in 1997, he signed a decree expropriating[21] nine farms that made up the land complex of the São João Sugar Mill.[22]

THE CREATION OF THE MST AND THE CPT

The success achieved in the expropriation of the land originally owned by the São João Mill also reflects the strength of the Catholic faith in rural Brazil. In Brazil, there is a history of Catholic involvement in situations of social conflicts, poverty, and hunger since the 1960s. At that time, the Catholic wing associated with liberation theology demanded that the Church should take a stand regarding the land conflicts happening in the Brazilian countryside. Thus, in 1971, attentive to those conflicts, Bishop Dom Pedro Casaldáglia wrote a pastoral letter, "A Church in the Amazon in Conflict with the Latifundium and Social Marginalization," in which he denounced the destruction of the natural resources of the Amazon rainforest and the poverty plaguing the region's inhabitants. This document gave birth to a new understanding of the relationship between parish life and the exploitation of rural workers in the Brazilian countryside.[23]

The letter reverberated internationally. Furthermore, two pastoral arms of the Catholic Church in Brazil stemmed from it: the Conselho Indigenista Missionário (CIMI–Indigenous Missionary Council), with a focus on law and the cultural diversity of indigenous people; and the Comissão Pastoral da Terra (CPT–Pastoral Land Commission), which promotes a wide range of work recording conflicts and denouncing violence perpetrated against rural workers.[24]

The official creation of the CPT is credited to the pastoral meeting of the Amazon, organized by the Conferência Nacional dos Bispos do Brasil (CNBB–National Conference of Bishops of Brazil), on June 22, 1975. Confronted by the needs of rural workers, squatters, and peasants, the CPT since its beginning took a stand against the military regime, which clearly represented national and transnational capitalist interests.[25] The CPT started helping rural community parishes by interacting with the Comunidades Eclesiais de Base (CEBs–Christian Base Communities), seeking to break the isolation of those people living in the Brazilian countryside. Starting in 1979, the CPT gained strength

---

[21] Land expropriation is a procedure by which a piece of unproductive land is removed from the owner by a juridical decision based on public utility or social interest in Brazil.
[22] Dew, "Samba revolucionário," 57–98.
[23] Michael Lowy, *A Guerra dos Deuses* (Petropólis: Vozes, 2000), 65–9.
[24] Ivo Polleto, "As contradições Sociais e a Pastoral da Terra," 130–40; and Siegfried Parter, *O Bispo dos Excluídos: Dom José Rodrigues* (Brazil: Fonte Viva, 1992), 45–7.
[25] Bernardo Mançano Fernandes and João Pedro Stédile, *Brava Gente: A Trajetória do MST e a Luta pela Terra no Brasil* (São Paulo: Editora Fundação Perseu Abramo, 2005); and Bernardo Mançano Fernandes, *A formação do MST no Brasil* (Petrópolis: Vozes, 2000), 34–6.

in Rio de Janeiro, with support from the parishes of Nova Friburgo. In the northern part of Rio de Janeiro, though, the commission earned little support from the Campos dos Goytacazes' diocese.[26]

The first CPT agents to arrive in Campos dos Goytacazes in 1997 intended to work with the waged sugarcane harvesters of the region.[27] At that time, 92 percent of the working population in the area were directly involved in sugarcane-related activities. To engage with this group, the CPT first targeted the issues of health and education.[28] By doing that, the CPT agents managed to get closer to the sugarcane harvesters.[29] Yet, the work of the CPT continued to receive no support from the local Catholic hierarchy. Instead, the bishops and other members of the Church's hierarchy in Campos dos Goytacazes wrote letters to the CNBB requesting the CPT to be removed from the town. Only priests of the Redemptorist Order offered support to the CPT in Campos.[30]

Even without institutional support, the CPT in association with the MST helped set up the encampment which later became the Zumbi dos Palmares land reform settlement.[31] In their view, that partnership allowed them to "reach out to a wider audience, and significantly contributed to the social and political training of the sugarcane harvesters and other landless rural or urban workers in Northern Rio de Janeiro state."[32] At the Zumbi dos Palmares Settlement, the CPT "helped mainly by keeping a medical clinic in the camp and by teaching the campers to tend a medicinal plant garden."[33] In terms of religious meetings, CPT promotes in the Zumbi dos Palmares settlement monthly masses held by the appointed priest in the Travessão District, who leads masses at the chapel located at the center of Unit 4 in the settlement. The CPT also supports a women's group and annual festivals that attract participants from the settlement and its surroundings. On top of that, the CPT has been involved in

---

[26]   Lowy, *A Guerra dos Deuses*, 203.

[27]   Dew, "Samba Revolucionário," 311.

[28]   Novick, "Governo Brizola, Movimentos de Ocupação de Terras," in *Assentamentos Rurias: Uma Visão Multidisciplinar* (São Paulo: EdUnesp, 1994), 201.

[29]   Dew, "Samba Revolucionário," 312.

[30]   The CPT in Campos is not part of the church's hierarchy, in the sense that it is not directly linked to the Diocesan Head Office. That is something that allows it some independence. See Gonçalves, *A Atuação da Comissão Pastoral da Terra*, 89. Due to this autonomy and because it is well known as a body "at the fringes of the church," the CPT has reached places that the Diocese does not manage to reach; and due to its ecumenical character, allegiance to the Catholic church is not mandatory for one to take part in the Commission. See Gonçalves, *A Atuação*, 210–6; and Novick, "Governo Brizola," 201.

[31]   Helena Lewin, *Uma Nova Abordagem da Questão da Terra no Brasil: O Caso do MST em Campos dos Goitacazes* (Rio de Janeiro: 7letras, 2005), 102–13.

[32]   Gonçalves, *A Atuação*, 111.

[33]   Lewin, *Uma Nova Abordagem,* 43.

conflict resolution and in the organization of pilgrimages.[34] In short, the CPT has played a crucial role in all spheres of life in the settlement. It is an important part of the local history and can be considered the backbone of the Zumbi dos Palmares settlement. Yet, there is more to be said about the current religious situation in the settlement.

RELIGION IN ZUMBI DOS PALMARES TODAY

In the 1990s, there was a strong Catholic dominance in the Brazilian rural set-tlements, among other things because of the influence of the CPT in the orga-nization of the struggles of rural workers throughout the Brazilian countryside. Since then, the Catholic presence in the Brazilian countryside—which used to claim 80 percent of the rural population in 1990—has dwindled, in large part because of the growing Evangelical presence, mostly Pentecostal.[35][29]

It is interesting to see how the case of the Zumbi dos Palmares settlement relates to the broader Brazilian religious scenario. As in other parts of the coun-try, in Zumbi dos Palmares the Assemblies of God is the most popular church among all Evangelical religious institutions (there are four Assemblies of God congregations in the settlement). Baptists and the *Universal Church of the Kingdom of God* (IURD) come second and third respectively. The members of the Assemblies of God and of the IURD do not have a good relationship with the CPT. Among these Evangelical churches, only the Baptist community, led by a pastor who identifies himself as a "settler,"[36] has a more positive view in the eyes of the local members of the CPT. However, the Baptist congregation is poorly attended (unlike the Assemblies of God—specifically the congregation in Unit 4).[37] The Zumbi dos Palmares settlement, thus, has a strong Evangelical presence (mostly Pentecostal), just as other rural landless workers' settlements around the country. This is something that scholars have often neglected in their analyses of the Zumbi dos Palmares settlement and of other settlements

---

[34] The XV State Land and Waters Pilgrimage, on July 24, 2016, was entitled "On the cry of the land and the wounded waters sprout cries of justice," and counted with the presence of bishop Roberto Francisco Ferreira Paz.
[35] Fábio Py and Marcos Pedlowski, "Atuação de Religiosos Luteranos," *Tempo* (2018): 232–50; Claudio Carvalhães and Fábio Py, "Liberation Theology in Brazil" (2017): 157–79; Fábio Py, "Lutheran Rebellion" (2016): 252–66.
[36] Alcimaro, interview with the author, December, 2017.
[37] Poeta, interview with the author, December, 2017.

both in northern Rio de Janeiro and in other parts of Brazil.[38] To illustrate this Evangelical prominence in the settlements today, I reproduce below an entry I made on my field diary after a visit to the Zumbi dos Palmares settlement:

> I woke up at 7:30 a.m. and went to the settlement; I took the Paraíso bus from the Jacarandá company at 10:30. There were many people [waiting for the bus]; too many for the few buses at the bus station. I was told they have cut some bus lines and reduced bus services. With the new itinerary, the buses to Zumbi now leave only in intervals of an hour and half. The lines are longer, and there is confusion all around. Standing on the line there are adults with children and pets. The companies provide poorly maintained, bumpy buses for the ever-neglected population going to or passing by the settlement. This is another form of veiled social restriction imposed upon the population who live in the camp. And it works against the people and families who have [built] their houses there. It is another way to prevent people from going to the city of Campos. Offering a poorly served bus line that does not run very often; it is a disguised form of social cleansing. On the way to the station, where I would meet Viviane, Ramiro and Alcimaro, as I looked around the outskirts of Campos, what most captured my attention was the drought. Also, my trained eyes [as a scholar of religion] saw the number of churches on the way, most of which are Pentecostal. On top of all other problems, the people who used to be landless also have to fight dire climate conditions to survive. Most of them have to work two jobs to contribute to their family income . . . . [T]hroughout the trek to Zumbi the bus collector listened to an Evangelical radio station playing early in the morning only hymns from the most traditional Protestant communities, hymns such as "The Message of the Cross" . . . and "Old Rugged Cross" . . . . I wondered if that happened by chance. Of course it did not. I am walking into an Evangelical site. The MST settlements are today a Pentecostal territory. With the music on the bus jammed with workers from settlements, I see that the situation of scarcity, the toil, and everything they go through becomes a reason for praising the Lord.[39]

---

[38]   Some analyses of the northern Rio de Janeiro settlements which did not address the issue of religion were: Lewin, 45–8; Novick, 200–3; Dew, 57–98; Gonçalves, 87–9. As for analyses that take religion into consideration, there are two texts that do offer some information. The first is a text by Fábio Py and Marcos Pedlowski, "Neo-Pentecostal Ethic and the Spirit of Northern Rio de Janeiro Rural Capitalism." As far as I know, the only other text that highlights the change in the religious scenario of the MST rural settlements, and specifically the decrease in Catholic influence, is one chapter in the book *The Diversity of Local and Regional Impacts in Rural Settlements in São Paulo*, by Sonia Maria Pessoa Pereira Bergamasco, Luiz Antonio Cabello Norder, Rosangela Aparecida de Oliveira and Leonardo de Barros Pinto. In this text, the authors point out the existence of data on the evangelical presence in MST settlements in the southeast up to 1994. However, little has been mentioned about its public significance in the rural settlements today. See Sonia Maria Pessoa Pereira Bergamasco, Luiz Antonio Cavello Norder, Rosangela Parecida de Oliveira and Leonardo de Barros Pinto, *The Diversity of Local and Regional Impacts in Rural Settlements in São Paulo* (Rio de Janeiro: Mauad, 2004).

[39]   Fabio Py, field diary, Campos dos Goytacazes, 2017.

I stressed in my field notes that the landless migrant population of the settlement is deprived of access to the city. In that account, I described only a small portion of the difficulties settlers in Zumbi dos Palmares face to have access to work, goods, and general services. I also described the fact that faith is made public even in the context of public transportation, bringing meaning to the struggle of workers who are trying to survive. Therefore, I concluded that listening to Protestant Evangelical hymns on the bus on the way to and from the settlement is not just a coincidence. In fact, most people who were on the bus crooned along. That is a sign that most settled rural workers recognize and engage Evangelical religious culture.[40]

With the prevalence of Evangelical religious culture in mind, it is important to analyze the role of the CPT and the role of the Catholic tradition in this community. This is particularly pertinent because the primacy of Evangelical religious expression is accompanied by a strong anti-Catholic point of view. In other words, I am interested in knowing how the Evangelicals take a public stand in regard to the settlement as a community (a venture initiated in many regards by a Catholic group, the CPT), to other Christians, and to nature. In order to do that, I chose two groups who live in the Zumbi settlement: (1) the first one is the IURD (Pentecostal), related to the Theology of Prosperity, which in this chapter is represented by my conversations with Vicente; and (2) the second one is made up of other Pentecostals, symbolized by Paulo Poeta, a writer and poet from Zumbi dos Palmares who, although being a Pentecostal, identifies himself as ecumenical. I will begin with Vicente's account.

AN EVANGELICAL PROSELYTIZING EXPRESSION IN THE SETTLEMENT

Vicente, now a member of the *Universal Church of the Kingdom of God* (IURD), and his family go to church in Travessão—a neighborhood of the Zumbi dos Palmares settlement. The path Vicente took before acquiring his plot led him to move from the impoverished northeastern region of Brazil to the southeast in the late 1970s, to work in sugarcane harvesting in the region of São Jesus de Itabapoana, a municipality near Campos dos Goytacazes. Then, he worked in banana farms in Casimiro de Abreu in the 1980s. In the same decade, he went back to work in sugarcane harvesting at a Campos do Goytacazes sugar mill. He says he kept migrating along northern Rio de Janeiro state searching for work "in the region so I could scrape some money together."[41] He concluded, however, that the only thing he managed to do was to run up debts. Because

---

[40]   See Fábio Py, "Ética Neopentecostal e Espírito do Capitalismo Rural Norte-Fluminense," 21–4. This information is also captured in the interview I had with Alcimaro.

[41]   Vicente, interview with the author, November 2017.

of his financial situation, only later in life he managed to have his own family. Having had a hard life, he stated that being white prevented him from suffering physical violence. Nevertheless, he says that on two occasions he was beaten by employees of the São João Mill who suspected that he had stolen stuff from the mill. He in fact admits to once stealing some stuff from the landowner because he "had no more credit to buy food for the house, his first wife and children."[42] It was then that Vicente made a promise to "the God of the *crentes* ['believers,' a term commonly used for Evangelicals in Brazil]—that if God protected him, he would go to an Evangelical church."[43] Prior to that event, he used to identify himself as Catholic.

At that time, he lived in a shantytown in Travessão, a district close to Zumbi Palmares, with his wife, three children, his mother-in-law, and a nephew. Initially, he started going to a small congregation called Igreja Evangélica da Palavra de Deus (Word of God Evangelical Church), associated with the Assemblies of God. Later on, however, he joined the IURD. He started going to Evangelical services after his divorce. At the IURD he met and later married his new wife. He has been in the IURD for ten years, having served as a teacher, a small-group leader, having also worked with pre-adolescents. Currently, he is a presbyter. The pastor likes him so much that "he lets him lead a prayer every Sunday at the church; he also allows some prayer campaigns to take place upon Vicente's request, such as the one that happens before sugarcane harvesting."[44] According to Vicente, "even though the people from Campos are not fond of the *paraibas* [a derogatory term commonly used in Rio de Janeiro in reference to migrants from the northeast], he has a good standing in the church, and they even allow him to take care of some of the finances."[45] According to Vicente, life is very difficult because in addition to the prejudice he suffers for being originally from the Northeast, he is also a settler (an *assentado*), a word severely frowned upon in Campos dos Goytacazes; and as a settler he is often "seen as a lazy person, a bum." During a conversation in his house, in the unit 2 of the settlement, Vicente showed me some fruits and vegetables he had planted in his lot. Then, he went to his bedroom to pick up something else he wanted to show: his best piece of clothing, the clothing he wears as an official presbyter at the IURD, which, according to him, "in light of his position, he can only wear at church, twice a week, usually on Sundays and on another day, to be properly dressed."[46] While he showed it, his wife placed her hand on his shoulder and proudly exhibited a light smile. Her reaction demonstrated that his clothing

---

[42]   Vicente, interview with the author.
[43]   Vicente, interview with the author.
[44]   Vicente, interview with the author.
[45]   Vicente, interview with the author.
[46]   Vicente, interview with the author.

(his position) was a source of pride for the family, as it also showed that they held a prominent position in the nearby church.

On my trips to and from the settlement, I also noticed that Vicente's house was better furnished and more equipped than others in the neighborhood. It had a well, two refrigerators, a number of beds, a closet just for clothes, and rugs all around the house. His lot boasts a greater diversity of crops. Later, Vicente took me outside and, looking all around his lot, he pointed to the crops and bags with harvested crops, and said, "If God is for us, who can be against us?"[47] At that moment, I noticed how different this family was from others I had met in the settlement. They did not share the crops they harvested. The ones already harvested had a certain destination. During the conversation, he pointed to a sack of maxixe and said that it "was worth 15 Brazilian *reals* [the Brazilian national currency], and the peeled pineapple bag was worth 10 *reals*."[48] All of them had been sold to merchants around that area. Then he added, "the establishment of the settlement was successful, it worked out . . . [so] there is no reason for causing trouble." He had "to work to get what God had promised him and his family."[49] He explained that since the moment he learned that principle in his church, his life in the settlement started to thrive. In sum, he articulated a narrative which has become very common among settlers associated with churches adept of the prosperity gospel. This adoption of the narrative is reflected in his discourse, which is permeated with commonly used neo-Pentecostal jargon, such as "a blessing from God," "the peace of the Lord," "fire man," "taking the keys for the blessing from God." He highlighted that "life is divided between those who are with God [that is, the Evangelicals who remain watchful not to falter], and the rest of the world who do not understand the things from God and God's salvation."[50] With great conviction he claimed that he "has experienced God on earth through the things he has achieved by faith. God has allowed him to have more and more because of his persistence, fasting and work."[51] He told me all those things while proudly staring at his crops and the material goods he had in his house. His trick to make God honor him was "knees on the ground, praying, fasting, [love for] family and working surrounded by brothers, not to disrupt what God had prepared for him, that is God's award on Earth."[52] In order to profit, he insists on prayer as an important key and then employs a pragmatic method, "harvesting sugarcane with brothers

---

47   Vicente, interview with the author. A recitation of Romans 8:31.
48   Vicente, interview with the author.
49   Vicente, interview with the author.
50   Vicente, interview with the author.
51   Vicente, interview with the author.
52   Vicente, interview with the author.

who know the region and the sugarcane crops very well so that at the end of the day they can have a greater amount of harvested cane stems to be weighed."

Vicente concludes his interesting account by saying that prayer and business acumen are the reasons he has more money than most other settlers, and he adds that if he had left idolatry earlier, he would be even in a better condition than he is now, for God does not "close his eyes to his children on Earth. God does not want them to suffer like this, non-stop."[53] The "idolatry" Vicente referred to was Roman Catholicism. According to him, using typical Evangelical dialect, those were "times of spiritual blindness, for although he had eyes to see, he did not see the truth."[54]

Vicente epitomizes an adaptation of a form of prosperity gospel into the environment of the Zumbi dos Palmares settlement. For him, true believers are entitled to enjoying material blessings while on Earth. In order for that to happen, he sets his own life in connection with the church to benefit from the opportunities that emerge, and also to help his Evangelical brothers. Thus, out of the settlement environment emerges a type of proselytizing faith which divides the Zumbi dos Palmares environment between the "elect" and the "non-elect." Then, they split the world and the settlement by putting fences around their religious discourse. For Vicente, everything he produces is to be transformed into material goods, or money.

THE POET AND HIS ENGAGED ECUMENICAL EVANGELICAL EXPRESSION IN ZUMBI DOS PALMARES

After writing about Vicente, a member of the IURD in Travessão, and his spirit of rural capitalism in association with a neo-Pentecostal spirituality, I will now address a well-known name in the Zumbi dos Palmares settlement, a native of the state of Minas Gerais known in Rio de Janeiro as Paulo Poeta (Paulo, the poet). Paulo Poeta's birth name is Paulo Roberto dos Santos. He was born in a small town called Bicas, near Juiz de Fora, where he was raised in a small farm. But in addition to working in the fields, he also worked as a baker. While working in the bakery, he ventured a few verses, rhyming and passing on the message about what was going on, or as he said, "the story of what was happening."[55] He left Minas Gerais in 1977. Initially, he tried to make a living in São Paulo, staying there for about six months. Then, he moved to coastal Rio de Janeiro in 1978, more specifically to the city of Macaé, where he initially worked as a fisherman, and later began to pick paper on the streets for recycling. In 1997, Paulo Roberto dos Santos started helping in the "mobilizations and meetings which

53   Vicente, interview with the author.
54   Vicente, interview with the author.
55   Paulo Poeta, interview with the author, December, 2017.

led to the occupation of the São João (Saint John) Sugar Mill."[56] Thus, along with the land settlement, Paulo Poeta from Zumbi dos Palmares was born. His birth as a poet was timid. He explains that his legs shook in the beginning. Encouraged by Mineirinho and Marina, two MST´s national leaders involved in organizing the occupation that led to the creation of the Zumbi dos Palmares settlement, he started reciting his verses in public. One of his poems speaks of the beginning of the settlement:

> *When I came from Macaé,*
> *I was well-meant*
> *I brought some tools,*
> *A knife and a machete.*
> *I also brought my scythe*
> *A hoe and a mattock*
> *At 9 o'clock in the evening*
> *I stepped aboard the bus*
> *Without a clue*
> *Of where it was going to.*
> *We did not know we were coming*
> *To the São João Mill Plant.*
>
> *On the 12th of April*
> *On the Occupation Day,*
> *My big watch showed*
> *Three o'clock a.m.*
> *The buses got here*
> *People were as one.*
> *Reporters were all around*
> *From papers and TV,*
> *We set up tents*
> *From scarce materials*
> *Since there was no bamboo*
> *To make poles.*[57]

These verses describe the first steps of the Zumbi dos Palmares settlement. He starts with the first scenes of the organization of the settlement in 1997. Buses were used to bring rural workers to set up the camp. Local newspapers and television stations covered the popular mobilization at a sugar mill, an old

---

[56]   Paulo Poeta, interview with the author.
[57]   Paulo Poeta, "Terra Conquistada, Esperança de Vida Nova." In *Poesias Paulo Poeta.* (Gráfica e Editora Lar Cristão, 2000), 6–7.

symbol of wealth and power in northern Rio de Janeiro.[58] In his poem, Paulo Poeta registered the time of arrival: 3 a.m. He also spoke about what they lacked: bamboo and canvas for the tents.[59] As he knew what living in the countryside was like, he brought tools such as a knife, a machete, and a hoe. Due to the leadership he showed from the outset of his involvement, he eventually became "a coordinator of some positions in the settlement."[60] According to Poeta, his verses are inspired by "a genre from Minas Gerais called *calango*,"[61] a rhymed genre sung around bonfires, where people talk about life and about the things one sees happening in life.

His new name (the nickname Poeta) connected him to the new life he experienced in Campos dos Goytacazes. His work and engagement in the rural workers' struggle for land did not go unnoticed. In the year 2000, the municipal government compiled his poems into a book called *Conquered Land, Hope for a New Life: Poems by Paulo Poeta*.[62] His poems address a number of topics, including his friendship with the MST activists who came to help set up the settlement—Boiadeiro, Mineirinho, Chiquinho, Marina and Nenê—who, he says, "live in our hearts."[63] His verses also speak of the first maize and bean crops which did not turn out good. For him, they lacked "divine protection."[64] In fact, at that point they had no water to irrigate what they planted. He wraps up the first poem of his book with the following verse:

> *Now I am going to wrap up*
> *With a simple prayer*
> *Asking the Virgin Mary*
> *And also Saint John,*
> *To bless the rulers*
> *And all my brothers,*
> *To promptly divide the lands*
> *Among all of us, all the citizens,*
> *So that we can*
> *Grow our own crops.*[65]

As we read through the verses written by the poet from Zumbi dos Palmares, we notice that he uses Catholic imagery to interpret what is happening around him: the organization of the settlement, the lack of support

---

[58] Paulo Poeta, "Terra Conquistada, Esperança de Vida Nova."
[59] Paulo Poeta, "Terra Conquistada, Esperança de Vida Nova."
[60] Paulo Poeta, interview with the author.
[61] Paulo Poeta, interview with the author.
[62] Paulo Poeta, "Terra conquistada, Esperança de Vida Nova," 7–8.
[63] Paulo Poeta, "Terra conquistada, Esperança de Vida Nova," 6.
[64] Paulo Poeta, "Terra conquistada, Esperança de Vida Nova."
[65] Paulo Poeta, "Terra conquistada, Esperança de Vida Nova," 7.

from society at-large, the scarcity of food, and the siege by the police. Paulo Poeta visited different Evangelical churches as the settlement was being set up and soon after he was officially assigned his lot. Despite his connections with the Catholic CPT, he and his two daughters are currently associated with the Assemblies of God at Unit 4, an association that is uncommon for someone who identifies as ecumenical in Brazil. A curious fact is that prior to attending that church he negotiated with the pastor. He told the religious leader that he cared for the education of his daughters. He would not like his daughters to follow a secluded religion. He told the Pentecostal pastor that as he teaches his daughters in church the pastor needs to respect all religions. Paulo Poeta had learned that kind of ecumenical respect through his involvement in the regional CPT. In contrast to Vicente, he shared the variety of mangoes he grew in his lot with others, beyond the members of his church, including all his visitors, always cooking for them the food he harvested or whatever food there was available in the settlement.

Nowadays, he devotes much of his time to the musical career of his daughters, who form an Evangelical duo. They sing in parties throughout the region, in activities organized by the regional CPT, and at the Assemblies of God congregation. Paulo Poeta writes most of the lyrics they sing. In his lyrics, which continue to be inspired by the *calango* from Minas Gerais, he blends the stories of life experiences in Rio de Janeiro countryside with his differentiated understanding of Pentecostal ecumenical Christianity, combined with popular Catholicism. He takes inspiration from nature to honor life, thus producing a theological thinking that is more open to others than what one commonly finds in other sorts of Brazilian Pentecostalism. Therefore, while being a member of the Assemblies of God, he understands the need to respect other religions, nature, and the land. The lyrics of the song "God, the Father of Nature," which he wrote for his daughters in 2015, says,

> *We live out here on the field*
> *In the middle of nature*
> *With divine protection*
> *Here we have no sadness*
> *God is the father of nature.*
>
> *I sow the seed on the soil*
> *It will spring up for sure*
> *It will soon grow and bear fruit.*
> *Bountifully and richly,*
> *Bringing a lot of abundance*
> *And chasing poverty away.*

> *The rain comes down and waters the earth*
> *Forming big dams,*
> *Feeding the nation.*
> *The waters of nature*
> *From the waters and earth*
> *All beauties emerge.*[66]

He hails nature because it grants abundance and wealth to everyone. Poeta believes that whatever takes place in nature is under divine protection. For him, it was not "God who made churches; men made them."[67] Poeta's lyrics do not put up fences around faith. Thus, he distances himself from proselytizing proclamations of faith. He does not make a list of sins to be avoided by everyone. Rather, together with his daughters, he prefers to describe the land as a gift from God to humankind. He speaks of the water that quenches the thirst and irrigates the delicious mango he carries in his bag. We can say that the Christian reasoning of Paulo Poeta is something unusual these polarized days, when we witness the spread of religious fundamentalism and intolerance in Brazil, many times also influenced by the cold calculations of profit. On the other hand, one notices that there are non-exclusivist religious expressions that stem from the life of rural workers in the small farms and settlements. That is something absolutely genuine. It is noteworthy that this is a kind of ecumenism that springs almost spontaneously, independent from the ecumenical literacy acquired in graduate programs or assumed by middle-class intellectual Protestants. In fact, it challenges assumptions which commonly associate ecumenical identity with elitism.

CONCLUSION

Some people may be surprised that given the significance conservative Evangelical churches have earned in settlements, there is still a sector within these groups that is willing to enter into dialogue with other Christians and people of other faiths. At the same time, the existence of such sector epitomized by Paulo Poeta is a trace of hope—a relief. Despite the hegemonic status that a presence of conservative Evangelicalism and neo-Pentecostalism in settlements of landless rural workers seems to imply, there is some deviation to dominant exclusivist theologies informing that kind of Christianity, as one can see in the case of Paulo Poeta and his family. That kind of faith formation does not happen by chance, but it is the result of a certain freedom to integrate different experiences from one's faith journey.

---

[66]   Paulo Poeta, "Terra conquistada, Esperança de Vida Nova," 15.
[67]   Paulo Poeta, interview with the author.

I have shown that Paulo Poeta and Vicente represent different poles in the religious experience one can find within Evangelical circles in the land reform settlements in Rio de Janeiro. In this brief chapter, I have taken those particular cases as representatives of different niches one can find in Brazilian Christian life, characterized by distinct paths, and cross-territorial migrations and journeys of faith, which are sometimes contrasting, although equally falling under the umbrella of Evangelical Protestant identities in Brazil. Vicente publicly displays a more exclusivist faith expression, connected to his journey as a member of a particular faith community, the IURD in Brazil, strongly informed by its prosperity theology. In his turn, Paulo Poeta exhibits a sui generis faith expression, that is an ecumenical Pentecostal faith intimately informed by his previous formation in the Catholic milieu of the CPT. That experience led him to negotiate with the pastor of the Assemblies of God in Campelo the conditions that would enable him and his family to join that church.

Both Paulo Poeta's and Vicente's adherence to Pentecostalism are indications of the adaptations that Pentecostal faith can experience in distinct geographies, but also, a clear sign that Brazil is gradually becoming an Evangelical country, a nation that is even more Evangelical in the peripheries, where people are constantly migrating. Therefore, it seems that there is an interweaving of Evangelical forces with the migrations, cooperating for greater plurality, even if still limited to the boundaries of Christianity, in social movements like the MST and also in the CPT.

BIBLIOGRAPHY:

Alcimaro, Interview. Campos dos Goytacazes, 2017.

Alencar, Gedeon. "Matriz Pentecostal Brasileira: Assembleia de Deus." *Revista Simpósio,* 10 (2008): 11–35.

Alentejano, Paulo. "Luta por terra e reforma agrária no Rio de Janeiro." *Revista Fluminense de Geografia,* 1/1 (2002): 109–24.

Alentejano, Paulo. "O Norte Fluminense, a Luta pela Terra e a Política de Reforma Agrária no Estado do Rio de Janeiro," in *Desconstruindo o latifúndio - a saga da reforma agrária no Norte Fluminense.* Edited by M. Pedlowski, J. C. Oliveira, and K. A. Kury, 19–55. *Rio de Janeiro: Apicuri,* 2011.

Carvalhaes, Claudio and Fábio Py. "Liberation Theology in Brazil." *CrossCurrents,* 6 (2017): 157–79.

Dew, Edward. "Samba Revolucionário: A Revolta Agrária que Quase Todo Mundo Apoia," in *Desconstruindo o Latifúndio: A Saga da Reforma Agrária no Norte Fluminense*. Edited by M. Pedlowski, J. C. Oliveira, and K. A. Kury, 57–98. *Rio de Janeiro: Apicuri,* 2011.

Domingues, Eliane. "O Movimento dos Trabalhadores Rurais Sem Terra, Contestado e Canudos: Algumas Reflexões sobre Religiosidade." *Memorandum. Belo Horizonte*, 4 (2005): 169–80.

Fernandes, Bernardo Mançano and João Pedro Stédile. *Brava Gente: A Trajetória do MST e a Luta pela Terra no Brasil*. São Paulo: Editora Fundação Perseu Abramo, 2005.

Fernandes, Bernardo Mançano. *A Formação do MST no Brasil*. Petrópolis: Vozes, 2000.

Gonçalves, Ricardo Luiz. "A Atuação da Comissão Pastoral da Terra (CPT) em Campos dos Goytacazes, RJ: Uma Análise do Assentamento Zumbi dos Palmares." Master's thesis in Rural Extension Studies, Federal University of Viçosa, Minas Gerais, 2012.

Hervieu-Léger, Danièle, *O Peregrino e o Convertido*. Petrópolis: Vozes, 2008.

Lewin, Helena, Ana Paula Alves Ribeiro, and Liliane Souza e Silva. *Uma Nova Abordagem da Questão da Terra no Brasil: O Caso do MST em Campos dos Goitacazes*. Rio de Janeiro: FAPERJ/ 7 Letras, 2005.

Lowy, Michael. *A Guerra dos Deuses*. Petrópolis: Vozes, 2000.

Martins, José de Souza. "A Reforma Agrária no Segundo Mandato de Fernando Henrique Cardoso," *Tempo Social* 15 (2004): 141–75.

Novick, Victor de Araújo. "Governo Brizola, Movimentos de Ocupação de Terras e Assentamentos Rurais no Rio de Janeiro (1983-1987). In *Assentamentos Rurais. Uma Visão Multidisciplinar*. Edited by L. S. Medeiros, 69–89. São Paulo: EdUnesp, 1994.

Nunes, Neila Ferraz Moreira. "A Experiência Eleitoral em Campos dos Goytacazes (1870 – 1889): Frequência Eleitoral e Perfil da População Votante." *Dados* 46/2 (2003): 311–43.

Pater, Siegfried. *O Bispo dos Excluídos: Dom José Rodrigues*. Paulo Afonso, Salvador: Fonte Viva, 1996.

Pedlowski, Marcos. "Os Limites da Reforma Agrária Desassistida na Região Norte do Estado do Rio de Janeiro: Entre o Descaso do Estado e a Resistência dos Assentados." In *Desconstruindo o Latifúndio: A Saga da Reforma Agrária no Norte Fluminense*. Edited by M. Pedlowski, J. C. Oliveira, and K. A. Kury, 119–36. Rio de Janeiro: Apicuri, 2011.

Pereira, Walter Luiz Carneiro de Mattos. "Francisco Ferreira Saturnino Braga: Negócios e Fortuna em Campos dos Goytacazes." *História* 31, no.2 (2012): 212–36.

Poeta, Paulo. Interview, 2017.

Poeta, Paulo. *Terra Conquistada, Vida Nova: Poesias Paulo Poeta*. Campos dos Goytacazes: Gráfica e Editora Lar Cristão, 2000.

Polleto, Ivo. "As Contradições Sociais e a Pastoral da Terra." In *Igreja e a Questão Agrária*. Edited by Vanilda Paiva, 130–40. São Paulo: Loyola, 1985.

Py, Fábio and Marcos Pedlowski. "Atuação de Religiosos Luteranos nos Movimentos Sociais Rurais do Brasil de 1975 à 1985." *Tempo* 74, no.2 (2018): 233–52.

Py, Fábio. "Lutheran Rebellion in the Brazilian Countryside." *CrossCurrents,* 66 (2016): 252–66.

Stédile, João Pedro ed. *A Questão Agrária Brasileira: História e Natureza das Ligas Camponesas (1954-1964)*. São Paulo: Expressão Popular, 2006.

Ribeiro, M. *Movimento Camponês, Trabalho e Educação: Liberdade, Autonomia, Emancipação: Princípios/Fins da Formação Humana*. São Paulo: Expressão Popular, 2013.

Vicente, Interview. Campos dos Goytacazes, 2017.

Weber, Max. *A Ética Protestante e o Espírito do Capitalismo*. Rio de Janeiro: Cultrix, 1983.

CHAPTER 15

THE DIASPORA OF BRAZILIAN PENTECOSTALISM[1]

David Mesquiati de Oliveira

INTRODUCTION

Brazilian Pentecostalism, as the other existing religions in Brazil—including indigenous ones—is a result of human movement. As other scholars have already pointed out, migration is not a new phenomenon in our times.[2] Y. Joy Harris-Smith is right in affirming that "part of the human story is migration, and it impacts culture, the communicative process and religion in particular."[3]

The study of Brazilian diasporic religious communities is not new either. Donizete Rodrigues has studied Brazilian Evangelical churches in the United States, highlighting the importance of transcontinental migration for the processes of "creating, expanding, scattering and globalizing religion."[4] He draws attention to the Pentecostal growth in the Brazil-United States-Europe migration triangle, using Paul Freston's understanding of reverse mission to the

---

[1]   This chapter stems from the paper "The Diaspora of Brazilian Religions," presented at the 4th Conference of the National Association for Graduate Studies and Research in Theology and Religious Studies (ANPTECRE), at the Pontifical Catholic University (PUC) GOIÁS, on September 13–15, 2017.

[2]   Gemma Tulud Cruz, "Between Identity and Security: Theological Implications of Migration in the Context of Globalization," *Theological Studies* 69, no.2 (2008): 357–75 (358). Cited in Yvette Joy Harris-Smith, "Uma Nova Fronteira: A Comunicação Intercultural e a Necessidade de uma Epistemologia Migratória," in *World Christianity as Public Religion*, edited by Raimundo C. Barreto, Jr., Ronaldo Cavalcante and Wanderley Pereira da Rosa. Series World Christianity and Public Religion, vol. 1. (Vitória, Brazil: Editora Unida, 2016), 385–94 (387).

[3]   Harris-Smith, "Uma Nova Fronteira."

[4]   Donizete Rodrigues, *O Evangélico Imigrante: O Pentecostalismo Brasileiro Salvando a América* (São Paulo: Fonte Editorial; Belém: PPGCR-UEPA, 2016), 193.

United States and to Europe to frame his study of the Brazilian Pentecostal diaspora.[5]

Like other countries, Brazil's history is deeply marked by outward and inward human flows. Before the European conquest 500 years ago, the many indigenous ethnic groups that lived in the region had already experienced a number of migratory flows and disputes. During the European colonization, Brazil became a Portuguese colony with an imposed foreign religion, namely Catholic Christianity. Two other European religious brands—Protestantism and Spiritism—would be brought to the country in the nineteenth century. With an agrigulturally based economy profoundly dependent on the work of enslaved peoples, for more than three centuries Brazil received a large migratory contingent of Africans, enslaved and trafficked to the country. They brought with them their African religions, such as Islam and the Orisha traditions, which gave rise to Afro-Brazilian religions such as Candomble and Umbanda.

When Brazilian emigrants go out into other parts of the world, they carry these and other Brazilian (or Brazilianized) religions with them. The focus of this chapter is on how Brazilian Pentecostalism has traveled with Brazilian migrants. As Cecilia Mariz points out, Brazil has become one of the leading countries exporting Protestant and Catholic missionaries to the world.[6] At one point in its history, Brazil was primarily a recipient in the missionary enterprise, receiving large numbers of European and North American missionaries. Now, it sends thousands of missionaries abroad. According to Mariz,

> Although there has been more research on the international missions of the IURD, other Brazilian churches, such as the Assemblies of God (AD) and God is Love Pentecostal Church (IPDA), also send pastors abroad and experience growth outside the country. Brazil, traditionally a "mission land," for both Catholics and Protestants, has become an exporter of missionaries.[7]

Migratory flows have multiple causes. When we consider the Brazilian exporting of Pentecostal missionaries in the last few decades, the question we ask is which have been the main factors informing recent migratory flows, and whether the exporting of missionaries stems primarily from a missiologic orientation of Brazilian Pentecostal churches or primarily as a result of an opportunity that emerged with migration driven by other reasons, such as economic factors. With this question in mind, in this chapter I address the links between globalization, migration flows, and Brazilian Pentecostal missions, in

---

[5]   See Paul Freston, "Reverse Mission. A Discourse in Search of Reality?" *PentecoStudies*, 9, no.2 (2010): 153–74.

[6]   Cecilia L. Mariz, "Missão Religiosa e Migração: 'Novas Comunidades' e Igrejas Pentecostais no Exterior," *Análise Social,* 44 (2009): 161–87.

[7]   Mariz, "Missão Religiosa e Migração," 163–64.

conversation with three recent studies of the Brazilian Pentecostal diaspora. The first one is the abovementioned article by Cecilia Mariz, which is the off-shoot of a research project aimed initially to study the new Catholic Renewal communities in Brazil and their diaspora throughout the world, and then was expanded to include the Protestant Pentecostal diaspora. The second one is the work of Donizete Rodrigues, also cited above, which analyzes the Brazilian Pentecostal presence in the United States. The third one is the work of Rafael Shoji on religious changes among Brazilians in Japan.[8] Based on the review of this literature and on my own research on Brazilian Pentecostalism,[9] I examine the motivations driving the Brazilian Pentecostal diaspora, arguing for their theological orientation. In other words, I demonstrate that they are related to a Pentecostal understanding of mission.

Brazilian Diaspora in Numbers

The migration map is today more complex and diversified than it was in previous centuries. On top of the increasing numbers of war refugees, the recent global economic crisis aggravated the situation of many families in different continents. According to Murialdo Gasparet, "the number of migrants might rise from current 232 million to 450 million by 2050."[10] In other words, migration flows will keep growing in the upcoming decades.

In 2016, the Ministry of Foreign Affairs (MRE) of the Brazilian government estimated that a total of 3,083,255 Brazilians live abroad, forming a large Brazilian diaspora.[11] Out of that total, almost half (1.4 million people) are now in the United States of America. The largest concentration of those Brazilians is located in the Boston area where there are over 350 thousand Brazilian people, then about 300 thousand Brazilians reside in the New York area, and another 300 thousand in the Miami area.[12] The second destination country for most

8   Rafael Shoji, "Religiões entre Brasileiros no Japão: Conversão ao Pentecostalismo e Redefinição Étnica," *Rever – Revista de Estudos da Religião*, 8 (2008): 46–85.
9   For some of my publications on Pentecostalism, see David Mesquiati de Oliveira, *Pentecostalismos em Diálogo* (São Paulo: Fonte Editorial, 2014), and *Pentecostalismos e Transformação Social* (São Paulo: Fonte Editorial, 2013). See also David Mesquiati de Oliveira et al eds., *Pentecostalismos em Perspectiva* (São Paulo: Terceira Via; RELEP, 2017).
10   Murialdo Gasparet, "Mobilidade e Evangelização: O Atendimento Pastoral de Brasileiros Católicos no Exterior." Doctoral Dissertation. (Departamento de Teologia. Pontifícia Universidade Católica do Rio de Janeiro, 2018), 63.
11   Governo Brasileiro, Ministério das Relações Exteriores, *Estimativas Populacionais das Comunidades Brasileiras no Mundo–2015* (números atualizados em 29/11/2016), accessed February 2, 2018, http://www.brasileirosnomundo.itamaraty.gov.br/a-comunidade/estimativas-populacionais-das-comunidades/Estimativas%20RCN%202015%20-%20Atualizado.pdf.
12   Darci Donizetti Silva, "Os Imigrantes Brasileiros na Região da Nova Inglaterra," in *Mobilidade Humana e Identidades Religiosas*, ed. Fabio Baggio, Paolo Parise, and Wagner Lopes Sanchez (São Paulo: Paulus, 2016), 165–71 (167).

Brazilian emigrants is Paraguay (332 thousand Brazilian people), followed by Japan (with around 170 thousand Brazilian people), the United Kingdom (120 thousand), and Portugal (116 thousand).

While helpful, the data available is not precise and varies depending on the agent responsible for collecting it. The inconsistency of figures in the past decades is a result of several factors such as the difficulty in counting the considerable number of undocumented people abroad; the number of families who did not respond to the last official Brazilian census (either because they were already abroad or because they had changed address); and the fact that some of the obtained data is based on remittances sent from abroad to Brazil (but often the exact situation of those who have not sent remittances is obscured).

As an example of inconsistent figures, according to the 2010 Brazilian Census undertaken by the Brazilian Institute of Geography and Statistics (IBGE), there were around 500 thousand Brazilians living abroad at that time. IBGE has acknowledged that that data underestimates the actual situation.[13] For the International Organization for Migration (IOM), on the other hand, the total number of Brazilians living abroad varies from one to three million. For the Brazilia Ministry of Foreign Affairs (MRE), it may have varied in the past decade between 2 and 3.7 million.[14] The analysis of available data is important not simply as an attempt to gauge how precise the various institutions are in their measurement, but also to verify the financial situation of those who feel the need to migrate or are displaced.

A report of the Pew Research Center shows that, in the United States, the total number of the foreign-born population reached the peak of 43.2 million people in 2015,[15] an amount that corresponds to 13.4 percent of the total US population. Out of that total, 76 percent of foreign born population in the US are documented immigrants, while a quarter of them are undocumented. Out of those with legal status, 44 percent were awarded American citizenship, 27 percent are permanent residents, and the other 5 percent are immigrants on a temporary visa. This data from 2015 shows that, in contrast to the previous two decades, the number of undocumented immigrants in the United States has since 2007 decreased by more than one million people.[16] That scenario has made an impact on the Brazilian diaspora in the United States. As Gasparet

---

[13]   See Governo Brasileiro, op. cit. Since then, they have tried to enhance their data colletion methodology.

[14]   See Brazilian Government, op. cit.

[15]   Gustavo Lopez and Kristen Bialik, "Key Findings about U.S. Immigrants," Pew Research Center, accessed April 30, 2018. https://goo.gl/dfX39E. See also D'Vera Cohn, "5 Key Factors about Lawful Immigrants," Pew Research Center, accessed December 15, 2017, https://goo.gl/t6hZMP.

[16]   Lopez and Bialik, "Key Findings about U.S. Immigrants."

points out, the current scenario reveals important changes in comparison to previous Brazilian migration waves to the United States:

> In the beginning, the Brazilians who migrated to the USA came from countryside towns and had little schooling. Today, people migrating from Brazil are from large urban centers and have higher levels of education; many of them have a college degree. It can be said that the last 25 years were dominated by the first generation of migrants, most of whom were from the states of Minas and Goiás. The second generation of migrants is the current one, coming from all the states of Brazil.[17]

The number of undocumented Brazilians in the United States varies from 116 thousand to over 500 thousand people, depending on the source generating the data.[18] The intensification of the crackdown on undocumented immigrants since President Donald Trump's Executive Order (EO) of January 25, 2017 has made life grimmer and is haunting the still large number of undocumented Brazilian immigrants in the United States.[19]

DIASPORA AND GLOBALIZATION

The process of globalization intensified and took on new contours in the twentieth century. Especially in the second half of the century, a "deep inversion in the relationship between politics and economics" took place in connection with a process "of profound changes caused by the impact of new technologies;" that is, "a fast-paced development of productive forces" turned production into a world chain.[20] In this new scenario, science and technology became a precondition for producing wealth, turning creative and intellectual work into a new valued capital, decentralizing the production process, revolutionizing the time and space experience, and generating new and larger migration flows. According to Manfredo Araújo de Oliveira,

> Globalization certainly means a new form of accumulating and regulating capital, which is now fully constituted as a world system, with an increasingly independent capacity for action. That has become visible in the first place by the internationalization of financial flows, making it possible to interpret globalization as a process geared toward the valorization of money, as capitalism

---

[17] Gasparet, "Mobilidade e Evangelização," 187.
[18] Gasparet, "Mobilidade e Evangelização," 80.
[19] According to a recent homeland security report, "58,766 known or suspected aliens were in DOJ custody at the end of FY 2017." See Homeland Security, The United States Department of Justice, "Alien Incarceration Report Fiscal Year 2017, Quarter 4," accessed April 30, 2018, https://goo.gl/G6A3W4.
[20] Manfredo Araújo Oliveria. *Desafios Éticos da Globalização*. 2nd ed. (São Paulo: Paulinas, 2002), 80.

has become an autonomous process in which money and finances run parallel to [independent from] the generation of income by production.[21]

Therefore, globalization, as a phenomenon above all informed by economic and technological factors, interferes directly in many migration flows, by concomitantly creating both imbalances and opportunities. No longer steered by policies of national states, but by interests of accumulating transnational capital, the new international order is not able to curb the worsening social and economic inequalities among nations, turning globalization into an economy whose core is the accumulation of money.[22]

At the same time, as Donizete Rodrigues points out, there is also a process of globalization of religious groups which has interconnected (semi) peripheral regions such as Latin America, Africa, and Asia to central regions, such as the United States, Europe, and Japan.[23] The globalization of different religions has created a large religious market that heats up the dispute for adherents.[24] Speaking of the relationship between globalization and the immigration phenomenon, Rodrigues says:

> The phenomenon of globalization and the extensive transcontinental migration flows are causing significant social, economic, ethnic, religious and identity-related changes, a factor that affects both migrants and citizens of host societies. Religion plays an important role among immigrants, helping them to keep their ethnic and religious identity while at the same time trying to adapt to the new culture and society in which they are now inserted.[25]

As Mariz highlights, the religious element is a very important factor impacting the decision to migrate:

> Despite assuming an economic and political role for the wider society, the missionary call will only be heeded and obeyed by individuals if it has a religious or cultural meaning for them, and if it meets their personal needs, both material and subjective. Religious beliefs and values will only be able to serve non-religious purposes if they are religiously legitimate, and socially and subjectively plausible.[26]

Religion is therefore important in the diaspora dynamics, having even more significant weight in the case of the Pentecostal diaspora, a "religion of

---

21   Oliveria. Desafios Éticos, 89.
22   Oliveria. Desafios Éticos, 102.
23   Rodrigues, O Evangélico Imigrante, 8.
24   There is an economic face of globalization and a religious one. The adherents of different religions are affected by both globalizing processes.
25   Rodrigues, O Evangélico Imigrante, 9.
26   Mariz, "Missão Religiosa e Migração," 175.

the Spirit" that encourages personal experiences with the divine, valuing the the experience of divine call, in which vocation can be redirected in the context of ecstatic events.

BRAZILIAN PENTECOSTALISM AND ITS VARIATIONS

The rapid expansion of Brazilian Pentecostalism can be sociologically explained by several factors. One of them is the missionary and conversionist disposition that stimulates Pentecostal churches. It is based on this vision of mission that they have set out to reach not only Brazilians in Brazil, but also those living abroad, in addition to reaching non-Brazilians in a number of countries. The history of Brazilian Pentecostalism dates back to the beginning of the twentieth century. From its inception, Brazilian Pentecostalism advanced in connection with several migration waves.[27] In 1910, Italian immigrant Louis Francescon (Luigi Francesconi) arrived in Brazil. Born in 1866, he was a Catholic when he migrated to the United States in 1890 and met a group of Waldensians.[28] In 1892, they founded the Italian Presbyterian Church in Ohio, where Louis became a deacon, and later an elder. He disagreed with the group in regard to the rite of Baptism, which he believed should be by immersion. He ended up leaving that church years later. After a brief visit to Italy, he returned in 1904 to the United States, this time to Chicago. In 1907, he met William H. Durham, one of the icons of American Pentecostalism, and Francescon had his first Pentecostal experience. In 1909, imbued with a Pentecostal perspective, he arrived in Argentina. In 1910, he moved to Brazil, where he founded the Christian Congregation of Brazil (CCB), a church with strong presence in the states of São Paulo and Paraná. In each case—in the United States, Argentina, and Brazil—Francescon appealed first of all to Italian immigrant communities. It was not until the mid-twentieth century that the CCB turned to other Brazilians. By the time of its centenary, it had over 2.3 million members throughout Brazil, according to the Brazilian Official Census of 2010.[29] In its mission to other countries, this church has changed its name from Christian Congregation of Brazil to Christian Congregation in Brazil.[30]

---

[27] Yara Nogueira Monteiro, "Congregação Cristã no Brasil: Da Fundação ao Centenário – A Trajetória de uma Igreja brasileira," *Revista Estudos de Religião*, 24/39 (2010): 122–63.

[28] The Waldensians were European migrants from a proto-Reformation movement in the twelfth and subsequent centuries. See Ernesto Combra, *Historia de los Valdenses* (Barcelona: Clie, 1987).

[29] Instituto Brasileiro de Geografia e Estatística–IBGE, *Censo demográfico 2010* (Rio de Janeiro: IBGE, 2012). 80.

[30] As a result of its expansion to other countries, the CCB did not want to be a church "of" Brazil, but "the" church of Christ that was in Brazil. There is a pretense here of being the "true church," which by its pricelessness would be supranational. Mendonça, Antônio Gouvêa and Prócoro Veslasques Filho, *Introdução ao Protestantismo no Brasil*. (São Paulo: Loyola), 1990.

The Assemblies of God (AG) is another important Brazilian Pentecostal community. The AG started in 1911 under the influence of two other Europeans, two Swedish Baptists, Daniel Berg and Gunnar Vingren. Their history is also connected to the United States. As for Berg, he entered into contact with William H. Durham, the same Baptist Pentecostal who influenced Francescon. After a schism in the First Brazilian Baptist Church in the city of Belem, in the northern part of Brazil, the newly founded church, the Assemblies of God, grew from twenty people in 1911 to about twelve million followers in 2010. It is the most popular Pentecostal church in the country, and its membership is twice as large as that of the North American Assemblies of God.[31] Both the AG and the CCB were founded by migrants who were not necessarily sent as missionaries. They were driven by their own initiative, and they received no financial support from their home churches, which is why the churches they established became Brazilian churches instead of missions. Also, this initiative of displacement is very telling as a model for Pentecostal mission which awakens the missionary vocation in each member or leader. The CCB and the AD formed the first wave of Brazilian Pentecostalism.

In the mid-twentieth century, other Pentecostal churches were founded in the country, among which the most prominent were the International Church of the Foursquare Gospel (ICFG), fruit of the movement of outdoor campaigns and crusades (at squares and soccer stadiums), and the Brazil for Christ Church (IPBC). Together they have today over two million members, according to the Brazilian census. Other migrants, such as Canadian and American missionaries, also contributed to this new Brazilian Pentecostal wave. Around that same time, there was a revival movement that led to the charismatic renewal/ pentecostalization of many Brazilian Protestant churches, such as in the Methodist (leading to the creation of the Wesleyan Methodist Church), Baptist (Renewed Baptist Churches) and Presbyterian (Renewed Presbyterian Churches), which eventually brought about new schisms.

In the 1970s and 1980s, a new group of Pentecostal churches emerged in Brazil. With an aggressively public presence, those churches have significantly altered the contours of the Brazilian religious scene. They formed a third Pentecostal wave, differing from the previous two because of their stronger use of mass media, presence in the political life of the country, and emphasis on the so-called "prosperity theology," which brought to religious life the logic of consumerism and utility, under strong North American influence.

---

[31]   See Gedeon F. Alencar, *Matriz Pentecostal Brasileira: Assembleias de Deus, 1911-2011* (Rio de Janeiro: Novos Diálogos, 2013).

The New Life Church (NLPC), a Pentecostal church founded by a Canadian missionary in the 1960s, and from which many Brazilian churches sprang—the most prominent being the Universal Church of the Kingdom of God (IURD)—set up a significant shift within the Brazilian Pentecostal movement. This latest group of churches is called neo-Pentecostal. It is estimated to have from four to five million members in Brazil. The figures are not very accurate because the IBGE Census classifies them as "other Pentecostal churches," bundling together neo-Pentecostals and other Pentecostals. The first two Pentecostal waves have had close ties and interaction with one another, but neither of them shares that same kind of connection with the neo-Pentecostal churches. However, when we talk about Pentecostal expansion in Brazil or about the diaspora of Brazilian Pentecostalism, those three groups must be taken into account, either separately or as a whole.

The three groups have in common the fact that they are Pentecostal, which means that they put the religious experience in prominence, having a special place for emotions and ecstasy in their spirituality. As for the specificity of each of the three groups, Pentecostals of the first group seek to create communities centered on ecstatic experience (speaking in tongues, dreams and visions, and performative biblical reading) as well as on personal evangelism. The second group focuses more acutely on a form of worship marked by healings and miracles, and their evangelization is oriented toward the masses (mass evangelism). The third group proposes a Christian life based on exchanges with the divine (mostly based on health and economic prosperity) and its preferential form of communication/announcement is via the so-called big media.

According to data from the IBGE 2010 Census, out of the 42 million Evangelicals in the country, 25 million are Pentecostal. The 2000 Census counted little over 17 million. The drastic growth of this group is largely due to their aggressive proselytist practices, but that is certainly not exclusive of them:

> All the diversity encompassing Assemblies of God and Baptists accounts for over half of the Evangelical growth of the past decade. Churches with a strong emphasis on proselytism, in whose regular services one always hears the call to "accept Jesus" [...] together account for 52 percent of Evangelical growth.[32]

Brazilian Pentecostals are, then, a strong missionary movement, which targets both their own country and the rest of the world. In regard to those who are displaced, this religious mission plays a very important role. Because they find themselves in a fragile situation, clinging to faith and seeking to live in their diasporic community becomes, for many Brazilian migrants, one

---

[32] Alexandre Brasil Fonseca, *Relações e Privilégios: Estado, secularização e Diversidade Religiosa no Brasil* (Rio de Janeiro: Novos Diálogos, 2011), 108.

of the several ways to survive in often hostile and vulnerable circumstances. Pentecostal churches find in those communities a fertile ground for pastoral care and mission. Below, we will demonstrate how religion becomes important for those living in diaspora.

THE ROLE OF RELIGION IN A DIASPORA CONTEXT

Stuart Hall[33] and James Clifford[34] carried out important anthropological studies on the topic of the diaspora, paying particular attention to the different diasporas created in the globalized and transnational "West" in a postcolonial perspective. In those studies, they made it clear that the diasporic environment is often unfavorable for migrants. Migrants experience many changes that demand complex human actions involving rupture, continuity, recreation of connections, and the imparting of meaning into the lives of people who are either temporarily or permanently displaced. In his turn, Donizete Rodrigues assesses the importance of religion in such an unfavorable diasporic environnment:

> Religion becomes especially important for immigrants. Besides the spiritual support [it offers], it plays a significant role in the process of maintaining ethnic, cultural and language identities. Religion provides positive values, greater social integration and a strong sense of belonging to (their) ethnic group. On top of the religious aspect, it develops a pragmatic solidarity, that is, activities which help them succeed in finding housing, jobs, education and health. Churches are places/meeting points where immigrants can meet other individuals from their home country and other immigrants in the same economic, social and legal situation. The places of worship promote not just liturgical events, but also social and commemorative events, facilitating the interaction of the newcomers and providing information, and new perspectives and possibilities.[35]

Whereas religion may be important for other human groups in the host society, all these ways as it touches the lives of migrants make it even more critical to their existence in a diasporic environment.[36]

Addressing the situation of Brazilians converting to Pentecostalism in Japan, Shoji says: "Those converted to Pentecostalism in Japan frequently speak about a crisis [faced] there that resulted in a pre-conversion phase, setting in

---

[33]   Stuart Hall, "Cultural Identity and Diaspora," in *Identity: Community, Culture, and Difference*, ed. Jonathan Rutherford (London: Lawrence & Wishart, 1990), 222-237.
[34]   James Clifford, "Diasporas," *Cultural Anthropology: Journal of the Society for Cultural Anthropology*, 9, no.3 (1994): 302–38.
[35]   Rodrigues, O Evangélico Imigrante, 193.
[36]   See Donizete Rodrigues e Marcos Silva, "Imigração e Pentecostalismo Brasileiro na Europa: O Caso da Igreja Universal do Reino de Deus," *Revista Angolana de Sociologia*, 13 (2014): 97–113 (108).

motion a gradual [conversion] process with well defined phases."[37] Discussing such a process of conversion in that setting, he says:

> Involving a search for meaning for the immigrant experience, health or family relationship problems, conversion starts with a first contact with a Pentecostal community, an initial doubt followed by a mystical or healing experience through the baptism in the Holy Spirit, which leads the new converts to turn that community into their main reference as for their social ties.[38]

In Japan, as in other places, such process is characterized by the recreation of social networks focused on the Brazilian culture, and marked by "human warmth" and by the notion of "family" the community provides. Religion thus plays a supportive role at a difficult time when many adjustments in the life of the migrant are necessary. According to Rodrigues, that is the main reason for the success of Brazilian Pentecostal churches in the Brazilian diaspora in Japan.

> Proportionally, Pentecostal churches are much more successful in Japan because of an optimized and relatively big offer to meet the demands of an ethnic religiosity, as Brazilian social institutions and support networks are missing. Thus, they especially attract mestizos [Japanese Brazilians] or Brazilians who are not of Japanese descent, working many times as an extended family, offering a way to solve problems through conversion . . . [and]occupying a communnal space with activities meant to preserve the Brazilian identity in Japan while working on problems which have not been sufficiently handled by other organizations, such as, for example, conflict prevention and mediation with the Japanese, on top of the rehabilitation of chemical dependents and Brazilians incarcerated in Japanese correctional facilities and prisons.[39]

In other words, the context of "exile" exacerbates certain subjective experiences which are largely accommodated into Pentecostalism through a "revival of religious symbols" that helps immigrants re-signify their new reality. According to Mariz, that "revival of religious symbols" ascribes "meaning to geographical displacements," propelling individuals to look for the realization of such meaning in their journey.[40] With this context in mind, we will discuss the missionary element of Pentecostalisn and its function in the Brazilian diaspora.

Diaspora and Pentecostal Missions

It is clear that the Brazilian Pentecostal churches have a strong conversionist orientation. The question we need to ask is, "When did they turn their

---

37   Shoji, "Religiões entre Brasileiros no Japão," 83.
38   Shoji, "Religiões entre Brasileiros no Japão."
39   Shoji, "Religiões entre Brasileiros no Japão," 51–2.
40   Mariz, "Missão Religiosa e Migração," 164.

attention to other countries?" As seen in the beginning of this chapter, in the past few decades Brazil has gradually ceased to be a mission field to other countries, to become a storehouse exporting missionaries to the world. According to Rodrigues, this change began to be noticed in the 1980s:

> Beginning in the late 1980s, the main Brazilian Evangelical churches and Charismatic groups started a rapid and extensive movement of international expansion, mainly to North America, Europe and Japan, having become today an important global religious phenomenon.[41]

Two important flows have cooperated for the Pentecostal international expansion since the 1980s. The first one was the increasing flow of emigrants, "many of whom were [already] Evangelicals or Charismatic at the time of departure."[42] The other important flow, according to Rodrigues, is the flow of missionaries, Catholic and mainly Protestant, who moved "to those more economically developed regions and, going beyond the Brazilian 'ethnic border,' have made evangelization efforts toward other [non-Brazilian] migrants and also locals."

According to Rodrigues, the motivation for engaging on a mission in the United States stems from the awareness of the Brazilian Pentecostal churches to consider themselves "responsible for the important 'divine mission' of (re) Christianizing the United States, which have deviated from 'true' Christian Protestant moral and practice."[43] In regard to "Europe, which used to be an exporter of religious institutions and doctrines," he adds, "it is a fertile territory for missionary work, mainly from Africa and Latin America."[44] In her analysis of the Brazilian Pentecostal diaspora, Mariz's initial hypothesis was that such internationalization was linked to the South–North migration flow of people searching for work. She correctly inferred that the large labor-motivated emigration generated a demand for religious services and pastoral care for those displaced abroad. However, in the process of her field work in many different places, she noticed that Pentecostal missions do not necessarily follow the emigration route:

> Would these missionaries be following the same migrant route, aiming at offering religious services in Portuguese or in the Brazilian style to fellow Brazilians in exile? The so-called "immigrant churches" and the arrival of religious leaders along with other immigrants are a phenomenon already largely described and

---

[41]   Rodrigues, *O Evangélico Imigrante*, 12.
[42]   Rodrigues, *O Evangélico Imigrante*.
[43]   Rodrigues, *O Evangélico Imigrante*, 13.
[44]   Rodrigues, *O Evangélico Imigrante*.

historically well known. However, the Brazilian missionaries of the IURD and other "new communities" do not necessarily follow that route.[45]

The missionary flow also caters to those newly-arrived, but what is behind this flow is precisely the mission ideal: to spread faith to other places; a sense of a special call, a vocation. According to Mariz, "the vocation to carry out such 'missions' is one among several legitimate religious meanings which individuals can ascribe to displacements of various types, propelled by contemporary global society and economy."[46] As a consequence of that finding, she reconsidered her hypothesis, affirming that displacements and trips "can be endowed with a sacred meaning in many religious traditions, not only in Christianity, and that they have taken up a variety of meanings in different religious discourses." Accordingly, "These trips may be mystical experiences, as those reported by shamans, or they may be physical or concrete experiences of individuals and groups moving for religious reasons across different geographical regions."[47]

Analyzing the Japanese context, where internal missions are self-sustaining in relation to Brazil, Shoji demonstrates that "Evangelical activity in Japan has depended little on help from Brazil."[48] Therefore although these churches and movements are recent in Japan, their missionary impetus has given birth to "reverse missions." In other words, these newly created Japanese-Brazilian churches have already begun to carry out missions back in Brazil. As Shoji points out, "these movements originated among Brazilians in Japan are already starting a reverse mission in Brazil is proof of their growth and transnational character."[49]

Rodrigues and Silva have highlighted how the migration wave of the past three decades, has contributed to create, expand, scatter, and globalize new religious movements. Pentecostalism has played a major role in that context, particularly in migration flows "moving from (semi)peripheral regions—Latin America, Africa and Asia—to central areas, namely, USA/Canada, Europe and Japan."[50] The Brazilian religious diaspora, particularly its Pentecostal diasporic experience, is increasingly catching the attention of scholars of religion, but its breadth and wealth still remains under-explored.

---

[45]   Mariz, "Missão Religiosa e Migração," 166.
[46]   Mariz, "Missão Religiosa e Migração," 164.
[47]   Mariz, "Missão Religiosa e Migração," 172.
[48]   Shoji, "Religiões entre Brasileiros no Japão," 66.
[49]   Shoji, "Religiões entre Brasileiros no Japão," 69.
[50]   Rodrigues and Silva, "Imigração e Pentecostalismo Brasileiro na Europa," 99. For a good collection of essays on this matter, see Christina Rocha and Manuel Vásquez eds. *The Diaspora of Brazilian Religions* (Leiden: Brill, 2013).

CONCLUSION

This chapter has enquired whether Brazilian Pentecostal diaspora is mainly driven by mission or by economic and ethnic reasons. In conversation with three major studies of that diaspora, we have noted that several factors have contributed to that phenomenon, being the search for better conditions of life, on the one hand, and Pentecostal mission theology, on the other hand, two major motivating factors. These have been two forces at work since the end of the twentieth century, and still reverberate in the twenty-first century, expanding on earlier migration scenarios. None of them seems to be the cause of the other.

The migrant communities stemming from migrations driven mainly by economic, social, ethnic, or political reasons are cared for by Brazilian Pentecostals who have, in the process, become transnational movements. But what seems to drive these Pentecostal missionaries to the diaspora cannot be reduced to a response to that specific demand. Instead, the very idea of mission held by Pentecostals urges them to publicly announce their faith, and turn their communities—both the Brazilian ones and those set abroad—into missionary groups, and the individuals into potential "called" people. This missional vocation has prompted several cases of "reverse missions," with diasporic Pentecostal communities developing missionary activities back in Brazil. Thus, the Pentecostal diaspora is also driven by missionary reasons. Without dismissing economic or corporate impulses, I am led to state that the religious and existential motivation is core to the Brazilian Pentecostal diaspora.

BIBLIOGRAPHY:

Alencar, Gedeon F. *Matriz Pentecostal Brasileira: Assembleias de Deus, 1911-2011*. Rio de Janeiro: Novos Diálogos, 2013.

Clifford, James. "Diasporas," *Cultural Anthropology: Journal of the Society for Cultural Anthropology*, 9, no.3 (1994): 302–38.

Cohn, D'Vera. "5 Key Facts about U.S. Lawful Immigrants," Pew Research Center. Accessed December 15, 2017, https://goo.gl/Ti2yu7.

Combra, Ernesto. *Historia de los Valdenses*. Barcelona: Clie, 1987.

Cruz, Gemma T. "Between Identity and Security: Theological Implications of Migration in the Context of Globalization." *Theological Studies*, 69, no.2 (2008): 357–75.

Fonseca, Alexandre B. *Relações e Privilégios: Estado, Secularização e Diversidade Religiosa no Brasil*. Rio de Janeiro: Novos Diálogos, 2011.

Freston, Paul. "Reverse Mission: A Discourse in Search of Reality." *PentecoStudies*, 9, no.2 (2010): 153–74.

Gasparet, Murialdo. "Mobilidade e Evangelização: O Atendimento Pastoral de Brasileiros Católicos no Exterior. Doctoral Dissertation. Departamento de Teologia. Pontifícia Universidade Católica do Rio de Janeiro, 2018.

Hall, Stuart. "Cultural Identity and Diaspora." In *Identity: Comummunity, Culture, and Difference*. Edited by Jonathan Rutherford. 222-237, London: Lawrence & Wishart, 1990.

Harris-Smith, Yvette Joy. "Uma Nova Fronteira: A Comunicação Intercultural e a Necessidade de uma Epistemologia Migratória." In *World Christianity as Public Religion*, Bilingual volume (English/Português). Edited by Raimundo Barreto, Ronaldo Cavalcante, and Wanderley P. da Rosa. 385–94, Vitóri, Brazil: Editora Unida, 2016 (Series World Christianity and Public Religion, vol.1).

Itamaraty. Governo Brasileiro. Ministério das Relações Exteriores. "Estimativas populacionais das comunidades brasileiras no Mundo, 2015 (números atualizados em 29/11/2016)." Accessed February 2, 2018, https://goo.gl/QNRJwk. IBGE. *Censo demográfico 2010*. Rio de Janeiro: IBGE, 2012. Accessed April 30, 2018, https://goo.gl/9ehg Jb.

Lopez, Gustavo and Kristen Bialik, "Key Findings about U.S. Immigrants," Pew Research Center. Accessed April 30, 2018, https://goo.gl/qQ7tf4.

Mariz, Cecília L. "Missão Religiosa e Migração: Novas Comunidades e Igrejas pentecostais no Exterior." *Análise Social*, 44 (2009): 161–87.

Mendonça, Antônio Gouvêa & Prócoro Veslasques Filho. *Introdução ao Protestantismo no Brasil*. São Paulo: Loyola, 1990.

Monteiro, Yara Nogueira. "Congregação Cristã no Brasil: Da Fundação ao Centenário—A Trajetória de uma Igreja brasileira." *Revista Estudos de Religião*, 24/39 (2010): 122–63.

Oliveira, Manfredo Araújo. *Desafios Éticos da Globalização*. 2nd ed. São Paulo: Paulinas, 2002.

Rocha, Christina and Manuel A. Vasquez eds.: *The Diaspora of Brazilian Religions*. Leiden: Brill, 2013.

Rodrigues, Donizete. *O Evangélico Imigrante: O Pentecostalismo Brasileiro Salvando a América*. São Paulo: Fonte Editorial; Belém: PPGCR-UEPA, 2016.

Rodrigues, Donizete. "The 'Brazilianization' of New York City: Brazilian immigrants and Evangelical Churches in a Pluralized Urban Landscape." In *Ecologies on Faith in New York City: The Evolution of Religious Institutions*. Edited by Richard P. Cimino et al. 120–42. Bloomington: Indiana University Press, 2013.

Rodrigues, Donizete and Marcos Silva. "Imigração e Pentecostalismo Brasileiro na Europa: O Caso da Igreja Universal do Reino de Deus." *Revista Angolana de Sociologia*, 13 (2014): 97–113.

Shoji, Rafael. "Religiões entre Brasileiros no Japão: Conversão ao Pentecostalismo e Redefinição Étnica." *Rever—Revista de Estudos da Religião*, 8 (2008): 46–85.

Silva, Darci Donizetti. "Os Imigrantes Brasileiros na Região da Nova Inglaterra, *Mobilidade Humana e Identidades Religiosas*. Edited by Fabio Baggio, Paolo Parise, and Wagner L. Sanchez, 165–71. São Paulo: Paulus, 2016.

INDEX

believers 101, 108, 109

Bellah, Robert Neelly (but by Robert Bellah) 219, 225

Benedict XVI, Pope 210

Berg, Daniel 276

Bolivia 36, 109

Bolshevik Revolution, the 104, 105, 112

Bonhoeffer, Dietrich 78, 80

border thinking xii, 4

Bowe, John 200, 211

Brazil ix, xiii, xiv, xv, xviii, xix, xxi, 5, 7, 10, 70, 74, 75, 79, 80, 99, 100, 101, 102, 103, 104, 105, 106, 107, 108, 109, 111, 112, 113, 114, 120, 187, 249, 250, 251, 252, 253, 255, 256, 257, 263, 264, 265, 269, 270, 271, 272, 273, 275, 276, 277, 280, 281, 282, 283

Brazil for Christ Church, the (IPBC) 276

Brazilian Baptists 6, 70, 72, 77

Brazilian diaspora 70, 72, 81, 271

Brazilian Diocese of the Russian Orthodox Church, the 110

Brazilian migrants 10, 270, 277

Brazilian (or Brazilianized) religions 269, 281, 283

Brazilian Pentecostal churches 10, 73, 270, 279, 280

Brazilian Pentecostal diaspora 270, 271, 280, 282

Brazilian Pentecostalism, Pentecostals x, 9, 10, 247, 263, 269, 270, 271, 275, 276, 277, 282

Brazil-United States-Europe migration triangle, the 269

Brazuca Baptists 72

Buddhism 32

Bulgaria, Bulgarians 102, 103, 109

Burundi 62

Bush, George W., President 70, 75, 197

C

Calvinism 46

Cameroon 151, 152, 153, 156, 162, 167, 169, 170, 174

Cameroonian migrants xxii, 7, 8, 153, 154

Cameroonian Migrants in Cape Town xviii, 151, 156, 175

Campese, Gioacchino x, xviii, xix, 8, 206, 209, 212, 215, 223, 224, 225, 237, 238, 239, 240, 242, 243, 245

Campo Limpo Paulista Hostel, the 106

Campos dos Goytacazes, the x, 9, 249, 252, 254, 256, 257, 258, 262, 265, 266, 267

Canada 6, 35, 51, 52, 69, 80, 100, 105, 113, 153, 174, 231, 232, 235, 244, 246, 281

Candomble 270

capital 3, 40, 45, 61, 103, 106, 107, 110, 112, 128, 234, 273, 274

caravan(s) 240

Cardoso, Fernando Henrique, President 252, 266

Caribbean x, xx, 4, 7, 10, 34, 35, 38, 49, 117, 118, 119, 120, 121, 122, 123, 124, 125, 126, 128, 129, 130, 131

Casaldáglia, Dom Pedro, Bishop 253

Catholic Church, the 8, 35, 39, 40, 179, 253

Catholics xix, 42, 50, 60, 224, 270

Cebulko, Kara 72

Central American countries 9, 37, 231, 235, 242

Central American Migration x, 3, 10, 229, 230, 232, 244. *See also* migration(s)

Central American Northern Triangle, the 5

Central America's Northern Triangle 5, 32, 235, 246

Charles K. Armstrong 89

Charlottesville 56, 57, 58

Cha, Teresa Hak Kyung 140, 141, 149

child rights 2

Cho, Jennifer 140, 149

Christian Congregation of Brazil (CCB), the 275, 276

Christianity ix, xi, xii, xiii, xiv, xv, xvii, xviii, xx, xxi, 1, 2, 3, 4, 5, 6, 9, 10, 11, 22, 25, 32, 33, 39, 52, 58, 60, 64, 65, 83, 84, 85, 86, 88, 89, 90, 91, 92, 93, 94, 95, 96, 97, 126, 155, 157, 158, 159, 163, 166, 170, 171, 172, 173, 175, 222, 236, 263, 264, 265, 269, 270, 281, 283

Cincinnatus, Lucius Quintus 53

citizens 52, 53, 55, 56, 58, 59, 63, 75, 78, 84, 89, 90, 91, 117, 194, 195, 196, 206, 207, 208, 210, 218, 219, 262, 274

civic responsibility(ies) 5, 6, 52, 53, 56, 59, 61, 62, 63

civil discourse 8

civil war(s) 34, 102

Clifford, James 278

climate change 2

co-ethnic churches 19

Cold War, the 34, 88, 91, 96

colonialism 216

colonial powers 3

colonization 33, 140, 141, 270

Comissão Pastoral da Terra, the (CPT - Pastoral Land Commission) xxii, 9, 253, 254, 255, 257, 263, 265, 266

communication xx, 3, 21, 26, 31, 34, 38, 48, 164, 277

Comunidades Eclesiais de Base, the (CEBs - Christian Base Communities) 253

Conferência Nacional dos Bispos do Brasil, the (CNBB - National Conference of Bishops of Brazil) 253, 254

Conselho Indigenista Missionário, the (CIMI - Indigenous Missionary Council) 253

conservatism 6, 38, 49, 70, 71, 72, 73, 79, 204

  political 6

  social 72, 79

  theopolitical 71, 73

continuity 6, 91, 95, 278

conversion 6, 83, 84, 85, 86, 87, 88, 90, 91, 92, 93, 94, 95, 239, 278, 279

corruption 9, 202, 240

Costa Rica 35, 203, 213, 232

courage 8, 77, 168, 200, 225

crime 9, 157, 241

Crucified People(s) 239, 242. *See also* Way of the Cross, the

Crüsemann, Frank 222, 223, 226

Cuban Revolution, the 34

cultural clashes 2, 186

cultural interweaving xii

culture xviii, 2, 6, 7, 8, 10, 20, 38, 45, 47, 55, 57, 77, 100, 108, 117, 119, 122, 123, 126, 138, 139, 140, 141, 142, 144, 146, 163,

Evangelicalism 69, 70, 72

  American 70

  Latin American 70

evangelical missionaries 69

Evangelical movement 39

Evangelicals xxiv, 69, 70

  American 69, 70

  in Brazil 258

  Latin American (also Evangelical Latinos) ix, 6, 42, 69

F

Faculdade Unida xiii, xv, xx, xxi

Faith x, xx, 2, 11, 17, 65, 108, 126, 154, 159, 161, 168, 171, 173, 174, 175, 283

familism 89, 90

Fanon, Franz 192, 205, 211

fear xii, 2, 54, 107, 112, 143, 144, 162, 183, 186, 192, 193, 194, 195, 196, 203, 207, 208, 217, 223, 233

feminization 5, 7, 117, 118, 129

Fitzsimmons, David 238

Fountain of Life Ministries (FOLM) 62

Francescon, Louis (Luigi Francesconi) 275, 276

Francis, Pope 8, 179, 181, 186, 218, 223

  the Holy Father 179, 181

freedom of religion and belief 2, 39

Freston, Paul 72, 73, 81, 269, 270, 283

G

García, Maria Cristina 232, 244

Gasparet, Murialdo 271, 272, 273, 283

gender xii, xiii, xiv, xxi, 2, 47, 54, 118, 130, 142

gender violence 2

genocide 208

Germany xvii, 22, 103, 104, 105, 110, 209, 211

Ghana xvii, xxi, 5, 17, 19, 20, 21, 22, 23, 26, 51, 58, 59, 62, 153, 154, 161, 163, 166, 168, 171, 173

Ghanaian ix, xviii, 5, 15, 17, 18, 19, 20, 21, 23, 25, 26, 27, 28, 29, 51, 55, 58, 59, 61, 62, 64, 153, 158, 161, 170, 171, 174, 175

  Ghanaian communities 5, 19, 26

  Ghanaian-led Christian churches 5

  Ghanaian migrants xvii, 15, 23, 28

ghetto churches 36

Gimenes, Edvar 75, 76, 81

globalization xiii, xvii, xxi, 3, 55, 56, 158, 207, 208, 209, 270, 273, 274

Global North, the xii

Global South, the xi, xii, xiv, 3, 193, 198, 223

God x, xxii, 8, 21, 22, 24, 43, 60, 61, 62, 72, 74, 75, 78, 80, 93, 110, 112, 126, 127, 129, 143, 148, 151, 152, 154, 156, 157, 158, 162, 165, 166, 167, 168, 169, 170, 171, 172, 175, 177, 182, 185, 186, 192, 195, 201, 202, 203, 204, 205, 206, 207, 215, 219, 220, 221, 222, 224, 225, 237, 250, 255, 257, 258, 259, 260, 263, 264, 265, 270, 276, 277

  God's identity 221

  God's Intervention x, 151

  God's memory 8, 219, 220

  God's presence 143

God's steadfast love 220

God's way of being and acting in history 202

God's will 78, 165, 168, 169

image of God, the 182, 207

understanding of God, the 215

word of God, the 21, 22, 204, 220

Gonzalez, Juan 3, 10

Good Samaritan, the 8, 61, 177, 178, 179, 181, 183, 184

Groody, Daniel 220

Guatemala 34, 35, 38, 42, 200, 232, 234, 235, 237, 240, 244, 246

guerrilla 34, 35

Gutiérrez, Gustavo 77, 78, 220

H

Haar, Ter 19

Hackett, Rosalind 153, 163, 164, 173

Haiti 36

Hall, Stuart 278

han 140, 141, 145, 149

Hanawon (House of Unity) 84, 85

Harris-Smith, Y. Joy 269, 283

healing xx, 8, 43, 152, 153, 154, 155, 156, 157, 158, 159, 160, 161, 162, 163, 164, 165, 166, 167, 168, 169, 170, 171, 172, 182, 183, 206, 279

divine healing 152, 153, 154, 158, 163, 167

healing churches 161

physical healing 156, 160, 165, 170, 171

prophetic healing 158

spiritual healing 153, 154, 160, 164, 165, 168, 172

Hispanics (also Latino) 42, 192, 199, 200

Holy Spirit, the 222, 279

the baptism in the Holy Spirit 279

homelands 2, 34

Hondagneu-Sotelo, Pierrette 238, 244

Honduras 34, 35, 42, 43, 200, 232, 233, 235, 243

Hoover, Herbert, President 195

hope xiv, 8, 10, 60, 61, 87, 104, 135, 137, 145, 148, 152, 156, 162, 163, 169, 170, 183, 200, 229, 236, 237, 238, 242, 264

Hospedaria de Imigrantes 100

hospitality 186, 202, 205, 207, 223

hostility 2, 8, 143, 161, 209, 223

Hughes, Theodore 87, 88, 96

human dignity 136, 142, 148, 182, 199

human mobility xix, 215, 216, 217, 218, 224

human movement 7, 32, 137, 269

human rights 2, 181, 210, 232, 233, 237, 240

Hungary 217

Huntington, Samuel P. 55, 56, 196, 197, 198, 199, 207, 211

Hwang, Jenny (but by Hwang) 70, 82, 196, 204, 209, 213

hybridity 238, 244

I

identity(ies) ix, xii, xiv, xix, 1, 2, 5, 6, 7, 16, 17, 18, 19, 20, 21, 25, 26, 32, 33, 38, 42, 44, 50, 55, 56, 61, 70, 73, 77, 85, 95, 103, 108, 113, 118, 124, 136, 137, 142, 146, 147, 148, 157, 158, 177, 185, 193, 197, 198, 199, 202, 207, 218, 219, 221, 222, 223,

224, 264, 265, 274, 278, 279.
See also religious identity

immigrant churches xx, 6, 25, 71, 73, 158, 280

immigrant generation 139, 144

immigrants xxii, 3, 4, 5, 6, 7, 8, 10, 16, 18, 19, 20, 23, 25, 36, 38, 40, 42, 43, 45, 46, 52, 54, 55, 57, 58, 59, 60, 61, 62, 63, 64, 70, 71, 72, 73, 74, 75, 76, 77, 79, 80, 99, 100, 101, 102, 103, 104, 106, 107, 108, 109, 110, 111, 113, 125, 128, 137, 138, 139, 141, 142, 143, 145, 146, 147, 148, 149, 158, 171, 192, 193, 194, 195, 197, 199, 200, 201, 204, 207, 208, 210, 216, 220, 221, 232, 235, 241, 272, 273, 274, 278, 279, 280, 283

legal immigrants 199

post-1965 immigrants 58

undocumented immigrants 72

Immigration and Nationality Act, the 56

immigration laws 72, 80

immigration policies 9, 18, 69, 79, 80

individual morality 45, 47

Information and Communication Technologies (ICTs) (also communication technologies) xxii, 21, 26, 38, 163, 164

ingenuity 8, 200

injustice xii, 2, 201, 206, 225

insecurity x, 2, 75, 76, 155, 157, 160, 161, 170, 171

insecurity theory 160

integration 7, 16, 85, 88, 99, 113, 120, 185, 186, 217, 223, 278

intercession 8

intercultural studies/dialogue xiii

interdisciplinarity 4

intergenerational dialogue xiv

intergenerational story 7, 137

internally displaced people 35, 84, 144, 218

International Church of the Foursquare Gospel (ICFG), the 276

International Organization for Migration (IOM) 58, 105, 272

internet 21, 26, 221

interview(s) 17, 20, 21, 22, 58, 86, 92, 102, 107, 110, 124, 126, 162, 240, 255, 257, 258, 259, 260, 261, 262, 264

invasión Brasileña (Brazilian invasion) 43

Irvin, Dale 199

Islam 32, 90, 96, 270

J

Jamaica 59, 120, 122, 124, 125, 126, 130

Japan xix, 271, 272, 274, 278, 279, 280, 281

the Nisei generation 146

the Sansei generation 146

Japanese American congregation 145

Jenny Hwang (but by Sorens and Hwang) 70, 82, 196, 204, 213

Jesus 70, 72, 78, 81, 93, 94, 127, 161, 162, 164, 166, 168, 173, 175, 177, 178, 203, 204, 205, 206, 219, 220, 221, 222, 225, 236, 237, 238, 239, 240, 242, 243, 246, 257, 277. *See also* Way of the Cross, the

actions of Jesus, the 166

Jesus's life 221

Jesus's passion 220, 242

international migration 5, 119, 185, 230, 231

labor migration 208, 209

migration studies xvii, 15, 16, 27, 28, 118, 131, 159, 173, 235, 236, 239, 243, 245

migration to South Africa (SA) 155

migration waves 32, 33, 231, 273, 275

migratory flows 4, 9, 42, 43, 47, 48, 270

migratory movements 31

pendular migration 5, 38, 43, 48

pendular migratory wave 38

south-south migration 5

transcontinental migration 269, 274

militias 36, 56

missionaries

Brazilian (or in Brazil) 281

Canadian and American 276

Evangelical 69

Pentecostal 270, 282

Missionaries of St. Charles, the (also Scalabrinians) xviii, 236, 237, 238, 245

missions

Brazilian Pentecostal missions 270

Pentecostal missions 270, 280

reverse mission 1, 269, 281

modernity 90, 96, 161, 171, 174, 200, 211

Movimento dos Trabalhadores Rurais Sem-Terra, the (MST) (also Landless Workers' Movement, the) 9, 249, 251, 252, 253, 254, 256, 262, 265, 266

multiculturalism 55, 88

Mumbere, Charles Wesley 51, 52, 63

Muslims 60, 208, 224

Myanmar, Rohingya 218

N

Nails, Thomas 229

narrative(s) 6, 21, 84, 90, 91, 136, 137, 141, 142, 143, 144, 145, 146, 147, 186, 205, 259

biblical exodus narrative 143

Nastácia Kozmekim 109, 110

nationalism xxi, 3, 55, 64, 91, 222, 223

nationalist xii, 90, 203

naturalization 54

Nausner, Michael 222, 224, 226

Neo-Conservatism 5

neo-Nazis 56

neo-Pentecostalism/ Pentecostal 40, 166, 171, 173, 259, 260, 277

Netherlands 15, 16, 17, 18, 19, 20, 22, 23, 24, 25, 26, 27, 29, 163, 172

New Life Church, the (NLPC) 277

New Mexico 41, 196, 211

Nicaragua 34, 35, 36, 42, 232, 234

North America ix, xiii, xiv, 5, 6, 51, 52, 57, 58, 59, 60, 63, 65, 71, 73, 136, 141, 210, 280

Northern Triangle ix, 5, 9, 31, 32, 34, 36, 37, 38, 40, 41, 42, 43, 44, 45, 46, 47, 48, 235, 236, 246

North Korea(n) 83, 84, 87, 88, 89, 90, 91, 92, 93, 94, 95, 96, 97, 98, 135, 146, 147. *See also* Democratic People's Republic of Korea, the

O

Old Believers (*Staroveri*) (also, Old Ritualists, *Staro-obriadtsi*) 101, 108, 109

Orisha traditions 270

Orthodox Church, the 101, 103, 108, 110, 111, 112, 113

Orthodox Russian immigrants in Brazil (also see Russian immigrants) 108. *See also* Russian immigrants

P

Pacific, the 4

paramilitary groups 35

participant observation 17, 162

Partlow, Joshua 234, 235, 245

Pastoral Commission of the Earth, the (CPT) xxii, 9, 253, 254, 255, 257, 263, 265, 266

Pentecostal church(es) 157, 158, 161, 276, 277

Pentecostal denominations 250

Pentecostalism x, xx, 9, 10, 43, 152, 153, 154, 155, 157, 161, 166, 168, 170, 171, 173, 174, 247, 249, 263, 264, 265, 269, 270, 271, 275, 276, 277, 278, 279, 281

Pentecostal missions 270, 280

perseverance 76, 152, 172

Poland 103, 109, 217

political subjectivity 93

post 9/11 attitudes 194

postcolonial/ decolonial theories xi

post-colonial period 33

postmodern secularism 46

postwar periods 33

prayers 21, 61, 73, 151, 152, 158, 167, 169, 237

Princeton Theological Seminary xi, xv, xix, 3, 10

private sphere 1

prophecies 153, 163

Prophet T.B. Joshua 167, 170, 172

prosperity gospel 46, 259, 260

prosperity theology 9, 265, 276

Protestantism xxiii, 33, 72, 197, 270

Protestants 6, 72, 87, 224, 264, 270

proximity 8, 178, 179, 180, 181, 183, 184, 186, 209

public concern 2

public discourses xii, 2, 4, 57, 193, 206, 207

public policy 8

public religion i, v, ix, xii, xvii, xx, 1, 2, 10, 11, 269, 283

public sphere x, xi, xxiii, 1, 52, 117, 139, 146, 147

public theologies xi

Q

queer xi

R

race x, xi, xii, 54, 55

racism 55, 64, 139, 193, 194, 196, 199, 205

Ramos, Jovelino xi

redemption 201, 239

reductionism 9

reenactment 9, 208, 229, 230, 236, 238, 240, 242

reenactment of the Way of the Cross, the 9, 229, 230, 236, 238, 242

reflexivity 7, 91, 94, 95

S

Salvadoran 9, 239

São João Sugar Mill, the 252, 253

São Paulo xx, xxi, xxiii, 7, 44, 99, 100, 101, 102, 103, 104, 105, 106, 107, 108, 109, 110, 111, 112, 113, 114, 115, 249, 252, 253, 254, 256, 260, 266, 267, 269, 271, 273, 275, 283, 284

São Paulo Philanthropic Society, the 107

second generation 5, 15, 19, 25, 26, 137, 138, 139, 144, 147, 273

sexual morality 45, 47

Shaull, Richard xi

Shin, Eun-Hee 90, 97

Shoji, Rafael 271, 278, 279, 281, 284

Sivanandan, Ambalavaner 193

Skype 21, 26

Slovakia 217

Smidt, Corwin E. 52, 61

Snowball sampling technique 17

Snyder, Susanna 193, 203, 209, 217, 227

Soccer War 35

social field 17, 22

socialist-oriented government 35

social marginalization 9

Soerens, Matthew 70, 196, 204

Solalinde, Alejandro, Father 240

solidarity x, xi, 75, 148, 201, 205, 237, 278

South Africa 7, 153, 154, 155, 156, 162, 169, 175

Southern Baptist Convention 69

South Sudan, the 218

Soviet Union, the (also the USSR) 34, 99, 102, 104, 107

Spain xix, 35, 114, 181

Spiritism 270

spirituality 8, 23, 160, 172, 260, 277

stories 6, 7, 8, 19, 52, 73, 87, 91, 103, 123, 124, 136, 137, 138, 139, 140, 141, 142, 143, 144, 145, 146, 147, 148, 149, 155, 179, 182, 186, 200, 203, 219, 236, 263

intergenerational story 7, 137

stories of the first generation of migrants, the 137

story transmission 137, 144

transmission of stories, the 137, 141

transmitted stories 139

storytelling 137, 142, 146

structural violence 9

subjectivity 6, 84, 88, 90, 91, 92, 93, 94, 95

Sub-Saharan African descent 15

suffering 2, 8, 76, 106, 142, 152, 180, 192, 200, 210, 220, 221, 222, 237, 238, 242, 258

Sung, Jung Mo 2

survival 2, 3, 7, 38, 91, 137, 138, 139, 145, 158, 160, 232

Sweden 217

T

Taesongkongsa 84

Tanzania 62

Televangelism 40

televangelist churches 41

televangelists 41, 159, 164

Texas 5, 41, 42, 50, 71

theological perspective 4, 207

theology(ies). *See also* liberation theology; *See also* prosperity theology

  for immigrants 71

  of Asian and Asian American people 137

  of borderlessness 74

  of Brazuca Baptist pastors 79

  of memory 219

  of migration 71, 200, 239

  Pentecostal mission 282

theopoetics xi

therapeutic communities 77

the role of religion 1

thinking in between 4

Transatlantic slave trade 33

transcultural dialogue xii

transformation 6, 7, 86, 107, 183, 220

trans-local and transnational religious xvii, 15, 17, 20, 22, 36, 50, 59, 64, 65, 153, 163, 171, 172

trans-local mobility 154, 167

transmigrants 158, 159

transmission of language 140

transmission of religio-cultural beliefs and values 142

transmitted and shared narratives 139. *See also* stories

transnationalism xxiii, 5, 16, 22, 154, 159, 172

transnational mobility 163, 169

transnational religious field 15, 17, 18, 20, 21, 24, 26

Trible, Phyllis 204, 213

U

Uganda 51, 52, 62

Umbanda 270

undocumented parents 143

United Kingdom, the 3, 11, 22, 272

United Nations, the (UN) 36, 37, 50, 84, 98, 105, 107, 217

United States of America, the (also the United States) xi, xii, xvii, xxi, xxiii, 3, 4, 5, 6, 10, 16, 28, 32, 33, 34, 35, 36, 37, 38, 39, 40, 41, 42, 43, 45, 47, 48, 50, 52, 53, 54, 55, 56, 57, 58, 59, 60, 62, 63, 64, 69, 70, 71, 72, 73, 75, 77, 78, 80, 81, 89, 100, 104, 105, 109, 110, 112, 113, 118, 120, 121, 124, 125, 128, 131, 136, 145, 146, 148, 192, 193, 195, 196, 197, 198, 199, 200, 201, 206, 207, 208, 212, 229, 230, 231, 232, 233, 234, 235, 236, 241, 244, 245, 246, 269, 270, 271, 272, 273, 274, 275, 276, 280

  American exceptionalism 141, 147

  American immigration policy 6, 71

  American Southwest 8, 200

  US evangelicalism 69, 72

  US immigration system 241

  US megachurches 5

Universal Church of the Kingdom of God, the (IURD) 43, 250, 255, 257, 258, 260, 265, 270, 277, 281

urbanization xii, 251

urban middle-class pendulum 34

US-Mexico border, the 229

V

value crisis 8

values 2, 24, 47, 61, 129, 137, 140, 142, 143, 148, 217, 274, 278

Vatican, the xx, 8, 217

Vetrivel, Steven 58

Viacrucis Migrante (Migrant Crossing) 242, 244

via crucis, the (also see Way of Cross, the) 229, 240, 241, 242

Vingren, Gunnar 276

violence 2, 9, 32, 36, 40, 56, 64, 143, 200, 202, 218, 220, 229, 230, 234, 235, 236, 241, 242, 253, 258

W

Walcott, Derek 191, 213

Wallace, Anthony 158

Walls, Andrew F. xxii, 60

war 2, 34, 35, 36, 38, 56, 64, 102, 104, 105, 106, 136, 140, 142, 146, 184, 218, 224, 271

Way of the Cross of the Migrant, the 230, 236, 237, 238, 239, 242, 243

Way of the Cross, the xviii, 9, 229, 230, 236, 237, 238, 239, 240, 242, 243, 245

Wells, David 39, 41, 50

white nationalists 56

white supremacists 56, 57

Wiesel, Elie 218

Wilfred, Felix x, 239, 243

William H. Durham 275, 276

women rights 2

woori/ woori-ness (Korean lament) 136, 139, 141

World Christianity i, iii, v, vi, ix, x, xi, xii, xv, xvii, xix, xx, xxii, xxiii, 1, 2, 3, 4, 5, 10, 11, 88, 96, 157, 158, 163, 166, 170, 172, 173, 269, 283

World Migration Report 58

world religions 32

world systems theory, the 231

World War II (1939-45) 100, 104, 107, 110

X

xenophilia 202, 203, 207

xenophobia 2, 8, 143, 156, 157, 193, 194, 196, 199, 200, 202, 203, 204, 205, 206, 208, 222, 225

xenophobic ideologies x

xenophobic sentiments 3

xenophobic white nativism 199

xeno-racism 193

Y

Yang, Fenggang 171, 175

yellow peril 143

Z

Zumbi dos Palmares settlement, the xviii, 9, 249, 250, 252, 254, 255, 256, 257, 260, 261, 262, 266

Zygmunt Bauman 200, 208, 211

SYMBOLS

38th parallel, the 145, 147

1882 Chinese Exclusion Act 194

2016 US Presidential election, the 69

πλησίον, rēa 177